Anton Chekhov

a reference guide to literature

A Reference Guide to Literature

Barry Scherr
Editor, Russian Literature

Anton Chekhov

a reference guide to literature

K.A. LANTZ

G.K.HALL &CO.

70 LINCOLN STREET, BOSTON, MASS.

Library of Congress Cataloging in Publication Data

Lantz, Kenneth.
Anton Chekhov: a reference guide.

(A Reference guide to literature)
Includes index.
1. Chekhov, Anton Pavlovich, 1860-1904—Bibliography.
I. Title. II. Series.
Z8165.4.L36 1985 [PG3458.Z8] 016.89172'3 85-16420
ISBN 0-8161-8701-0

This publication is printed on permanent/durable acid-free paper
MANUFACTURED IN THE UNITED STATES OF AMERICA

Contents

The Author

K.A. Lantz is Associate Professor of Russian at the University of Toronto. He is the author of *Nikolay Leskov* and the editor-translator of *The Sealed Angel and Other Stories* by Nikolay Leskov.

Preface

Anton Chekhov: A Reference Guide is intended for use by scholars, critics, and students. It consists of four parts: an introduction, a list of works by Chekhov, an annotated bibliography of Chekhov criticism, and an index.

The introduction provides an outline of Chekhov's life and literary career and of the major trends in his critical reception in his homeland and in the West.

The checklist of Chekhov's own writings is arranged by order of publication date and is complete for works written after 1887; writings before that year have been selected according to their importance, their representative nature, and their mentions in the bibliography of Part Three of this work. Unfinished or unpublished works are not included. Full indices of Chekhov's writings can be found in 1952.4, pp. 393-432 (in English) and in Polnoe sobranie sochinenii i pisem v tridtsati tomakh [Complete collected works and letters in thirty volumes], by A.P. Chekhov, Moscow: Nauka, 1974-1983, vol. 18, pp. 524-40 (in Russian).

Writings about Chekhov are limited to 1200 titles. These have been selected from a large body of Chekhov criticism in Russian, English, French, and German. Items were chosen to give a representative sampling of the development of critical attitudes to Chekhov; emphasis is on more recent material, but items of note from earlier years have also been included. Criteria for selection were also weighted toward English-language material, although I think that no Russian work of real merit has been omitted. Relatively few newspaper articles and reviews of Chekhov's plays have been included; those that have were chosen because they made important statements about Chekhov and his art. I have examined all works listed, except for a few marked with an asterisk. In order to save space not all reprints have been listed; for the more significant material I have noted the first appearance and its latest or most accessible reprint. The annotations are not judgements but concise descriptions that are sufficient, I hope, to inform the reader of the scope of the work and help him decide whether he wants to read the original.

The index combines authors, titles of Chekhov's works, and selected subjects. Stories by Chekhov discussed in general surveys and monographs have not been indexed individually unless the treatment is substantial. I have been able to include annotated listings of complete contents of only a few of the most important collections of articles. Other collections have only their most significant articles listed separately, but the remaining articles are described briefly under the principal entry and are included in the Index.

* * * *

Work on the book was supported by a research grant and a grant-in-aid from the University of Toronto. Some of the research was done at the University of Illinois Summer Research Laboratory, and I gratefully acknowledge this assistance as well.

K.A. Lantz
May, 1985

Abbreviations

A. Periodicals

(Abbreviations of periodicals follow those of the MLA International Bibliography).

ALitASH	Acta Litteraria Academiae Scientiarum Hungaricae
BuR	Bucknell Review: A Scholarly Journal of Letters, Arts and Science
CalSS	California Slavic Studies
CASS	Canadian-American Slavic Studies
CompD	Comparative Drama
ConL	Contemporary Literature
CR	The Critical Review (Australia)
CRCL	The Canadian Review of Contemporary Literature
CSP	Canadian Slavonic Papers
ÉSl	Études Slaves et Est-Européennes
FN	Filologicheskie nauki
GaR	Georgia Review
HudR	Hudson Review
IAN	Izvestiia Akademii Nauk SSSR, Seriia literatury i iazyka
IFR	International Fiction Review
JGE	The Journal of General Education
JML	The Journal of Modern Literature
KR	The Kenyon Review
LO	Literaturnoe obozrenie
MD	Modern Drama
MelbSS	Melbourne Slavonic Studies
MLR	Modern Language Review
NLH	New Literary History: A Journal of Theory and Interpretation
NovM	Novyi mir
NovŽ	Novyi Zhurnal
NRF	Nouvelle Revue Française
NZSJ	New Zealand Slavonic Journal
Okt	Oktiabr'
OSP	Oxford Slavonic Papers
PCP	Pacific Coast Philology

PMLA	Publications of the Modern Language Association of America
PsyR	Psychoanalytic Review
RBPH	Revue Belge de Philologie et d'Histoire
ReAL	RE: Artes Liberales
RHT	Revue d'Histoire du Théâtre
RJŠ	Russkii iazyk v shkole
RLC	Revue de Littérature Comparée
RLit	Russkaia literatura
RLJ	Russian Language Journal
RLT	Russian Literature Triquarterly
RusL	Russian Literature
RusR	Russian Review
RusRe	Russkaia rech'
SEEJ	Slavic and East European Journal
SEER	The Slavonic and East European Review
SlavR	Slavic Review
SovL	Soviet Literature
SQ	Shakespeare Quarterly
SR	Sewanee Review
SSASH	Studia Slavica Academiae Scientiarum Hungaricae
SSF	Studies in Short Fiction
SSl	Scando-Slavica
SSLit	Soviet Studies in Literature
TDR	The Drama Review
TN	Theatre Notebook
TQ	The Texas Quarterly
UlbR	Ulbandus Review
VAN	Vestnik Akademii nauk
VLit	Voprosy literatury
VLU	Vestnik Leningradskogo universiteta
VMU	Vestnik Moskovskogo universiteta
Voz	Vozrozhdenie
VRL	Voprosy russkoi literatury
WHR	Western Humanities Review
WSl	Die Welt der Slaven: Halbjahresschrift für Slavistik
WSlA	Wiener Slawistischer Almanach
YCGL	Yearbook of Comparative and General Literature
YR	Yale Review
ZS	Zeitschrift für Slawistik
ZSP	Zeitschrift für slavische Philologie

B. Other

AN SSSR	Akademiia nauk SSSR
gos.	gosudarstvennyi
im.	imeni
MAT	Moscow Art Theater
PSSP	Polnoe sobranie sochinenii i pisem. 30 vols. By A.P. Chekhov. Moscow: Nauka, 1974-1983.

Introduction: Images of Chekhov

A hundred years of Chekhov criticism have created no single, dominant picture of him, either as a writer or as a personality; what emerges, rather, is a series of very different, even contradictory images, each of which captures only some aspects of this elusive and complex figure. The image of the author most commonly derived from his best-known stories and plays has been that of a gloomy and cold man obsessed with the grayness of life and with the failings of his characters. The material images of Chekhov--the photographs taken, for the most part, in his last years when he was already dying--support that view, depicting as they do a haggard, suffering man who seems to maintain his aloofness even on paper. Yet one need read only a few of his delightful letters to discover a very different Chekhov, a man of bubbling humor, gentle self-mockery, and immense charm. Memoirs of his contemporaries are near-unanimous in confirming his gregarious nature and his love of fun. Conflicting images arise even from within his own literary work. His early stories, with their lighthearted and often grotesque humor, seem, at first glance at least, scarcely to have been written by the author of "Peasants" and _The Three Sisters_. Thus the diversity of images of Chekhov created by critical literature over the past century is not suprising. Is he fundamentally an optimist or a pessimist? A writer who shuns his social responsibilities to create "pure art" or one deeply committed to a set of humanitarian values? An impressionist? A realist? A naturalist? A symbolist? An absurdist? A tragic dramatist or a writer of great comedies? One can find ample support for all of these views in critical literature.

A brief sketch of Chekhov's life and his treatment at the hands of the critics cannot reconcile these conflicts but can at least attempt to clarify some of the most important trends that have created these images.

Chekhov's early life--to use his own famous and

memorable phrase--was a process of "squeezing the slave out of himself drop by drop." His early years, from his birth on January 17, 1860 to his emergence from Moscow University in 1884 as a medical doctor, make up an almost Dickensian tale of triumph over a grim childhood. His father, a stern and narrow-minded man who was born a serf, kept a small general store in the south-Russian town of Taganrog. Anton was the third of his six children. His childhood memories were principally of being roused long before dawn to sing in the church choir directed by his father, of tedious work in his father's shop, of beatings, and of long hours of homework. As Chekhov later wrote to his brother, "despotism and lying so distorted our childhood as to make it a frightful and nauseating memory" (PSSP 3.122).

When Anton was sixteen his father had to flee to Moscow to escape being jailed for debt after the bankruptcy of his business. Anton remained in Taganrog to finish high school and then, in 1879, joined the family in Moscow to study medicine. The family was barely ekeing out a living, and Anton, in his spare time from medical studies, helped supplement it by writing sketches and anecdotes for the popular comic weeklies. The work had few rewards either intellectual or financial, yet Chekhov had a gift for writing humor and a seemingly inexhaustible supply of material. He quickly developed a reputation and a considerable following among readers of this new form of popular entertainment. Even while establishing his medical practice he continued to write, moving on to become a regular contributor of stories to the more prestigious literary sections of the daily newspapers. By 1888 his career had reached a turning point: his first long story "The Steppe" had appeared in a respectable literary journal, and he was received, with some qualifications, into the ranks of serious literature with the award of the Academy of Sciences Pushkin Prize (he was awarded only half of the thousand-ruble prize).

Chekhov had few kind words for critics; he once compared them to gadflies, buzzing restlessly around a horse that is straining to pull the plow and hindering its work. "For twenty-five years I have been reading criticisms of my stories, but I don't remember one useful hint or one word of valuable advice" (quoted in 1905.4). And indeed many responses of his contemporaries to his work were attempts to make him conform to the critic's own narrowly-defined conception of what the writer ought to be. The dominant critical approach through most of the nineteenth century was to judge a writer's worth by the degree to which his works illuminated social problems. But critics were often hard pressed to find evidence of social concerns in Chekhov's writings, and so took him severely to task for irresponsibility.

Serious critical attention to Chekhov's work dates from 1886, when his second collection, Motley Stories was reviewed in some of the leading newspapers and literary journals by some of the era's leading critics. The book contained stories published in the humor magazines and daily newspapers, and critics regarded their author within that context rather than as a full-fledged, "serious" man of letters. They had few doubts, however, that Chekhov was far more talented than his humor-magazine colleagues. A.M. Skabichevsky, a prominent populist critic, expressed this reaction most forcefully. He found Motley Stories to be an uneven collection, but had high praise for some individual works. His concerns, however, were less with Chekhov's writings than with the medium in which they appeared and with Chekhov's likely fate should he continue working in that medium. He wrote of the "suicide" of a "young, fresh talent" slowly wearing itself out in the daily grind of newspaper work. He concluded, with an unfortunate choice of metaphors, by saying that "it ends by him being turned into a squeezed lemon, and like a squeezed lemon he is fated to die somewhere in a ditch, utterly forgotten and considering himself fortunate if his comrades place him in a public hospital at the expense of the Literary Fund" (1886.2).

As Chekhov continued to produce works showing unquestioned talent, the socially-minded critics found it increasingly difficult to label him as merely an exceptionally clever comic writer. The seemingly irresponsible humoresques he tossed off for the humor magazines gave way to serious, sensitive, but dispassionate treatments of characters from all strata of Russian society. Yet so many of these stories seemed concerned only with the trivial events of daily life, and no easily-defined set of values could be discerned in them. His talent was undeniable, but what sort of talent was it? The critics, accustomed to judging writers primarily by their ideology, could find none in Chekhov and were uncertain how to evaluate him. Thus the question of Chekhov's "ideals" (or rather his lack of ideals)--ideals being understood as a socially responsible attitude--were at the center of Chekhov criticism for much of his lifetime.

In the front rank of those lamenting Chekhov's lack of ideals was the influential populist critic N.K.

Mikhailovsky. Although Mikhailovsky was severe in his judgements, he was by no means hostile to Chekhov's art; indeed, in the half-dozen or more articles he wrote on Chekhov he consistently praises his talent. His tone is that of the elderly uncle watching with dismay as his favorite nephew turns his back on the family business to take up motorcyle repair. Mikhailovsky essentially accuses Chekhov of irresponsibility in his art; he pays full tribute to his talent but laments the fact that this talent is not put to better use. His works are not filled with the same passionate social concern expressed by the older generation of writers of the 1860s (see 1890.1); Chekhov, he says, recognizes nothing beyond the "everyday reality in which he is destined to live." Chekhov himself writes "in cold blood," indifferent to his characters; and because he has no all-embracing ideology to guide him, he has no proper sense of values or framework on which to evaluate his material. He writes with equal indifference about anything that catches his eye; thus his works present a confusing kaleidoscope of fragments of life in which the truly significant is jumbled together with the utterly trivial. (It is interesting to note that Mikhailovsky holds up as a flaw this tendency to throw together seemingly unnecessary details and motifs. Many years later, A.P. Chudakov (1971.6) argues that this sense of "randomness" is a cornerstone of Chekhov's art and an essential feature of his vision of life.)

Mikhailovsky's views were echoed by a dozen lesser critics who, acknowledging Chekhov's stature as a leading writer of his generation, deplored the fact that he could not harness his talent to an acceptable ideology. His "Dreary Story" became the center of critical attention. Chekhov's professor's admission of the absence of a "general idea" in his life was taken as Chekhov's own admission of his lack of ideology and of the fact that life without some such guiding principle was impossible. Chekhov was explained, rather sadly, as a product of the 1880s, a dreary decade that did not allow his talent to come to full flower. Chekhov criticism of the late eighties and early nineties abounds in phrases that quickly became critical clichés, some of which persisted for many years: his lack of ideology (bezideinost'); Chekhov as "a victim of Russia's dead years" (zhertva bezvremen'ia); Chekhov as "the poet of Russia's twilight years" (poet sumerek).

While Chekhov was not by nature a political man, he did have a very deep concern for his society and for his fellow citizens, and the carping of critics clearly disturbed him. Perhaps the angriest letter he ever wrote was to the editor of a journal whose anonymous reviewer had called his writing "unprincipled" (PSSP 4.54-57). His life contains ample evidence that he took his social responsibilities very seriously indeed. In 1890 he undertook a trying and hazardous journey to the penal colony of Sakhalin on Russia's Pacific coast, nearly as far from Moscow as one could travel within the Russian empire. His motives were more humanitarian and scientific than literary: he wished to draw attention to the prisoners whom, he said, society had abandoned there to rot (PSSP 4.32) and to write a scholarly study of the island so as to "repay his debt to medicine." Only a few post-Sakhalin stories directly reflect impressions of his journey. During the summer of 1890 he interviewed convicts, compiling some 10,000 census cards that provided raw data for his study The Island of Sakhalin, published in 1893-94. His philanthropic efforts continued at Melikhovo, the modest estate south of Moscow which he purchased in 1892. He was busily engaged in both famine relief and in fighting a cholera epidemic in that same year; his literary work at Melikhovo was frequently interrupted by calls to treat ailing peasants; a few years later he participated as a volunteer census taker. He also organized campaigns to send books to libraries on Sakhalin and in his native Taganrog, helped raise funds to supply his native town with a statue of Peter the Great, served on the local county council (zemstvo) and as a school trustee, and organized the building of two new community schoolhouses near Melikhovo. All the critics who accused Chekhov of indifference or social irresponsibility could, taken together, scarcely compile a more impressive list of philanthropic activities.

Critical opinion slowly began to shift in the 1890s in response to developments in Chekhov's art. Mikhailovsky's views were still influential, but became increasingly challenged. Chekhov produced a series of detailed studies of various levels of Russian society; while critics still struggled to find specific ideological stances in these stories, they reacted positively on the whole to his treatment of social reality and social problems. His journey to Sakhalin and his "Ward Six" in particular seemed to show that he was far from indifferent to the life around him. His stories of peasant life conveyed an unflinchingly honest view of Russia's largest social class and made an especially strong impact. As Ivan Bunin remarks in his memoirs:

> Chekhov was muffled for a long time. Until "Peasants," which is by no means his best work, he was very popular with the broad masses of the public, but they regarded

> him only as an amusing storyteller, author of "Vint" and "The Complaint Book" [early humorous stories, K.L.]. Serious people, people with "ideas," took little interest in him on the whole. They acknowledged his talent but did not take him very seriously. I remember how a few of them fankly laughed at me, a young man, when I ventured to compare him with Garshin or Korolenko, and there were those who said they would never read an author who began writing under the name of Chekhonte: "One simply can't imagine," they would say, "Tolstoy or Turgenev changing their names for such a vulgar alias" (1960.26).

Gradually, then, Chekhov was seen to have, if not a full-fledged ideology, at least a basically healthy set of values. His stories might be gloomy, his view of life jaundiced, but his work seemed to show a vague faith in, or at least a definite longing for, a decent and more humane life. He was held to be the poet of the Russian intelligentsia, a people he portrays as weak-willed, unhappy, and with small talent for living, but who, nonetheless, have his affection and sympathy. By the mid-1890s he had become one of Russia's most popular writers.

Toward the end of the century, as the pattern of evolution of Chekhov's art could be seen more clearly, the notion of Chekhov as an irresponsible writer became much more difficult to support. Skabichevsky (1895.1) answered his own question "Does Mr. Chekhov Have Any Ideals?" with a resounding "Yes." Mikhailovsky himself modified his opinion, noting that Chekhov's work had evolved considerably (1900.3) and that Chekhov himself at least displayed a very respectable "longing for an ideal" in his latest work. Maxim Gorky wrote about "In the Ravine," insisting that Chekhov was neither wholly pessimistic nor indifferent to his characters. (Gorky's article appeared in a provincial newspaper, however, and it is doubtful that it had much immediate influence, although it certainly aided in Chekhov's admission into the pantheon of writers approved by the Soviet regime some years later). The publication of his Collected Works by A.F. Marks (1899-1902) also provided critics with a better perspective on Chekhov's career and so helped them make a more profound examination of it.

Chekhov's dramatic work was also slow in gaining acceptance among the critics. Much of the theatrical criticism in Chekhov's own day appeared in daily newspapers and was concerned largely with evaluating specific performances rather than assessing his status as a dramatist. But a brief review of his early dramatic career can set the context for later criticism. Ivanov's premiere, in November 1887, created a considerable uproar, with both hisses and wild applause, a reaction caused by a combination of the actors' poor performance and the audience's bewilderment over Chekhov's apparent abstention from moral judgements of his characters. Reviews were brief and had few kind words; the play closed after three performances. After substantial revision the play was restaged on January 31, 1889, this time with considerable popular and critical success. Critics on the left of the spectrum, led by Mikhailovsky, were less receptive; they objected to the play's lack of redeeming social message, accusing Chekhov of preaching "reconciliation with reality" rather than engaging in social criticism. His Wood Demon, staged in December 1889, was met coldly by critics and public alike. The Seagull, in its October 1896 premiere, was a complete fiasco, again because of an indequate production that was unequal to the play's striking dramatic innovations. Chekhov abandoned the theater for nearly six years. Not until the Moscow Art Theater [MAT] staged The Seagull (December 17. 1898), a performance described by Nemirovich-Danchenko as a "collosal success," was Chekhov's reputation as a dramatist established. The MAT's productions of subsequent plays confirmed and raised his status as a dramatist. But for all the brilliance of these productions they set a precedent in interpreting Chekhov as a dramatist of "lyric melancholy," an approach that Chekhov himself chafed at but which remained dominant for many years.

The last years of Chekhov's life were ones of increasingly deteriorating health due to tuberculosis and correspondingly decreased activity. Much more of his time was devoted to the drama, although some of his finest short stories also date from this period. His final years were spent in Yalta, whose Black Sea climate was more beneficial to his lungs. His marriage in 1901 to Olga Knipper, a young actress from the MAT, did not fundamentally alter his life. By the time of his death in 1904 he was acknowledged as an artist of the first magnitude.

Chekhov's death brought a reassessment of his significance. Not only the usual obituaries and summaries of his career but also the publication of some of his letters and memoirs of his friends and colleagues (see Bunin, Kuprin, Korolenko and Gorky in 1960.26) created an image of a more genial and life-loving author than the one imagined by most readers. In the writings of Chekhov's last years critics found signs of a transcendence of the gloom and pessimism they had perceived in his earlier work. The Cherry Orchard in particular was seen as a valedictory work which expressed a much deeper faith in the future.

The enormous changes in the literary climate at the turn of the century in Russia also added new touches to the image of Chekhov the artist. Writers from newly-developing literary schools strove to include Chekhov in their numbers. Critics from the decadent and symbolist movements saw Chekhov's abstention from narrowly ideological concerns as a virtue rather than a flaw and as a sign that his works anticipated the "new art" that was being created in Europe and in Russia. The first studies appeared that focused on his craftsmanship rather than on his ideology. As early as 1888 Merezhkovsky (1888.1) had defended Chekhov against the civic-minded critics (and had spoken of Chekhov's "impressionism", a topic prominent in later Chekhov criticism). He called for a reappraisal of Chekhov's work, arguing that it proved a non-tendentious art could still deal meaningfully with social issues. In keeping with the increasingly apocalyptic mood of the end of the century, Merezhkovsky later argued that Chekhov (together with Gorky) personified the mood and the ideal of the contemporary Russian intelligentsia; his works express the new "religion of humanity" and progress and point to the end of the era of Christian culture (1906.5). Shestov's influential study (1905.9) also sees Chekhov's complete independence from ideology as one of his principal achievements, reflecting his sense of the death of the old culture and his longing for something new. Basing himself largely on "A Dreary Story" and Ivanov, Shestov views Chekhov as a "poet of hopelessness." His characters are isolated and alienated, stripped of all hope and so, potentially at least, able to create their selves and their world anew.

Andrey Bely proposed that Chekhov was in fact a symbolist, whose works suggest the essence of true reality through their portrayal of the banal texture of daily life: in The Cherry Orchard, Bely wrote, Chekhov drew apart "the folds of life, and that which from a distance seems but shadowed creases turns out to be a stairway to Eternity" (1904.5). A few years later Mayakovsky (1914.6) argued that Chekhov was a quasi-futurist, "a craftsman of the word," whose chief concern was not social reform but exploring the possibilites of language itself. Leonid Grossman (1914.5) placed Chekhov within the tradition of naturalism. This profusion of new images of Chekhov, many of which are flawed by the extremes to which their arguments are taken, at least expanded critical horizons by drawing attention away from the tiresome debate over Chekhov's ideals.

In all this, however, the prevailing (but by no means exclusive) image of Chekhov was as a pessimist. Those who now acknowledged his "ideal" saw the source of his pessimism in the gap between that ideal and the grim reality depicted in his writings. Those who admired his independence from the tradition of socially-conscious literature also maintained that his works expressed disillusionment over the inevitable vulgarity of daily life. The notion of Chekhov as a writer consumed by despair and longing, the "poet of Russia's twilight years," was to persist for a long time.

Chekhov's critics abroad were not so preoccupied with ideology as were their Russian counterparts, but they were, initially at least, uncomfortable with what they perceived as the thorough pessimism of his writings. The gloomy atmosphere of many of his works was explained as an accurate reflection of the dreariness of Russia itself and as a result of the sadness inherent in the "Russian soul." To fit him into a familiar frame of reference, they labelled Chekhov "the Russian Maupassant." Only a few works of criticism show sensitivity to the innovations of his stories and plays.

In the first decade of the twentieth century Chekhov gained some qualified recognition among the English, but was slow to win any broad popularity. Early comments on his writings tend to summarize the reactions of the Russian critics. Chekhov's obituary in the London Times Literary Supplement (July 22, 1904) could only equivocate that he "may or may not have been a genius."

R.E.C. Long, Chekhov's first major English translator spoke of his "hopeless pessimism." In his 1902 article (1902.3), Long says that the final impression produced by Chekhov's stories is "that life is a nightmare of abysmal emptiness, that all men are ridiculous in one another's eyes and contemptible in their own, that no man is a master of his own fate, and that genius, courage and virtue are, by a law of nature, inevitably shipwrecked in a world for which they are by nature unfitted..." Of Chekhov's plays (not yet translated into English) he can find very little good to say.

Long's translations (one collection appeared in 1903,

a second in 1908) were generally well received, however, and began to arouse serious interest in Chekhov's stories. Arnold Bennett gave an enthusiastic review of the translations, paying tribute to Chekhov's mastery of the short story form and ranking him together with Tolstoy, Turgenev, and Dostoevsky (1909.2). Maurice Baring, who had seen Chekhov's plays in Russia, made the first serious attempt to explain them to British readers (1908.2). He wrote sensitively and perceptively about Chekhov's art, stressing Chekhov's dramatic technique of conveying inner rather than outer action. George Calderon, the only other British critic of the pre-war era who appreciated Chekhov's true originality as a dramatist, also made efforts to bring Chekhov to a wider audience. Calderon's introduction to his translations of The Seagull and The Cherry Orchard (1912.2) set the plays within the context of the very different Russian theatrical tradition and attempted to raise the level of his audience to a point where it could appreciate Chekhov's new art. Chekhov's plays, he argued, were unlike existing ones, being "centrifugal" in drawing their audience outward to the larger world beyond the events on the stage. Calderon's production of The Seagull in Glasgow in 1909 was the first performance of a Chekhov play in English; it attracted little critical attention, however.

The Seagull, The Cherry Orchard and Uncle Vanya were all staged in Britain before World War I; reviews, with few exceptions, were unenthusiastic. Critics spoke of the plays' formlessness, their strangeness, and their unremitting gloom.

The post-war era, however, saw Chekhov at the forefront of the British theater and found leading writers and critics hailing him as a new master of the short story. The explanation for this sudden popularity is to be found in part in the change in intellectual climate produced by the war. Audiences who had survived the collapse of the old order in Europe and who had seen the truths and standards they assumed to be unshakeable blasted to pieces in the trenches of Flanders were far more sensitive to the images of cultural collapse in Chekhov's plays and to the uncertainties that dominate the world of his stories. Russia had also been an ally in the war; this fact, plus the dramatic events of the 1917 revolution, roused considerable curiosity about things Russian. This change in climate, coupled with the fifteen volumes of Constance Garnett's translations of Chekhov's stories and plays (published between 1916 and 1923) provided the basis for the "Chekhov cult" of the 1920s.

Chekhov's plays were very popular on the British stage in the 1920s. Critical reaction, although often dissatisfied with specific productions, was near unanimous in praising Chekhov's genius as a playwright. The scale of his popularity can be judged by Virginia Woolf's remark, in her review of a 1920 production of The Three Sisters, that every member of the audience had "probably read Chekhov's Cherry Orchard several times" (1920.5).

British writers and critics of the early 1920s heaped more praise on Chekhov than he had hitherto received anywhere. They were attracted by the freshness of his art and admired his moral and intellectual honesty, the apparent simplicity of his manner, and his deep and sympathetic understanding of human behavior and human suffering. The absence of political concerns in Chekhov's writings was seen as a virtue: critics applauded his political and intellectual freedom and saw it as the very basis of his new art. Middleton Murry hailed Chekhov's modernity, describing him as "a good many phases in advance of all that is habitually described as modern in the art of literature" (1920.4) and placing him far ahead of Joyce and Proust (1924.5). Edward Garnett also wrote of Chekhov's modernity: his independence and skepticism, coupled with his scientific outlook, "equipped him for seizing and judging modern life from fresh angles" (1921.3). William Gerhardi (later spelled Gerhardie) focused on Chekhov's sensibility in his study, the first English-language monograph on Chekhov (1923.6). This sensibility is expressed through irony, melancholy, philosophical relativism, deep humanity, and absolute honesty. Gerhardie's Chekhov is a skeptic but not a pessimist; he is a man with a deep faith in humanity's capacity to build a humane culture. Virginia Woolf also praised Chekhov's "subtle and delicate" analysis of human relations (1925.8). She admired his fundamental honesty, his refusal "to manipulate the evidence so as to produce something fitting, decorous, agreeable to our vanity." His is a fiction with "soul," and in reading it "the soul gains an asonishing sense of freedom."

But by the end of the decade Chekhov's popularity in Britain had begun to wane. One sign of the times was D.S. Mirsky's essay "Chekhov and the English" (1927.4), in which he took English intellectuals to task for their "Chekhov cult." Mirsky maintains Chekhov's style is "undistinguished;" moreover, his values--specifically his rejection of the heroic--are fundamentally unhealthy. Several years later, John Galsworthy, an unqualified admirer of Chekhov, cautioned young writers about the perils of trying to imitate the inimitable Chekhov, whom he described as "the most potent magnet to young writers in several countries for the last twenty years" (1932.1).

The American image of Chekhov formed rather more slowly than did the British one. No Chekhov cult developed, even though his plays became very popular in the later 1920s. His short stories were particulary slow to find a wide audience.

The first American study of Chekhov, by Abraham Cahan (1899.1), essentially echoed earlier Russian views, noting he was a writer without a "general idea;" nonetheless Cahan ranked him as Russia's greatest short-story writer after Tolstoy. W.L. Phelps (1917.3) provided a rather unenthusiastic appraisal of Chekhov's art, rating it below that of Turgenev, Tolstoy, or Dostoevsky, and criticizing his plays as "formless." Henry Seidel Canby (1915.2) admired Chekhov's freedom from sentimentality and the typical formulas of American magazine writing, although he found the stories excessively gloomy.

Chekhov's plays had been performed in New York and Chicago before World War I (in Russian) by emigré groups and touring companies; amateur groups had also staged his one-act farces and _The Cherry Orchard_. But it was the American tours of the MAT in 1923 and 1924 that aroused serious interest in Chekhov's drama. Constance Garnett's translations had also appeared in the United States by this time, and many individual stories were published in American magazines. Yet evidence suggests that his audience was very small: Robert Littel, writing in the _New Republic_ (June 22, 1927), could say that Chekhov "is accepted, though ignorantly and vaguely, as a 'big man' in the literature of somewhere or other, but he is simply not current at all."

Eve Le Galliene appeared in the first professional English-language performance of Chekhov in the United States when _The Three Sisters_ was staged in New York in 1927. Reviews were enthusiastic, and a series of her productions, which were influenced by the methods of the MAT, followed to continuing critical acclaim.

Chekhov's reception in France follows the same general pattern as his rise to popularity in England. At the beginning of the century Tolstoy, Turgenev, and Dostoevsky were only becoming popular and, as Edmond Jaloux has noted, "this newcomer seemed pretty thin next to them" (1925.5). Early critics of his short stories make comparisons, not always favorable, with Maupassant and stress Chekhov's pessimism and lack of a systematic world view. He did win admiration from a small circle of littérateurs in the years preceding World War I, but only in the twenties did he gain widespread popularity as a dramatist, principally because of the enormously successful productions of Georges Pitoëff (Uncle Vanya, 1921 and 1922; The Seagull, 1922; The Three Sisters, 1929). The publishing house of Plon issued Chekhov's Collected Works in the mid-1920s. In Paris in 1924 the critic Charles du Bos gave a series of influential public lectures that were one of the most discerning analyses of Chekhov's new art produced in any country to date. His Chekhov is one who can reveal the depths of life precisely as they are reflected on its surface. In France as in England, however, Chekhov's popularity waned in the 1930s only to be revived in the 1950s.

Thus by 1930 Chekhov had become firmly established as a classic in Europe, on the stage to a broad audience, and as a short-story writer to a much smaller but influential group of writers and readers. Productions of his plays continued through the thirties and forties, although the number of critical studies of his prose dropped off sharply.

In the USSR the image of Chekhov inherited by post-revolutionary critics was generally that of the pessimist, the "poet of a dying era" whose major concern was the fate of the intelligentsia in the last decades of the previous century. To a society concerned with repairing the physical and emotional damage wrought by six years of war, revolution, and civil war, a society with its eyes fixed firmly on the future, a society in which optimism and confidence were the slogans of the day, the image of a wistful Chekhov could have little relevance. Yet Chekhov was undeniably a great artist. The problem was how to redefine his greatness and make him significant to a very different society in which a new set of literary demands were gradually being elaborated. Two general trends are present in the period 1917-1934: one, to revise the image of Chekhov in Soviet terms and establish that he was not only acceptable but also "useful" to the new Soviet state; and another, very productive effort to collect Chekhov's literary legacy and to examine his art apart from questions of ideology. Given the remarkable cultural energy and comparative tolerance of the 1920s a number of interesting and valuable studies emerged.

Anatoly Lunacharsky, Commissar of Education and a man of broad culture, posed the question directly in his article "What Can Chekhov Be for Us?" (1924.4).

Lunacharsky asserted that the gloom and pessimism of Chekhov's writings reflected the general mood of his era. Confronted with the horror of life around him, Chekhov escaped into art. This could have little relevance to Soviet life, but Lunacharasky attempted to "save" Chekhov for the Soviet reader by arguing that his works satirize and denounce the sordidness of pre-revolutionary life; his works could serve a purpose in helping build a new Soviet culture by combatting those same elements of "petty-bourgeois vulgarity" that had survived the revolution. Lunacharsky also held up Chekhov as a master craftsman whose technique was worthy of emulation by young Soviet writers.

The notion of Chekhov as the exemplary short story writer was an important one in that it shifted attention away from his lack of an approved ideology. Considerable attention was paid to his craftsmanship, and through the twenties and early thirties there appeared a series of valuable studies of his artistic technique (1924.7, 1926.1, 1927.2, 1929.15, 20, and others). The short story was the dominant genre in Soviet literature in the 1920s; not surprisingly, Chekhov had a deep influence on the first generation of Soviet writers.

Considerable effort was devoted to collecting memoir and biographical material, particluarly in connection with the twenty-fifth anniversary of Chekhov's death, marked in 1929. Archival material was studied and published; early writings that had been omitted from the Marks edition of his Collected Works were published as were his letters. The first systematic description of Chekhov's growing archives was published (1939.5); bibliographies appeared (1929.13, 1930.2). A twelve-volume Collected Works appeared in 1929, another between 1930 and 1933.

The first Soviet monographs on Chekhov also appeared in the 1920s. Balukhatyi's study (1927.2) shows the influence of the formalist school in its avoidance of any extra-literary factors in tracing the development of Chekhov's plays. He finds a common structural principle in the plays which, he argues, is essentially musical. Iuryi Sobolev's Chekhov (1930.4) uses much of the recently collected material to give a detailed account of his life. He stresses Chekhov's scientific interests and sees the notion of evolution as central to his outlook and an important influence on his art. Sobolev's explanation of Chekhov's career relies on a class-based approach (later to be condemned as "vulgar sociologism"). Chekhov, he argues, evolved from a typically petty-bourgeois apolitical stance through conservatism and eventually to liberalism. A more interesting attempt to capture the essence of Chekhov's personality both as man and as artist is found in Avram Derman's _A Portrait of Chekhov as an Artist_ (1929.6). Derman also argues that Chekhov's class origins weighed heavily on his writing. His repulsion toward the "slave mentality" of his childhood milieu was seen as one of the driving forces behind his art. But Derman took a quite unorthodox psychological approach to his subject, examining the "disharmony" in Chekhov's personality, noting the absence of passion in his life and arguing that he lacked the capacity to experience deep emotion. This fundamental coldness is reflected throughout his literary work.

The delicate and subtle art of Chekhov's plays seemed scarcely in tune with the bold themes and experimental techniques that dominated Soviet drama in the years following the revolution. Lunacharsky, himself a playwright, did not extend his apology for Chekhov (1924.4) to the plays: he was ready to bury "the whining, sentimental intelligentsia, _The Three Sisters_ and all their many kin." Chekhov's one-act vaudevilles were popular, however: Vakhtangov staged a very original production of _The Wedding_ in 1920 and Meyerhold's 1935 production, _Thirty-Three Swoons_ combined _The Anniversary_, _The Bear_, and _The Proposal_ to form what he called a "tragic grotesque." But the major plays were considered to be overly concerned with the fate of the pre-revolutionary intelligentsia, a group little in favor in Soviet Russia. _The Cherry Orchard_ was an exception since it was more amenable to a Marxist interpretation in its depiction of the collapse of the landowning aristocracy and the rise of a new, energetic class.

Although efforts were being made to secure an honored place for Chekhov in the Soviet pantheon, his position was by no means secure among those who saw themselves as the guardians of the new Soviet culture. A 1929 survey of some twenty of the more party-minded writers, critics, poets, and directors (1929.9) revealed that only a few of those polled admired Chekhov's work and that most considered him to be quite passé.

A direct and impassioned plea for a new, Soviet image of Chekhov came in Mikhail Koltsov's 1928 article (1928.4). Koltsov called for a Chekhov "without makeup", a Chekhov cleansed from the pre-revolutionary notions of him as the "poet of twilight people," the image which, he suggests, was created largely by the MAT. Koltsov's Chekhov was not only a marvellous craftsman of the word but a deeply socially-conscious writer, "a materialist, a socially-minded skeptic," who pointed out the injustices and flaws of his society and who satirized its weaknesses. Chekhov is thus useful (as Lunacharsky had suggested) in helping to destroy the same flaws that persist in Soviet society.

The First Congress of Soviet Writers (1934), the meeting that proclaimed the full domination of literature by the party and by party concerns, also confirmed Chekhov as a full-fledged classic. Gorky's speech, on August 17, 1934, included Chekhov in the tradition of "critical realists" whose legacy, reexamined and reinterpreted, was to become an essential part of Soviet culture.

The full acceptance of Chekhov's plays began with the MAT's 1940 production of The Three Sisters by Nemirovich-Danchenko. This production downplayed the play's tragic elements, stressed the characters' faith in the future, and even adjusted the play's ending by omitting Chebutykin's final speech ("...It doesn't matter...") in order to give prominence to Olga's expression of hope ("We shall live!")

One of the first critics to begin creating a new image of Chekhov in accordance with the new literary standards of the Stalin era was A. Roskin. In a series of articles and books of the later thirties and forties, studies that were devoted mainly to Chekhov's drama, Roskin creates an image of Chekhov that is neither the strident satirist and proto-Bolshevik proposed by Koltsov nor the pessimistic and wistful poet of ineffectual intellectuals as seen by many pre-revolutionary critics. Roskin's Chekhov has social concerns and a joy of life; he is essentially an optimist, compassionate yet critical toward his characters. And Roskin makes an important point that helped create an image of Chekhov acceptable even to the most dedicated Bolshevik when he argues that the gloomy notes in Chekhov's writings belong to his characters, not to their author.

The Stalinist critic par excellence, however, was V.V. Ermilov. Ermilov's books were issued in large printings and frequently translated. They, more than any other, set forth the "official" image of Chekhov in Stalin's time and for some years thereafter. Ermilov's critico-biographical study (1946.4) paints a portrait of Chekhov as the indefatigable champion of the underdog, a healthy, cheerful, relentlessly optimistic writer who was tireless in his attacks on the abuses of pre-revolutionary Russian society and who delighted in puncturing "liberal illusions" about the possibility of Russia's peaceful capitalist development. Ermilov's Chekhov is, in the words of one western critic, "a Gorky in glasses." Ermilov's technique is to suggest rather than to prove, and he suggests clearly that the values implicit in Chekhov's writings are those that are at the basis of the Soviet state. Ermilov's study was in fact criticized for its overly idealized portrait of Chekhov and later editions were toned down somewhat, but still left no doubt that Chekhov was to be found in the front ranks of the "progressive" pre-revolutionary intelligentsia.

In the Soviet Union Chekhov had definitely ceased to be the "poet of twilight Russia."

With Chekhov established as an officially approved classic, a new series of studies appeared placing him in the context of literary and intellectual history. Considerable attention was paid to linking Chekhov with the "progressive" ideologies of the 1880s and 90s (1954.20). Even though few overtly political statements can be found in Chekhov's writings, a common argument was that an innate sense of democracy (and therefore an implicit opposition to the pre-revolutionary Russian political order) was a fundamental feature of his work. Such was proposed, for example, by G.A. Bialyi in the authoritative History of Russian Literature (1956.2). Chekhov's scorn for the banality of daily life was read as his protest against the social order; his compassion for the suffering was seen as his championing of the oppressed; notes of gloom or pessimism were explained as his reaction to Russian social evils. Soviet studies of the fifties and sixties such as Papernyi's (1960.49) and Berdnikov's (1961.2) have much value; but their overall tendency is to simplify Chekhov and sentimentalize his work, to overlook the very subtleties and ambiguities that are the whole basis of his art, to seek out villians and positive heroes and so to resurrect the very stereotypes that Chekhov's art sets out to destroy.

The hundredth anniversary of Chekhov's birth (1960) brought a veritable explosion of new studies, both in the USSR and in the West, studies that created a body of Chekhov scholarship and criticism so large that only its major outlines can be indicated here. A host of considerably more sophisticated monographs, collections, and essays created new images of Chekhov by taking a much closer look at his writings.

Even before the centenary year Ronald Hingley

(1950.3) and David Magarshack (1952.5) had challenged the image of a melancholy and resigned Chekhov that had persisted since the turn of the century. They drew attention to his humor and derived a much healthier and more optimistic view of life from his writings. Magarshack particularly took issue with the MAT's "misinterpretations" of his plays. Documentary material published in the USSR helped western biographers such as Simmons (1962.17) produce detailed accounts of his life. More intimate biographies followed: French biographers (1967.5, 1971.1) again proposed a pessimistic, despairing Chekhov; British biographers examined Chekhov's relations with women (1973.17, 1976.14, 1979.19). The result was a more complex and less idealized image than that found in Soviet biographies. Chekhov was seen not only as a selfless philanthropist but also as a detached, fundamentally cold man who was not above exploiting those closest to him, a man who is all the more human for having some flaws.

Western critics (1971.31, 1972.17, 1973.21, 1977.3) have devoted much attention to Chekhov's plays in recent years, shedding new light on his dramatic technique and examining the nuances and subtleties of his texts. Chekhov's relationsip to western dramatists has been the subject of numerous studies, and surveys of modern drama routinely assign him a place of honor. The question of the actual nature of Chekhov's drama has been a favorite topic: his plays have been seen as tragicomedies (1964.8), as anticipations of the theater of the absurd (1965.3, 1972.21, 1973.11, 1977.11), as part of the modernist movement (1970.20), as comedy (1967.13), as tragedy (1968.20, 1981.5), and within the tradition of naturalism (1965.17, 1968.13, 27, 1977.15). Finally, the publication of The Oxford Chekhov (Oxford and London: Oxford University Press, 1964-80), with its colloquial translations by Ronald Hingley, provides a modern rendering together with notes and commentary that complements Constance Garnett's versions.

The 1960 jubilee year left no question about Chekhov's status as a classic in the USSR. The relatively tolerant climate for literary criticism in the 1960s and 70s allowed freer expression of divergent opinions on Chekhov; new studies appeared that focused on his writings themselves and paid much less attention to matters of ideology. Ilya Ehrenburg attempted to find a contemporary answer to Lunacharsky's question of Chekhov's relevance to Soviet society. In his "Rereading Chekhov" (1959.7) he set forth his notion of Chekhov as a writer who neither preached nor drew morals, who "did not set out to teach anything, yet taught millions of people." Ehrenburg argues Chekhov's non-ideological art still has a positive social value: "if [the artist] is able to see beneath the surface, if he can look into the depths of the human heart, he will produce works that will help men face hardships and will move their children and grandchildren many years after history has given its verdict and the dust of the archives has settled on the old burning problems." Even before Ehrenburg, and in fact during the Stalin years, A. Skaftymov had published several studies that focused on the art of Chekhov's writings rather than on their supposed message. He argues that Chekhov's plays are by no means clear-cut depictions of heroes and villains; he stresses Chekhov's use of conflicting emotions to convey complex and contradictory aspects of character. Skaftymov's articles first appeared in rather obscure journals but were republished (1958.20-23, 1972.25) and had considerable influence in establishing a more sophisticated appreciation of Chekhov's plays. More recently, some studies of the author-character relationship in Chekhov have appeared that are particularly interesting, given the traditional Russian preoccupation with deriving an acceptable ideology from his work. Critics such as Vladimir Kataev (1979.11) and V.Ia. Linkov (1982.23) have argued for a clear distinction between Chekhov's own views and those expressed by his characters and have attempted to define with greater precision the role ideas play in his work. Another trend is that of formal and stylistic analyses, chiefly of Chekhov's prose. One of the most remarkable studies is Chudakov's Chekhov's Poetics (1971.6, 1983.5), a thorough, if perhaps overly schematic examination of Chekhov's narrative technique and of his world view generally. Finally, Soviet Chekhovists continue to produce high-quality scholarship, illuminating aspects of his biography and his attitudes to events and personalities of his time. Most of these have arisen in connection with work done for the thirty-volume Complete Collected Works and Letters (Moscow: Nauka, 1974-83). Although not without shortcomings this edition provides authorative texts and detailed commentary, creating a solid basis for further research.

A study of Chekhov in criticism shows most strikingly how different the Russian and the western images of him are. From the very beginning Russian critics have viewed Chekhov first as a short-story writer and only second as a dramatist; the situation in the West is quite the reverse. Western writings on Chekhov's stories have been overwhelmingly a product of professional scholars of

Russian literature (as opposed to professional critics writing for mass media) and of short-story writers themselves (Somerset Maugham, Frank O'Connor, H.E. Bates, Sean O'Faolain, Thomas Mann, and others). The image produced by western criticism is predominantly of Chekhov as a dramatist, that by Russian criticism of Chekhov as a short story writer.

Why should this be? Part of the explanation seems to lie in the differing status of the short story in Russian and western literatures. One is hard put to find any characters in English or French short stories that have assumed the archetypical significance of Pushkin's Hermann ("The Queen of Spades") or Gogol's Akaky Akakievich ("The Overcoat"), characters who are as well-known and as important in Russian literature as are the heroes of any novel in the West. The short story in the West simply does not have the mass appeal it has in Russian literature, and Chekhov's revolutionary transformation of the genre, while influential on practitioners and studied by specialists, has made relatively little impact on the western common reader.

A second reason for the western interest in Chekhov's plays lies in the fact that his first widespread popularity abroad came as a dramatist. His real introduction to British, French, and American audiences came in the numerous stage performances of his works in the 1920s. His beginnings as a dramatist in Russia, however, were far from auspicious. Although the MAT had enormous successes with his plays, these still did not appeal to the mass audience that his stories did. For some years after the 1917 revolution the plays were considered "highbrow" and far too concerned with the fates of pre-revolutionary intellectuals to be appropriate for citizens of a new workers' state.

The most significant pattern in Chekhov criticism, however, has been the attempt to pin him down, to label or categorize him, from the earliest debates over his "ideals" (a debate that still continues in more sophisticated forms), through the continuing arguments over his essential optimism or pessimism, his impressionism or realism. Is he a naturalist or an absurdist or a symbolist? Are his plays tragedies or comedies? Such questions have provided fodder for many a critical article; none can be considered resolved.

Indeed, the greatest tribute to the complexity and depth of Chekhov's elusive, multifaceted art is that so many have found so much in his writings. Chekhov continues to intrigue and to provoke and so is very much alive.

Writings by Anton Chekhov

1880

"A Letter to a Learned Neighbour" [Pis'mo k uchenomu sosedu]. Strekoza, no. 10 (March 9), p. 6.

"For Apples" [Za iablochki]. Strekoza, no. 33 (August 17), pp. 6-7.

1881

"St. Peter's Day" [Petrov den']. Budil'nik, no. 26 (June 29), pp. 404-05, 408.

"The Sinner from Toledo" [Greshnik iz Toledo]. Zritel', no. 25-26 (December 23), pp. 13-14.

Platonov. Written 1880-81? First published in Neizdannaia p'esa A.P. Chekhova [An unpublished play by Chekhov]. Dokumenty po istorii literatury i obshchestvennosti, no. 5 [Documents on the history of literature and society]. Edited by N.F. Bel'chikov. Moscow: Novaia Moskva, 1923, 253 p.

1882

"The Green Scythe (A Little Novel)" [Zelenaia kosa (malen'kii roman)]. Literaturnoe prilozhenie zhurnala "Moskva", no. 15 (April 23), p. 108, and no. 16 (April 30), pp. 109-112.

"An Unnecessary Victory" [Nenuzhnaia pobeda]. Budil'nik, nos. 24-27 (June), and 29-34 (July and August).

"A Lady" [Barynia]. Moskva, no. 29 (July 30), pp. 239-41; no. 30 (August 7), pp. 245-47; and no. 31 (August 17), pp. 255-56.

"Late-blooming Flowers" [Tsvety zapozdalye]. Mirskoi tolk, no. 37 (October 10), pp. 197-99; no. 38 (October 17), pp. 212-14; no. 39 (October 23), pp. 225-28; no. 41 (November 11), pp. 243-45.

1883

"Two in One [Dvoe v odnom]. Zritel', no. 3 (January 8), p. 2.

"The Death of a Civil Servant" [Smert' chinovnika]. Oskolki, no. 27 (July 2), pp. 4-5.

"A Daughter of Albion" [Doch' Al'biona]. Oskolki, no. 33 (August 13), pp. 4-5.

"In Autumn" [Osen'iu]. Budil'nik, no. 37 (September 24), pp. 343-44.

"The Fat Man and the Thin Man" [Tolstyi i tonkii]. Oskolki, no. 40 (October 1), p. 5.

"At Sea" [V more]. Mirskoi tolk, no. 40 (October 29), pp. 470-71.

"On Christmas Eve" [V Rozhdestvenskuiu noch']. Budil'nik, no. 50 (December 22), pp. 509-11.

1884

"The Swedish Match" [Shvedskaia spichka]. Al'manakh "Strekozy" na 1884 god, St. Petersburg, n.p., 1884.

"The Complaint Book" [Zhalobnaia kniga]. Oskolki, no. 10 (March 10), p. 6.

"Minds in Ferment" [Brozhenie umov]. Oskolki, no. 24 (June 16), pp. 4-5.

"Surgery" [Khirurgiia]. Oskolki, no. 36 (August 11), pp. 3-4.

"The Chameleon" [Khameleon]. Oskolki, no. 36 (September 8), p. 4

"Vint" [Vint]. Oskolki, no. 39 (September 29), p. 4.

"Oysters" [Ustritsy]. Budil'nik, no. 48 (December 6), pp. 585-86.

The Shooting Party [Drama na okhote]. Novosti dnia, nos. 212, 213, 219, 226, 233, 241, 247, 254, 261, 275, 282, 289, 296, 303, 310, 317, 331, 338, 345, 353 (August to December) and 1885, nos. 26, 45, 54, 61, 62, 75, 80, 95, 98, 102, 107, and 111 (January to April).

"On the Highway" [Na bol'shoi doroge]. Written 1884-85; first published in Slovo. Sbornik vtoroi: k desiatiletiiu smerti A.P. Chekhova [The word. Second collection: for the tenth anniversary of Chekhov's death]. Edited by M.P. Chekhova. Moscow: Knigoizdatel'stvo pisatelei v Moskve, 1914, pp. 8-36.

1885

"The Captain's Tunic" [Kapitanskii mundir]. Oskolki, no. 4 (January 26), pp. 4-5.

"The Burbot" [Nalim]. Peterburgskaia gazeta, no. 177 (July 1), p. 3.

"A Horsey Name" [Loshadinaia familiia]. Peterburgskaia gazeta, no. 183 (July 7), p. 3.

"The Huntsman" [Eger']. Peterburgskaia gazeta, no. 194 (July 18), p. 3.

"The Malefactor" [Zloumyshlennik]. Peterburgskaia gazeta, no. 200 July 24), p. 3.

"The Cook's Wedding" [Kukharka zhenitsia]. Peterburgskaia gazeta, no. 254 (September 16), p. 3.

"Sergeant Prishibeev" [Unter Prishibeev]. Peterburgskaia gazeta, no. 273 (October 5), p. 3.

"Grief" [Gore]. Peterburgskaia gazeta, no. 324 (November 25), p. 3.

1886

"Heartache" [Toska]. Peterburgskaia gazeta, no. 26 (January 27), p. 3.

"An Upheaval" [Perepolokh]. Peterburgskaia gazeta, no. 33 (February 3), p. 3.

"Smoking is Bad For You" [O vrede tabaka].

Peterburgskaia gazeta, no. 47 (February 17), p. 3.

"Anyuta" [Aniuta]. Oskolki, no. 22 (February 22), p. 4.

"The Night Before the Trial" [Noch' pered sudom]. Oskolki, no. 5 (February 1), pp. 4-5.

"The Service for the Dead" [Panikhida]. Novoe vremia, no. 3581 (February 15), pp. 1-2.

"The Witch" [Ved'ma]. Novoe vremia, no. 3600 (March 8), p. 2.

"A Little Joke" [Shutochka]. Sverchok, no. 10 (March 12), pp. 74-78.

"A Nightmare" [Koshmar]. Novoe vremia, no. 3621 (March 29), pp. 1-2.

"Grisha" [Grisha]. Oskolki, no. 14 (April 5), p. 4.

"On Holy Night" ("Easter Eve") [Sviatoiu noch'iu]. Novoe vremia, no 3636 (April 13), pp. 1-2.

"A Gentleman Friend" [Znakomyi muzhchina]. Oskolki, no. 18 (May 3), p. 4.

"The Privy Councillor" [Taynyi sovetnik]. Novoe vremia, no. 3657 (May 6), pp. 2-3.

"The Chorus Girl" [Khoristka]. Oskolki, no. 27 (July 5), pp. 4-5.

"Mire" [Tina]. Novoe vremia, no. 3832 (October 29), pp. 2-3.

"Dreams" [Mechty]. Novoe vremia, no. 3849 (November 15), p. 2.

"On the Road" [Na puti]. Novoe vremia, no. 3889 (December 25), pp. 3-4.

"Vanka" [Van'ka]. Peterburgskaia gazeta, no. 354 (December 25), p. 4.

1887

"Champagne" [Shampanskoe]. Peterburgskaia gazeta, no. 5 (January 5), p. 3.

"The Swan Song (Calchas)" [Lebedinaia pesnia (Kalkhas)]. Sezon, no. 1, pp. 52-53.

"The Beggar" [Nishchii]. Peterburgskaia gazeta, no. 18 (January 19), p. 3.

"Enemies" [Vragi]. Novoe vremia, no. 3913 (January 20), pp. 2-3.

"Polinka" [Polin'ka]. Peterburgskaia gazeta, no. 32 (February 2), pp. 3-4.

"An Inadvertence" [Neostorozhnost']. Oskolki, no. 8 (February 21), p. 4.

"Verochka" [Verochka]. Novoe vremia, no. 3944 (February 21), pp. 2-3.

"Typhus" [Tif]. Peterburgskaia gazeta, no. 80 (March 23), p. 3.

"In Holy Week" [Na strastnoi nedeli]. Peterburgskaia gazeta, no. 87 (March 30), p. 3.

"The Letter" [Pis'mo]. Novoe vremia, no. 3998 (April 18), p. 2.

"The Investigator" [Sledovatel']. Peterburgskaia gazeta, no. 127 (May 11), p. 3.

"Volodia" [Volodia]. Peterburgskaia gazeta, no. 147 (June 1), p. 3.

"Happiness" [Shchast'e]. Novoe vremia, no. 4046 (June 6), pp. 1-2.

"A Rolling Stone" [Perekati-pole]. Novoe vremia, no. 4084 (July 14), pp. 2-3.

"The Siren" [Sirena]. Peterburgskaia gazeta, no. 231 (August 24), p. 3.

"The Shepherd's Pipe" [Svirel']. Novoe vremia, no. 4130 (August 29), p. 2.

"The Kiss" [Potselui]. Novoe vremia, no. 4238 (December 15), pp. 2-3.

"Boys" [Mal'chiki]. Peterburgskaia gazeta, no. 350 (December 21), p. 3.

"Kashtanka" [Kashtanka]. Novoe vremia, no. 4248 (December 25), pp. 1-2.

1888

Ivanov (First edition). Moscow: Litografiia Moskovskoi teatral'noi biblioteki E.N. Rassokhinoi.

"Sleepy" [Spat' khochetsia]. Peterburgskaia gazeta, no. 24 (January 25), p. 3.

"The Steppe" [Step']. Severnyi vestnik, no. 3, pp. 75-167.

"Lights" [Ogni]. Severnyi vestnik, no. 6, pp. 1-36.

"An Unpleasantness" [Nepriiatnost']. Novoe vremia, no. 4404 (June 3), p. 2, and no. 4408 (June 7), pp. 2-3.

"The Bear" [Medved']. Novoe vremia, no. 4491 (August 30), pp. 2-3.

"Beauties" [Krasavitsy]. Novoe vremia, no. 4513 (September 21), p. 2.

"The Name-Day Party" [Imeniny]. Severnyi vestnik, no. 11, pp. 49-89.

"The Cobbler and the Devil" [Sapozhnik i nechistaia sila]. Peterburgskaia gazeta, no. 355 (December 25), p. 2.

"The Proposal" [Predlozhenie]. Moscow: Litografiia Moskovskoi teatral'noi biblioteki E.N. Rassokhinoi.

1889

"The Bet" [Pari]. Novoe vremia, no. 4613 (January 1), pp. 1-2.

"A Fit of Nerves" ("A Nervous Breakdown") [Pripadok]. In Pamiati V.M. Garshina: khudozhestvenno-literaturnyi sbornik [In memory of V.M. Garshin: a literary anthology]. St. Petersburg: V.I. Shtein, pp. 295-319.

Ivanov (Second edition). Severnyi vestnik, no. 3, pp. 135-94.

"The Princess" [Kniaginia]. Novoe vremia, no. 4696 (March 26), p. 3.

"A Forced Declaration" [Vynuzhdennoe zaiavlenie]. Novoe vremia, no. 4721 (April 22), p. 2.

"A Tragedian in Spite of Himself" [Tragik ponevole]. St. Petersburg: Teatral'naia biblioteka V.A. Bazarova.

"A Dreary Story" ("A Boring Story") [Skuchnaia istoriia]. Severnyi vestnik, no. 11, pp. 73-130.

Tatyana Repina. St. Petersburg: A.S. Suvorin.

1890

"Horse Thieves" ("Thieves") [Vory]. Novoe vremia, no. 5061 (April 1), pp. 2-3.

"The Wedding" [Svad'ba]. Moscow: Litografiia Obshchestva russkikh dramaticheskikh pisatelei S.F. Rassokhina.

The Wood Demon [Leshii]. Litografiia Obshchestva russkikh dramaticheskikh pisatelei S.F. Rassokhina.

"From Siberia" [Iz Sibiri]. Novoe vremia, nos. 5142-5147 (June 24-29), no. 5168 (July 20), no. 5172 (July 24), and no. 5202 (August 23).

"Gusev" [Gusev]. Novoe vremia, no. 5326 (December 25), pp. 1-2.

1891

"Peasant Women" [Baby]. Novoe vremia, no. 5502 (June 25), pp. 2-3.

"The Duel" [Duel']. Novoe vremia, nos. 5612, 5622, 5624, 5628, 5629, 5635, 5642, 5643, 5649, 5656, and 5657 (October 22 to November 27).

"In Moscow" [V Moskve]. Novoe vremia, no. 5667 (December 7), p. 2.

1892

"My Wife" [Zhena]. Severnyi vestnik, no. 1, pp. 125-66.

"The Grasshopper" ("The Butterfly") [Poprygun'ia]. Sever, no. 1 (January 5) and no. 2 (January 12).

"The Anniversary" ("The Jubilee") [Iubilei]. Moscow: Litografiia komissionera Obshchestva russkikh dramaticheskikh pisatelei S.F. Rassokhina.

"After the Theater" [Posle teatra]. Peterburgskaia gazeta, no. 94 (April 7), p. 3.

"A Fragment" [Otryvok]. Oskolki, no. 16 (April 18), p. 5.

"The History of A Business Enterprise" [Istoriia odnogo torgovogo predpriiatiia]. Oskolki, no. 18 (May 2), p. 4.

"From a Retired Teacher's Notebook" [Iz zapisnoi knizhki starogo pedagoga]. Oskolki, no. 21 (May 23), p. 5.

"In Exile" [V ssylke]. Vsemirnaia illiustratsiia, no. 20 (May 9), pp. 354-55.

"A Fishy Affair" [Ryb'ia liubov']. Oskolki, no. 24 (June 13), p. 4.

"Neighbours" [Sosedi]. Knizhki Nedeli, no. 7, pp. 88-114.

"Ward Six" [Palata No. 6]. Russkaia mysl', no. 11, pp. 76-123.

"Terror" [Strakh]. Novoe vremia, no. 6045 (December 25), pp. 1-2.

1893

"An Anonymous Story" [Rasskaz neizvestnogo cheloveka]. Russkaia mysl', no. 2, pp. 153-86 and no. 3, pp. 8-129.

"The Two Volodias" ("Big Volodia and Little Volodia") [Volodia bol'shoi i Volodia malen'kii]. Russkie vedomosti, no. 357 (December 28), pp. 2-3.

The Island of Sakhalin [Ostrov Sakhalin]. (Chapters 1 to 19). Russkaia mysl', no. 10, pp. 1-33; no. 11, pp. 149-70; no. 12, pp. 77-114; and 1894, no. 2, pp. 26-60; no. 3, pp. 1-28; no. 5, pp. 1-30; no. 6, pp.

1-27; and no. 7, pp. 1-30.

1894

"The Black Monk" [Chernyi monakh]. Artist, no. 1, pp. 1-16.

"A Woman's Kingdom" [Bab'e tsarstvo]. Russkaia mysl', no. 1, pp. 154-89.

"Rothschild's Fiddle" [Skripka Rotshil'da]. Russkie vedomosti, no. 37 (February 6), p. 2.

"The Student" [Student]. Russkie vedomosti, no. 104 (April 15), p. 2.

"The Russian Master" ("The Teacher of Literature") [Uchitel' slovesnosti]. Chapter One: Novoe vremia, 1889, no. 4940 (November 28); Chapter Two: Russkie vedomosti, 1894, no. 188 (July 10).

"At a Country House" [V usad'be]. Russkie vedomosti, no. 237 (August 28).

"The Head Gardener's Story" [Rasskaz starshego sadovnika]. Russkie vedomosti, no. 356 (December 25).

1895

"Three Years" [Tri goda]. Russkaia mysl', no. 1, pp. 1-53, and no. 2, pp. 115-56.

"His Wife" [Supruga]. Pochin: sbornik Obshchestva liubitelei rossiiskoi slovesnosti na 1895 god [New enterprise: anthology of the Society of Lovers of Russian Literature for 1895]. Moscow: Russkoe tovarishchestvo pechatnogo dela, pp. 279-285.

"Whitebrow" ("Spot") [Belolobyi]. Detskoe chtenie, no. 11, pp. 1531-39.

"Murder" [Ubiistvo]. Russkaia mysl', no. 11, pp. 1-27.

"Anna Round the Neck" ("The Order of St. Anne") [Anna na shee]. Russkie vedomosti, no. 292 (October 22).

The Island of Sakhalin: From Travel Notes [Ostrov Sakhalin: iz putevykh zametok]. (Complete edition).

Moscow: Russkaia mysl', 520 pp.

"Ariadne" [Ariadna]. *Russkaia mysl'*, no. 12, pp. 1-26.

1896

"The Artist's Story" ("The House with a Mansard," "The House with an Attic") [Dom s mezoninom]. *Russkaia mysl'*, no. 4, pp. 1-17.

"My Life" [Moia zhizn']. *Ezhemesiachnye literaturnye prilozheniia k zhurnalu "Niva"* [Monthly literary supplements to the journal *Niva*], no. 10, pp. 224-60; no. 11, pp. 481-524; no. 12, pp. 705-42.

The Seagull [Chaika]. *Russkaia mysl'*, no. 12, pp. 117-61.

1897

"Peasants" [Muzhiki]. *Russkaia mysl'*, no. 4, pp. 167-94.

"The Savage" [Pecheneg]. *Russkie vedomosti*, no. 303 (November 2), p. 3.

"At Home" [V rodnom uglu]. *Russkie vedomosti*, no. 317 (November 16), pp. 2-3.

"In the Cart" [Na podvode]. *Russkie vedomosti*, no. 352 (December 21), p. 4.

Uncle Vanya [Diadia Vania]. In *P'esy* [Plays]. By A.P. Chekhov. St. Petersburg: A.S. Suvorin.

1898

"A Visit to Friends" [U znakomykh]. *Cosmopolis. Mezhdunarodnyi zhurnal*, no. 2, pp. 103-20.

"Ionych" ("Dr. Startsev") [Ionych]. *Ezhemesiachnye literaturnye prilozheniia k zhurnalu "Niva"* [Monthly literary supplements to the journal *Niva*], no. 9, pp. 1-24.

"The Man in a Case" ("The Man in a Shell") [Chelovek v futliare]. *Russkaia mysl'*, no. 7, pp. 120-31.

"Gooseberries" [Kryzhovnik]. *Russkaia mysl'*, no. 8, pp.

145-54.

"About Love" [O liubvi]. Russkaia mysl', no. 8, pp. 154-62.

"A Case History" [Sluchai iz praktiki]. Russkaia mysl', no. 12, pp. 189-98.

1899

"On Official Duty" ("On Official Business") [Po delam sluzhby]. Knizhki Nedeli, no. 1, pp. 16-36.

"The Darling" [Dushechka]. Sem'ia, no. 1 (January 3), pp. 2-4, 6.

"The New Dacha" [Novaia dacha]. Russkie vedomosti, no. 3 (January 3), pp. 2-3.

"The Lady With the Little Dog" ("The Lady With the Pet Dog") [Dama s sobachkoi]. Russkaia mysl', no. 12, pp. 149-64.

1900

"At Christmas" [Na sviatkakh]. Peterburgskaia gazeta, no. 1 (January 1), p. 5.

"In the Ravine" [V ovrage]. Zhizn', no. 1, pp. 201-234.

1901

The Three Sisters [Tri sestry]. Russkaia mysl', no. 2, pp. 124-78.

1902

"The Bishop" [Arkhierei]. Zhurnal dlia vsekh, no. 4, pp. 447-62.

1903

"Betrothed" [Nevesta]. Zhurnal dlia vsekh, no. 12, pp. 1413-1432.

1904

<u>The Cherry Orchard</u> [Vishnevyi sad]. <u>Sbornik tovarishchestva "Znanie" za 1903 god</u> [Anthology of the "Znanie" group for 1903]. Vol. 2. St. Petersburg: Znanie, pp. 29-105.

Writings About Anton Chekhov

1886

1 OBOLENSKII, L.E. "Molodye talanty g. Chekhova i g. Korolenko: sravnenie mezhdu nimi" [The young talents of Mr. Chekhov and Mr. Korolenko: a comparison]. Russkoe bogatstvo, no. 12, pp. 166-79.

Acknowledges Chekhov's "remarkable" talent and argues that it is superior to Korolenko's. Chekhov does not create his plots but discovers them everywhere in life itself. He has the ability to take only the essentials and express them in a single detail which powerfully moves the reader.

2 [SKABICHEVSKII, A.M.] Review of Motley Stories. Severnyi vestnik, no. 6, pp. 123-26.

Pays tribute to Chekhov's "young, fresh talent," although finds the quality of the stories in the collection uneven. Skabichevsky views Chekhov as a representative of "secondary literature" ("malaia pressa"), more talented than his colleagues but wasting his talent in the unrewarding milieu of the daily newspapers. Chekhov will probably end, after squandering his talents, by dying forgotten in a ditch.

1887

1 ARSEN'EV, K.K. "Belletristi poslednego vremeni: A.P. Chekhov" [Current writers: A.P. Chekhov]. Vestnik Evropy, no. 12, pp. 766-76.

Most of Chekhov's Motley Stories are of little value because they are simply anecdotes or involve wholly improbable characters. In his second collection, In the Twilight, he abandons the anecdote and writes in a much more polished manner. But many stories are so short that the characters cannot be fully motivated. He is at his best when describing fleeting states of mind that do not require detailed treatment. His descriptions of nature are also original and remarkable. Reprinted: 1907.3.

2 [MIKHAILOVSKII, N.K.]. Review of In The Twilight. Severnyi vestnik, no. 9, pp. 81-85.

Reviews Chekhov's second collection of stories and criticizes the fragmentary nature of his writings. Chekhov has undeniable talent, but he is largely indifferent to his characters and so is unable to arouse the reader's interest in them.

1888

1 MEREZHKOVSKII, D.S. "Staryi vopros po povodu novogo talanta" [An old question posed for a new talent]. Severnyi vestnik, no. 11, pp. 77-99.

Reviews Chekhov's work to date and argues that critics have not yet taken it sufficiently seriously. Although his stories lack plot and his characters do not develop, the stories are perceptive studies of weak-willed, idealistic natures. His work is non-tendentious and impressionistic and proves that "pure art" can still concern itself with topical issues.

1889

1 BYCHKOV, A.F. "Otchet o chetvertom prisuzhdenii pushkinskikh premii v 1888 godu" [Report on the fourth awarding of the Pushkin Prizes, 1888]. Sbornik otdeleniia russkogo iazyka i slovesnosti Imperatorskoi Akademii nauk [Collection of the section on Russian language and literature of the Imperial Academy of Sciences] 46:46-53.

Discusses the contents of Chekhov's second collection of stories, In The Twilight, and argues that it is markedly superior to his first. A typical feature of his talent is the ability to select significant details, often ones that seem trivial or accidental but which express much in few words. Although the stories "do not fully satisfy the demands of higher artistic criticism", they still represent a remarkable literary achievement and merit half the Pushkin Prize for 1888.

2 MILIUKOV [Milyoukov], PAUL. "Russia." Athenaeum, July 6, pp. 26-28.

Contains what is probably the first mention of Chekhov in English. Within the context of a general review of contemporary Russian literature notes that Chekhov, "a most sympathetic writer" of small psychological sketches, has "unfortunately" turned to the drama in Ivanov. In the play "there is no action, and the principal character presents an impossible combination of contradictions, leaving the reader hopelessly bewildered."

1890

1 MIKHAILOVSKII, N.K. "Ob otsakh i detiakh i o Chekhove" [About fathers and sons and about Chekhov]. Russkie vedomosti, no. 140 (April 18), pp. 2-3.

Reviews Chekhov's sixth collection of stories, Gloomy People; argues that Chekhov denies all principles and ideals, specifically those of the generations of the 1840s and 1860s, and recognizes only the power of everyday actuality. Thus nature in his works is animated and exists on the same level as humans. Chekhov is "indifferent," like his professor in "A Dreary Story" (the one work in the collection that stands out), and writes about whatever happens to fall into his view. "I know of no sadder sight that this talent being vainly wasted." Several reprints, including 1957.9.

2 OBOLENSKII, L.E. [Sozertsatel']. "Novyi povorot v ideiakh nashei belletristiki: 'Skuchnaia istoria', povest' A. Chekhova" [A new turn in our literature's ideas: "A Boring Story," Chekhov's tale]. Russkoe bogatstvo, no. 1, pp. 95-113.

Pessimism is the prevailing mood in the literature of the 1880s; Chekhov undertakes a critical examination of that pessimism in "A Boring Story." The spiritual bankruptcy of the professor shows that life is impossible without the "general idea" provided by religion.

3 STRUNIN, D.M. "Vydaiushchiisia literaturnyi tip: ob"ektivno-kriticheskii ocherk" [An outstanding literary type: an objectively critical sketch]. Russkoe bogatstvo, no. 4, pp. 106-25.

Compares Tolstoy's "Death of Ivan Ilych" with Chekhov's "Boring Story" and argues that both deal with characters whose spiritual qualities have atrophied while they pursued other goals. Tolstoy presents a more detailed picture of the falsity of his protagonist's life and, unlike Chekhov, provides a solution to his dilemma.

1891

1 DILLON, E.J. "Recent Russian Literature." Review of Reviews 4:79-83.
Sees Chekhov as the "Russian Maupassant" and successor to Turgenev. His main achievement is in creating a remarkable portrait gallery of Russian types.

1892

1 MIKHAILOVSKII, N.K. Review of "Ward Six." Russkie vedomosti, no. 335 (December 4), pp. 2-3.
Compares the story to Garshin's "The Red Flower" and finds it artistically inferior. Chekhov's talent continues to lack focus. Several reprints.

2 PROTOPOPOV, M.A. "Zhertva bezvremen'ia: povesti g. Antona Chekhova" [A victim of Russia's empty years: the tales of Mr. Anton Chekhov]. Russkaia mysl', no. 6, pp. 95-122.
Chekhov has no ideals or defined outlook on life and he denies even the right to pose the question of life's ultimate purpose. Because he lacks a "general idea" his individual works are disconnected and fragmentary. Still, his descriptions of nature are remarkable; he is a sensitive psychologist and an astute observer of everyday life.

1893

1 FLEKSER, A.L. [Volynskii]. Review of "Ward Six" and "An Anonymous Story." Severnyi vestnik, no. 5, pp. 130-41.
Pays tribute to Chekhov's talent but criticizes the narrowness of his vision and the fragmentary nature of his art. Although the characters of "Ward Six" are psychologically convincing, Gromov's madness does not ring true. "An Anonymous Story" leaves many questions unanswered about its characters' motivations.

2 *MEREZHKOVSKII, D.S. "O prichinakh upadka i o novykh techeniiakh sovremennoi russkoi literatury." [On the reasons for the decline of and the new currents in contemporary Russian literature]. St.

Petersburg, n.p., 192 pp.

Argues that Chekhov is an impressionist in the tradition of Turgenev; his works are "on the way to the new, approaching idealism." The secret of his short "poems" is in the way they suddenly reveal bright flashes of beauty in the midst of the drab reality they depict. The elusive moods of his works and the ultrasensitivity of their author reveals new and hitherto uncharted worlds. Chekhov is one of the first writers to break with the traditions of the Russian realist novel; his simple, laconic prose will help renew literature. Several reprints.

1895

1 SKABICHEVSKII, A.M. "Est' li u g. Chekhova idealy?" [Does Mr. Chekhov have any ideals?]. In Sochineniia [Works]. Vol 2. 3d. ed. St. Petersburg: F. Pavlenkov, pp. 349-80.

Critics are wrong to accuse Chekhov of lacking ideals; he simply does not formulate his ideals systematically. The author's basically healthy set of values can be discerned even in the gloom of "Ward Six" and "An Anonymous Story."

1896

1 MEDVEDSKII, K.P. [K. M-skii]. "Zhertva bezvremen'ia: povesti i rasskazy Antona Chekhova" [A victim of Russia's empty years: the tales and stories of Anton Chekhov]. Russkii vestnik, no. 7, pp. 231-45 and no. 8, pp. 279-93.

Chekhov chose to free himself from tendency, but his stories have no point or purpose whatsoever. "The Steppe" is a failure; it is a large work only because of its number of pages. Laevsky in "The Duel" is unconvincing and reveals that Chekhov is a superficial writer who cannot see into the human heart.

1897

1 GOLOVIN, K.F. Russkii roman i russkoe obshchestvo [The Russian novel and Russian society]. St. Petersburg: A.A. Porokhovshchikov, pp. 451-62. Reprint. Leipzig Zentralantiquariat der Deutschen Demokratischen Republic, 1974.

Demokratischen Republic, 1974.

Chekhov is typical of a new group of writers who are indifferent to ideology and who write short works which fail to separate significant phenomena from trivialities. "An Anonymous Story" is the best of an undistinguished lot.

2 MIKHAILOVSKII, N.K. "Literatura i zhizn'" [Literature and life]. Russkoe bogatstvo, no. 6, pp. 116-26.

In "Peasants" as in his other work Chekhov did not employ his full talents as a writer. His characters here are drawn sketchily and much remains unsaid. The waiter Nikolai is an unreal, abstract figure transported to a village that is portrayed in far too somber colors. Although he has talent there is no unified vision in Chekhov's work because he himself lacks a "general idea." Reprinted: 1907.3.

1899

1 CAHAN, ABRAHAM. "The Younger Russian Writers." Forum 28:119-28.

Because Chekhov lacked social ideas he suffered at the hands of socially-minded critics. but his immense powers of capturing life have overcome this obstacle and he is now acknowledged as the leading living Russian writer after Tolstoy.

2 MEN'SHIKOV, M.O. "Bol'naia volia: 'Palata No. 6.' Rasskaz A.P. Chekhova [A sick will: "Ward Six. A story by Chekhov]. In Kriticheski ocherki. St. Petersburg, n.p., pp. 158-88.

Reviews the story, considering it a tale of a "contemporary Oblomov." The whole story is an attack on Tolstoy's doctrine of non-resistance and a reproach to the ineffectualness of the intelligentsia.

1900

1 FLEKSER, A.L. [Volynskii]. "Anton Chekhov. Chelovek v futliare. Kryzhovnik. O liubvi. Ionych. Sluchai iz praktiki. Po delam sluzhby. Novaia dacha" [A.P. Chekhov: "The Man in a Case," "Gooseberries," "About Love," "Ionych," "A Case History," "On Official Duty," "The New Dacha"]. In Bor'ba za idealizm: kriticheskie stat'i [The

struggle for idealism: critical studies]. St. Petersburg: N.G. Molostvov, pp. 334-43.

Discusses seven stories, paying tribute to Chekhov's talent and noting that his art touches the depths of the spirit of contemporary man. Several of these stories speak prophetically about spiritual rebirth and hint at the coming regeneration of humanity.

2 *GOR'KII, MAKSIM. "Po povodu novogo rasskaza A.P. Chekhova 'V ovrage'" [A propos of a new story by Chekhov, "In the Ravine"]. Nizhegorodskii listok, no. 29 (30 January), p. 2.

Comments on Chekhov's importance as a writer and argues that he has more than an outlook on life; he rises above the life he describes and his vantage point thus defies description and labelling. His works may treat the harsh realities but they are not gloomy; they are full of courage and love of life. Many reprints. Translated: 1982.10.

3 MIKHAILOVSKII, N.K. "Koe-chto o g. Chekhove" [Something about Mr. Chekhov]. Russkoe bogatstvo, no. 4, pp. 119-40.

Reviews the A.F. Marks collection of Chekhov's stories. The main subject of these early writings is life's interminable banality. His works first poke fun at this, then gradually portray it as hateful and depressing. Because he lacks an overall point of view to guide him he is uncertain how to reconcile the positive things he finds in life amid all the banality and vulgarity. But with "Ward Six" and "The Black Monk" his work begins seeking out worthy ideals.

1901

1 BOGDANOVICH, A.I. [A.V.]. "Kriticheskie zametki" [Critical remarks]. Mir bozhii, no. 4, pp. 1-12.

Argues that when one reads Uncle Vanya and The Three Sisters their artistic weaknesses are revealed: the plays lack action and their characters are more allegorical than human. But when the plays are performed by the MAT the characters come alive and the spectator is thoroughly enthralled.

1902

1 CAHAN, ABRAHAM. "The Mantle of Tolstoy." Bookman

(New York) 16:328-33.

Discusses some leading Russian contemporary writers and notes that "from a purely artistic point of view Chekhoff is the Tolstoy of the Russian short story." His is an art without didacticism however.

2 DE VOGÜÉ, E.M. "Anton Tchekhof." Revue des deux mondes. Vol. 7 (January 1), pp. 201-16.

Reviews Chekhov's work generally and notes that his short stories display amazing economy of means; they focus on the transitory, fragmentary aspects of life. An ineluctable fate determines the lives of the characters of his plays. He lacks an all-encompassing outlook on life, apart from a deep-rooted pessimism which is tempered by a vague faith in progress. His heroes are spiritually empty.

3 LONG, R.E.C. "Anton Tchekhoff." Fortnightly Review 72:103-18.

Attempts to introduce Chekhov to English readers and argues that he is a pessimist whose works convey his sense of the emptiness of life and the futility of human pretentions. Although his powers as an artist are obvious in his stories, his focus on the trivialities of life in his dramas makes for very undramatic plays. His few characters who aspire to better things end in lunacy or suicide.

4 MEN'SHIKOV, M.O. "Tri stikhii: 'V ovrage', povest' A.P. Chekhova" [Three elements: "In The Ravine," a tale by A.P. Chekhov]. In Kriticheskie ocherki [Critical sketches]. Vol. 2. St. Petersburg: Trud, pp. 101-34.

Chekhov has a deep understanding of peasant life, as shown by his "In the Ravine," which deals with the catastrophic effects of the new and foreign forces of capitalism in the Russian village. All characters in the story fit into one of three categories exemplified by a female character: Aksinya is the predatory type; Varvara stands passively between good and evil; Lipa personifies meekness and Christian humility. But Lipa emerges as the strongest of the three. Reprinted in part: 1906.6. Reprinted: 1907.3.

5 STRUVE, PETR. "Muzhiki Chekhova" [Chekhov's peasants]. In Na raznye temy (1893-1901 gg.): sbornik statei [On various topics (1893-1901): a collection of articles]. St. Petersburg: A.E. Kolpinskii, pp. 121-32.

Chekhov is the outstanding representative of post-narodnik literature. His "Peasants" is a pessimistic, if somewhat over-simplified, depiction of peasant brutality. Reprinted in part: 1907.3.

1903

1 DE VOGÜÉ, E.M. Anton Chekhov: etiud [Anton Chekhov: a study]. 2d ed. Moscow: D. Efimov, 39 pp.

Russian translation of 1902.2.

2 GLINKA, A.S. [Volzhskii]. Ocherki o Chekhove [Sketches of Chekhov]. St. Petersburg: M.M. Stasiulevich, 179 pp.

Reviews the debate over Chekhov's ideals between Skabichevsky (1895.1) and Mikhailovsky (1890.1) and argues that Chekhov is both a coldly pessimistic idealist and a warmly optimistic pantheist. His main subject is the power that everyday reality exerts on the lives of his characters: some submit to it, some struggle against it, some seek to escape it in self-delusion, but none are free of its influence. Reprinted in part: 1906.6.

3 LUNACHARSKII, A.V. "O khudozhnike voobshche i nekotorykh khudozhnikakh v chastnosti" [On the artist generally and on certain artists in particular]. Russkaia mysl', no. 2, pp. 58-60.

Reviews The Three Sisters and takes Chekhov to task for his overly-sympathetic portrayal of "provincial martyrs;" urges Chekhov to create an energetic, positive hero who can rise above such provincial dullness "and show us the seeds of a new life." Perhaps the play is a very subtle satire on weak-willed characters but is too subtle to be effective. Reprinted in part: 1907.3.

4 SOLOV'EV, E.A. [Andreevich]. "A.P. Chekhov." In Ocherki po istorii russkoi literatury XIX veka [Sketches in the history of Russian Literature of the 19th century]. St. Petersburg: A. Kolpinskii, pp. 513-23.

Discusses Chekhov's work generally, noting that he was the greatest writer to emerge from the 1880s. His characters are engaged in a losing battle with the forces of vulgarity and phariseeism. He portrays life as a kaleidoscope governed only by chance. His satire is directed not at individuals but at life itself.

5 VENGEROV, S.A. "Chekhov." Entsiklopedicheskii slovar' Brokgauza i Efrona 76:777-81.

Divides Chekhov's career into two phases: his

early compact comic sketches with their undercurrent of sadness, and his later work, beginning with "A Dreary Story", in which he deals seriously with much broader areas of life. Along with the pessimism that infuses his work is a longing for something better, and this compensates for the absence of precisely-defined social attitudes. He is the historian of "the period of neurasthenic enfeeblement of Russian society." Reprinted in part: 1906.6.

1904

1 AIKHENVAL'D, Iu.I. Review of The Cherry Orchard. Russkaia mysl', no. 2, pp. 255-63.

Describes the play as a delicate elegy with characters whose psychology is conveyed with remarkable subtlety. His Lopakhin especially has much more depth than the usual stereotyped stage businessman. The play and its staging by the MAT create a "festival of art." Reprinted: 1907.3.

2 BATIUSHKOV, F.D.. "Predsmertnyi zavet A.P. Chekhova" [Chekhov's testament]. Mir Bozhii, no. 8, pp. 1-12.

Chekhov is not a pessimist; his works generally, and The Cherry Orchard in particular, show a world that has not developed to its full potential. The play can be seen as his last testament in that it expresses his faith in a better future and summons people to work toward it. Reprinted: 1907.3.

3 BUGAEV, BORIS N. [Andrei Belyi]. "Chekhov." Vesy, no. 8, pp. 1-9.

Argues that genuine symbolism is the equivalent of genuine realism and that Chekhov was such a realist-symbolist who discovered new areas of meaning in the ordinary and everyday. Reprinted: 1910.4.

4 ----- "Ivanov na stsene Khudozhestvennogo teatra" [Ivanov on the stage of the Art Theater]. Vesy, no. 11, pp. 29-31.

Reviews Ivanov, "the weakest of Chekhov's plays," as staged by the MAT, and argues that it reveals the fantastic, nightmarish aspects of an era of the recent past. Reprinted: 1911.3.

5 ----- "Vishnevyi sad" [The Cherry Orchard]. Vesy, no. 2, pp. 45-48.

Argues that Chekhov is a realist and thus a

symbolist: he reveals genuine reality as glimpsed through the elaborate but meaningless texture of daily life that is found in his art. But his Cherry Orchard presents less of a total artistic impression that does The Three Sisters. Reprinted: 1911.3. Translated: 1981.39.

6 CHEREDA, Iu. "O poshlosti" [On vulgarity]. Novyi put', no. 4, pp. 228-38.

Argues that Chekhov, like Dostoevsky, loves life as it is, with all its trivialities and its vulgarity.

7 GIPPIUS, Z.N. [Anton Krainii]. "Eshche o poshlosti" [On vulgarity once again]. Novyi put', no. 4, pp. 238-43.

Takes issue with Chereda (1904.6), arguing that vulgarity is in fact deadness and immobility and is opposed to life. Chekhov and Dostoevsky both despise and fear it, but apart from that they have absolutely nothing in common.

8 ----- "Vishnevye sady" [Cherry orchards]. Novyi put', no. 5, pp. 251-57.

Reviews the MAT's production of The Cherry Orchard and comments on Chekhov generally, arguing that the MAT should move away from Chekhov's plays.

9 KARPOV, N.N. Chekhov i ego tvorchestvo: etiud [Chekhov and his work: a study]. St. Petersburg: Privately published, 47 pp.

A general survey of Chekhov's literary career that distinguishes three currents in his work: his early period of carefree humor; his middle period of melancholy and pessimism; and his last period of hope and faith in the future. His many idealistic characters are unhappy because they cannot realize their ideals. He began a new era in Russian literature.

10 KOROLENKO, V.G. "Pamiati Antona Pavlovicha Chekhova" [In memory of Chekhov]. Russkoe bogatstvo, no. 7, pp. 212-23.

Contains personal reminiscences of Chekhov; surveys his career, taking issue with those who see him as lacking in ideals or who identify him with his passive characters. His career falls into three periods: his early humor, full of the joy of life; the quest for an ideal or world view; and his final plays and stories that express striving for a better world and faith in the future. Reprinted: 1960.26.

11 LIATSKII, E.A. "A.P. Chekhov i ego rasskazy: etiud" [Chekhov and his stories: a study]. Vestnik

<u>Evropy</u>, no. 1, pp. 104-62.

Reviews Chekhov's treatment at the hands of several contemporary critics (Mikhailovsky, Skabichevsky, Volzhsky); notes that his works are not tragic but simply melancholy. Chekhov's most typical characters are his intellectuals, bewildered by the complexity of their world. His most serious formal shortcoming is the almost official "dryness" of his narrative. His works are too much a product of their era to endure for long.

<u>1905</u>

1 AIKHENVAL'D, Iu.I. "Chekhov: osnovnye momenty ego proizvedenii" [Chekhov: basic features of his works]. <u>Nauchnoe slovo</u>, no. 1, pp. 110-36.

The basic mood of Chekhov's work is melancholy, but this is tempered by his affection for his characters. Passive, dreamy types are generally treated more sympathetically than are active, practical ones. Although his works deal with the vulgarity of life they also contain glimpses of better things and reveal his high ideals. Reprinted in part: 1906.6.

2 BATIUSHKOV, F.D. "Teatral'nyi zametki: Meterlink i Chekhov v ispolnenii artistov Moskovskogo Khudozhestvennogo teatra" [Theatrical notes: Maeterlinck and Chekhov as performed by the artists of the Moscow Art Theater]. <u>Mir Bozhii</u>, no. 7, pp. 13-30.

Comments on the MAT's first production of <u>Ivanov</u> in 1905 and on the play generally, which is seen as a study of provincial barrenness and boredom.

3 BULGAKOV, S.N. <u>Chekhov kak myslitetel'</u> [Chekhov as a thinker]. Kiev: S.I. Ivanov, 32 pp.

Seeks to elucidate Chekhov's world view. Through his art he sought after truth and a higher purpose in life. His outlook can best be termed "optimopessimism," in that he recognizes the triumph of Evil yet calls for active resistance against it and maintains his belief in the ultimate victory of Good. His later works in particular are filled with religious spirit. Reprinted in part: 1906.6 and 1907.3.

4 GOR'KII, MAKSIM. "A.P. Chekhov: otryvki iz vospominanii" [Chekhov: excerpts from reminiscences]. <u>Nizhegorodskii sbornik</u>. St. Petersburg: Znanie, pp. 3-16.

An intimate portrait of Chekhov that conveys his

lack of pretence, his "subtle skepticism," and his gentle humor. "He had the art of revealing everywhere and driving away banality..." Many reprints, including 1960.26. Translated: 1959.12 and 1967.9.

5 KROPOTKIN, PETER. Russian Literature. New York: McClure, Phillips & Co., pp. 308-17.

Surveys Chekhov's work generally and argues that he is the most deeply original of contemporary Russian writers. His distinctive theme is the defeat of the intellectual by "the all-invading meanness of everyday life." He is not a pessimist, however, for he retains his faith in progress.

6 LYSKOV, IVAN P., ed. A.P. Chekhov v ponimanii kritiki [Chekhov as understood by the critics]. Moscow: A. Gattsuk, 263 pp.

Summarizes seventy-five critical articles on Chekhov that appeared from 1877 to 1905.

7 MEREZHKOVSKII, D.S. "O Chekhove" [About Chekhov]. Vesy, no. 11, pp. 1-26.

Chekhov and Gorky are the first real writers from the intelligentsia, and their works express the new, middle-class religion of man and of human progress. Chekhov's work conveys in precise, meticulous detail the daily routine (byt) of Russian life, but the life he protrays is utterly empty and barren. "Chekhov's heroes have no life; there is only the daily routine without any event, or with only one event: death, the end of the daily routine, the end of being. Daily routine and death: these are the two fixed poles of Chekhov's world. Like Gorky, Chekhov wanted to show that man without God becomes a god himself; but both showed that without God man is nothing. Several reprints, including 1906.5.

8 SHAPIR, NIKOLAI. "Chekhov kak realist-novator: opyt nauchno-psikhologicheskoi kritiki" [Chekhov as an innovative realist: an essay in scientific-psychological criticism]. Voprosy filosofii i psikhologii 79:335-553 and 80:633-82.

Argues that Chekhov's works are the first to reflect the psyche of characters independent of the individual life situation and moment of inner development in which the character might be found. His characters are taken from the ranks of average and ordinary people generally.

9 SHESTOV, LEV. "Tvorchestvo iz nichego: A.P. Chekhov" [Creation from the void: Chekhov]. Voprosy zhizni, no. 3, pp. 101-41.

Argues, largely on the basis of "A Dreary Story" and Ivanov, that Chekhov was a "poet of hopelessness." In his works he rejects ideas of every kind and even loses the sense of a connection between the events of life: "sovereign accident reigns everywhere and in everything, this time boldly throwing the gauntlet to all conceptions." Stripped of all consolation, lonely and alienated, Chekhov's characters are left to create everything for themselves, "from the void." Several reprints and translations, including 1908.6 and 1966.17.

10 SKABICHEVSKII, A.M. "Anton Pavlovich Chekhov." Russkaia mysl', no. 6, pp. 29-56.

Reviews Chekhov's career. "Objectivity" is only apparent in his works: he states his views very subtly through the debates of his characters. He was a firm believer in social progress, had great sympathy for the plight of the peasants, and consistently argues for the value of culture and enlightenment. Reprinted in part: 1906.6.

11 *VOROVSKII, V.V. [Iu. Adamovich]. "Lishnie liudi" [Superfluous people]. Pravda (Journal, Moscow), no. 4, pp. 113-44.

A Marxist analysis of Chekhov's plays, it argues that their characters are "superfluous people," the latest representatives of what was once an active and progressive class but who now have no role to play in society. Chekhov's plays suggest that some of these social groups are disappearing while others are joining different classes. Reprinted: 1975.16.

1906

1 ANNENSKII, I.F. "Drama nastroenii" [The drama of mood]. In Kniga otrazhenii. [The book of reflections]. St. Petersburg: Trud, pp. 147-67. Reprint. Munich: Wilhelm Fink, 1969.

Discusses each of the major characters in The Three Sisters and examines their interrelationships.

2 *BATIUSHKOV, F.D. "Chekhov i osvoboditel'noe dvizhenie" [Chekhov and the liberation movement]. Mir Bozhii 4:34-52.

Examines Chekhov's politics, arguing that he was neither hostile nor indifferent to the reformist ideas of the 1860s; however he does satirize those who continue to repeat the clichés of that era a generation later. Likewise he takes issue with the populist tendency to idealize peasant life. His works help the progressive cause by destroying prejudice and by showing life as it really is. Lida, in "The Artist's Story," conveys his positive ideal, which is close to that of the Constitutional Democratic Party. Reprinted: 1907.3.

3 BUDDE, E.F. "Osnovnaia ideia khudozhestvennykh proizvedenii A.P. Chekhova" [The basic idea of Chekhov's artistic works]. Russkaia mysl', no. 1, pp. 1-29.

Examines some of the principal themes of Chekhov's work. His characters suffer from paralysis of will, fear of life, and spiritual isolation. They cannot be happy because they are all too aware of their own weaknesses.

4 GLINKA, A.S. [Volzhskii]. "Vishnevyi sad Chekhova v Khudozhestvennom teatre" [Chekhov's Cherry Orchard at the Art Theatre]. In Iz mira literaturnykh iskanii: sbornik statei [From the world of literary explorations: a collection]. St. Petersburg: D.E. Zhukovskii, pp. 163-80.

The Cherry Orchard adds little new to Chekhov's art but advances his previous traits and themes to their perfection. The conflict of ideal and actual is much sharper here than in his previous works.

5 MEREZHKOVSKII, D.S. Chekhov i Gor'kii [Chekhov and Gorky]. St. Petersburg: M.V. Pirozhkov, 67 pp.

Contains 1905.7. Several reprints.

6 POKROVSKII, N.A., ed. A.P. Chekhov v znachenii russkogo pisatelia-khudozhnika: iz kriticheskoi literatury o Chekhove [Chekhov and his significance as an artist and writer: from the critical literature on Chekhov]. Moscow: V.S. Spiridonov and A.M. Mikhailov, 238 pp.

Contains eighteen articles on Chekhov, most in somewhat abbreviated form, written between 1890 and 1905. Includes portions of 1902.4, 1903.2, 1903.5, 1905.1, 1905.3, and 1905.10.

7 POLNER, TIKHON. Simvoly "Vishnevego sada" [The symbols of The Cherry Orchard]. Moscow: n.p., 46 pp.

Argues that The Cherry Orchard is a symbol of culture, carefully built up over many years but now no longer valid and so doomed to destruction. The characters in the play can be grouped according to their attitudes to this culture. Chekhov does not indicate if the new culture will be better, but this play is more hopeful than his previous ones.

8 SKABICHEVSKII, A.M. Istoriia noveishei russkoi literatury: 1848-1906 gg. [The history of recent Russian literature: 1848-1906]. 6th ed., rev. St. Petersburg: Shmidt, pp. 379-80.

Contains a brief sketch of Chekhov's life and works that argues he was a pessimist typical of the writers of the 1880s. His gloom and almost pathological concerns prevented him from becoming a truly popular writer.

1907

1 BLOK, ALEKSANDR. "O drame" [On the drama]. Zolotoe runo, nos. 7-9, pp. 122-31. Several reprints, including 1962.2.

Notes that Chekhov's dramatic talent comes by chance and by intuition; thus he has neither predecessors nor followers since his dramatic gifts cannot be imitated. Translated: 1981.39.

2 BUGAEV, BORIS [Andrei Belyi]. "Anton Pavlovich Chekhov." V mire iskusstv (Kiev), no. 11-12, pp. 11-13.

Argues that Chekhov occupies a key position in Russian literary history: the opposing tendencies of symbolism and realism meet in his work His writings seem to belong to the realist tradition, but a close examination reveals their truly symbolic features. He has "exhausted realism" and so has ended an epoch in Russian literature. Reprinted: 1911.3.

3 POKROVSKII, V.I., ed. Anton Pavlovich Chekhov, ego zhizn' i sochineniia: sbornik istoriko-literaturnykh statei [Chekhov, his life and works: a collection of historico-literary articles]. Moscow: V. Spiridonov and A. Mikhailov, 1062 pp.

Contains reprints of 108 articles by Chekhov's contemporaries. These include general assessments of his work and his place in Russian literature, his reception abroad, his relationship with his own time, stylistic studies, comparative studies (Balzac, Ibsen, Gorky, Maupassant), studies of early stories and individual later works ("A Dreary Story," The Island of Sakhalin, "A Woman's Kingdom," "Murder," "Anna Round the Neck," "Ariadne," "His Wife," "My Life," "Peasants," "The Man in a Case," "Gooseberries," "About Love," "On Official Duty,"

"A Case History," "The New Dacha," "The Lady with the Little Dog," "In the Ravine," "Betrothed," "The Steppe," Ivanov, The Seagull, The Wood Demon, The Three Sisters, Uncle Vanya, and The Cherry Orchard. Includes, complete or in part, 1887.1, 1897.2, 1902.4-5, 1903.2, 1094.1, 1095.3, 10, and 1906.2.

1908

1 AIKHENVAL'D, Iu.I. "Deti u Chekhova" [Children in Chekhov's work]. In Siluety russkikh pisatelei [Silhouettes of Russian writers]. Vol. 2. Moscow: Nauchnoe slovo, pp. 165-80.

Examines a number of stories in which children appear and characterizes these children generally; pays tribute to the delicate psychology Chekhov uses to describe them. His children enter life trustingly, but their trust is often abused by the harshness and vulgarity of a life they do not understand. They grow old to become unhappy or vulgar themselves. Reprinted: 1923.1.

2 ALEKSANDROVICH, Iu. Posle Chekhova: ocherk molodoi literatury poslednego desiatiletiia, 1898-908 [After Chekhov: an outline of the young literature of the last decade, 1898-1908]. Vol. 1. Moscow: Obshchestvennaia pol'za, pp. 9-15, 243-56.

Argues that Chekhov's writings are filled with the "heroic pessimism" that results from the conflict of individual ideals with reality; this sense of tragedy is Chekhov's legacy to the writers who followed him.

3 *BARING, MAURICE. "The Plays of Anton Tchekov." New Quarterly, no. 1, pp. 405-29.

Characterizes Chekhov's plays generally within the context of Russian dramatic history, noting that the Russian tradition has been one of simply depicting life clearly. But Chekhov discovered that real life need not be dramatic in order to be interesting. The Seagull and The Cherry Orchard are discussed in detail: the former is more conventional, but the latter shows Chekhov at his best, capable of building an intricate edifice "in air," an edifice which never ceases to fascinate. "Tchekov's plays are a thousand times more interesting to see on the stage than they are to read." Reprinted: 1910.2.

4 CHUKOVSKII, KORNEI. Ot Chekhova do nashikh dnei: literaturnye portrety. Kharakteristiki [From Chekhov to our time: literary portraits and characteristics]. 3d ed., rev. and expanded. St.

Petersburg and Moscow: M.O. Vol'f, pp. 1-17.

Argues that Chekhov is a most secretive writer who carefully camouflages his real likes and dislikes. He loves his weak and confused characters and scorns the strong and decisive who claim to know why they are living.

5 MEIERKHOL'D, VSEVOLOD. "Naturalisticheskii teatr i teatr nastroenii" [Naturalistic theater and the theater of mood]. In _Teatr. Kniga o novom teatre: sbornik statei_ [Theater. A book about the new theater: a collection of articles]. St. Petersburg: Shipovnik, pp. 136-50.

The naturalistic tendency of the MAT attempts a precise reproduction of reality and so denies the audience its opportunity to imagine; this also weakens its production of Chekhov's plays. Its other tendency, "the theater of mood," was prompted by Chekhov's work and is the way the theatre should develop. Several reprints and translations, including 1967.9, 1969.16, and 1977.3.

6 SHESTOV, LEV. "Tvorchestvo iz nichego: A.P. Chekhov" [Creation from the void: A.P. Chekhov]. In _Nachala i kontsy_ [Beginnings and ends]. St. Petersburg: M.M. Stasiulevich, pp. 1-68.

Reprinted from 1905.9

1909

1 ALEKSANDROVICH, Iu. _Posle Chekhova: nigilizm-modern i nashi moralisty_ [After Chekhov: neo-nihilism and our moralists]. Vol. 2. Moscow: Osnova, pp. 55-106.

Argues that Russian literature as a national phenomenon ended with Chekhov. With antipopulism and the loss of national ideals came a loss of social responsibility. Ideals and responsibility were replaced by materialism in economic life and modernism in artistic life resulting in a new nihilism.

2 *BENNETT, ARNOLD [Jacob Tonson]. "Anton Chekhov." _New Age_, March 18, p. 423.

Reviews of R.E.C. Long's translations, _The Kiss and Other Stories_; ranks Chekhov with Dostoevsky, Turgenev, Gogol, and Tolstoy. Chekhov "seems to have achieved absolute realism." Reprinted as "Tchehkoff": 1917.1.

3 EZHOV, N.M. "Anton Pavlovich Chekhov: opyt kharakteristiki" [Chekhov: an attempt at a

characterization]. Istoricheskii vestnik 117:499-519.

Reviews contemporary reminiscences of Chekhov and argues that they attempt to "canonize" him. Ezhov surveys his biography with the aim of decanonizing him, arguing that his best work was his early comic stories. His later stories are weak, and his plays do not deserve the success they have had.

4 OVSIANIKO-KULIKOVSKII, D.N. "Etiudy o tvorchestve A.P. Chekhova" [Studies of Chekhov's works]. In Sobranie sochinenii [Collected works]. Vol. 5. St. Petersburg: Obshchestvennaia pol'za and Prometei, pp. 114-74. Reprint. Slavistic Printings and Reprintings, no. 102/9. Edited by C.H. van Schooneveld. The Hague and Paris: Mouton, 1969.

Consists of four sections: the first, largely theoretical, argues that Chekhov belongs to that group of artists which seizes on only a few of life's aspects rather than presenting a complete, multifaceted picture of life. The second section analyzes "Ionych" and argues that Chekhov is able to illuminate the life of a man, a town, and its inhabitants fully yet without portraying them in detail. In "In the Ravine" Chekhov deals with the rural "neo-bourgeoisie," motivated only by their passion for gain. The final section places The Cherry Orchard in the context of nineteenth-century Russian literature, arguing that it sums up many earlier portrayals of the decline of old, serfowning Russia. Chekhov portrays Gaev and Ranevskaia as the last of the "superfluous people;" his Lopakhin, however, suggests that Russia's future intelligentsia will be infused with new healthy and active forces.

5 ----- Istoriia russkoi intelligentsii [A history of the Russian intelligentsia]. Part 3, 80-e gody i nachalo 90-kh [The 1880s and the beginning of the 1890s. In Sobranie sochinenii [Collected works]. Vol. 9. St. Petersburg: Obshchestvennaia pol'za and Prometei, pp. 45-128. Reprint. Slavistic Printings and Reprintings, no. 102/9. Edited by C.H. van Schooneveld. The Hague and Paris: Mouton, 1969.

Surveys Chekhov's writings of the late 1880s and the early 1890s within the context of Russian intellectual history. His "Dreary Story" reflects the spirit and the color of the 1880s and also helps clarify Chekhov's own state of mind at that time. Ivanov deals with the antithesis between the poverty of material culture and the wealth of moral and intellectual life in the 1880s. The inability of the educated classes to bridge this gap is a theme of "My Wife" as well.

6 SOLOV'EV, E.A. [Andreevich]. "Poeziia Chekhova" [Chekhov's poetry]. In <u>Opyt filisofii russkoi literatury</u> [An essay in the philosophy of Russian literature]. 2d ed. St. Petersburg: Znanie, pp. 287-93.

Comments on Chekhov's works generally, noting that his main concern is to show how Russian life crushes his characters. His works make up one great "poem" of Russian life akin to Gogol's "poem" in <u>Dead Souls</u>.

<u>1910</u>

1 <u>A.P. Chekhov: sbornik statei</u>. Russkaia byl', seriia III [A.P. Chekhov: a collection of articles. Russian life, series 3]. No. 2. Moscow: Obrazovanie, 183 pp.

Contains a general appreciation; an account of the first half of his career; and two critical articles: one, by M. Novikova, deals with Chekhov's theme of work as a solution to human problems; a second discusses Chekhov's first collection of stories, <u>Tales of Melpomene</u>. Illustrated.

2 BARING, MAURICE. "The Plays of Anton Tchekov." In <u>Landmarks in Russian Literature</u>. London: Methuen, pp. 163-85.

Reprinted from 1908.3.

3 BOTSIANOVSKII, V.F. "Chekhov i simvolisty" [Chekhov and the symbolists]. <u>Teatr i iskusstvo</u>, no. 3, pp. 55-57.

Comments favorably on Bely's article on Chekhov (1904.5) and argues that Chekhov does indeed have a kinship with the Symbolists.

4 BUGAEV, BORIS [Andrei Belyi]. "Chekhov." In <u>Lug zelenyi: kniga statei</u> [The green meadow: a book of articles]. Moscow: Al'tsion, pp. 122-33. Reprint, with introduction by Zoia Iur'eva. New York and London: Johnson Reprint Corporation (The Slavic Series), 1967.

Reprinted from 1904.3.

5 CHUKOVSKII, KORNEI. "Chekhov i khristianstvo" [Chekhov and Christianity]. <u>Mir</u>, no. 5, pp. 356-59.

Argues that critics who reproach Chekhov for lack of interest in Christianity are wrong: the beauty of his writings about the ordinary things of life brings his readers closer to God than do most pious tracts. The Three Sisters is an example of how his works are informed by Christian virtues; it not only evokes sympathy for the downtrodden and suffering but makes them an image of beauty.

6 Iubileinyi Chekhovskii sbornik [A Chekhov jubilee collection]. Moscow: Zaria, 148 pp.
Contains five articles on various aspects of Chekhov and his work. Includes 1910.8.

7 IZMAILOV, A.A. "Mezhdu veroi i neveriem: religiia Chekhova" [Between faith and disbelief: Chekhov's religion]. Russkoe slovo, no. 13, pp. 204-7.
Examines Chekhov's own statements on his lack of faith but argues that few writers could describe believers more sympathetically. The contradiction between his emotional attraction to religion and his intellectual attraction to skepticism was typical of his generation.

8 ROZANOV, V.V. "A.P. Chekhov." In Iubileinyi chekhovskii sbornik [A Chekhov jubilee collection]. Moscow: Zaria, pp. 117-32.
A general appreciation that regards Chekhov as a keen observer of life's mysteries; his works express the essence of Russia.

9 SEMENOV, M. and TULUPOV, N., eds. Chekhovskii iubileinyi sbornik [A jubilee collection on Chekhov]. Moscow: I.D. Sytin, 544 pp.
Contains material that appeared in the Russian press marking the fiftieth anniversary of Chekhov's birth, including poems in his memory, reprints of some of his early stories, excerpts from his letters and fiction, a selection of appreciations and evaluations of his achievement, critical assessments, reminiscences, and illustrations.

10 *VOROVSKII, V.V. [Profan]. "A.P. Chekhov." Nashe slovo (Odessa), January 17.
A general assessment of Chekhov's significance from a Marxist point of view. He was a merciless and analytical critic of his society but was unable to formulate a clear idea of how that society should develop. His later works, beginning with Uncle Vanya, do express the notion of working for a better future, however. Reprinted: 1975.16.

1911

1 ALEKSANDROVICH, Iu. Istoriia noveishei russkoi literatury 1880-1910 g. Part 1, Chekhov i ego vremia [A history of recent Russian literature, part 1: Chekhov and his time]. Moscow: Sfinks, pp. 105-283.

Examines Chekhov's career within the general context of the literary and intellectual currents of his day. Considerable attention is paid to the outlooks of the journals in which Chekhov published.

2 BATIUSHKOV, F.D. "Anton Pavlovich Chekhov." In Istoriia russkoi literatury XIX veka [The history of Russian literature in the nineteenth century]. Edited by D.N. Ovsianiko-Kulikovskii. Vol. 5. Moscow: Mir, pp. 187-215. Reprint. Slavistic Printings and Reprintings, no. 153/5. Edited by C.H. van Schooneveld. The Hague and Paris: Mouton, 1969.

A general survey of Chekhov's career which divides his work into three periods: 1880-1886; 1887-1893; 1893-1904. In the first his technique is typically impressionistic. The middle period is one of considerable gloom and pessimism and focuses on life's vulgarity. But the writings of the final period express faith in humanity. His work brings Russian literature back to the classical, non-tendentious realism of the Pushkin period.

3 BUGAEV, BORIS [Andrei Belyi]. "A.P. Chekhov." In Arabeski: kniga statei [Arabesques: a book of articles]. Moscow: Musaget, pp. 395-408.

Contains 1904.4, 1904.5, and 1907.2.

4 IVANOV, R.V. [Ivanov-Razumnik]. Istoriia russkoi obshchestvennoi mysli: individualizm i meshchanstvo v russkoi literatury i zhizni XIX v. [A history of Russian social thought: individualism and philistinism in Russian literature and life of the 19th century]. Vo. 2. 3d ed., expanded. St. Petersburg: M.M. Stasiulevich, pp. 388-408, 443-46. Reprint. Slavistic Printings and Reprintings, no. 229/2. Edited by C.H. van Schooneveld. The Hague and Paris: Mouton, 1969.

Surveys Chekhov's writings within an overall framework that sees the conflict of individualism and philistinism as central to Russian intellectual history. Chekhov's early writings are absolutely hostile to philistinism but are also absolutely pessimistic because they show that philistinism is deeply engrained everywhere in life. In the works of his middle period he sought salvation from pessimism through faith in progress. But he also realized that future harmony could do nothing to improve life now, and the pessimistic note remains in his writings. Both Chekhov and Gorky are divided between an inborn individualism and an acquired anti-individualism.

5 KNIAZEV, G.A. O Chekhove: literaturnyi ocherk [On Chekhov: a literary sketch]. St. Petersburg: A.S. Suvorin, 48 pp.

Contains a sketch of Chekhov's artistic outlook; argues that in his early stories he treated the specific and the "accidental" qualities of people, whereas his later work deals with their typical qualities. The tone of his works generally is melancholic and his attitude is one of sorrow and compassion.

1912

1 AMFITEATROV, A.V. "A.P. Chekhov." In Sobranie sochinenii [Collected works]. Vol. 14. St. Petersburg: Samoobrazovanie, pp. 3-233.

A collection of independent articles that include personal reminiscences, criticism (studies of Chekhov and the novel and of The Cherry Orchard), and general appreciations.

2 CALDERON, GEORGE. "Tchekhof." In Two Plays by Tchekhof. Translated by George Calderon. London: Grant Richards, pp. 7-22.

Argues that Chekhov's plays are centrifugal, not self-centered, meaning that they draw our attention to the larger world and not inward as we consider the events represented. They demonstrate the truth that group emotions and experiences rather than individual ones are what chiefly characterize human conduct. His plays are complex blends of the comic and the pathetic ("tragedies with the texture of comedy") and his characters complex mixes of virtue and vice. His famous faith in Progress should be seen as a symbol: life itself does not improve, but man's faith in an ideal progresses.

3 DUKES, ASHLEY. "Anton Tchekhov." In Modern Dramatists. London: F. Palmer, pp. 190-210. Reprint. Freeport, N.Y.: Books for Libraries Press, 1967.

Characterizes Chekhov's plays generally and examines The Seagull in detail, noting that the plays involve characters who constitute an aristocracy of thought and feeling and thus have a capacity for great drama. Chekhov is not a great dramatist, however: his plays are "a series of original experiments" that present life only as a "picture puzzle of existence in fragments."

1913

1 ANDREEV, LEONID. "Tri sestry" [The Three Sisters]. In Polnoe sobranie sochinenii [Complete collected works]. Vol. 6. St. Petersburg: A.F. Marks, pp. 321-25.

Praises the MAT's production of the play as "a fact" of life rather than a piece of art. The play had a powerful effect on the audience. It is not a pessimistic work; the sisters thirst to live and strive toward a new and a better life.

2 GLINKA, A.S. [Volzhskii]. "Dostoevskii i Chekhov: parallel'" [Dostoevsky and Chekhov: a parallel]. Russkaia mysl' 5:33-42.

Chekhov and Dostoevsky are the best representatives in Russian literature of two opposite aspects of the human soul: Chekhov of the bright, chaste, Apollonian side, and Dostoevsky of the dark, passionate Dionysian.

3 STEPANOV, M.M. Religiia A.P. Chekhova [A.P. Chekhov's religion]. Religiia russkikh pisatelei, no. 1. Saratov: Volga, 59 pp.

Surveys Russian studies of Chekhov and religion; examines references to religion in his letters and his treatment of it in his stories. Notes that he has many sympathetic characters who express faith in God and immortality. Many of his stories deal with various sacraments of the church and with religious ritual. The sympathy and understanding with which he treats religion leads to the conclusion that he was a believer.

1914

1 ANDREEV, LEONID. "Pis'ma o teatre" [Letters on the theater]. In Literaturno-khudozhestvennye al'manakhi izdatel'stva Shipovnik, no. 22. St. Petersburg: Shipovnik, pp. 21-66. Reprint. Russian Titles for the Specialist, no. 56. Letchworth, Herts.: Prideaux Press, 1974.

Argues that Chekhov is a "panpsychologist" who animates everything that meets his eye: landscapes, objects, characters, and time itself. The MAT's success with Chekhov arises because it understands this secret. But the MAT is wrong the transform every play it produces into a psychological drama. Translated: 1981.39.

2 CHANDLER, FRANK W. Aspects of Modern Drama. New York: Macmillan, pp. 221-24.
Argues that Chekhov's plays present character instead of action. His outlook is gloomy and his method naturalistic.

3 DOLININ, A.S. "Putnik-sozertsatel': tvorchestvo A.P. Chekhova" [The contemplative traveller: the work of A.P. Chekhov]. Zavety, no. 7, pp. 64-102.
A general examination of Chekhov's literary personality that stresses his characteristic of seeing life as a multiplicity of individual, unrelated facts and events. He strove to find some connecting link between these but never could.

4 GOLDMAN, EMMA. The Social Significance of the Modern Drama. Boston: Richard G. Badger, pp. 283-93.
Discusses The Seagull and The Cherry Orchard, considering the first as a picture of the "wretchedness and horror" of Russian life. Treplyov is struggling to achieve his ideals in art; his suicide is an indictment of his society. The Cherry Orchard also deals with the spirit of idealism, personified by Trofimov. He and Anya free themselves from aristocratic traditions and from the materialism of Lopakhin. "Far from being a pessimist, as charged by unintelligent critics, [Chekhov's] faith was strong in the possibilities of liberty."

5 GROSSMAN, LEONID. "Naturalizm Chekhova" [Chekhov's naturalism]. Vestnik Evropy, no. 7, pp. 218-47.
The example of French naturalism strengthened the tendency toward a scientific approach to art which was already a part of Chekhov's make-up. He was influenced by Zola's and Maupassant's stress on human animality and pessimism, as he was by Flaubert's strict objectivity and contempt for philistinism and predatory females. Yet Chekhov's compassion and his awareness of man's spiritual capacity reveal his ultimate acceptance and love of the world. Translated in part: 1967.9.

6 MAIAKOVSKII, V.V. "Dva Chekhova" [Two Chekhovs]. Novaia zhizn', no. 7, pp. 140-46.
Argues that Chekhov was a "craftsman of the

word" whose aim was not to teach or to moralize but simply to play with language. Discussed in 1981.28. Several reprints.

7 MEREZHKOVSKII, D.S. "Chekhov i Gor'kii" [Chekhov and Gorky]. In Polnoe sobranie sochinenii [Complete collected works]. Vol. 14. Moscow: I.D. Sytin, pp. 60-115.
Reprinted from 1906.4.

8 PERSKY, SERGE. "Anton Tchekoff." In Contemporary Russian Novelists. Translated by Frederick Eisemann. London: Frank Palmer, pp. 40-75.
Surveys Chekhov's literary work, noting his major themes and character types. His attitude is one of "profound melancholy," and this is even more pronounced in his last works. His writings are not satirical since he sympathizes too much with his characters.

9 SHAKHOVSAKAIA, N.D. "O Chekhove" [About Chekhov]. Russkaia mysl', no. 7, pp. 1-15.
Commemorates the tenth anniversary of Chekhov's death by reviewing his literary career. His works did not provide answers to life's burning questions; he himself was tormented by the lack of answers.

10 SOBOLEV, Iu.V. "Bez illiuzii: o Chekhove" [Without illusions: on Chekhov]. Novaia zhizn', no. 7, pp. 110-17.
Discusses Chekhov's powers of observation and his ability to imagine the hidden, inner side of those he met by examining their exterior. This same ability forms the basis of his approach to characterization in fiction.

11 TALANKIN, V. "Chekhov kak reformator russkogo iazyka" [Chekhov as a reformer of the Russian language]. Novaia zhizn', no. 7, pp. 118-39.
Examines Chekhov's language and style in a broad sense, including characterization, description, syntax, and lexicon. He was an impressionist who tried to capture the transitoriness of life by seizing only its most essential traits. His method of characterization is also impressionistic and quite different from traditional technique.

1915

1 AIKHENVAL'D, Iu.I. Pis'ma Chekhova, s ego portretom [Chekhov's letters, with his portrait]. Moscow:

Kosmos, 37 pp.

Argues that a writer reveals himself most completely in his private letters, and that Chekhov's letters are works of art in themselves. The beauty, modesty, and purity of Chekhov's spirit shows clearly in his letters, as do his loneliness and private sorrows. Reprinted: 1923.1.

2 CANBY, HENRY SEIDEL. "Free Fiction." Atlantic Monthly 116 (July):60-68.

In spite of their "needless dinginess," Chekhov's short stories are a model for American writers. They are free of the sentimentality and formula writing which magazine editors and the public demand from American authors.

1916

1 BAKSHY, ALEXANDER. The Path of the Modern Russian Stage and Other Essays. London: Cecil Palmer & Hayward, pp. 3-53.

Discusses the historical background of the Russian theater, the origin and the evolution of the MAT, and the nature of Chekhov's plays as staged by the MAT.

2 IZMAILOV, A.A. Chekhov: 1860-1904. Biograficheskii nabrosok [Chekhov: 1860-1904. A biographical outline]. Moscow: I.D. Sytin, 592 pp.

A general survey of his life and literary career based on Chekhov's letters and on recollections of contemporaries. Izmailov devotes some attention to the role of religion in Chekhov's life and works. He argues that Chekhov was essentially a pessimist who portrayed the people of Russia's "twilight years" but who longed for a brighter future.

3 McAFEE, HELEN. "Tchekhov, and the Spirit of the East." North American Review 204:282-91.

Argues that Chekhov's art, like Russian art in general, is a blend of Eastern and Western attitudes and techniques. The simple plots of his plays, his characters' passive submission to Fate, his loosely-constructed dialogue, the attitudes of his women, and his characters' preoccupation with the meaning of existence are all Eastern elements in Chekhov's work.

4 TROFIMOV, M.V. "Chekhov's Stories and Dramas." Modern Language Teaching 12:176-86.

Makes a general survey of Chekhov's literary

career, noting the "kaleidoscopic" impression created by his stories. "The Man in a Case" displays his genius at its highest point. Ivanov is a typically Chekhovian intellectual, quickly excited and quickly exhausted. His plays convey the actual texture of life, but make great demands on both actors and audience.

1917

1 BENNETT, ARNOLD. "Tchehkoff." In Books and Persons. Being Comments on a Past Epoch, 1908-1911. London: Chatto & Windus, pp. 117-19.
Reprinted: 1909.2

2 FYFE, H. "Chekoff and Modern Russia." English Review 24:408-14.
Argues that Chekhov "has been praised in England vastly beyond his deserts," particularly as a dramatist. The chief characteristic of his plays is their "smooth, soothing harmony;" they leave an utterly wrong impression of the Russians themselves, however, and he is quite out of date as an interpreter of the Russian character.

3 PHELPS, WILLIAM LYON. "Chekhov." In Essays on Russian Novelists. New York: Macmillan, pp. 234-47.
Describes Chekhov's writings generally, commenting on his reception in Russia and abroad and comparing him with his writer-contemporaries. He loves the imagination, and his works condemn those who try to repress it; his ideal is the man of vision. Although he is not on a level with Tolstoy, Turgenev, or Dostoevsky, he is an "exquisite artist."

4 WOOLF, L.S. "Tchehov." New Statesman 9 (August 11):446-48.
Reviews the third volume of Constance Garnett's translations of Chekhov and notes that his stories raise questions about the nature of his realism. His object is not "unflinching realism;" he himself has a "mental stammer" in that he is bewildered by life's many unanswered questions. He takes refuge from them in irony and aloofness.

1918

1 NOYES, G.R. "Chekhov." The Nation 107:406-8.

Reviews six collections of Chekhov's works translated into English and notes that his sketches mingle "ironic humor and cynicism." His longer tales are inferior to his short stories; his plays, which show his characters' futile attempts to escape from the tedium of existence, have been influenced by the Symbolist movement. He is not a pessimist but a meliorist.

1919

1 EFROS, NIKOLAI. "Tri sestry:" p'esa A.P. Chekhova v postanovke Moskovskogo Khudozhestvennogo teatra [The Three Sisters: Chekhov's play as performed by the MAT]. Petrograd: Svetozar, 74 pp.

Describes the preparations for and the staging of The Three Sisters by the MAT in 1901.

2 LYND, ROBERT. "Tchehov: The Perfect Story-teller." In Old and New Masters. London: T. Fisher Unwin, pp. 171-77.

One of Chekhov's great talents was to portray ordinary people and make them interesting. "Tchehov is, for his variety, abundance, tenderness and knowledge of the heart ... the greatest short-story writer who has yet appeared on the planet."

3 SHAW, GEORGE BERNARD. Preface to Heartbreak House. London: Constable Co., pp. vii-xlvii.

Notes that Chekhov has produced studies of "Heartbreak House" ("cultured, leisured Europe before the war") in each of his last four plays. The characters in these plays are the sole repositories of culture, but their detachment from practical concerns and the moral vacuum in which they live lead to their doom. Many reprints.

1920

1 CHEKHOV, A.P. Letters of Anton Chekhov to His Family and Friends. Edited and translated by Constance Garnett. London: Chatto & Windus, 424 pp.

Contains 165 letters or excerpts from letters dating from 1876 to 1904, together with a biographical sketch. The letters are chosen "to throw most light on his character, his life, and his opinions." Unannotated. Illustrated.

2 JAMESON, STORM. Modern Drama in Europe. London: W. Collins Sons, pp. 245-53.

Discusses Chekhov's plays within the framework of a history of modern European drama, seeing them as part of a trend of reaction against realism. His plays are not concerned with the facts of everyday life but with life itself and its meaning. His plays, however, are weak, both technically and in spirit.

3 MacCARTHY, DESMOND. Review of The Three Sisters. New Statesman 14 (March 13):676-77.

Reviews the 1920 London production and compares the play to Shaw's Heartbreak House.

4 MURRY, J. MIDDLETON. "Thoughts on Tchehov." In Aspects of Literature. London: W. Collins & Sons, pp. 76-90.

Argues that Chekhov is not an impressionist; he has discerned "a unity in multiplicity" but he takes no attitude toward this unity. He has more creative vigor and is more modern because he is less preoccupied with non-aesthetic matters. His letters reveal his humanism and his moral and intellectual honesty.

5 WOOLF, VIRGINIA. "The Cherry Orchard." New Statesman 15:446-47.

Reviews the 1920 London production of the play and notes that it is utterly unlike anything in English literature. Although the production has flaws the play itself reveals life as it is, "visible to the depths."

1921

1 CHEKHOV, A.P. Note-book of Anton Chekhov. Translated by S.S. Koteliansky and Leonard Woolf. New York: B.W. Huebsch, 146 pp.

Contains Chekhov's diary (1896 to 1903) and his note-books (1892 to 1904).

2 FAGIN, N. BRYLLION. "Anton Chekhov: The Master of the Gray Short-Story." Poet Lore 32:416-24.

Notes that Chekhov's works deal with defeated people living a monotonous existence. His is a humorist, but his humor is ironic, even somewhat cynical. "His laugh quite eloquently suggests the ominous combination of submission to Fate and Mephistophelian despair." But his later stories do show some pity for his characters.

3 GARNETT, EDWARD. "Tchehov and his Art." <u>Quarterly Review</u> 236:257-69.

Chekhov fits into the Russian tradition of "candour of the soul." His modernity can be explained by his fusion of the detached, impartial attitude of the scientist with deep humanism, humor, and sensitivity. Several reprints.

4 MAIS, S.P.B. "Tchekov." In <u>Why We Should Read</u>. London: G. Richards, pp. 292-311. Reprint. Freeport, N.Y.: Books for Libraries, 1967.

Surveys Chekhov's writings generally, noting that even though his plays are "laden with gloom" they still convey his hopes for the future. As a short story writer "he has certainly no equal in Russia and few in any other country."

<u>1922</u>

1 De SCHLOEZER, BORIS. "Anton Tchekhov: considérations actuelles." <u>NRF</u> 19:528-36.

Attempts to sketch a portrait of Chekhov's artistic personality and argues that he is elusive, even for those who know and love his work. Simplicity is his hallmark, and his achievement lies in creating the illusion of the total absence of art and form. Modifying Shestov's view (1905.9), de Schloezer argues that Chekhov kills hopes only in the sense of ridding humans of those superfluities and social <u>personae</u> which are not properly theirs. He creates "l'homme nu."

2 LYND, ROBERT. "The Alleged Hopelessness of Tchehov." In <u>Books and Authors</u>. London: Richard Cobden-Sanderson, pp. 233-39.

Takes issue with those who see Chekhov as the "poet of hopelessness," arguing that in his personal life he was a reformer and an activist. Although "he often writes like a doctor going his rounds in a sick world," he cares deeply about that world.

3 PHELPS, WILLIAM LYON. "The Life and Art of Chekhov." <u>Yale Review</u> 11:399-406.

Reviews four collections of Chekhov's works and reminiscences of him; notes that the charm and the gaiety of the personality reflected in his letters seem absent from his stories. His stories are quite unlike American ones: their object is not to tell a "snappy story"; they do not amuse, but challenge and provoke the reader to thought.

4 ROGACHEVKSII, V.L. [L'vov-Rogachevskii]. "Chekhov i novye puti: 1860-1904" [Chekhov and the new ways: 1860-1904]. In Noveishaia russkaia literatura [Recent Russian literature]. Moscow: Vserossiiskii tsentral'nyi soiuz potrebitel'skikh obshchestv, pp. 122-30.

Discusses Chekhov in the context of a Marxist history of literature; argues that as a "free artist" he began a new relationship to art, free from tendency and accurately reflecting the new realities. Several reprints.

5 WILLCOCKS, M.P. "Tchechov." English Review 34:207-16.

A general appreciation of Chekhov that notes some of his similarities to and differences from Shaw.

1923

1 AIKHENVAL'D, Iu.I. Siluety russkikh pisatelei [Silhouettes of Russian writers]. No. 1. Noveishaia literatura [Recent literature]. 4th ed., revised. Berlin: Slovo, pp. 32-59. Reprint. Slavistic Printings and Reprintings. Edited by C.H. van Schooneveld, no. 191/3. The Hague and Paris, 1969.

Contains three articles on Chekhov. One, a general appreciation of Chekhov's work, argues that he found the close relationship between the tragic and the comic in life. His hallmark is his unique combination of objectivity and delicate intimacy. His characters either come to terms with the vulgarity of life around them and so sink into complacency, or they are stifled by it and become "superfluous." These superfluous, passive types are portrayed with sympathy and affection. Also included are studies of Chekhov's letters (1915.1) and of children in his work (1908.1).

2 CHEKHOV, M.P. Chekhov i ego siuzhety [Chekhov and his plots]. Moscow: 9-e ianvaria, 158 pp.

Describes various details and incidents from Chekhov's biography, chiefly from his early life, that were used in his writings. Illustrated. Excerpt translated: 1925.6.

3 COPPARD, A.E. "Chehov." Spectator 131 (December 8):902-3.

Reviews Gerhardie's Anton Chekhov (1923.6),

noting that Chekhov was a "noble creature" who inspires genuine love in his readers. His attitude is one of "a deep compassion for moral frailty with its slender holds upon happiness." Asserts, contrary to Gerhardie, that there are many points of contact between Chekhov and Maupassant.

4 DERMAN, A.B. Akademicheskii intsident: istoriia ukhoda iz Akademii Nauk V.G. Korolenko i A.P. Chekhova, v sviazi s "raz"iasneniem" M. Gor'kogo [The Academy incident: a history of the resignation of Korolenko and Chekhov from the Academy of Sciences in connection with Gorky's "explanation"]. Simferopol': Krymizdat, 63 pp.

Describes the two writers' resignations from the Academy in protest of the refusal to elect Gorky a member. Consists largely of letters and documents with Derman's commentary.

5 DOLININ, A.S. "Turgenev i Chekhov: parallel'nyi analiz 'Svidaniia' Turgeneva i 'Egeria' Chekhova" [Turgenev and Chekhov: a parallel analysis of Turgenev's "The Meeting" and Chekhov's "The Huntsman"]. In Tvorcheskii put' Turgeneva: sbornik statei [Turgenev's creative path: a collection of essays]. Edited by N.L. Brodsky. Petrograd: Seiatel', pp. 277-318.

Although the two stories analyzed share a common theme and have a similar structure, Chekhov's attitude is less emotional and more objective than Turgenev's and his treatment is more economical and dynamic.

6 GERHARDIE, WILLIAM A. Anton Chekhov: A Critical Study. London: Richard Cobden-Sanderson, 192 pp.

The first major non-Russian study of Chekhov, it focuses on his sensibility, described as a feeling compounded of introspection, lyricism, and hard fact. He fully succeeds in capturing reality; his casual, subtle plots convey the "fluidness" of life. His attitude is one of emotional restraint, impartiality, and irony tinged with melancholy. "To Chehov literature is life made intelligible by the discovery of form--the form that is invisible in life but which is seen when, mentally, you step aside to get a better view of life." Reprinted: 1974.13.

7 *GOR'KII, MAKSIM. "Iz dnevnika." Beseda (Berlin), no. 2.

Continues Gorky's reminiscences (1905.4), noting that Chekhov placed great store in work as the basis of all culture and commenting on his attitude to Tolstoy.

Many reprints, including 1960.26. Translated: 1959.12.

8 IVANOV, R.V. [Ivanov-Razumnik]. "Chekhov." In Russkaia literatura ot semidesiatykh godov do nashikh dnei [Russian literature from the sixties to the present]. 6th ed., rev. Berlin: Skify, pp. 280-98.

Reprinted from 1911.4.

9 KAUN, ALEXANDER. "Chekhov's Smile." Bookman (New York) 57:93-95.

Argues that Chekhov is "a profound pessimist" whose expression of faith in a better life in the future ("optimism deferred") is like the weary smile with which he masked his aversion for the senseless life around him.

1924

1 BREWSTER, DOROTHY and BURRELL, ANGUS. "Soundings: Fiction of Anton Chekhov and Katherine Mansfield." In Dead Reckonings in Fiction. New York: Longmans, Green, pp. 42-100.

Compares the attitudes and the techniques of the two writers, arguing that each offers a new literary form, the story with neither plot nor climax.

2 CHEKHOV, ANTON. Letters on the Short Story, the Drama and Other Literary Topics. Edited by Louis Friedland. New York: Minton, Balch, 346 pp.

Contains letters on literary matters, including his own writings, remarks on others writers and their work, and opinions on literature and drama generally. The letters are arranged by subject. Unannoted. Index. Several reprints.

3 GORNFEL'D, A.G. "V masterskoi Chekhova" [In Chekhov's workshop]. In Boevye otkliki na mirnye temy [Bellicose comments on peaceful topics]. Leningrad: Kolos, pp. 184-90.

Discusses Chekhov's notebooks and argues that the brief entries here testify to his brilliance in inventing subjects for stories.

4 LUNACHARSKII, A.V. "Chem mozhet byt' A.P.Chekhov dlia nas?" [What can Chekhov be for us?]. Pechat' i revoliutsiia, no. 4, pp. 19-34.

Attempts to show Chekhov's significance for Soviet society. Chekhov, like Tchaikovsky, tried to sublimate sorrow and death by transforming them into beauty. He chose not to struggle against the nightmare of the life of his day but to escape into art, first with humor and then with "lyrical sadness." His acute powers of observation and his ability to express what he saw accurately make him the "greatest Russian realist-impressionist" and a model stylist. His attacks on middle-class complacency are still relevant to Soviet society. Several reprints.

5 MURRY, J. MIDDLETON. "Anton Tchehov." In Discoveries: Essays in Literary Criticism. London: W. Collins & Sons, pp. 81-101.

Reviews Gerhardie's study (1923.6) and pays tribute to the humanity and simplicity of Chekhov's art. His simplicity "is an achievement wrung out of much knowledge and surpassing inward honesty," a simplicity that, when we try to analyze it, we find astonishingly complex. His humanity is that of the perfectly free man.

6 NABOKOFF, C. "Chekhov and His Plays." Contemporary Review 125:338-46.

Reviews Chekhov's drama and argues that the whole spirit of his work is expressed in the concepts of Irony and Pity. Dr. Astrov is one of his finest dramatic creations, and the last act of Uncle Vanya is his dramatic masterpiece.

7 RYBNIKOVA, M.A. "Dvizhenie v povestiakh i rasskazakh Chekhova" [Movement in Chekhov's tales and stories]. In Po voprosam kompozitsii [On matters of composition]. Moscow: V.V. Dumnov, pp. 46-61.

Argues that Chekhov had difficulty managing plot; thus his longer works are generally less successful than his shorter ones, where the maintenance of a unified action is not so critical. He could not cope with the novel form and frequently complained of his difficulties when composing his longer tales. His genius lay in psychology, in his choice of detail, and in portraying daily life. These features are best expressed in his shorter works.

8 STANISLAVSKY, KONSTANTIN. My Life in Art. Translated by J.J. Robbins. Boston: Little, Brown & Co., pp. 345-76; 415-24, and passim.

Describes his first encounters with Chekhov's work and his productions of Chekhov's last four plays. The MAT succeeded with Chekhov when other theaters failed because of its new approach to his art. His plays are effective because of their inner, not outer development; to convey this on stage actors must not perform Chekhov, they must live their roles. Chekhov's plays are by no means dated; they are inexhaustible. Several reprints.

9 WEINER, LEO. The Contemporary Drama of Russia. The Contemporary Drama Series. Edited by Richard Burton. Boston: Little, Brown, pp. 94-124.
Surveys Chekhov's drama before and after his association with the MAT and argues that he had had "enormous successes" before the Art Theater's founding. Weiner generally plays down the MAT's importance in Chekhov's dramatic career, arguing that its interpretations suffered from excessive literalism.

1925

1 BELIAEV, M.D. and DOLININ, A.S., eds. A.P. Chekhov: zateriannye proizvedeniia, neizdannye pis'ma, vospominaniia, bibliografiia [A.P. Chekhov: lost works, unpublished letters, reminiscences, bibliography]. Leningrad: Atenei, 304 pp.
Contains a collection of previously unpublished writings, Dolinin's article on "Tat'iana Repina" (1925.3), several letters of Chekhov, and reminiscences of him by Suvorin, A.F. Koni, and T.L. Shchepkina-Kupernik, as well as a bibliography of Chekhov's works.

2 CHEKHOV, ANTON. The Letters of Anton Pavlovich Tchekhov to Olga Leonardovna Knipper. Edited and Translated by Constance Garnett. New York: George H. Doran, 387 pp. Reprint. New York: Benjamin Blom, 1966.
Contains 434 letters of Chekhov to his wife together with an introduction by her. Annotated.

3 DOLININ, A.S. "Parodiia li Tat'iana Repina?" [Is Tatyana Repina a parody?]. In A.P. Chekhov: zateriannye proizvedeniia, neizdannye pis'ma, vospominaniia, bibliografiia [A.P. Chekhov: lost works, unpublished letters, reminiscences, bibliography]. Edited by M.D. Beliaev and A.S. Dolinin. Leningrad: Atenei, pp. 59-86.
Discusses the migratory plot used by Turgenev and Suvorin (in his Tatyana Repina) concerning an actress who actually committed suicide while playing the role of a suicide on stage. Dolinin compares Suvorin's and Chekhov's plays and concludes that although Chekhov had Suvorin's work very much in mind, he did not write a parody. The play is an experiment for Chekhov and presages his later dramatic work.

4 GIPPIUS, ZINAIDA. Zhivye litsa [Living people]. Vol. 2. Prague: Plamia, pp. 132-39.

Argues that Chekhov's most characteristic trait was the static nature of his writings and his personality, the gift "not to move in time." He is essentially a writer of the moment who can portray only the ordinary and the normal as apprehended statically. His works are deeply pessimistic because he has no life-affirming ideals.

5 JALOUX, EDMOND. "Anton Tchékhov." In Figures étrangères: première série. Paris: Plon, pp. 162-79.

Discusses "Ward Six," "Peasants," and "A Dreary Story;" comments on Chekhov's influence in France and compares him with Maupassant. Maupassant tends to exaggerate in order to give his reader a sudden shock; Chekhov's method is one of deliberate nuance and slow revelation of his subject. "Anguish and nostalgia" form the basis of Chekhov's work. "His art consisted principally in finding the means to express this anguish and nostalgia, not in lyricism or effusive confessions ... but in the plainest and humblest pictures of everyday life, using them to show us, in the cheap mirror of this life, what is universal, significant, and human."

6 KOTELIANSKY, S.S. and TOMLINSON, PHILIP, trs. and eds. The Life and Letters of Anton Tchekhov. London: Cassel & Co., 315 pp. Reprint. New York: Benjamin Blom, 1965.

Includes a biographical note by Evgenyi Zamiatin, excerpts from "Chekhov and his Plots" (1923.2) and "Chekhov and the Theater" by Mikhail Chekhov, as well as a selection of letters from 1876 to 1904. A bibliography of Chekhov's writings is included. Illustrated.

7 WERTH, ALEXANDER. "Anton Chekhov." SEER 3:622-41.

Describes Chekhov's world view and the world of his stories, arguing that he is a fatalist who has no faith in human progress. His sympathies are with those who seek but who have not found; his aversion is to the "mechanical in men." His stories convey a sense of continuity, a sense that their life continues long after the story itself has ended. His greatest achievment is his ability to give emotional and psychological significance to the atmosphere in his stories.

8 WOOLF, VIRGINIA. "The Russian Point of View." In The Common Reader. First Series. London: The Hogarth Press, pp. 219-31.

Examines the "alien" point of view of Russian fiction and suggests that much of its apparent strangeness to the English reader derives from the characteristic Russian honesty and direct concern with fundamental human problems. Chekhov's seeming inconclusiveness, for instance, is due to his awareness that human relations generally are inconclusive. Chekhov's primary concern is "the soul's relation to health." Many reprints.

1926

1 BALUKHATYI, S.D. "Etiudy po istorii teksta i kompozitsii chekhovskikh p'es" [Studies in the history of the text and composition of Chekhov's plays]. Poetika: sbornik statei [Poetics: a collection of articles]. Vol. 1. Leningrad: Academia, pp. 138-54. Reprint. Slavistic Printings and Reprintings, no 66. Edited by C.H. van Schooneveld. The Hague: Mouton, 1966. Reprint. Slavische Propyläen, vol. 104. Edited by Dmitrij Tschiževskij. Munich: Wilhelm Fink, 1970.

A resume of Balukhatyi's full-length study of Chekhov's plays (1927.2), it attempts to describe the course of the creative process of Chekhov the dramatist as revealed in drafts and variants of the plays and to summarize the significance of each play for Chekhov's dramatic work as a whole.

2 LAVRIN, JANKO. "Chekhov and Maupassant." SEER 5:1-24.

Discusses points of similarity such as "laconic reserve," simplicity, raciness, and the use of life's trivialities as subject matter. Both writers share a similar perspective on life, although Chekhov is more concerned with finding a purpose in it. Neither feels at home in the drab world he inhabits, but Maupassant's scorn is expressed openly in sarcasm whereas Chekhov is charitable. Both are "wounded idealists," and both are essentially short story writers who refined their chosen genre.

3 MacCARTHY, DESMOND. "Tchehov." New Statesman 26:645-6.

Comments on the current popularity of Chekhov's plays on the English stage and argues that it is due both to Constance Garnett's translations and to the imaginative productions of Kommissarzhevskii. Chekhov's conception of life may seem a depressing one, but his art moves and exalts its audience.

4 MIRSKY, D.S. Contemporary Russian Literature, 1881-1925. London: George Routledge & Sons: New York, Alfred A. Knopf, pp. 79-96.

Argues that, with few exceptions, Chekhov's pre-1886 stories are buffoonery, but after that date he gradually developed his essentially poetic style. His most characteristic theme is human isolation and mutual incomprehension. His characters are "all alike," but this is not a fault since his fundamental intuition was of life as homogeneous matter. Reprint, with slight revisions: 1949.6.

5 NABOKOFF, C. "Chekhov on the English Stage." Contemporary Review 129:756-62.

Comments on Chekhov's sudden success on the English stage; outlines his critical reception in Russia; reviews London productions of his five major plays in 1925-26. Producers often fail to convey the emotional atmosphere of the plays and sometimes err in attempting to reproduce Russian customs and manners. Constance Garnett's translations also have shortcomings.

6 SHERMAN, STUART. "Chekhov, Chekhovians, Chekhovism." In Critical Woodcuts. New York and London: Charles Scribner's Sons, pp. 122-37.

Discusses the current popularity of Chekhov in England and America; argues that many critics have overemphasized Chekhov's pessimism. His letters prove that "the center of the man is positive." "Chekhovism" should be seen as skepticism and positive faith.

1927

1 BALUKHATYI, S.D. [Baluchatyj]. "Die Čechov-Forschung seit 1918." ZSP 4:443-62.

Lists and summarizes the main Russian contributions to the study of Chekhov from 1918 to 1924. Bibliography.

2 ----- Problemy dramaturgicheskogo analiza: Chekhov [Problems of dramatic analysis: Chekhov]. Voprosy poetiki [Questions of poetics], no. 9. Leningrad: Academia, 186 pp. Reprint. Munich: Wilhelm Fink Verlag. Slavische Propyläen, no. 68, 1969.

Outlines a theoretical model for the analysis of drama and applies it to Chekhov's major plays. Ivanov represents Chekhov's attempt to absorb contemporary dramatic practices in his own way. The Wood Demon, however, is a new departure in its attitude to plot and structure generally; The Seagull, a psychological drama of everyday life, employs many new techniques which are continued and elaborated in Uncle Vanya (his first play without a central hero) and in The Three Sisters, where Chekhov makes new advances in the art of building character through dialogue. The Cherry Orchard has a distinct comedic structure. Chapter translated: 1967.9.

3 KOTELIANSKY, S.S., ed. Anton Tchekhov: Literary and Theatrical Reminiscences. London: Routledge & Kegan Paul, 249 pp. Reprint. New York: Benjamin Blom, 1965.

Contains a chronology of Chekhov's life and works, excerpts from Alexander Chekhov's reminiscences, and reminiscences, mainly by other writers or actors, on Chekhov's literary-theatrical views and methods. Also includes eight previously unpublished works of Chekhov.

4 MIRSKY, D.S. "Chekhov and the English." Monthly Criterion 6:292-309.

Discusses the "Chekhov cult" among English intellectuals of the 1920s and argues that his attraction lay, first, in his attitude to culture as a system of negative values and, second, in his smooth, bland style. The balance of his art and his approach to it via the "middle way" have great appeal as well. His narrative technique may have some healthy influence in English literature, but his ethics are "debilitating." Reprinted: 1965.2.

1928

1 DANIEL-ROPS, HENRY. "Anton Tchekhov." In Carte d'Europe: Strindberg-Conrad-Tchekhov-Unamuno-Pirandello-Duhamel-Rilke. Ouvrage ornée de sept portraits gravés sur bois par Henri Martin. Paris: Perrin, pp. 85-120.

Characterizes Chekhov's work generally, noting his simplicity, his ability to create atmosphere, and his "profound Russianness." He is the interpreter of the nineteenth-century intelligentsia, and his characters, aware of the huge gap between themselves and the mass of their countrymen, uncertain of their purpose, and with small talent for living, are filled with anxiety. The theme of death is prominent in his works. Chekhov has a remarkable talent for creating a story from a minimum of material, largely because of his ability to distinguish the essence of his characters from their appearance.

2 DERMAN, A.B. "Chekhov-publitsist: po neizdannym materialam" [Chekhov as a publicist: based on unpublished materials]. Pechat' i revoliutsiia, no. 7, pp. 42-59.

Examines Chekhov's early journalism, its principal subjects (ten of which are listed), its style, and its development; argues that it provides essential evidence in tracing his evolution as a writer.

3 FEIDER, V.A., ed. A.P. Chekhov: literaturnyi byt i tvorchestvo. Po memuarnym materialom [A.P. Chekhov: literary life and work. Based on memoirs]. Leningrad: Academia, 464 pp.

A biographical study composed entirely of excerpts from Chekhov's letters, his notebooks, and eyewitness accounts of contemporaries that aims to depict in strictly objective fashion the material conditions under which he lived and worked. The scope of the study is limited to the external facts of Chekhov's literary career.

4 KOL'TSOV, MIKHAIL. "Chekhov bez grima" [Chekhov without makeup]. Pravda, no. 163 (July 15), p. 6.

Argues that creating a new, Soviet interpretation of Chekhov should be a major concern of those responsible for marking the twenty-fifth anniversary of his death in 1929. Chekhov himself was not a sickly intellectual; in his writings he carried on an active campaign against the moral flaws of his society and expressed only scorn for his weak-willed characters. His journalism, humor stories, stories of peasant life, and his account of Sakhalin should be better known. The Cherry Orchard should be performed as its author intended, as a comedy.

5 KRUTCH, JOSEPH WOOD. "The Greatness of Chekhov." Nation 127 (October 31):461.

Reviews Eve Le Gallienne's 1928 New York production of The Cherry Orchard and comments on Chekhov's revolutionizing of modern drama. "The very soul of his method had always been the avoidance of anything artificially 'dramatic,' and he was wise enough not to alter it when he came to write drama."

6 STANISLAVSKII, K.S. Moia zhizn' v iskusstve [My life in art]. 2d ed. Leningrad: Academiia, pp. 341-44, 374-408, 458-78, and passim.

The Russian version of 1924.8 (which was first published in the U.S.). Many reprints.

1929

1 ALESHINA, T. "Tvorchestvo Chekhova: k peresmotru ustarevshei traditsii" [Chekhov's work: toward a re-examination of an outmoded tradition]. Pechat' i revoliutsiia, no. 7, pp. 3-22.

A Marxist reappraisal of Chekhov's work which argues that his positive achievement lies in the series of active, healthy characters he created who are seeking knowledge and building culture.

2 CARR, E.H. "Chekhov: Twenty-Five Years After." Spectator 143 (July 20):72-73.

Notes that Chekhov's reputation has diminished in Russia while it has risen in the West. The Russians view him as a poet of trivialities and have consigned him to the second rank of literature; in the West his skepticism reflected the post-war mood of disillusionment and he has been overestimated.

3 DERMAN, A.B. "Odna iz chekhovskikh magistralei: k 25-letiiu so dnia smerti" [One of the main currents in Chekhov's work: for the twenty-fifth anniversary of his death]. NovM, no. 7, pp. 173-90.

Examines Chekhov's process of "squeezing out the slave" in his own character and traces this same process in his writings. Derman argues that Chekhov's style, with its combination of simplicity and freshness, was arrived at through conscious effort as a means of overcoming slavish deference to the authority of accepted forms. His works assert human dignity and decry obscurantism and banality.

4 ----- "Optimizm Chekhova" [Chekhov's optimism]. Literaturnaia gazeta, 15 July, p. 2.

Argues that Chekhov's reputation as a pessimist arises from his essential joy of life and his wish to see it better than it is.

5 ----- "Ranee tvorchestvo Chekhova" [Chekhov's early work]. In Chekhovskii sbornik: naidennye stat'i i pis'ma. Vospominaniia, kritika, bibliografia [A Chekhov collection: newly-discovered articles and letters. Reminiscences, criticism, bibliography]. By Obshchestvo Chekhova i ego epokhi. Moscow: n.p., pp. 131-71.

Examines the early years of Chekhov's career and argues that his literary debut was utterly unlike those of other writers: the work of Chekhov's first year is marked by its sharp humor, its very close attention to matters of literary form, its extremely critical attitude to literary banality, and by its total absence of personal expression. The fact that Chekhov was forced to write quickly to earn money, and the general repressive atmosphere of his age caused him to develop slowly and unevenly as a writer.

6 ----- Tvorcheskii portret Chekhova [A portrait of Chekhov as an artist]. Moscow: Mir, 351 pp.

Examines the impact of Chekhov's personality on his work; argues that he lacked the ability to experience deep emotions. He compensated for this through a very rational and consciously-assumed sensitivity and kindness. His second major personal problem was overcoming his inherited slave mentality. The contradictions in Chekhov's personality are reflected in his writing; only a dialectical criticism can explain them.

7 ELTON, OLIVER. Chekhov. The Taylorian Lecture. Oxford: The Clarendon Press, 24 pp.

Surveys Chekhov's literary career and discusses the principal characteristics of his art. Chekhov is a humorist first to last, but the satirical humor of his early stories flashes only occasionally in his later works. Many of his writings deal with an impasse: an imprisoned spirit longs to escape but cannot. His plays convey "his peculiar strain of poetic musing" and rely on a symbol to provide a center for the action.

8 HEIFETZ, ANNA. "Bibliography of Chekhov's Works Translated into English and Published in America, with Introduction and Annotations." Bulletin of Bibliography 13:172-76.

Lists forty-six collections of stories or plays translated into English.

9 "Kak my otnosimsia k Chekhovu" [How we regard Chekhov]. Na literaturnom postu, no. 17, pp. 59-63.

A survey in which nine writers are questioned about their attitudes to Chekhov's work before and after the Revolution, whether his work should be encouraged among a mass readership, and what his significance is for contemporary literature. The answers range from one who consigns Chekhov to the trash heap to others much more enthusiastic. Several stress the importance of Chekhov's stories as models for young writers to emulate.

10 KRUTCH, JOSEPH WOOD. "The Tragic-Comedy of Chekhov." Nation (May 22) 128:626-7.

Comments on The Seagull, à propos of a New York production of the play by Leo Bulgakov, and argues that

Chekhov's mood is not one that blends tragedy and comedy: "it is something generated by the perception that certain tragic patterns have repeated themselves so frequently and so futilely...as to have become comic at last."

11 KUBIKOV, I.N. "Palata No. 6 v razvitii tvorchestva A. Chekhova" ["Ward Six" in the development of Chekhov's work]. In Chekhovskii sbornik: naidennye stat'i i pis'ma. Vospominaniia, kritika, bibliografia [A Chekhov collection: newly-found articles and letters. Reminiscences, criticism, bibliography]. By Obshchestvo A.P. Chekhova i ego epokhi. Moscow: n.p., pp. 192-219.

Examines the development of Chekhov's outlook within the socio-political context of his day and the events of his own biography. His journey to Sakhalin exposed him to the inadequacy of Aurelian stoicism; his new outlook, much more one of active protest rather than passive acceptance, is reflected in "Ward Six."

12 KUGEL', A.P. [Homo Novus]. "Teatr Chekhova" [Chekhov's theater]. In Profili teatra [Profiles of the theater]. Edited by A.V. Lunacharskii. Moscow: Teakinopechat', pp. 220-75.

Discusses Chekhov's "indifferentism," arguing that it is a basic feature of his outlook. The outward humor of much of his work covers an ironic, even cold attitude to the world. He had no ideology or credo and no passions; life therefore seemed monotonous and gray. The Cherry Orchard is his most characteristic work; in it he smiles ironically and sadly at the vanity of life. His plays generally capture the rhythm of the gloomy period in which he lived.

13 MASANOV, I.F. Chekhoviana: sistematicheskii ukazatel' literatury o Chekhove i ego tvorchestve [Chekhoviana: a systematic guide to literature on Chekhov and his work]. Introduction by A.B. Derman. Moscow: Gosudarstvennaia tsentral'naia knizhnaia palata SSSR, 121 pp.

Lists 2766 items, including works on individual stories and plays and on other aspects of Chekhov's works as well as biographical and bibliographical material. Unannotated.

14 MYSHKOVSKAIA, L.M. Chekhov i iumoristicheskie zhurnaly 80-kh godov [Chekhov and the humor magazines of the 1880s]. Moscow: Moskovskii rabochii, 128 pp.

Examines Chekhov's early work in its context of the humor magazines. These magazines were designed to appeal to the urban lower-middle class, and their point of view and contents were remarkably uniform. Items were invariably short, reflected the season of the year, and involved a small stock of easily recognizable characters. The young Chekhov worked within these conventions but gradually developed their potential as well as working out his own new devices to create serious literature.

15 ----- "Chekhov-novellist" [Chekhov as a short-story writer]. Okt, no. 8, pp. 177-89.

Argues that the new short story form created by Chekhov arose from the conditions under which he worked: the tempo of life speeded up; a new readership appeared; and Chekhov himself began his career in the humor magazines, where the requirements were different from those of previous literary organs. His new, short forms embodied new middle-class subjects.

16 ----- "Molodoi Chekhov" [The young Chekhov]. Okt, no. 6, pp. 221-28; no. 7, pp. 191-203.

Surveys Chekhov's early writings generally, examines his work in the humor magazines, and describes the magazines themselves. Overlaps with but does not duplicate 1929.13.

17 OBSHCHESTVO A.P. CHEKHOVA I EGO EPOKHI [The society of A.P. Chekhov and his epoch]. Chekhovskii sbornik: naidennye stat'i i pis'ma. Vospominaniia, kritika, bibliografia [A Chekhov collection: newly-discovered articles and letters. Reminiscences, criticism, bibliography]. Moscow: n.p., 352 pp.

Contains previously unpublished articles and letters of Chekhov, a reminiscence by his younger brother (reprinted in 1960.26), a bibliography, and eight articles on various aspects of his career, including 1929.5, 1929.11, 1929.18 and 1929.19, as well as studies of Chekhov as a doctor and of his relations with the Russian intelligentsia. Illustrated and indexed.

18 PIKSANOV, N.K. "Romanticheskii geroi v tvorchestve Chekhova: obraz konokrada Merika" [The romantic hero in Chekhov's work: the portrait of the horse thief Merik]. In Chekhovskii sbornik: naidennye stat'i i pis'ma. Vospominaniia, kritika, bibliografiia [A Chekhov collection: newly-discovered articles and letters. Reminiscences, criticism, bibliography]. By Obshchestvo A.P. Chekhova i ego epokhi. Moscow: n.p., pp. 172-91.

Investigates links between four of Chekhov's

works: his play Platonov; his story "In Autumn;" his play On the Highway; and his story "Horse Thieves." Each of these works contains a central figure, unusual for Chekhov's work, of a bold and colorful horsethief. Piksanov argues that Chekhov created these as a relief from his more common mundane and melancholy characters. Reprinted in slightly revised form: 1933.5.

19 POPOV, P.S. "Tvorcheskii genezis povesti A.P. Chekhova 'Tri goda'" [The genesis of Chekhov's tale "Three Years"]. In Chekhovskii sbornik: naidennye stat'i i pis'ma. Vospominaniia, kritika, bibliografiia [A Chekhov collection: newly-discovered articles and letters. Reminiscences, criticism, bibliography]. By Obshchestvo A.P. Chekhova i ego epokhi. Moscow: n.p., pp. 251-94.

Examines Chekhov's notebook entries for "Three Years" and attempts to trace the gradual evolution of the work.

20 SHKLOVSKII, VIKTOR. O teorii prozy [On the theory of prose]. Moscow: Federatsiia, pp. 74-79 and passim.

Examines some of the devices Chekhov uses in plot construction such as mistaken identity, surprise endings, parallelism; argues that Chekhov often destroys traditional and outworn plots in his stories. His most popular and most formally accomplished writings are his early stories.

1930

1 BEL'CHIKOV, N.F., ed. Chekhov i ego sreda [Chekhov and his milieu]. Leningrad: Academia, 466 pp.

Contains articles on Chekhov's views on literature, his uncompleted project to write a history of medicine in Russia, and on his library, as well as a previously unpublished story, twenty-three letters, and the diary of his father.

2 FRIDKES, L.M. Opisanie memuarov o Chekhove [A description of memoirs about Chekhov]. Moscow-Leningrad: Academia, 152 pp.

Lists 214 reminiscences of Chekhov, each with a detailed annotation including a summary of contents, the period of Chekhov's life treated, and works of Chekhov mentioned. Personal and subject indices. Supplemented in 1960.51.

3 SOBOLEV, Iu.V. "Kak sdelana 'Poprygun'ia'" [How "The Grasshopper" is made]. In Chekhov: stat'i, materialy, bibliografiia [Chekhov: articles, materials, bibliography]. Moscow: Federatsiia, pp. 132-44.

Using the reminiscences of Shchepkina-Kupernik, discusses the prototypes behind the marital triangle in "The Grasshopper" and argues that Chekhov created a very unpleasant character in Olga because of personal antipathy to her real-life prototype.

4 ----- Chekhov: stat'ti, materialy, bibliografiia [Chekhov: articles, materials, bibliography]. Moscow: Federatsiia, 347 pp.

Contains eighteen essays on various aspects of Chekhov and his art. Their general tendency is to dispel the image of Chekhov as a melancholy poet of the superfluous man and to create an image of him as an optimist who exposed the weaknesses of his decaying society. The essays include general surveys of his career, studies of individual works, comments on aspects of his biography, and a bibliography. Includes 1930.3. Indexed.

1931

1 BALUKHATYI, S.D. Ot "Trekh sester" k "Vishnevomu sadu" [From The Three Sisters to The Cherry Orchard]. Literatura, no. 1. Trudy instituta novoi russkoi literatury AN SSSR [Literature, no. 1. Papers of the Institute of Modern Russian Literature, Academy of Sciences of the USSR]. Leningrad: AN SSSR, 69 pp.

Describes the changes in Chekhov's attitude to his art in the last decade of his career and how these changes were perceived by contemporary critics. Chekhov's art evolved not by discarding old methods but by adding new ones to those already existing.

1932

1 GALSWORTHY, JOHN. "Four Novelists in Profile: An Address." English Review 55:485-500.

Describes Chekhov as "more modern than the moderns;" argues that he has been "the most potent magnet to young writers in several countries for the last twenty years." Cautions young writers not to copy Chekhov's manner: his stories appear to be "all middle," and young writers often try to achieve the same effect, forgetting that Chekhov's stories do have beginnings and endings which are carefully concealed within the stories themselves. It is the atmosphere of his works which makes them memorable.

2 HOPPE, HARRY R. "Form in Chekhov's Short Stories." _University of California Chronicle_ 34:62-67.

Argues that matters of form are especially critical in the short story, a genre which has few formal conventions for writers to fall back on. The secret of Chekhov's mastery of form was his vision of the whole trend of the life of a character, a trend which he could suggest in only a few incidents.

3 PATRICK, GEORGE Z. "Chekhov's Attitude Towards Life." _SEER_ 10:658-68.

Argues that many of Chekhov's characters express his own thoughts about life; analyzes a number of such expressions. His characters are confused and tormented by the reality of Russian life in their present, but education and enlightenment will create a beautiful life in the future.

1933

1 CHEKHOV, M.P. _Vokrug Chekhova: vstrechi i vpechatleniia_ [Around Chekhov: meetings and impressions]. Moscow-Leningrad: Academia, 299 pp.

The reminiscences of Chekhov's younger brother, they give an intimate picture of Chekhov's youth, his family and friends; the account of his later life is less detailed. Illustrated, annotated, and indexed. Several reprints.

2 ELIZAROVA, M.E. "Chekhovskii rasskaz i gazetnaia khronika" [The Chekhov story and the newspaper chronicle]. _Literaturnaia ucheba_ 9:20-35.

Chekhov found ideas for a number of early stories in the newspaper "chronicles"--lurid accounts of crimes or bizarre events. But he eliminated most of the sensational aspects of the material to bring it closer to ordinary life. His aim was to shock his readers with the horror of the everyday.

3 HALM, HANS. _Anton Tschechows Kurzgeschichte und deren Vorläufer_. Forschungen zur neueren Literaturgeschichte, edited by Walther Brecht, no.

67. Weimar: Alexander Duncker, 181 pp.

Examines the concept of the short story generally and places Chekhov's stories in the context of European theory and practice of the genre. Chekhov created a new type of story that combines epic, dramatic, and lyrical elements.

4 MYSHKOVSKAIA, L.M. "Chekhov: master malogo rasskaza" [Chekhov: master of the little story]. Literaturnaia ucheba, no. 9, pp. 3-19.

Examines Chekhov's stories of the 1880s and describes the devices he elaborated to help achieve the brevity required by his editors.

5 PIKSANOV, N.K. "Romanticheskii geroi v tvorchestve Chekhova: obraz konokrada Merika" [The romantic hero in Chekhov's work: the portrait of the horsethief Merik]. In O klasskikakh: sbornik statei [On the classics: a collection of articles]. Moscow: Moskovskii t-vo pisatelki, pp. 271-92.

Reprinted from 1929.18, with slight revisions.

1934

1 BALUKHATYI, S.D. "Zapisnye knizhki Chekhova" [Chekhov's notebooks]. Literaturnaia ucheba, no. 2, pp. 49-64.

Chekhov's notebooks show his method of creation was inductive: from a single, trivial incident he could generalize to reach a conclusion of deep importance. Thus virtually anything could provide a subject for a story.

2 GEBEL', V.A.; GOL'BERG, M.; KAGAN, L.V.; and TSUKERMAN, L.E. "Chekhov, Anton Pavlovich." Bol'shaia sovetskaia entsiklopediia [The great Soviet encyclopedia]. Vol. 61, pp. 459-69.

Surveys Chekhov's literary career and argues that the writings of his early period (until 1886) were marked by an absence of ideology and a superficial humor. From 1887 onwards his emphasis shifted to the psychological story. His writings of the 1890s are sharply critical of bourgeois mentality; his stories of peasants attack the populist view of village life. He is Russia's first master of the short story and raised that genre to full literary respectability. His plays are impressionistic and are essentially plotless since they are based on conveying mood rather than action.

3 KURDIUMOV, M.G. Serdtse smiatennoe: o tvorchestve

A.P. Chekhova, 1904-1934 [A troubled heart: on the work of Chekhov, 1904-1934]. Paris: YMCA Press, 210 pp.

Argues that as a thinker Chekhov reflected the postivist, materialist values of the era in which he lived; yet as an artist he had an instinctively Christian sense of life which his acquired humanism could not suppress. He portrays a series of believers with sympathy and understanding; his non-believers are painfully aware of the emptiness of their lives. "Chekhov's tragedy lay in the fact that throughout his life he stood before the door which his heart and soul beckoned him to enter, but which remained all but closed to him by his own consciousness."

4 ----- "Où situer Tchékhov parmi les grands écrivains russes." Revue bleue 72:853-57.

Discusses Chekhov's writings within the context of his times and in relation to the writings of Tolstoy and Dostoevsky. Chekhov's work lacks heroic figures; his protagonists are not déclassé but "a-classé". His writings treat the whole of Russia.

5 VAL'BE, B. "Etapy pisatel'skoi raboty A.P. Chekhova" [The stages of Chekhov's writing career]. Literaturnaia ucheba, no. 2, pp. 26-48.

Attempts to explain the evolution of Chekhov's genres by sociological factors.

1935

1 BALUKHATYI, S.D., and PETROV, N.V. Dramaturgiia Chekhova: k postanovke p'esy "Vishnevyi sad" v Khar'kovskom Teatre Russkoi Dramy [Chekhov's drama: on the staging of The Cherry Orchard in the Kharkov Theater of Russian Drama]. Khar'kov: Teatr Russkoi Dramy, 208 pp.

Contains two articles and a bibliography of Russian and Soviet works on Chekhov's drama by K.D. Muratova. Balukhatyi's article surveys Chekhov's drama generally, describing its innovative features and its major themes. Petrov's article deals with the staging of The Cherry Orchard. Illustrated.

2 BALUKHATYI, S.D. "Vokrug 'Stepi'" [Around "The Steppe"]. In A.P. Chekhov i nash krai: k 75-letiiu so dnia rozhdeniia. Sbornik [A.P.Chekhov and our region: for the 75th anniversary of his birth. A collection]. Rostov-on-the-Don:

Azovo-chernomorskoe kraevoe knigoizdatel'stvo, pp. 115-44.

Examines the place of "The Steppe" in Chekhov's literary development and argues that it marks his emergence into serious literature. Contemporary reaction to the story is described in detail.

3 LEWIS, F.R. "Anton Chekhov." <u>London Quarterly Review</u> 160:484-87.

A general appreciation of Chekhov's dramatic art that argues that the apparent inconsequence of the action in his plays reflects the disconnected quality of life itself. Much of his drama can be called "the tragedy of inaction" and as such it is universal even when it reflects specifically Russian problems.

4 LININ, A.M., ed. <u>A.P. Chekhov i nash krai: k 75-letiiu so dnia rozhdeniia. Sbornik</u> [Chekhov and our region: for the 75th anniversary of his birth. A collection]. Rostov-on-the-Don: Azovo-chernomorskoe kraevoe knigoizdatel'stvo, 233 pp.

Contains eleven articles dealing with Taganrog and southern Russia as reflected in Chekhov's life and works. Also includes a two-hundred-and-one item bibliography of works dealing with the same topic. Includes 1935.2 as well as studies of Chekhov's reception in Russia, his use of folklore, the origins of "The Steppe" and <u>The Seagull</u>, the language of his peasant characters, and the biographical sources of "The Man in a Case."

5 PERL'MUTTER, L.B. "Iazyk i stil' rasskaza 'Khameleon' kak tipichnogo obraztsa rannego tvorchestva Chekhova" [The language and style of "The Chameleon" as a typical example of Chekhov's early work]. <u>Literaturnaia ucheba</u>, no. 4, pp. 69-90.

Examines the genre, style, and structure of "The Chameleon" in the context of the humor magazines.

6 SCHNEIDER, ELISABETH. "Katherine Mansfield and Chekhov." <u>Modern Language Notes</u> 50:394-97.

Compares Mansfield's "The Child-Who-Was-Tired" and Chekhov's "Sleepy," arguing that the many similarities are more likely due to Mansfield's "unconscious memory" than to plagiarism or a deliberate reworking of the same plot.

1936

1 BALUKHATYI, S.D. Chekhov-dramaturg [Chekhov the dramatist]. Leningrad: Khudozhestvannaia literatura, 321 pp.

Surveys Chekhov's entire dramatic output, discussing the writing of each play, its main idea, its style, and commenting on its initial staging and critical reception. His dramas are seen in the context of the social and political life of the last decades of the nineteenth century. Chekhov was an innovator in the drama because of his use of "undercurrent;" the absence of any central hero in his plays; their apparent lack of plot; and their generally lyrical atmosphere. Balukhatyi argues that the new form of Chekhov's plays originated as his means of expressing the basic tendency of the "most advanced groups" of his era.

2 BELGION, MONTGOMERY. "Verisimilitude in Tchekhov and Dostoevsky." Criterion 16:14-32.

Argues that the appeal to the reader's notion of moral truth expressed in "Ward Six" is "negative and silent" rather than explicit. Chekhov, like Dostoevsky, only implies his underlying belief about life.

3 NEMIROVICH-DANCHENKO, V.I. Iz proshlogo [From the past]. Leningrad: Academia, pp. 1-78, 144-233, 357-58.

Contains an account of the author's acquaintance with Chekhov, including discussion of his personal characteristics and of his early dramatic career; also includes a detailed account of the MAT's production of The Seagull. Translated: 1936.4.

4 -----. My Life in the Russian Theatre. Translated by John Cournos. Boston: Little, Brown, 358 pp. Reprint. With an Introduction by Joshua Logan, a Foreword by Oliver M. Sayler, and a Chronology by Elizabeth Hapgood. New York: Theatre Arts Books, 1968.

Translation of 1936.3.

1937

1 BALUKHATYI, S.D., ed. M. Gor'kii i A. Chekhov: perepiska, stat'i i vyskazyvaniia [Gorky and Chekhov: correspondence, articles, opinions]. Moscow-Leningrad: AN SSSR, 288 pp.

Contains the two writers' letters to one another and Gorky's articles on Chekhov as well as excerpts from his other articles and letters in which he mentions Chekhov. A comparative chronology of the two writers' lives is also included. Annotated and indexed.

2 DERMAN, A.B. "Chekhovskii smekh" [Chekhov's laughter]. Tridtsat' dnei 8:91-96.

Examines the elements of humor and satire in Chekhov's work. The main objects of his satire are the stagnancy of life, abuse of authority, and the absence of human dignity in personal relations. Chekhov's satirical tendencies can best be seen when his stories are grouped thematically rather than chronologically.

3 TOUMANOVA, NINA ANDRONIKOVA. Anton Chekhov: The Voice of Twilight Russia. London: Jonathan Cape, 239 pp.

A critico-biographical study that surveys Chekhov's whole career but focuses on the development of the unique Chekhovian "misty autumnal" mood, compounded of "symbolism and reality, of hope and despair." His own illness and the political stagnation of his age gave rise to his pessimism. His Cherry Orchard sums up all his previous work and conveys his sense of the imminent collapse of his society.

1938

1 BALUKHATYI, S.D., ed. "Chaika" v postanovke Moskovskogo khudozhestvennogo teatra: Rezhisserskaia partitura K.S. Stanislavskogo [The Seagull as staged by the MAT: The director Stanislavsky's production score]. Moscow: Iskusstvo, 297 pp.

Contains Balukhatyi's detailed introduction which discusses Chekhov's work on the play, its initial failure in St. Petersburg, the origins of the MAT, and the theater's work on the play for its production. Stanislavsky's own text of the play with his notes and production score is included. Translated: 1952.1.

2 EIGES, IOSIF. "K istorii sozdaniia rasskaza Chekhova 'Pripadok'" [On the history of the creation of Chekhov's "A Fit of Nerves"]. Literaturnaia ucheba, no. 7, pp. 31-61.

Examines the influence of Garshin's personality and Tolstoy's ideas on the story and argues that it has three levels: a Garshin one, in the portrait of Vasilev, a Tolstoyan one, in some of its ideas, and a Chekhovian one, which is its essence.

3 MAUGHAM, W. SOMERSET. The Summing Up. Garden City, N.Y.: Doubleday, Doran, pp. 124-25, 208-9.
Notes that Chekhov's are "plays of atmosphere" in which interest is concentrated on a group rather than on a few individuals. Such plays are difficult to write and to perform since the audience's interest is easily lost. Comments, unfavorably, on Chekhov's influence on the English short story. "He had no gift for devising a compact, dramatic story..." and his characters "are not sharply individualized."

4 MYSHKOVSKAIA, L.M. "Gor'kii i Chekhov" [Gorky and Chekhov]. Okt, no. 6, pp. 206-14.
Describes the correspondence and acquaintance of the two writers and outlines Chekhov's influence on Gorky's prose and drama.

5 POLIAK, L.M. "Gor'kii i Chekhov" [Gorky and Chekhov]. Literaturnaia ucheba, no. 6, pp. 25-42.
Examines the acquaintance of the two writers (1898 to 1904), focusing on their similarities rather than on their differences and arguing that Gorky continued Chekhov's literary quest for a better life.

6 ROSKIN, A.I. "Staryi spor" [An old argument]. Literaturnyi kritik, no. 9-10, pp. 128-53.
Examines Chekhov's relationship to the MAT and outlines critical disagreements over the interpretation of his plays. Reprinted: 1959.25.

7 *-----. "Chekhov v sovetakh dramaturgam" [Chekhov's advice to dramatists]. Literaturnaia ucheba, no. 10.
Surveys Chekhov's views on drama as outlined in his theatrical reviews, in his advice to would-be playwrights, in his letters to established dramatists, and in his remarks about his own plays. He stressed that the "personal element" should be avoided; the language should be simple and elegant, and everything superficial should be deleted. Reprinted: 1959.25.

8 -----. "Istoriia odnogo provala i odnogo triumfa" [The history of a failure and of a triumph]. Krasnaia nov', no. 9, pp. 186-201.
Discusses the premiere of The Seagull within the context of the Russian theater of the 1880s and the general mood of the era; these factors explain the play's initial failure. Stanislavsky's production was a success

because it was sensitive to the play's undercurrents and other innovative features. Reprinted: 1959.25.

1939

1 DERMAN, A.B. Anton Pavlovich Chekhov: kritiko-biograficheskii ocherk [Chekhov: a critico-biographical sketch]. Moscow: Khudozhestvennaia literatura, 211 pp.

The major theme of Chekhov's work after 1883 is human dignity and the offences against it. Medical training and his work in the humor magazines were the main forces at work on the early Chekhov. His sense that he lacked an ideology made him incapable of writing a long work. He was not a pessimist but a man who truly loved life. His literary reforms, like Pushkin's, restored simplicity and economy as virtues in prose but, again like Pushkin, his influence was not immediately felt.

2 GORNFEL'D, A.G. "Chekhovskie finaly" [Chekhov's endings]. Krasnaia nov', nos. 8-9, pp. 286-300.

Chekhov's early stories had sudden, surprise endings which nonetheless were organic parts of the whole. Many of his later stories break off with the protagonist only beginning to think about his weaknesses and to face up to his dilemma, realizing the true complexity of his situation.

3 GURBANOV, V.V. "O masterstve dialoga Chekhova" [On the craftsmanship of Chekhov's dialogue]. RJŠ, no. 1, pp. 22-30.

Examines Chekhov's methods of reproducing speech of characters from various social groups. He uses specific turns of phrase and frequently comments on a character's intonation and other speech traits in order to individualize his characters' dialogue.

4 KOROTAEV, A.V. "Chekhov i malaia pressa 80-kh godov" [Chekhov and the popular press of the 1880s]. Leningradskii gos. pedagogicheskii institut im. A.I. Gertsena. Kafedra russkoi literatury. Uchenye zapiski 24:87-136.

Surveys Chekhov's writings of the period 1880 to 1887; discusses the principal humor magazines, their general characteristics, their readership, and their problems with censorship. Popular demand and the conditions of censorship largely determined their content. Topical and seasonal themes predominated. Chekhov's works in the humor magazines can be divided into two periods:

in the first, 1880-1883, he observed the standards of the humor magazines closely; but in the second period, 1883 to 1886, he began to develop in his own manner.

5 LEITNEKKER, E.E. Arkhiv A.P. Chekhova. Annotirovannoe opisanie pisem k A.P. Chekhovu. No. 1. [Chekhov's archive: an annotated description of letters to Chekhov]. Moscow: Gosudarstvennoe sotsial'no-ekonomicheskoe izdatel'stvo, 115 pp.

Lists 753 letters to Chekhov from correspondents with surnames beginning with the letters from A to K. The annotation includes details about the correspondent and his relations with Chekhov as well as a summary of the contents of each letter. Continued: 1941.3.

5 ROSKIN, A.I. "Zametki o realizme Chekhova" [Remarks on Chekhov's realism]. Literaturnyi kritik, no. 7, pp. 58-77.

The origins of Chekhov's realism can best be seen in his early long stories--"Belated Flowers," "The Shooting Party," and "The Green Scythe"--since here he was not constrained by the limitations of the humor magazines. As a young writer his views on literature were nearly identical with those of Claude Bernard and Émile Zola. But his attitude to beauty and his sense of its reality in life took him beyond the canons of naturalism. Reprinted: 1959.25.

1940

1 BALUKHATYI, S.D. "A.P. Chekhov." In Klassiki russkoi dramy [Classics of the Russian drama]. Edited by V.A. Desnitskii. Leningrad-Moscow: Iskusstvo, pp. 329-60.

Surveys the development of Chekhov's drama within a historical and cultural context. His first major play, Ivanov, presented few innovations in dramatic technique; The Wood Demon marks his first real attempt to portray people on the stage as they are in life. The Cherry Orchard is different from Chekhov's other plays because of the importance of its comic strains.

2 BOICHEVSKII, V. "A.P. Chekhov o tvorchestve" [Chekhov on creative work]. Literaturnaia ucheba, no. 10, pp. 8-28.

Summarizes Chekhov's views on literary criticism, the role of science in his fiction, the objectivity of the artist, and other literary matters.

3 CLARK, BARRETT H. "Anton Chekhov." In A Study of the Modern Drama. Rev. ed. New York: Appleton-Century, pp. 56-62.

Discusses briefly Chekhov's dramatic technique, arguing that his plays are "tightly woven" and their apparent aimlessness is a result of his delicate art. The plot, characters, and structure of The Seagull are examined in more detail.

4 GOL'DINER, V.D. "Temy i problemy tvorchestva Chekhova" [Themes and problems in Chekhov's work]. Literaturnaia ucheba, no. 1, pp. 7-30.

Takes issue with those who regard Chekhov's major theme as life's vulgarity, arguing that his humane attitude raises him above such simple depiction of everyday reality. His major theme is the right of human beings to a happy and reasonable life. This theme develops gradually as Chekhov examines and then transcends a pessimistic view of life. "The Student" is the first expression of the mature outlook elaborated in his later writings.

5 GURBANOV, V.V. "O stile A.P. Chekhova" [On Chekhov's style]. Literaturnaia ucheba, no. 2, pp. 36-52.

Chekhov achieves the effect of objectivity by describing things "from without." He uses impersonal forms of visual, acoustic, and olfactory verbs to activate the reader's perceptions and to evoke the inner life by describing the outer.

6 IAGOLIM, B. "Priroda v tvorchestve Chekhova" [Nature in Chekhov's work]. Literaturnaia ucheba, no. 1, pp. 31-40.

Examines the style of Chekhov's nature descriptions and argues that they are simple and laconic like his style in general; they are also musical and marked by original, colorful metaphors. Nature is not merely a background but is an organic and essential element in Chekhov's stories.

7 KRZHIZHANOVSKII, S. "Chekhonte i Chekhov: rozhdenie i smert' iumoreski" [Chekhonte and Chekhov: the birth and death of the humor story]. Literaturnaia ucheba, no. 10, pp. 67-87.

Examines Chekhov's early writings in the context of the humor magazines. A common device in these early stories is to combine or identify things that are totally disparate. In the mid-1880s he began to reverse the elements of the serious and non-serious, creating happy openings and sad endings.

8 KVIATKOVSKII, A. "'Duel'' A.P. Chekhova" [Chekhov's "The Duel"]. Literaturnaia ucheba, no. 7, pp. 39-52.

Makes a detailed study of the story, examining its major characters, its style, and its technique of characterization. Samoilenko is one of Chekhov's most memorable creations. Although Chekhov usually regards his characters with objectivity, his antipathies and sympathies occasionally show through in this story.

9 NIKITIN, N.I. "Sreda i geroi: khudozhestvenno-izobrazitel'nye priemy Chekhova v rasskaze 'Ionych'" [Environment and hero: Chekhov's devices of representation in "Ionych"]. Literaturnaia ucheba, nos. 4-5, pp. 118-39.

Examines the story as an example of Chekhov's ability to express a great deal in very few words. Through brilliant economy of means Chekhov is able to show in only a few pages how Startsev changes from an eager young doctor into an ill-tempered miser; at the same time he conveys Startsev's surroundings vividly and in detail.

10 ROSKIN, A.I. Antosha Chekhonte. Moscow: Sovetskii pisatel', 186 pp.

An unfinished biographie romancée closely based, however, on both published and unpublished archival material. It takes Chekhov's life to 1886. Reprinted: 1959.26.

11 -----. "Ob Antoshe Chekhonte i Antone Chekhove" [On Antosha Chekhonte and Anton Chekhov]. Literaturnoe obozrenie, no. 3, pp. 77-87.

Examines Chekhov's early years and argues that the cultivation of an "official" bureaucratic style of writing, much valued by his father, awoke in Chekhov an early sense of form and an aversion for such pompous writing. Reprinted: 1959.25.

12 -----. "Teatr i iskusstvo Chekhova: zametki o Trekh sestrakh v Khudozhestvennom teatre" [The theater and Chekhov's art: remarks on The Three Sisters in MAT]. Literaturnyi kritik, nos. 7-8, pp. 112-45.

Discusses the MAT's 1940 version of The Three Sisters and examines the question of how the play, and Chekhov's plays generally, should be staged. Reprinted: 1959.26.

1941

1 BATES, H.E. "Tchehov and Maupassant." In The Modern Short Story: A Critical Survey. Boston: The Writer, pp. 72-94.

Examines Chekhov's work in the context of the development of the short story and in comparison with Maupassant. In spite of many superficial similarities, the two writers are fundamentally different: Maupassant's attitude to his characters is akin to a lawyer's, Chekhov's to a doctor's. Many reprints.

2 MAUGHAM, W. SOMERSET. Introduction to Tellers of Tales: 100 Short Stories from the United States, England, France, Russia and Germany. New York: Doubleday, Doran, pp. xxi-xxiiii.

Notes that Chekhov's characters are neither vivid nor sharply distinguished from one another and that his plots are not memorable, yet his stories do produce a powerful effect. Chekhov is unique in that he "fills you with an overpowering sense of the mystery of life." Several reprints.

3 VSESOIUSNAIA BIBLIOTEKA SSSR IMENI V.I. LENINA. Arkhiv A.P. Chekhova. Kratkoe annotirovannoe opisanie pisem k A.P.Chekhovu [Chekhov's archive: a brief annotated description of letters to A.P. Chekhov]. No. 2. Moscow: Ogiz-Gospolitizdat, 95 pp.

Continues 1939.5, listing 902 letters to Chekhov from correspondents with surnames from "L" to "Ia." The annotation includes details about the correspondent and his relations with Chekhov as well as a summary of the contents of each letter.

1942

1 BITSILLI, PETR. "Tvorchestvo Chekhova. Opyt stilisticheskogo analiza" [Chekhov's work: an essay in stylistic analysis]. Godishnik na universiteta sv. Kliment Okhridski (Sofia). Istoriko-filologicheski fakultet. Vol. 38, no. 6. 138 pp.

Attempts to define the essence of Chekhov's style and so to reveal his artistic individuality. His prose is laconic, impressionistic, and musical; it is synthetic rather than analytic because it conveys reality as perceived by some specific observer. His stories attempt to show a segment of life which itself is a process of continuous change, a process whose essential features are obscured by its accidental ones. His plays, however, are his weakest work because the dramatic form was inadequate for expressing his vision. The real expression of Chekhov's view of life lies in his symbolism rather than in logical argument. Translated: 1983.3.

2 LAVRIN, JANKO. "The Chekhov Period." In _An Introduction to the Russian Novel_. London: Methuen, pp. 126-35.

Discusses Chekhov's work in the context of the literature of his day and notes that it marks the beginning of the disintegration of "monumental Russian realism."

1943

1 NEMIROVICH-DANCHENKO, Vl.I. "_Tri sestry_" [_The three sisters_]. In _Ezhegodnik Moskovskogo Khudozhestvennogo Teatra_. 1943 [MAT yearbook, 1943]. Edited by V.E. Meskheteli. Moscow: Muzei Moskovskogo khudozhestvennogo akademicheskogo teatra, pp. 149-57.

Nemirovich-Danchenko's lecture to the cast before rehersals of his 1940 production of the _The Three Sisters_, this argues that the "kernel" of the play is the characters' sense of duty, their duty to live and work for a better future.

2 ----- "_Vishnevyi sad_ v Moskovskom khudozhestvennom teatre" [_The Cherry Orchard_ in the MAT]. In _Ezhegodnik Moskovskogo Khudozhestvennogo Teatra_. 1943 [MAT yearbook, 1943]. Edited by V.E. Meskheteli. Moscow: Muzei Moskovskogo khudozhestvennogo akademicheskogo teatra, pp. 167-83.

Nemirovich-Danchenko's speech marking the twenty-fifth anniversary of the play's first production, this describes the history of its staging, the MAT's interpretation, and Chekhov's reaction to it.

3 STANISLAVSKII, K.S. "A.P. Chekhov v MKhAT" [Chekhov in the MAT]. In _Ezhegodnik Moskovskogo Khudozhestvennogo Teatra_. 1943 [MAT yearbook, 1943]. Edited by V.E. Meskheteli. Moscow: Muzei Moskovskogo khudozhestvennogo akademicheskogo teatra, pp. 95-148.

Stanislavsky's reminiscences of Chekhov, these

discuss their acquaintance and describe Chekhov's reactions to the MAT's productions of his plays. Several reprints, including 1960.26.

1944

1 CHERNOV, VIKTOR. "A.P. Chekhov: k sorokaletiiu ego smerti" [Chekhov: for the fortieth anniversary of his death]. Novž 7:342-54.

A general study of Chekhov's personality that focuses on some of its contradictory aspects. He was fundamentally restless, yet also had a love of the settled life; he declared himself an atheist, yet had a love for the church. But the "mystery of Chekhov" can be explained when one keeps in mind his origins as the son of a serf and his struggle to eradicate the slave in himself.

2 EIKHENBAUM, BORIS. "O Chekhove" [On Chekhov]. Zvezda, nos. 5-6, pp. 75-79.

Chekhov's method attempts to transcend "the contradictions between the social and the personal, the historic and the intimate, the general and the particular, the large and the small." His writings thus capture the whole of human life. Translated as "Chekhov at Large": 1967.9.

3 MURATOVA, K.D. A.P. Chekhov. Bibliografiia [Chekhov: a bibliography]. Leningrad: Leningradskaia knizhnaia lavka pisatelei, 58 pp.

Lists 370 editions and reprints of Chekhov's works and letters published in Russia and the Soviet Union between 1884 and 1943. Unannotated.

4 ----- "Iumor molodogo Chekhova" [The humor of young Chekhov]. Zvezda, nos. 5-6, pp. 84-87.

Examines the humor magazines, some of their prominent contributors, and surveys Chekhov's work in them. Here he learned to write with brevity and developed sharp and rapid powers of observation.

5 ZASLAVSKII, D.I. "Mechta Chekhova" [Chekhov's dream]. Okt, nos. 7-8, pp. 156-61.

Examines the debates on the purpose of life found in a number of Chekhov's works and argues that his ideal was one of an active quest for a better life as Vershinin proposes in The Three Sisters and that this "beautiful life" is possible in socialism.

1945

1 BROOKS, CLEANTH and HEILMAN, ROBERT B. Notes on The Seagull. In Understanding Drama: Twelve Plays. New York: Holt, Reinhart & Winston, pp. 490-502.

Discusses the tone of the play and notes that it is not a tragedy, yet hardly a comedy either. Chekhov maintains aesthetic distance from his characters so that his attitude, and the one he wishes his audience to adopt, is one of "wise pity." The major themes of the play and some of its links to Shakespeare's Hamlet are also discussed.

2 FARRELL, JAMES T. "On the Letters of Anton Chekhov." In The League of Frightened Philistines and Other Papers. New York: Vanguard Press, pp. 60-71.

Characterizes Chekhov on the basis of his letters. He has influenced both the form and the content of the short story. His letters contain a wealth of valuable observations on literature and also reflect vividly his attractive personality.

1946

1 BALUKHATYI, S.D. "K perepiske Vl.I. Nemirovich-Danchenko i K.S. Stanislavskogo s A.P. Chekhovym" [On Nemirovich-Danchenko's and Stanislavsky's correspondence with Chekhov]. In Ezhegodnik Moskovskogo Khudozhestvennogo Teatra, 1944 g. [MAT yearbook, 1944]. Vol. 1. Edited by V.E. Meskheteli. Moscow: Muzei Moskovskogo Khudozhestvennogo akademicheskogo Teatra, pp. 61-251.

Provides biographical and theatrical background for the correspondence between the three. 152 letters from Nemirovich-Danchenko and nine from Stanislavsky are included, complete with detailed annotations.

2 DU BOS, CHARLES. Journal. Paris: Corrêa, Vol. 1, pp. 113, 145-48, 295-97; Vol. 2, pp. 90-91, 93-94, 103-05, 126-32, 141-42; Vol. 3, pp. 53, 97-98, 227.

A series of personal impressions of Chekhov's writings that stresses his ability to convey the precise essence of life. Du Bos suggests Chekhov was a poet of hopelessness but that his very despair contains "something bracing." Translated in part: 1967.9.

3 EFROS, N.E. "Chaika" A.P. Chekhova na stsene Moskovskogo Khudozhestvennogo teatra" [The Seagull on the stage of the MAT]. In Ezhegodnik Moskovskogo Khudozhestvennogo teatra, 1944 g. [MAT yearbook, 1944]. Vol. 1. Edited by V.E. Meskheteli. Moscow: Muzei Moskovskogo Khudozhestvennogo akademicheskogo teatra, pp. 257-94.

Describes the genesis of the play and its initial failure; discusses the MAT's production of it and summarizes its reception by critics and public.

4 ERMILOV, V.V. Chekhov. Zhizn' zamechatel'nykh liudei [Chekhov. The lives of remarkable people]. Moscow: Molodaia gvardiia, 444 pp.

A full-length biography that attempts to revise the image of Chekhov from one of a kindly, idealistic, understanding intellectual into one of a heroic, healthy fighter for the truth whose roots ran deep into the life of his country. Ermilov argues that Chekhov was not a liberal but a "democrat" who mocked the shortcomings of the old order and sympathized with the coming revolution.

5 NÉMIROVSKY, IRÈNE. La vie de Tchekov. Introduction by Jean-Jacques Bernard. Paris: Albin Michel, 261 pp.

A biographie romancée that treats Chekhov's youth and his family life in considerable detail and deals only briefly with his writings. Translated: 1950.5.

6 PEACOCK, RONALD. "Chehov." In The Poet in the Theatre. London: Routledge, pp. 79-87. Reprint. New York: Hill & Wang, 1960.

Examines Chekhov's drama within the context of a general study of the relations between poetry and theater. Chekhov altered the dramatic form to reflect the spiritual malaise of his age, which he conveys with subtlety and poetry.

7 ROSKIN, A.I. "Tri sestry" na stene Khudozhestvennogo teatra. Monografii o spektakliakh, no. 6. [The Three Sisters on the stage of the Art Theater. Monographs on performances, no. 6]. Edited by Iu. Iuzovskii. Leningrad-Moscow: Vserossiiskoe teatral'noe obshchestvo, 127 pp.

Discusses the fate of Chekhov's plays on the post-revolutionary stage, specifically as interpreted by the MAT; comments on Chekhov's reception as a dramatist; makes a detailed study of The Three Sisters, arguing for a new and much more optimistic interpretation and discussing the MAT's attempts at such an interpretation in their new production of 1940. Reprinted: 1959.26.

8 THOMPSON, ALAN REYNOLDS. "Chekhov and Naturalism." In The Anatomy of Drama. 2d ed. Berkeley and Los Angeles: University of California Press, pp. 333-41.

Describes the ways in which Chekhov violated dramatic traditions: his plays have no protagonist; they have no plots; the dialogue does not seem to advance the action; the plays lack a unity of action. He "achieved the nearest approach to pure naturalism ever likely to be seen in the theater."

1947

1 AVILOVA, LIDIIA. "A.P. Chekhov v moei zhizni" [Chekhov in my life]. In A.P. Chekhov v vospominaniiakh sovremennikov: sbornik [Chekhov in the reminiscences of contemporaries: an anthology]. Edited by A.K. Kotov. Moscow: Khudozhestvennaia literatura, pp. 323-95.

Describes the author's friendship with Chekhov from 1889 to 1899. Avilova provides explanations for some supposedly autobiographical references in The Seagull. Her claim that Chekhov was in love with her has been discounted by Ernest J. Simmons (1962.17) and Virginia Llewellyn-Smith (1973.17) among others, but is supported by C. Wilczkowski (1960.76). Several reprints. Translated: 1950.1.

2 CLARK, BARRETT H. and FREEDLEY, GEORGE, eds. A History of Modern Drama. New York: Appleton-Century-Crofts, pp. 400-21.

Surveys Chekhov's career as a playwright and discusses his association with the MAT. The writing and staging of each of his major plays is described. As a playwright he was "unflinchingly honest."

3 DERMAN, A.B., ed. A.P. Chekhov: sbornik dokumentov i materialov. Literaturnyi arkhiv, vol. 1 [Chekhov: a collection of documents and materials. Literary archive]. Moscow: Khudozhestvennaia literatura, 270 pp.

Contains the texts of four early works, including a rough copy of "Two in One", 299 letters of Chekhov, and thirteen reports from censors regarding Chekhov's writings.

4 KHIZHNIAKOV, V.V. Anton Pavlovich Chekhov kak vrach [Chekhov as a doctor]. Moscow: Medgiz, 135 pp.

Contains a brief survey of Chekhov's medical career and a three-hundred-and-seventy-two item bibliography of material, including Chekhov's own works, which relates to medicine.

5 KOTOV, A.K., ed. A.P. Chekhov v vospominaniiakh sovremennikov: sbornik [Chekhov in the reminiscences of his contemporaries: an anthology]. Moscow: Khudozhestvennaia literatura, 520 pp.

Contains twenty-three reminiscences by family members, colleagues, and friends, ranging from his childhood through various aspects of his career until the final days of his life. Annotated and indexed. Includes 1947.1.

6 MALOVA, M.I. "Rukopisi Chekhova v sobraniiakh Instituta literatury (Pushkinskogo doma) Akademii nauk SSSR: nauchnoe opisanie" [Chekhov's manuscripts in the collection of the Institute of Literature (Pushkin House) of the Academy of Sciences of the USSR: a scholarly description]. Biulliteni rukopisnogo otdela Akademiia nauk SSSR. Institut literatury (Pushkinskii dom), no. 1, pp. 33-57.

Lists manuscripts and drafts, letters, inscriptions on books and photographs and other biographical manuscripts held in the Pushkin House. 292 items are included. Annotated.

7 YARMOLINSKY, AVRAHM. Introduction to The Portable Chekhov. Edited by Avrahm Yarmolinsky. New York: Viking Press, pp. 1-27.

Contains a biographical sketch and a general survey of Chekhov's writings. Chekhov lacked the dramatic instinct but compensated for it by giving his plays a lyrical quality His stories are more rewarding: although they lack a purely narrative interest they seize the imagination through the way the seem to convey direct experience, and through their humanity and candor. Several reprints.

1948

1 BRUFORD, W.H. Chekhov and His Russia: A Sociological Study. International Library of Sociology and Social Reconstruction, edited by W.J.H. Sprott. London: Routledge & Kegan Paul, 233 pp. Reprint. 1971.

Argues that Chekhov's works paint a detailed and

accurate picture of Russian society. Bruford examines how Chekhov portrays the geography of the country and the various social groups--peasants, landowners, officials, clergy, intelligentsia, and merchants. A concluding chapter finds that Chekhov had a non-dogmatic, "entirely secular" ideal of freedom. Bibliography.

2 CHEKHOV, A.P. The Personal Papers of Anton Chekhov. Translated by S.S. Koteliansky, Leonard Woolf, and Constance Garnett. Introduction by Matthew Josephson. New York: Lear, 235 pp.

Includes translations of Chekhov's notebooks, selected letters on literature and the theatre, "A Moscow Hamlet," and his diary.

3 DERMAN, A.B. Moskva v zhizni i tvorchestve A.P. Chekhova [Moscow in Chekhov's life and work]. Moscow: Moskovskii rabochii, 200 pp.

Describes Chekhov's life in and around Moscow and discusses the role played by the city in his development as a writer and as a setting for many of his stories.

4 ERMILOV, V.V. Dramaturgiia Chekhova [Chekhov's drama]. Moscow: Sovetskii pisatel', 271 pp.

Analyzes Ivanov, The Seagull, Uncle Vania, The Three Sisters, and The Cherry Orchard. The plays are seen in the context of Russian drama and theater and, specifically, of the MAT. Chekhov's main trait as a dramatist was his combination of realistic portrayal with the use of undercurrent to convey the play's meaning. The plays organically fuse comedy and drama; their comedy results from the discrepancy between the characters' idealistic dreams and their practical incapacity. Chapter translated: 1967.9.

5 LAVRIN, JANKO. "The Dramatic Art of Chekhov." In From Pushkin to Mayakovsky: A Study in the Evolution of Literature. London: Sylvan Press, pp. 174-91. Reprint. Westport, Conn.: Greenwood Press, 1971.

Characterizes Chekhov as an artist and describes the major themes and techniques of his plays. He stands largely outside the Russian dramatic tradition, discarding plot and reducing external action to a minimum. By means of their atmosphere his plays show the tragic nature and the drabness of ordinary life; but Chekhov is able to turn this material into great art.

6 SHCHEPKINA-KUPERNIK, T.L. "O.L. Knipper-Chekhova v roliakh p'es A.P. Chekhova" [Olga Knipper-Chekhova

and her roles in Chekhov's plays]. In Ezhegodnik Moskovskogo Khudozhestvennogo teatra, 1945 g. [MAT yearbook, 1945]. Vol. 1. Moscow-Leningrad: Iskusstvo, pp. 317-37.

Surveys Olga Knipper's biography and describes her roles as Arkadina in The Seagull, Elena in Uncle Vanya, Masha in The Three Sisters, Ranevskaia in The Cherry Orchard, and Sara in Ivanov.

7 TRAUTMANN, REINHOLD. "Tschechow als Novellist." In Turgenjew und Tschechow. Ein Beitrag zum russischen Geistesleben. Die Humboldt-Bücherei, no. 5. Leipzig: Volk und Buch Verlag, pp. 45-76.

Sets Chekhov's short stories in historical and literary context and discusses their sociological significance.

8 YOUNG, STARK. Immortal Shadows: A Book of Dramatic Criticism. New York and London: Charles Scribner's Sons, pp. 15-19 and 200-10.

Contains a review of the MAT's 1923 touring productions of Chekhov, a review of a 1938 New York production of The Seagull, and a review ("Heartbreak Houses") comparing Shaw's play to The Cherry Orchard.

1949

1 BENTLEY, ERIC. "Chekhov as Playwright: Reconsiderations, No. XI." KR 11:226-50.

Attempts to account for the continuing popularity of Chekhov's plays by taking Uncle Vania as a case study and comparing it to its earlier variant, The Wood Demon. The main quality of the plays is "grace," meaning "the least possible number of movements over some definite Action." Several reprints and revisions, including 1953.1 and 1977.3.

2 FERGUSSON, FRANCIS. "Ghosts and The Cherry Orchard: The Theater of Modern Realism." In The Idea of a Theater: A Study of Ten Plays. The Art of Modern Drama in Changing Perspective. Princeton: Princeton University Press, pp. 146-77.

Examines the two plays as examples of modern theatrical realism. The mode of action of The Cherry Orchard is pathetic: by means of his plot--the unsuccessful attempt to cling to the orchard--Chekhov shows "the suffering and perception of change." Act Two shows Chekhov's method at work: the scenes, themselves made up of prosaic material, are "composed" to make poetry. Chekhov's dramatic art brings modern realism to its perfection and, at the same time, returns it to its ancient sources. Many reprints, including 1967.9, 1977.3, and 1981.1.

3 GORDON, CAROLINE. "Notes on Chekhov and Maugham." SR 57:401-10.

Takes issue with Somerset Maugham's comments on Chekhov's method (1938.3) in which he argues that Chekhov's stories are essentially plotless vignettes that tell us nothing. Like the paintings of the French impressionists, every detail of Chekhov's canvas vibrates with animation and shows us life in a new and brilliant light.

4 HEIFETZ, ANNA. Chekhov in English: A List of Works by and About Him. Edited and with foreword by Avrahm Yarmolinsky. New York: New York Public Library, 35 pp.

Lists 205 titles of Chekhov's works translated into English and 263 English-language articles about him. The editor's foreword discusses Chekhov's reception in the United States and Britain.

5 MAUGHAM, W. SOMERSET. A Writer's Notebook. New York: Doubleday, pp. 150-52. Reprint. Westport, Conn.: Greenwood Press, 1970.

Notes that Chekhov is "a writer of real substance...who amazes, inspires, terrifies and perplexes." He, unlike any other, can reveal "the secret of Russia." His stories are not slices of life, they are scenes, only partially seen, of life itself.

6 MIRSKY, D.S. A History of Russian Literature from Its Beginnings to 1900. Edited and abridged by Francis J. Whitfield. New York: Alfred A. Knopf, pp. 353-67. Many reprints.

Contains, in slightly revised form, 1926.4.

7 NICOLL, ALLARDYCE. "The Poetic Realism of Chekhov." In World Drama from Aeschylus to Anouilh. London: George Harrap, pp. 682-89. Several reprints.

Argues that an appreciation of Chekhov's one-act comedies, with their humor and irony, is essential for understanding his full-length plays. His later plays seem utterly naturalistic, yet leave us with a sense of the poetry of life. He can "invest the particular with universal attributes" so that his plays have great power and appeal. "His subtlety is supreme."

1950

1 AVILOVA, LYDIA. Chekhov in My Life. Translated and with Introduction by David Magarshack. New York: Harcourt, Brace & Co., 159 pp. Reprint. Westport, Conn.: Greenwood Press, 1971.

Translation of 1947.1.

2 BERDNIKOV, G.P. Anton Pavlovich Chekhov. Russkie dramaturgi: nauchno-populiarnye ocherki [Chekhov. Russian dramatists: scholarly-popular sketches]. Moscow-Leningrad: Iskusstvo, 194 pp.

Surveys Chekhov's career as a dramatist and describes his relations with the Russian theatre of his day. His works are seen as stages in his attempt to elaborate a clear and integral outlook on life; thus there is a continual progression in the form and the content of his drama. The emphasis in the study is on his last four plays.

3 HINGLEY, RONALD. Chekhov: A Biographical and Critical Study. London: George Allen & Unwin, 278 pp.

A study of Chekhov's life and work that attempts to destroy the image of Chekhov as a passive pessimist who wrote about the aimlessness of life, but also strives to avoid the Soviet view of the writer as an inexorably optimistic opponent of the prerevolutionary regime. His biography and writings are discussed concurrently, and several chapters are devoted to his outlook at various stages of his career and to the critical reception of his works. Chekhov's best-known stories are discussed within the context of his literary development; separate sections deal with his approach to fiction and to the drama.

4 MAGARSHACK, DAVID. Stanislavsky: A Life. London: Macgibbon & Kee, pp. 168-73, 181-86, 189-203, 253-56, and passim. Reprint. Westport, Conn.: Greenwood Press, 1975.

Describes Stanislavsky's productions of Chekhov's plays, his roles in them, and discusses the relations between the two men generally.

5 NÉMIROVSKY, IRÈNE. A Life of Chekhov. Translated by Erik de Mauny. London: Gray Walls Press, 181 pp. Reprint. New York: Haskell House, 1974.

Translation of 1946.5.

6 SCHORER, MARK, Comment to "Gooseberries." In The Story: A Critical Anthology. Edited by Mark

Schorer. New York: Prentice-Hall, pp. 61-65.

Discusses the functions of the anecdote and its "frame" in the story and argues that each illuminates the other. Ivan's story (the anecdote) tries at once to prove and disprove its point; the frame judges the anecdote and reveals the confusion of fact and dream that it contains.

1951

1 ERMILOV, V.V. Anton Pavlovich Chekhov: 1860-1904. Moscow: Molodaia gvardiia, 430 pp.

The third edition of 1946.4, it devotes less space to arguing Chekhov's distinctly Russian roots. Translated: 1954.13 and 1959.8.

2 O'FAOLÁIN, SEÁN. "Anton Chekhov, or The Persistent Moralist." In The Short Story. New York: Devin-Adair, pp. 76-105.

Chekhov's overall characteristics are hatred of falsity; love of simplicity and normalcy; reserve; a scientific approach; faith in humanity. He began as a naturalist but goes beyond naturalism. He is a moral writer and a realist who believes in a permanent norm of human nature and behavior by which his characters are judged. Several reprints.

3 STEPHENSON, ROBERT C. "Chekhov on Western Writers." Texas University Studies in English 30:235-42.

Discusses Chekhov's views, as expressed in his letters, on western writers and western literature generally. These show that he especially admired Hauptmann, Ibsen, Thoreau, Zola, Maupassant, and Maeterlinck.

1952

1 BALUKHATYI, S.D., ed. The Seagull Produced by Stanislavsky. Translated by David Magarshack. International Theatre and Cinema. Edited by Herbert Marshall. London: Dennis Dobson, 292 pp.

Translation of 1938.1. A postscript by Herbert Marshall comments on the value of Stanislavsky's production score and on Magarshack's translation of The Seagull.

2 KOTOV, A.K., ed. Chekhov v vospominaniiakh sovremennikov. Seriia literaturnykh memuarov

[Chekhov in the reminiscences of contemporaries. Literary memoirs series]. Edited by N.L. Brodsky, F.V. Gladkov, F.M. Golovenchenko, and N.K. Gudzii. Moscow: Khudozhestvennaia literatura, 567 pp.

An expanded version of 1947.5, it contains six additional reminiscences.

3 LAMM, MARTIN. "Anton Chekhov." In Modern Drama. Translated by Karin Elliott. Oxford: Basil Blackwell, pp. 194-215.

Surveys Chekhov's plays within the context of the development of modern drama. His genius lies in his mastery of dialogue and his ability to convey the tedium of life without being tedious.

4 MAGARSHACK, DAVID. Chekhov: A Life. London: Faber & Faber, 431 pp.

A detailed biography that views Chekhov as an enigmatic personality; not even those closest to him were able "to break through the impenetrable wall which he had erected between himself and the outside world." This extraordinary reserve and passion for privacy can be explained partly by his unhappy childhood and partly by his incurable illness, which he tried to conceal from those around him. Major turning points in his literary career were his first visit to St. Petersburg (1885), the receipt of the Pushkin Prize (1888), his journey to Sakhalin (1890), and his relationship with the MAT (1898). Contains a bibliographical index of Chekhov's works. Illustrated. Several reprints.

5 ----- Chekhov the Dramatist. New York: Auvergne, 301 pp. Reprint. New York: Hill & Wang, 1960.

Analyzes the development of Chekhov's dramatic art and deals in detail with his four major plays. His dramatic work divides itself into two phases: in the first, 1880 to 1888, Chekhov wrote one-act and full-length plays of direct action ("plays in which the main dramatic action takes place on the stage in full view of the audience"); in the second period, 1895 to 1904, he evolved a whole series of techniques to keep his audience informed of the action occurring offstage. Magarshack also takes issue with critics and producers who view Chekhov as a poet of disillusionment, ineffectualness, and inaction; he argues that the plays have a basically comic texture.

6 MAUROIS, ANDRÉ. "Anton Tchékhov." In Destins exemplaires. Paris: Plon, pp. 13-22.

A general appreciation of Chekhov's art and personality that views him as a modern version of the "honest man." He hoped that decency would become a natural quality of human beings. His unpretentious personality is reflected in his simple, honest prose.

7 NEMIROVICH-DANCHENKO, V.I. Teatral'noe nasledie [Theatrical legacy]. Vol. 1. Stat'i. Rechi. Besedy. Pis'ma [Articles, speeches, conversations, letters]. Moscow: Iskusstvo, pp. 79-109; 111-13.

Contains excerpts from 1936.3, thirteen letters of Nemirovich-Danchenko to Chekhov concerning the MAT's first production of The Seagull, Nemirovich-Danchenko's speech on The Cherry Orchard (1943.2), and letters and remarks on Chekhov and Gorky.

8 POPKIN, HENRY. "Chekhov, the Ironic Spectator." Theatre Arts, no. 3, pp. 17, 80.

Argues that Chekhov's notion of comedy meant "the irony of the chaotically conflicting actions and speeches presented on the stage." Much of the supposed melancholy of scenes in his plays disappears when one becomes attuned to the faintly ludicrous undercurrent within them. His stance is ironic, and one must appreciate this to keep the genres of his plays, as well as the political views of his characters, in perspective

9 WILSON, EDMUND. "Seeing Chekhov Plain." New Yorker, 22 November, pp. 180-98.

Reviews Ronald Hingley's Chekhov: A Biographical and Critical Study (1950.3) and David Magarshack's Chekhov the Dramatist (1952.5) and comments on some of the obstacles western readers must overcome to appreciate Chekhov. Reprinted: 1972.28.

1953

1 BENTLEY, ERIC. "Craftsmanship in Uncle Vanya." In In Search of Theater. New York: Alfred A. Knopf, pp. 342-64. Several reprints, including 1977.3

A slightly revised version of 1949.1.

2 EIGES, I.R. Muzyka v zhizni i tvorchestve Chekhova [Music in Chekhov's life and work]. Moscow: Gos. muzykal'noe izdatel'stvo, 95pp.

Surveys the many instances in which music is used in Chekhov's stories and plays; comments on its artistic functions; provides specific sources of the music used. Chekhov's attitude to Tchaikovsky and Rachmaninoff are also treated in detail.

3 MEISTER, CHARLES W. "Chekhov's Reception in England

and America." SlavR 12:109-21.
Surveys English and American criticism of Chekhov from 1888 to 1951 and comments on the production and reception of his plays in England and America during that period.

4 MYSHKOVSKAIA, L.M. "Khudozhestvennoe masterstvo Chekhova-novellista" [Chekhov's craftsmanship in the short story]. Okt, no. 2, pp. 153-65.
Analyzes the various elements of Chekhov's short stories--plot, use of detail, language, nature descriptions, and the various devices he used to achieve economy of means--that enabled him to expand the possibilities of the short form.

1954

1 AL'TSHULLER, A.Ia. "Chekhov na zarubezhnoi stsene" [Chekhov on the foreign stage]. Teatr, no. 7, pp. 94-105.
Surveys productions of Chekhov's plays in Eastern and Western Europe and, briefly, in the United States.

2 Anton Pavlovich Chekhov: sbornik. Stat'i, issledovaniia, publikatsii [Chekhov: an anthology. Articles, scholarly research, publications]. Rostov-on-the-Don: Rostovskoe knizhnoe izdatel'stvo, 215 pp.
Contains previously unpublished letters, biographical researches, and reminiscences; also includes studies of Gogol's influence on Chekhov, of Chekhov's story "Lights," and of his style.

3 BARRAULT, JEAN-LOUIS. "Pourquoi La Cerisaie?" In Cahiers, no. 6. Anton Tchékov et "La Cerisaie." By Compagnie Madeleine Renaud-Jean-Louis Barrault. Paris: René Julliard, pp. 87-97.
Argues that The Cherry Orchard is Chekhov's masterpiece. It is a play of the present that deals with the passing of time; its structure is musical and its movement slow. Gaev represents the past, Lopakhin the present, Trofimov the future, and Ranevskaia humanity itself: together they make tangible the passage of time.

4 BIALYI, G.A. "Dramaticheskoe masterstvo Chekhova" [Chekhov's craftsmanship in the drama]. Teatr, no. 7, pp. 41-51.
Argues that Chekhov's plays are able to depict

life in such breadth and depth because they involve a group rather than a single central hero; they reveal the characters' complex experiences through the language of the everyday, and they create typical life situations. The evolution of his drama is also discussed: Bialyi argues that The Cherry Orchard represents the beginning of a new phase in Chekhov's drama.

5 ----- "Iumoristicheskie rasskazy A.P. Chekhova" [Chekhov's comic stories]. IAN 13:305-16.

The early comic stories express scorn for people by stressing their dehumanization. Later stories depict characters who become more human as they suffer.

6 BREWSTER, DOROTHY. East-West Passage: A Study in Literary Relationships. London: George Allen & Unwin, pp. 185-86, 202-04, 232-42, and passim.

Discusses the reasons for Chekhov's appeal to the English and examines his influence on the plays of Shaw and on the English and American short story generally. Katherine Mansfield's stories introduced the Chekhovian manner in the 1920s; his plays were not popularized until somewhat later but have had a deep if not always obvious influence on English and American drama.

7 CADOT, MICHEL. "Tchékhov, un faux pessimiste." Europe, nos. 104-105, pp. 41-54.

Argues that Chekhov is not a pessimist in the manner of Maupassant but a writer full of the joy of life. He exposes the flaws in his own society but has faith in man's future. He believed that happiness could be achieved through the perfection of the individual and the general progress of humanity.

8 COLLINS, H.P. "Chekhov: The Last Phase." Contemporary Review 186:37-41.

Surveys Chekhov's life and writings from 1895 to his death, noting that it would be a mistake to call this his "mature" phase (he was always mature) in which he freed himself from Tolstoy's influence (this was done long before). The knowledge that he was dying helped him detach himself from day-to-day experience and focus his vision of life.

9 COMPAGNIE MADELEINE RENAUD--JEAN-LOUIS BARRAULT. Cahiers, no. 6. Anton Tchékov et "La cerisaie". Paris: René Julliard, 127 pp.

Contains general appreciations of Chekhov's art, extracts from his letters dealing with The Cherry Orchard, a sketch of the French theatre at the time of the play's debut, and three articles on the play. Includes 1954.3.

10 DIKII, ALEKSEI. "Nesygrannaia p'esa Chekhova" [Chekhov's unperformed play]. Teatr, no. 7, pp. 69-83.

Argues that in spite of its defects Ivanov is a truly important play, "a tragedy of Russian life." Ivanov himself is an unfortunate product of his times, a man who finds nowhere in life to realize his high ideals. The play itself anticipates Chekhov's later drama.

11 EEKMAN, THOMAS. "Anton Čechov et sa 'Pièce sans titre'." Revue des Études slaves 31:56-70.

A general study of Platonov that examines its place within Chekhov's drama and discusses the play's characters and major issues.

12 EMMER, HANS. "Die Wandlung des Bildes Tschechows." Osteuropa 4:422-30.

Surveys the history of Chekhov criticism and argues that it has moved from seeing Chekhov primarily as a pessimist (prerevolutionary Russian critics, early English critics) to seeing him as an optimist (Soviet criticism, David Magarshack). Includes a brief bibliography.

13 ERMILOV, V.V. Anton Pavlovich Chekhov: 1860-1904. Translated by Ivy Litvinov. Moscow: Foreign Languages Publishing House, 415 pp. Several reprints.

Translation of 1951.1.

14 EUROPE. Revue Mensuelle. Nos. 104-105. Special issue on Chekhov.

Contains twelve items on Chekhov's life and works and French translations of three early stories. Includes 1954.7, a portion of 1947.1, as well as general assessments, studies of Chekhov and Tchaikovsky, Chekhov and Pirandello, and of Chekhov's reception in the French theater.

15 EVNIN, F.I. "'Shchast'e:' ob odnom rasskaze A.P. Chekhova" ["Happiness:" on a story by Chekhov]. NovM, no. 7, pp. 223-32.

Examines the theme of happiness in the story and suggests that Chekhov proposes it as a great mystery which man never tires of trying to solve. The story has little apparent plot, but it does have development. Its composition is musical, and its theme of happiness is developed as in a symphony.

16 GASSNER, JOHN. "Chekhov and the Sublimation of Realism." In Masters of the Drama. 3d ed., rev. and enlarged. New York: Dover, pp. 508-20.

Argues that Chekhov was the Sophocles of modern Europe, possessing a balance and simplicity of temper even while keenly aware of the harsh nature of life. In The Seagull he develops his characteristic technique by dramatizing a group rather than an individual and by creating a "poetry of environment" through his subtle shiftings of mood.

17 GEIZER, I.M. Chekhov i meditsina [Chekhov and medicine]. Moscow: Medgiz, 140 pp.

Describes Chekhov's career as a doctor, including his medical training, his life-long practice, and his statements about medicine. The role doctors and medicine play in his writings is also discussed, and Chekhov's own illness and death are treated in detail. His depictions of illness in his writings are medically accurate. He was an exemplary doctor who prided himself on his profession and regarded the practice of medicine as his obligation to society. A chronology of his life and a bibliography are included. Illustrated.

18 GRANI, no. 22, pp. 5-8; 102-25.

Special issue on Chekhov. Contains eight articles, including surveys of his reception in Italy, France, England, Sweden, Denmark, and Yugoslavia, as well as a general assessment of his art and a study of Soviet censorship of his letters.

19 GRIBOV, A.N. "Pravda obraza" [The truth of an image]. Teatr, no. 7, pp. 84-89.

Takes issue with Ermilov (1948.4) and argues that Chebutykin in The Three Sisters is not meant as a satirical figure or a villain; he is like a homeless dog who is all too aware of his own superfluity. He has been deeply wounded in the past and is more to be pitied than scorned.

20 GUSHCHIN, M.P. Tvorchestvo A.P. Chekhova: ocherki [Chekhov's work: sketches]. Khar'kov: Khar'kovskogo universiteta, 210 pp.

Contains seven chapters: the first discusses Chekhov's early humor stories; the remaining deal respectively with "A Dreary Story," "Ward Six," "The Black Monk," "Three Years," "Peasants," and "The Man in a Case." The stories are discussed with frequent reference to the socio-political events of their day to support the argument that Chekhov was not an apolitical writer but a strong critic of reactionary tendencies.

21 HUDSON, LYNTON. "The Loose-end Drama and the Elusiveness of Life." In Life and the Theatre. New York: Roy, pp. 16-33.

Argues that Chekhov's plays convey the texture of actual life. His influence on the drama was profound: he introduced a new type of play in which every character is important in his own right; and he solved the problem of conveying unspoken thoughts on stage.

22 KOTOV, A.K., ed. A.P. Chekhov v vospominaniiakh sovremennikov: sbornik [Chekhov in reminiscences of contemporaries]. 2d ed., rev. and enlarged. Moscow: Khudozhestvannaia literatura, 682 pp.

Contains the material from 1952.2 plus four new selections.

23 MacCARTHY, DESMOND. "A Master of Natural Dialogue." In Theatre. London: MacGibbon & Kee, pp. 21-27.

Discusses Chekhov's ability to compose dialogue that is absolutely natural and ordinary yet is expressive and revealing. This is because he selects significant detail, creates atmosphere in his dialogue, and uses it to contrast the mood of one character with another.

24 MANN, THOMAS. "Versuch über Tschechow." Sinn und Form 5-6:783-804. Many reprints.

Argues that Chekhov's narrative art is "unsurpassed in European literature." His writings project a keen sense of responsibility for human fate and life. His only answer to the question of "what is to be done" was to work, even with the awareness that one has no answers to the final questions. The fact that his works are not monumental has caused his talent to be underestimated, but together they encompass the whole of life and so attain epic magnitude. Translated: 1965.2.

25 PAPERNYI, Z.M. A.P.Chekhov: ocherk tvorchestva [A.P. Chekhov: an outline of his work]. Moscow: Khudozhestvennaia literatura, 191 pp.

Examines the whole of Chekhov's career by focusing on a selection of key stories and attempts to counter the earlier image of the writer as a pessimist who wrote about boredom and misery. "The Student" is seen as an important stage in Chekhov's development of the theme of the "people" (narod). His work after this shows greater faith in humanity. His last story, "Betrothed," reveals Chekhov's hopes for the future in that it involves a character who breaks with the past and seeks a new life. Chekhov's drama is not discussed. Revised and expanded in 1960.49.

26 ----- "O liubvi" [About love]. Znamia, no. 7, pp. 149-65.

Surveys Chekhov's handling of the love theme from his earliest farcical stories to the sensitive treatments of his mature works. The inhuman social conditions in which his characters live are most often responsible for the failure of love. However his "Lady With the Little Dog" shows that love can summon up an individual's best qualities.

27 PHELPS, GILBERT. "'Indifference' in the Letters and Tales of Anton Chekhov." Cambridge Journal 7:208-20.

Examines some of Chekhov's beliefs as expressed in his letters and fiction. A recurrent motifs of a character set within "indifferent" Nature. This does not imply his pessimism; rather it highlights his fascination with the human will to survive. "'Indifference' in Chekhov ... is to a large extent a technique evolved to demonstrate his own particular faith in humanity..."

28 PLOTKIN, L.A. "Satiricheskoe u Chekhova" [Satirical elements in Chekhov's work]. Zvezda, no. 7, pp. 153-62.

Although few of Chekhov's writings are wholly satirical, many have elements of satire which exist as undercurrents in his mature work. His early writings use typically satirical techniques such as hyperbole and the grotesque; his later works manage to convey their satire while remaining within the conventions of realism. Reprinted: 1958.16.

29 REVIAKIN, A.I, "Dramaturgicheskoe masterstvo Chekhova" [Chekhov's dramatic craftsmanship]. Okt, no. 8, pp. 179-88.

Discusses the ideological stance Chekhov takes in his plays, arguing that with their social concerns and questioning of established values they fit into the tradition of "critical realism."

30 ----- O dramaturgii A.P. Chekhova. Vsesoiuznoe obshchestvo po rasprostraneniiu politicheskikh i nauchnykh znanii, series 6, no. 18. [Chekhov's drama. The all-union society for the dissemination of political and scientific knowledge]. Moscow: Znanie, 32 pp.

Surveys the general outlook expressed in Chekhov's plays; examines their plots and the nature of their conflicts, their principles of characterization, the language of their dialogue, and Chekhov's methods of developing the action. A concluding section deals with the overall significance of Chekhov's drama.

31 STROEVA, M.N. "Rabota Vl.I. Nemirovich-Danchenko nad spektaklem 'Tri sestry'" [Nemirovich-Danchenko's work on the production of The Three Sisters]. Teatr, no. 7, pp. 53-67.

Describes the MAT's second production, under Nemirovich-Danchenko, of The Three Sisters in 1940. His production stressed the "three truths:" social truth, theatrical truth, and truth to life. He saw the play as a conflict between duty and the hope for a better life; he stressed optimism rather than pessimism in Act 4.

32 TRIOLET, ELSA. L'histoire d'Anton Tchekhov: sa vie--son oeuvre. Paris: Les Éditeurs Françats Réunis, 205 pp.

A critico-biographical study that relies heavily on quotations from Chekhov's letters and accounts of his contemporaries; discusses briefly his major writings. His personal credo was that of "un homme bien élevé." Love played a large role in his work and his life and he had an extraordinary talent for understanding women. The nearer he approached his own death the more his works turned to the future.

33 ZAITSEV, BORIS. Chekhov: Literaturnaia biografiia [Chekhov: a literary biography]. New York: Izdatel'stvo im. Chekhova, 257 pp.

A biography based in part on Zaitsev's personal acquaintance with Chekhov's friends, it offers brief analyses of the major works in Chekhov's literary career, largely from the point of view of how they contribute to a picture of his artistic personality. Zaitsev devotes considerable attention to Chekhov's spiritual side and sees him as a seeker after faith who was sympathetic to Orthodoxy but who, nonetheless, remained in uncertainty.

1955

1 ALDANOV, MARC. "Reflections on Chekhov." Translated by Ida Estrin. RusR 14:83-92.

Assigns Chekhov fourth place among Russian prose writers (after Tolstoy, Gogol, and Dostoevsky); discusses his reception in Russia and abroad, and examines some of the contradictory aspects of his personality.

2 BUNIN, IVAN. O Chekhove: nezakonchennaia rukopis' [On Chekhov: an unfinished manuscript]. Foreword by Mark Aldanov. New York: Izdatel'stvo im. Chekhova, 414 pp.

An incomplete critico-biographical study based on Bunin's own recollections of Chekhov, Chekhov's letters, and remarks of contemporaries assembled as a collection of brief notes and fragments. Bunin discusses Lidia Avilova's relationship with Chekhov at some length. Part 2 includes excerpts from Chekhov's letters on literary matters and also contains Bunin's reactions to later criticism and reminiscences of Chekhov.

3 CHEKHOV, A.P. A.P. Chekhov o literature [Chekhov on literature]. Moscow: Khudozhestvennaia literatura, 403 pp.

Contains excerpts from Chekhov's letters from 1879 to 1904 in which he expressed views on literature; also contains excerpts from reminiscences of contemporaries who recorded his views. Annotated and indexed.

4 -----. The Selected Letters of Anton Chekhov. Edited by Lillian Hellman. Translated by Sidonie Lederer. Great Letters Series, edited by Louis Kronenberger. New York: Farrar, Straus, 331 pp.

Contains 204 letters from 1885 to 1904 arranged in chronological groups, each with an introduction by the editor. Also contains a general introduction by Lillian Hellman and biographical notes on the individuals mentioned in the letters.

5 CORRIGAN, ROBERT W. "Some Aspects of Chekhov's Dramaturgy." Educational Theatre Journal 7:107-14.

Argues that Chekhov carried the realistic tradition of drama to its completion. His plays attempt to show the true nature of human existence and do so by heightening the apparent reality until it becomes ludicrous. His characters try to hide their flaws behind masks but, ironically, they are exposed all the more when they do.

6 GITOVICH, N.I. Letopis' zhizni i tvorchestva A.P. Chekhova [A chronicle of the life and creative work of Chekhov]. Moscow: Khudozhestvennaia literatura, 880 pp.

A detailed day-by-day chronology of Chekhov's life and career compiled on the basis of letters, memoirs, and other archival material. The work establishes many previously uncertain dates and clarifies many formerly dubious areas of his biography. Contains indices of sources used, of Chekhov's works mentioned, and of persons.

7 KRONENBERGER, LOUIS. "Chekhov: the Four Plays."

In Republic of Letters: Essays on Various Writers. New York: Knopf, pp. 178-204.

Characterizes Chekhov as the "truest artist" among modern playwrights. His plays show that "feeling can create more intensity than drama." Discusses his last four plays, arguing that The Three Sisters is his finest and is the finest in the whole of modern theater. The play is optimistic in that the sisters refuse to be defeated inwardly.

8 LAFFITTE, SOPHIE. Tchékhov par lui-même. Écrivains de toujours. Paris: Éditions du seuil, 192 pp.

A biographical study that details his views, as expressed in letters and remarks to contemporaries, on science, ethics, religion, drama, literature, and the other arts. A chapter on Chekhov the man stresses his detachment and dispassionate attitude as well as the absence of emotion in his life. A chronology of his life is included. Illustrated.

9 LEZHNEV, I.G. "Kratkost'--sestra talanta" [Brevity is the sister of talent]. NovM, no. 5, pp. 218-30.

Examines "The Steppe" as an example of Chekhov's fundamentally laconic style. All details within the work are integrated; its characters are made vivid through their expressive speech; its imagery evokes many associations. All these techniques enable Chekhov to say much in few words.

10 POLOTSKAIA, E.A. Anton Pavlovich Chekhov: rekomendatel'nyi ukazatel' literatury [Chekhov: a guide of recommended literature]. Velikie russkie pisateli, no. 13 [Great Russian writers, no. 13]. Moscow: Biblioteka im. Lenina, 190 pp.

Contains a chronology of Chekhov's life and works, a list of his writings, and a selected, annotated list of critical and biographical works.

11 RAHV, PHILIP. "The Education of Anton Chekhov." New Republic 133 (18 July):18-19.

A review of Lillian Hellman's edition of Chekhov's Selected Letters (1955.4). Rahv stresses the importance of Chekhov's letters in contributing to an understanding of him and his work since they chronicle the "education toward freedom" that was his life. Several reprints, including 1965.10.

12 SEMANOVA, M.L., ed. "A.P. Chekhov." In Russkie pisateli o literaturnom trude [Russian writers on literary work]. Vol. 3. Edited by B. Meilakh.

Leningrad: Sovetskii pisatel', pp. 329-428.

Contains excerpts from Chekhov's letters on literary matters organized by topics such as style, the creative process, advice to young writers, drama and the theater, and literary criticism. An editor's introduction summarizes Chekhov's views.

13 SHKLOVSKII, VIKTOR. "A.P. Chekhov." In Zametki o proze russkikh klassikov [Remarks on the prose of the Russian classics]. 2d ed., rev. Moscow: Sovetskii pisatel', pp. 413-59.

Surveys the development of Chekhov's literary style and examines some of the influences on it. Pushkin provided a model for simple, powerful prose. Chekhov also created a new type of plot, utterly unlike the traditional, which seems fragmentary but which reveals what is significant and essential in the given situation. Chekhov is not an impressionist; he is not concerned with conveying merely the details of his subject but its very essence.

14 SOSNITSKAIA, M.D. 'Ionych' i 'Vishnevyi sad' A.P. Chekhova [Chekhov's "Ionych" and The Cherry Orchard]. Moscow: Uchpedgiz, 63 pp.

Analyzes in detail each of the five chapters of "Ionych" and each of the four acts of The Cherry Orchard with the aim of showing the unity of form and content in each work. Comparisons between the two works are not made, but the significance of each is pointed out.

15 STRELKOV, P.G. "Rabota Chekhova nad iazykom svoikh proizvedenii" [Chekhov's work on the language of his writings]. Voprosy iazykoznaniia, no. 1, pp. 42-59.

Examines in detail the stylistic changes Chekhov made in two stories from 1886, "A Little Joke" and "An Upheaval," as he revised them for his Collected Works. Notes that his revisions eliminated vulgarisms and clichés, made descriptive details more effective, created more subtle means of expressing emotion, and adjusted his narrative to reflect more closely the attitudes of a character. The revised stories are much more concentrated and more dramatic than the originals.

16 STROEVA, M.N. Chekhov i khudozhestvennyi teatr: rabota K.S. Stanislavskogo i Vl.I. Nemirovicha-Danchenko nad p'esami A.P. Chekhova [Chekhov and the MAT: Stanislavsky's and Nemirovich-Danchenko's work on Chekhov's plays]. Moscow: Iskusstvo, 315 pp.

Focuses on the innovative dramatic techniques of Stanislavsky and Nemirovich-Danchenko as applied to

Chekhov's plays and argues that the MAT did not distort or misinterpret them. A chapter is devoted to describing the MAT's productions of each of the five major plays; Nemirovich-Danchenko's second production of The Three Sisters in 1940 is described in an additional chapter. Illustrated. Translated in part: 1966.20.

17 -----. "Protivorechiia Ivanova" [Ivanov's contradictions]. Teatr, no. 6, pp. 39-51.
Makes a character study of Ivanov, prompted by a 1955 Moscow production of the play at the Pushkin Theater. This production stresses Ivanov's positive qualities; he emerges as an exceptional man, totally at odds with his milieu. His complex character is full of contradictions.

18 -----. "Rezhissura K.S. Stanislavskogo v chekhovskikh spektakliakh MKht: Chaika, Diadia Vania, Tri sestry, 1898-1901 gg." [Stanislavksy the director in the MAT's productions of Chekhov's plays: The Seagull, Uncle Vanya, The Three Sisters, 1898-1901]. In K.S. Stanislavskii: Materialy, pis'ma, issledovaniia. Teatral'noe nasledstvo [Stanislavsky: documents, letters, scholarly studies. Theatrical legacy]. Vol 1. Moscow: Akademiia nauk, pp. 613-70.
Describes the first production of the plays in 1901. In each play Stanislavsky stressed the characters' struggle with vulgarity. Although philistinism and vulgarity triumph in The Three Sisters, the finale shows a moral victory with the sisters surmounting suffering. Nemirovich-Danchenko, however, emphasized the sisters' passive acceptance of their fate. In The Seagull Stanislavsky stressed the gap between the characters' dreams and their reality. The staging of Uncle Vanya created new disagreements between Stanislavsky and Nemirovich-Danchenko. Translated in part: 1967.9.

19 STRUVE, GLEB. "Chekhov in Communist Censorship." SEER 33:327-41.
Discusses the 1944-51 twenty-volume edition of Chekhov's Collected Works and Letters and provides examples of editorial tampering with his letters.

20 ZAMIATIN, EVGENYI. "Chekhov." In Litsa [Faces]. New York: Izdatel'stvo im. Chekhova, pp. 39-49. Reprinted with foreword by Mikhail Koriakov and introduction by Vladimir Bondarenko. New York: Inter-Language Literary Associates, 1967.
In this speech made in 1925 but first published here Zamiatin attempts to show Chekhov's relevance to new, post-revolutionary conditions by arguing that he was not a

melancholy pessimist nor was he old-fashioned. He was a writer profoundly concerned with social themes and was a genuine realist whose works provide a model for contemporary writers. Translated: 1970.23.

1956

1 AUZINGER, HELENE. Die Pointe bei Čechov. Wiesbaden: Otto Harrassowitz, 151 pp.

Examines the notion of the "point" in the anecdote and the short story and argues that Chekhov uses it as an indirect means of expression that forces the reader to discover the essence of the story for himself. The effect of the point is created in part by Chekhov's restrained, understated, and typically impressionist style.

2 BIALYI, G.A. "Chekhov." In Istoriia russkoi literatury [The history of Russian literature]. Vol. 9, part 2. Edited by B.I. Bursov, B.S. Meilakh, and M.B. Khrapchenko. Moscow-Leningrad: AN SSSR, pp. 345-432.

Surveys Chekhov's literary career, discussing his major writings, commenting on his critical reception, and providing a historical context. The years 1888 and 1889 are seen as a turning point in his career, a time when he reassessed his work and turned it in a new direction. In his last creative period his hopes for change were placed in the process of history itself.

3 KANNAK, E. "Neizvestnaia p'esa Chekhova" [Chekhov's unknown play]. NovŽ 44:114-23.

Discusses the origins and the fate of Platonov, pointing out some links with Chekhov's other dramatic work and examining some of the revisions he made in the play.

4 MEILAKH, B.S. "Dva resheniia odnoi temy" [Two different treatments of a single subject]. Neva, no. 9, pp. 184-88.

Compares Tolstoy's and Chekhov's treatments of marital infidelity, arguing that in "The Lady With the Little Dog" Chekhov transfers the marital triangle from an aristocratic milieu to one of ordinary life. Tolstoy's Anna perishes because of the harsh standards of her society; Chekhov's Anna shows that there is still hope for a solution. This view is disputed in 1971.23.

5 PHELPS, GILBERT. The Russian Novel in English Fiction. Hutchinson's University Library. English

Literature, edited by Basil Willey. London: Hutchinson, pp. 187-92.

Discusses Chekhov's reception in England and outlines his influence on British dramatists and short story writers. Along with Turgenev, Chekhov "appeared to many practising writers to constitute the quintessence of Russian Realism."

6 SEMANOVA, M.L. "K voprosu o traditsiiakh A.P. Chekhova v sovremennoi proze" [On the question of Chekhovian traditions in contemporary prose]. Voprosy sovetskoi literatury [Questions of Soviet literature]. Vol. 3. Edited by V.A. Kovalev and V.V. Timofeev. Moscow and Leningrad: AN SSSR, pp. 244-87.

Examines Chekhov's influence on Soviet prose generally, making case studies of the "Chekhov tradition" in the works of P. Pavlenko and S. Antonov.

7 WILSON, EDMUND. Preface to Peasants and Other Stories by Anton Chekhov. A Doubleday Anchor Book. Translated by Constance Garnett. Garden City, New York: Doubleday & Co., pp. vii-xi.

Criticizes the lack of chronological sequence in the volumes of Constance Garnett's translations of Chekhov. His stories of 1894-1903 "constitute a kind of analysis of Russian society, a miniature Comédie Humaine."

8 WINNER, THOMAS G. "Chekhov's Seagull and Shakespeare's Hamlet: A Study of a Dramatic Device." SlavR 15:103-11.

Analyzes Hamletian elements in The Seagull and discusses their role in the overall meaning of the play. The Hamlet theme functions as "an ironic commentary on Treplyov's pretensions" and also as a means of heightening the tension. Reprinted: 1977.3.

9 YOUNG, STARK. Introduction to Best Plays by Chekhov. Translated by Stark Young. New York: Modern Library, pp. vii-xiii.

Discusses problems of translating Chekhov's plays and argues that his most impressive achievement in the drama is his ability to create a lyrical mood which is neither comedy nor tragedy nor a mixture of the two.

1957

1 ALEKSANDROV, B.I. Seminarii po Chekhovu: posobie

dlia vuzov [A Chekhov seminar: a university textbook]. Moscow: Gos. uchebno-pedagogicheskoe izdatel'stvo, 272 pp.

Contains an essay on Chekhov's literary significance and a list of topics for study of his work with appropriate bibliographical references. Also included is an essay on Chekhov in Russian criticism which discusses in detail his reception among prerevolutionary critics and summarizes and discusses the principal Soviet studies to 1956.

2 BERDNIKOV, G.P. *Chekhov-dramaturg: traditsii i novatorstvo v dramaturgii Chekhova* [Chekhov the dramatist: tradition and innovation in Chekhov's drama]. Leningrad-Moscow: Iskusstvo, 246 pp.

Makes a literary analysis, in chronological order, of Chekhov's plays, from the one-act vaudevilles to *The Cherry Orchard*. Berdnikov argues that many of the features usually considered innovative in Chekhov's art--the absence of plot, the avoidance of dramatic convention, the attempt to make the plays resemble real life--are in fact the result of his following the Russian dramatic tradition of Turgenev and Gogol. Unlike his predecessors, Chekhov can manage without a strong plot to focus the action; his characters are all linked by their conflict with everyday life, and it is this conflict that provides the dramatic interest. He also created "lyrical comedies" whose basis is the disparity between a character's conduct and Chekhov's own ideal. Chapter translated: 1967.9.

3 BON, ANNE-MARIE. "La figure du premier héros de Tchékhov." *Mercure de France* 329:660-72.

Discusses Chekhov's early play *Platonov*, focusing on the character of the title figure and pointing out some of his links with Ivanov in the play of the same name. Both characters are seeking redemption.

4 BRISSON, PIERRE. "Tchékhov et sa vie." In *Propos de théâtre*. Paris: Gallimard, pp. 169-233.

Consists principally of a biographical sketch that emphasizes his career as a dramatist.

5 BRUFORD, W.H. *Anton Chekhov*. Studies in Modern European Literature and Thought. Edited by Erich Heller. London: Bowes & Bowes, 62 pp.

Contains three sections: the first discusses a selection of Chekhov's early stories and his technique in them; the second deals with the post-1888 mature stories and examines "The Name-Day Party" as typically Chekhovian; and the third analyzes each of the major plays and discusses Chekhov's dramatic technique.

6 ----- "Goethe and Tschechow as Liberal Humanists." In Gestaltung Umgestaltung. Festschrift zum 75. Geburtstag von Hermann August Korff. Edited by Joachim Müller. Leipzig: Koehler & Amelang, pp. 118-28.

Notes a number of similarities between the two writers, including a profound interest in science, with its concomittant objectivity of attitude, a sense of values derived in large measure from the Greeks, a desire to be free as artists and as men, and a mistrust of dogmatic religion. There are many differences as well, brought about by the differing historical and cultural milieus; but Chekhov's ideal of the educated, free man owes much to the ideas of the Enlightenment and German Idealism.

7 FADEEV, ALEKSANDR. "O Chekhove" [On Chekhov]. NovM, no. 2, pp. 214-16. Several reprints.

An entry from Fadeev's notebook of 1944, this pays tribute to Chekhov's talent but argues that his works have no heroic or outstanding figures; his stories, taken as a whole, are monotonous and fail to capture the true strengths of the Russian character. His plays are more moving and have an "educational" function. Translated into French: 1980.34.

8 LIUL'KO, N.P. "Iazyk i stil' dramaturgii A.P. Chekhova" [The language and style of Chekhov's drama]. In Izucheniia iazyka pisatelia: sbornik statei [The study of a writer's language: a collection of articles]. Edited by N.P. Grinkova. Leningrad: Uchpedgiz, pp. 157-98.

Clarifies Chekhov's views on language by summarizing his main pronouncements and examines the language of his last four plays; divides the language in these plays into a number of categories on the basis of function. Each category is discussed.

9 MIKHAILOVSKII, N.K. "Ob otsakh i detiakh i o g. Chekhove" [About fathers and sons and about Mr. Chekhov]. In Literaturno-kriticheskie stat'i [Literary criticism]. Moscow: Khudozhestvennaia literatura, pp. 594-607.

Reprinted from 1890.1.

10 POGGIOLI, RENATO. "Storytelling in a Double Key." In The Phoenix and the Spider: A Book of Essays about some Russian Writers and their View of the Self. Cambridge, Mass.: Harvard University Press,

pp. 109-30.

Examines six stories from Chekhov's "transitional period" (1886-87) which use a "contrapuntal" technique: comic and pathetic strains are attuned to each other to create the effect of dissonance. Chekhov is a writer who attempts "to interpret the comedy of life in pathetic rather than in comic terms." A second part of the essay studies Chekhov's use of the Psyche myth in two stories. Reprinted: 1979.14.

11 POSPELOV, G.N. "Ob ideinykh i khudozhestvennykh osobennostiakh tvorchestva A.P. Chekhova" [On the ideological and artistic features of Chekhov's work]. VLit, no. 6, pp. 154-83.

Argues that Chekhov's works convey a basically democratic outlook and reflect accurately the vagaries of Russian social thought of his era. At the same time he evolved new principles of prose narration and dramatic structure.

12 RODIONOVNA, V.M. "A.P. Chekhov i iumoristicheskaia zhurnalistika vos'midesiatykh godov" [Chekhov and the humor journalism of the 1880s]. Moskovskii gos. pedagogicheskii institut im. V.I. Lenina. Kafedra russkoi literatury. Uchenye zapiski, vol. 115, no. 7, pp. 339-63.

Examines Chekhov's work from 1880 to 1884, arguing that it was considerably different from the writing of other contributors to the humor magazines. Many of his earliest stories are marked by his protests against violations of human dignity. He was not only a humorist but a satirist whose targets were the slavish mentality of his characters and their worship of money and rank.

1958

1 AIKEN, CONRAD. "Chekhov, Anton." In A Reviewer's ABC: Collected Criticism of Conrad Aiken from 1916 to the Present. Introduction by Rufus A. Blanshard. New York: Meridian Books, pp. 148-53.

Characterizes Chekhov as "possibly the greatest writer of the short story who has ever lived" and argues that the appeal of his stories lies in their sense of actuality and seeming artlessness. His manner disarms us so that we are willing to believe him; then he shows us life as it really is. He is a "poet of the actual."

2 BORDINAT, PHILIP. "Dramatic Structure in Čexov's

Uncle Vanja." <u>SEEJ</u> 16:195-210.

Argues that the play does have a solid dramatic structure which is evident once one accepts the notion that there is no one single protagonist; the role shifts from character to character so that the protagonist is the individual in the abstract. The play's central motivating force is this "individual's" desire for happiness. Reprinted: 1981.1.

3 CELLI, ROSE. <u>L'art de Tchékhov</u>. Le demi-siècle des idées. Edited by Pierre de Lescure. Paris: del Duca, 172 pp.

A general survey of the world of Chekhov's literary works. The greatest flaws in this world are corruption and fear; his ideal is one of talent, freedom, and physical and spiritual health. His economical style, his objectivity, and his narrative techniques revolutionized the short story form. Nature is always a presence in his works, and its beauty and sense of time provide a contrast with and an inspiration for the human world. Chekhov sees, and makes us see, the world as it really is.

4 CLURMAN, HAROLD. "Anton Chekhov." In <u>Lies Like Truth: Theatre Reviews and Essays</u>. New York: Macmillan, pp. 131-35.

Argues that Chekhov was both a social and a universal playwright. <u>The Seagull</u>, as staged in New York in 1954, proves this. His goodness and generosity transform the undramatic stuff of his plays into pure poetry.

5 DEER, IRVING. "Speech as Action in Chekhov's <u>The Cherry Orchard</u>." <u>Educational Theatre Journal</u> 10:30-34.

Discusses the "apparent formlessness" of Chekhov's dialogue and the problem of communication in his plays generally. The characters' rambling remarks are functional, however, because they convey their inner conflicts and doubts.

6 ELIZAROVA, M.E. <u>Tvorchestvo A.P. Chekhova i voprosy realizma kontsa XIX veka</u> [Chekhov's work and questions of realism of the end of the nineteenth century]. Moscow: Khudozhestvennaia literatura, 200 pp.

Examines various aspects of Chekhov's outlook and aesthetics, attempting to show what these have in common with developments in Russian and European literature of Chekhov's day. Chekhov's works find drama in ordinary life and ordinary subjects and are hostile to the new tendencies of the decadent movement; he affirms the intellectual's responsibility to promote social good. His works contain a series of positive, active, and selfless characters.

7 FAGIN, N. BRYLLION. "In Search of an American *Cherry Orchard*." *TQ* 1, no. 3: pp. 132-41.

Examines some American attempts to create a Chekhovian play like *The Cherry Orchard*: Thomas Wolfe's *Mannerhouse*, Joshua Logan's *The Wisteria Trees*, and Paul Green's *The House of Connelly*. The drama of Tennessee Williams, Lillian Hellman, and Clifford Odets also shows traces of Chekhov's influence. He is inimitable, however, and his plays come from a social reality quite unlike that of the American South.

8 GEROULD, DAVID CHARLES. "*The Cherry Orchard* as Comedy." *JGE* 11:109-22.

Argues that the play is an appropriate one to include in a general humanities course, not because of its treatment of social problems but as a means of deducing some general principles of comedy. Its action is "one of the most perfect comic plots ever created" and its characters are comedically conceived.

9 GOLUBKOV, V.V. *Masterstvo A.P. Chekhova* [Chekhov's craftsmanship]. Moscow: Uchpedgiz, 199 pp.

Examines Chekhov's technique as represented in a selection of short stories. The stories are divided into three categories: humorous, satirical, and lyrical-dramatic. Specific qualities of each, as well as the qualities of Chekhov's prose generally, are discussed. A common device in the lyrical-dramatic stories is the use of a double level: there is a conflict between the public, external lives of his characters and their inner, essential lives. Translated in part: 1976.15.

10 IUZOVSKII, Iu.I. "Traditsii russkoi dramy: opyt kharakteristiki. Ostrovskii. Chekhov" [The traditions of Russian drama: an attempt at characterizing them. Ostrovsky. Chekhov] *Teatr*, no. 2, pp. 133-36.

Surveys Chekhov's dramatic work against a background of Russian drama of his day. Conflict in his plays comes from the struggle between the world within the play and the world outside it. The world outside thus plays the role of antagonist. Although his characters are generally overpowered, Chekhov's plays still convey the notion of personal responsibility to continue the struggle.

11 KERNAN, ALVIN B. "Truth and Dramatic Mode in the Modern Theater: Chekhov, Pirandello, and Williams." MD 1:101-14.

Discusses the modern dramatists' search for an adequate dramatic mode and argues that The Seagull, Pirandello's Six Characters in Search of An Author, and Williams' Streetcar Named Desire deal explicitly with that very problem. Each character in The Seagull has his own "theory of drama," his own idea of what a play should be in order to reflect life truly, and each acts as if life itself were his own kind of play.

12 LAKSHIN, V.Ia. Iskusstvo psikhologicheskoi dramy Chekhova i Tolstogo: "Diadia Vania" i "Zhivoi trup" [The art of the psychological drama of Chekhov and Tolstoy: Uncle Vanya and A Living Corpse]. Moscow: Izdatel'stvo MGU, 87 pp.

Compares the two plays generally and argues that the similarity in basic dramatic concept is the result of the era in which both writers lived rather than one of conscious influence. Chekhov's and Tolstoy's plays are "psychological dramas" typical of the turn of the century. The nature of the conflict in each play is compared, as is their language and their use of pauses and monologues.

13 LATHAM, JACQUELINE E.M. "The Cherry Orchard as Comedy." Educational Theatre Journal 10:21-29.

Argues that Chekhov criticizes his comically-conceived characters in the play and creates a complex comedy with "occasional overtones of pathos and tragedy." The original production of the was one-sided and ignored its comic elements, thus setting a bad precedent. James R. Brandon disputes this view in 1960.11.

14 MAUGHAM, W. SOMERSET. Points of View. London: Heinemann, pp. 159-76.

Makes a brief survey of Chekhov's life, work and comments on the short story. Unlike Maupassant, Chekhov deliberately eschews the dramatic to focus on the everyday, which he conveys impassively and with extraordinary reality; his very objectivity, however, gives his stories their powerful effect.

15 NILSSON, NILS ÅKE. "Čechov und Ibsen." In Ibsen in Russland. Acta Universitatis Stockholmiensis. Études de Philologie Slave, no. 7. Stockholm: Almqvist & Wiksell, pp. 221-33.

Examines Chekhov's pronouncements on Ibsen and investigates some parallels between The Wild Duck and The Seagull; argues that although Chekhov did profit from his acquaintance with Ibsen's dramatic technique, he developed his own technique much further. There was no thematic or ideological influence on Chekhov, and direct technical influence can scarcely be measured.

16 PLOTKIN, L.A. Literaturnye ocherki i stat'i. [Literary sketches and articles]. Leningrad: Sovetskii pisatel', pp. 366-412.

Contains 1954.28 as well as an article on Chekhov and Turgenev that reviews previous scholarship on the two writers' relationship and examines some specific parallels between The Three Sisters and Turgenev's story "The Duellist."

17 REEVE, F.D. "Tension in Prose: Čexov's 'Three Years'." SEEJ 16-99-108.

Examines Chekhov's revisions to the work, arguing that he attempted to make the "area of intensions ... as specific and as vast as possible."

18 ROY, CLAUDE. "Tchekhov." In Descriptions critiques, IV: La main heureuse. Paris: Gallimard, pp. 226-33.

Argues that Chekhov perfected the short story form; his technique puts great demands on the reader since so much is left unsaid. His innovations in prose and in the theater have made possible the modern forms we now accept.

19 SILVERSTEIN, NORMAN. "Chekhov's Comic Spirit and The Cherry Orchard." MD 1:91-100.

Argues that Chekhov's treatment of the commonplace was comic, evoking "thoughtful laughter." His Cherry Orchard is a comedy. Its characters are basically comic, and the play itself is a development of farce that still manages to achieve pathos. At its end the characters abandon their unproductive society and go to an new beginning.

20 SKAFTYMOV, A.P. "K voprosu o printsipakh postroeniia p'es A.P. Chekhova" [On the question of the structural principles of Chekhov's plays]. In Stat'i o russkoi literature [Articles on Russian literature]. Saratov: Saratovskoe knizhnoe izdatel'stvo, pp. 313-38.

Unlike his predecessors Chekhov places "the peaceful flow of life as it is lived" at the center of his plays; the events of the plot do not alter this humdrum of life. Conflicts in the plays are not between strong characters but result from contradictions in life itself. The plays develop as the characters hope for happiness and renewal only to find their dreams shattered. Still, the plays express confidence that life will become "beautiful." Reprinted: 1972.25. Translated in part: 1967.9.

21 -----. "O edinstve formy i soderzhaniia v Vishnevom sade A.P. Chekhova" [On the unity of form and content in Chekhov's Cherry Orchard]. In Stat'i o russkoi literarture [Articles on Russian literature]. Saratov: Saratovskoe knizhnoe izdatel'stvo, pp. 356-90.

A detailed study of the play that examines some of its basic features. Its dramatic conflict is grounded in the everyday life of its characters; the essence of that conflict is the contradiction between the secret, individual hopes of each character and the force of external circumstance. Each character's most cherished dreams are inaccessible to each other character, resulting in their essential loneliness. Characters are portrayed both as ridiculous and as pathetic; the contrast between their inner and outer selves helps create Chekhov's "undercurrent." Reprinted: 1972.25.

22 -----. "O povestiakh Chekhova 'Palata No. 6' i 'Moia zhizn''" [On Chekhov's tales "Ward Six" and "My Life"]. In Stat'i o russkoi literature [Articles on Russian literature]. Saratov: Saratovskoe knizhnoe izdatel'stvo, pp. 295-312.

Discusses the ideas in the two stories and argues that Chekhov was not debating with Tolstoy in either one. Ragin's quietism does not come from Tolstoy but from Schopenhauer; in any case; Chekhov takes issue less with Ragin than with the society that produced him. Similarly, the ethical basis of "My Life" is largely Tolstoyan; the enemies are moral blindness and social tyranny. Reprinted: 1972.25.

23 -----. "P'esa Chekhova Ivanov v rannikh redaktsiiakh" [The early editions of Chekhov's "Ivanov"]. In Stat'i o russkoi literature [Articles on Russian literature]. Saratov: Saratovskoe knizhnoe izdatel'stvo, pp. 339-355.

Examines Chekhov's early versions of the play and the changes he made in it, arguing that it presages his later dramatic work. Chekhov proposes the notion of "involuntary guilt:" Ivanov has caused someone else's misfortune without intending to. The play's innovative features include a new concept of dramatic conflict in which everday life is an important factor; Chekhov continues to portray his characters' inner lives by the traditional technique of the monologue, however.

Reprinted: 1972.25.

24 STROUD, T.A. "Hamlet and The Seagull." SQ 9:367-72.
Examines the extent to which the characters, the plot, and the overall mood of The Seagull were drawn from Hamlet. The relationship between the two plays is intricate but close; even Chekhov's insistence that The Seagull is a comedy may mean that he intended it as an inversion of a tragedy (Hamlet).

1959

1 ADAMOVICH, GEORGII. "O chem govoril Chekhov" [What Chekhov was talking about]. NovŽ 58:135-42.
A general appreciation of Chekhov's art that sees him as "an afterword to Pushkin." His works do treat the great issues of nineteenth-century literature, but do so calmly and without histrionics.

2 BALUKHATYI, S.D. "Rannii Chekhov" [The early Chekhov]. In Literaturnyi muzei A.P. Chekhova, A.P. Chekhov: sbornik statei i materialov [A.P. Chekhov: a collection of articles and materials]. Rostov-on-the-Don: Rostovskoe knizhnoe izdatel'stvo, pp. 7-94.
Characterizes generally Chekhov's early writings, noting that he developed his own original techniques for creating comic stories. He had a keen sense of literary form and altered existing genres, usually by greatly simplifying them. He also selected material from the simplest and most ordinary events of everyday life. His descriptive passages become "subjective," i.e., they are associated with the psychological states of specific characters. Seemingly trivial details assume great importance.

3 BERDNIKOV, G.P. "Zametki o rannem tvorchestve A.P. Chekhova" [Remarks on Chekhov's early work]. RLit 4:87-107.
Surveys Chekhov's early writings; argues that his parodies reveal an awareness of the shortcomings of the literrary milieu in which he began his career. His early satire shows the strong influence of Saltykov-Shchedrin, but is a satire of manners rather than a political satire.

4 CHUDAKOV, A.P. "Stil' i iazyk rasskaza Chekhova 'Ionych'" [The style and language of Chekhov's "Ionych"]. RJŠ, no. 1, pp. 64-69.

Discusses Chekhov's "objective" narration in the story, noting that he filters his narrative through the mind of his central character. Ionych evolves and the language of the narrative evolves with him. The story serves as a good illustration of Chekhov's style and narrative technique.

5 DERMAN, A.B. O masterstve Chekhova [On Chekhov's craftsmanship]. Moscow: Sovetskii pisatel', 207 pp.

Examines the innovative nature of Chekhov's work from the earliest stories, which parody literary clichés, to later efforts to create new forms of prose and drama that demand much more active participation by the reader. Chekhov's new approach to plot meant that any fragment of ordinary life could provide material for a work of art; his endings are designed to stimulate the reader to examine these mundane fragments more closely. Such innovations were acknowledged more quickly in Chekhov's drama than in his prose. Derman makes detailed analyses of "The Grasshopper" and "The Man in the Case" to show the workings of Chekhov's poetics. Translated in part: 1979.14 and 1976.15.

6 DICK, GERHARD. "Die deutsche Čechov-Interpretation der Gegenwart." ZS 4:686-704.

Compares the East and West German interpretations of Chekhov since 1945 and surveys the debate in West Germany over Chekhov's optimism versus his pessimism. Includes a bibliography of German translations of Chekhov for the period 1945 to 1958.

7 ERENBURG, I.G. "Perechityvaia Chekhova" [Rereading Chekhov]. NovM, no. 5, pp. 193-208; no. 6, pp. 174-96.

Argues that Chekhov's continuing appeal derives from his view of life and his closeness to the spiritual world of his readers. Taken together his writings make up one great novel or poem that catches the wonder and the poetry of everyday life. Several reprints. Translated: 1963.3.

8 ERMILOV, V.V. [Yermilov]. A.P. Chekhov: 1860-1904. Translated by Ivy Litvinov. Moscow: Foreign Languages Publishing House, 415 pp.

Translation, with some modifications, of 1951.1.

9 -----. "Nekotorye osobennosti poetiki Chekhova: o khudozhestvennykh printsipakh izobrazheniia deistvitel'nosti" [Some features of Chekhov's

poetics: on his artistic principles of depicting reality]. VLit, no. 10, pp. 152-68.

Examines "Vanka," "Sleepy," and The Three Sisters, arguing that they illustrate Chekhov's technique of transferring his perspective from the subjective world of a character to the larger reality of life itself. The inability of many characters to realize their hopes in their present is meant to lead the reader to look to the future. Translated: 1961.9.

10 -----. "O svoeobrazii komicheskogo u Chekhova" [On the distinctive features of Chekhov's comedy]. VLit, no. 11, pp. 100-16.

Surveys the forms and functions of Chekhov's humor, arguing that it touches all aspects and all periods of his work. Closely linked with tragedy, his comedy is sometimes concealed; it is comedy of situation, based on the incongruities within the texture of life itself. Translated: 1961.9.

11 -----. "Tema krasoty u Chekhova" [Chekhov's theme of beauty]. VLit, no. 12, pp. 129-42.

Argues that Chekhov's works identify the beauty of nature with the potential beauty of human life. Nature's beauty exists as a criterion in evaluating social reality and as a reminder of what life could and should be like. Examines this theme in a series of stories and plays. Translated: 1961.9.

12 GOR'KII, MAKSIM [Gorki]. "Reminiscences of Anton Chekhov." In Reminiscences of Tolstoy, Chekhov and Andreyev. New York: Viking Press, pp. 67-126.

Translation of 1905.4 and 1923.7. Also includes twenty letters from the Chekhov-Gorky correspondence.

13 IUZOVSKII, Iu.I. "Gor'kii i Chekhov" [Gorky and Chekhov]. In Maksim Gor'kii i ego dramaturgiia [Maxim Gorky and his drama]. Moscow: Iskusstvo, pp. 275-316.

Argues that Chekhov's plays expose the weaknesses of liberalism and populism and express faith in the historical process, attitudes which Gorky shared. Both dramatists' work expresses a deep respect for human beings.

14 IVASK, GEORGE. "Annenskij und Čechov." ZS 27:363-74.

Compares Annenskii's "Parting" with Chekhov's "Lady With the Little Dog", arguing that the two share a similar theme. The stress on the mundane, everyday details of life and the tendency to understatement as well as the treatment of the deeply tragic in very ordinary terms are features of both Chekhov's and Annenskii's poetics. Both use an impressionistic technique.

15 KELSON, JOHN. "Allegory and Myth in The Cherry Orchard." WHR 13:321-24.
Argues that there is a very definite patterning beneath the play's surface. It operates on the literal, allegorical, and mythical levels. On the allegorical level each character represents an element of Russian society. On the mythical level the play is a mimesis of the seasonal cycle; Ranevskaya represents the continuing, life-giving power of Nature.

16 KHALIZEV, V.E. "Russkaia dramaturgiia nakanune Ivanova i Chaika" [Russian drama on the eve of Ivanov and The Seagull]. FN, no. 1, pp. 20-30.
Argues that in spite of their many differences from Russian drama of their day, Chekhov's early plays have links with the work of some of his contemporaries. Examines plays by several minor Russian dramatists of the 1880s that also attempted to free themselves from conventions of the day.

17 KNIAZEVA, K.I.; KULESHOV, F.I.; and TEPLINSKII, M.V., eds. Anton Pavlovich Chekhov: sbornik statei [Chekhov: a collection of articles]. Iuzhno-Sakhalinsk: Sakhalinskoe knizhnoe izdatel'stvo, 231 pp.
Contains thirteen articles: five deal with various aspects of his work, including his views on literature and on peasant life, his reception by pre-revolutionary Marxist critics, and general evaluations; three deal with his reception abroad; and five with his journey to Sakhalin and his study The Island of Sakhalin.

18 KUČEROVSKIJ, N.M. "Bemerkungen zur künstlerischen Meisterschaft A.P. Čechovs: analyse einer Erzählung." ZS 4:518-33.
Makes a detailed stylistic and structural analysis of "Sleepy," showing its links with Chekhov's other writings.

19 LAFFITTE, SOPHIE. "Le style de Tchékhov." In Stil- und Formprobleme in der Literatur: Vorträge des VII. Kongresses der Internationalen Vereinigung für moderne Sprachen und Literaturen in Heidelberg. Edited by Paul Böckmann. Heidelberg: Carl Winter, pp. 406-13.
Describes Chekhov's style as a combination of

simplicity with unexpected and bold expressions. The development of his style can be seen in part as a reaction to the dominant Turgenev manner of the 1880s. His lyrical style succeeds in moving the reader.

20 MYSHKOVSKAIA, L.M. "Osobennosti tvorcheskoi individual'nosti Chekhova" [Distinctive features of Chekhov's creative individuality]. Okt, no. 12, pp. 212-19.

Examines Chekhov's work in the context of nineteenth-century Russian literature and attempts to isolate specific qualities of his artistic make-up. He tends to focus not on the events of the plot but on the effects those events have on his characters. Dialogue is a major means of conveying character, thus requiring little authorial comment. This is a particularly prominent feature of his early humor stories. Expanded in 1967.20.

21 NAGIBIN, Iu. "O Chekhove" [On Chekhov]. Znamia, no. 12, pp. 191-95.

Takes issues with the myth of Chekhov as a kindly, sickly ascetic. His story "Horsethieves" is seldom discussed because it does not conform to this image; here Chekhov obviously sympathizes with the rebellious spirit of the protagonist.

22 NIKULIN, L.V. "Khudozhnik zhizni" [An artist of life]. Okt, no. 6, pp. 211-225.

Discusses Chekhov's reception in Russia and abroad, his personality, and some attitudes of contemporaries toward him. Expanded: 1960.46.

23 OKHOTINA, G.A. "Literaturnye parodii A.P. Chekhova" [Chekhov's literary parodies]. Don, no. 11, pp. 150-54.

Argues that even early in his career Chekhov had an acute sensitivity to falsity in literature; surveys Chekhov's parodies of the 1880s.

24 PRUTSKOV, N.I. "K voprosu ob evoliutsii realizma A.P. Chekhova" [On the question of the evolution of Chekhov's realism]. In Iz istorii russkikh literaturnykh otnoshenii XVIII-XX vekov [From the history of Russian literary relations, 18th-20th centuries]. Edited by S.V. Kastorskii. Moscow and Leningrad: AN SSSR, pp. 266-78.

Traces the evolution of Chekhov's approach to his art in the 1880s and 1890s as exemplified in three related works: "Autumn" (1883), "On the High Road" (1885), and "Thieves" (1890). The emphasis shifts from plot to character and mood, and the implications of each work grow ever wider, suggesting the "unreasonableness of life."

25 ROSKIN, A.I. A.P. Chekhov: stat'i i ocherki [Chekhov: articles and sketches]. Moscow: Khudozhestvennaia literatura, 432 pp.

Contains reprints of Roskin's biographical sketch of Chekhov, nine articles, and his study of The Three Sisters. Includes 1938.6, 1938.7, 1938.8 and 1940.11.

26 ----- Stat'i o literature i teatre. Antosha Chekhonte [Articles on literature and the theater. Antosha Chekhonte]. Moscow: Sovetskii pisatel', 438 pp.

Contains 1940.12, 1946.8, and Roskin's unfinished biography, Antosha Chekhonte (1940.10).

27 SAKHAROVA, E.M. Anton Pavlovich Chekhov: 1860-1904. Bibliograficheskie i metodichiskie materialy v pomoshch' bibliotekariu [Chekhov: 1860-1904. Bibliographical and methodological materials to aid the librarian]. Moscow: Biblioteka im. Lenina, 104 pp.

Contains a biographical note, a survey of Chekhov's principal writings, a list of basic editions, a brief annotated survey of criticism, and suggestions for librarians wishing to publicize Chekhov's work.

28 SHKLOVSKII, VIKTOR. Khudozhestvennaia proza: razmyshleniia i razbory [Literary proze: reflections and analyses]. Moscow: Sovetskii pisatel', pp. 482-509. Several reprints.

Surveys the development of the short story form in Chekhov's work. His plots are constructed along lines radically different from those of traditional poetics: he abandons intrigue, avoids extended psychological motivation, and often bases a story on simple encounters or "collisons." His endings are not final; thus his characters are portrayed dynamically with room for further development. He shows the gap between what his characters are and what they ought to be. Expanded: 1966.18.

29 WINNER, THOMAS. "Čexov's 'Ward No. 6' and Tolstoyan Ethics." SEEJ 17:321-34.

Discusses the waxing and waning of the influence of Tolstoy's moral teachings, specifically non-violent resistance to evil, on Chekhov's prose. His most direct attack on non-resistance occurs in "Ward Six" where Ragin's views are so thoroughly discredited that he becomes, in fact, a parody of Tolstoyan ethics.

1960

1 AKADEMIIA NAUK SSSR. Literaturnoe nasledstvo [Literary legacy] Vol. 68, Chekhov. Moscow: Akademiia nauk, 974 pp.

Includes newly-discovered manuscripts and letters of Chekhov, letters to Chekhov, reminiscences, surveys of his reception abroad, general appreciations of his art and his significance, previously unpublished early works, excerpts from letters outlining Tolstoy's opinions of Chekhov, and a bibliography of reminiscences. Indexed and illustrated. Includes 1960.4, 1960.21, 1960.25, 1960.33, 1960.34, 1960.36, 1960.51, 1960.52, 1960.54, 1960.60, 1960.73, 1960.74, 1960.75 and 1960.77.

2 AUZINGER, HELENE. Anton Tschechow: Russlands heiter-melancholischer Dichter. Schriftenreihe Osteuropa, no. 4. Stuttgart: Deutsche Verlags-Anstalt, 107 pp.

A brief biography derived largely from evidence of Chekhov's letters. A concluding section compares Chekhov's reception in Germany with that in the English-speaking world.

3 ----- "Čechov und das Nicht-zu-Ende-sprechen." WSl 5:233-44.

Discusses Chekhov's technique of indirectness, which forces the reader to complete what the author only hinted at; argues that this is linked with Poe's ideas on the short story and with impressionism and symbolism.

4 BABORENKO, A.K., and GITOVICH, N.I. "Chekhov i Bunin" [Chekhov and Bunin]. In Literaturnoe nasledstvo [Literary legacy] Vol. 68, Chekhov. By Akademiia nauk SSSR. Moscow: Akademiia nauk, pp. 395-416.

Describes the acquaintance of the two writers and Bunin's later efforts to perpetuate the memory of Chekhov. Discusses early critical articles on the topic of Bunin and Chekhov; also includes seventeen of Bunin's letters to Chekhov.

5 BEL'CHIKOV, Iu.A. and KARPOV, E.L. "Nabliudeniia nad stilem avtorskogo povestvovaniia v rasskazakh A.P. Chekhova" [Observations on the style of authorial narration in Chekhov's stories]. RJŠ, no. 1, pp. 39-43.

Distinguishes between author's narration, narrator's speech, and character's speech; outlines the different relationship between these three elements in Chekhov's early and later works.

6 BERDNIKOV, G.A. "A.P. Chekhov v kontse 80-kh godov: Chekhov i Garshin" [Chekhov at the end of the eighties: Chekhov and Garshin]. RLit, no. 1, pp. 3-25.

Examines Chekhov's work of 1888 and 1889, arguing that these were crucial years in his literary career. He took a new aproach to literature which involved, among other things, dealing directly with topical issues (such as pessimism in "Lights"). His sympathy for Garshin is expressed in "A Fit of Nerves;" unlike Garshin, however, Chekhov keeps himself separate from his hero.

7 -----. "Problemy russkoi zhizni v povesti A.P. Chekhova 'Step''" [Problems of Russian life in Chekhov's tale "The Steppe"]. Zvezda, no. 1, pp. 164-70.

Examines "The Steppe" as both a new departure in Chekhov's literary career and as a continuation of his stories of peasants and children. His subject is an individual who seeks to live fully and that individual's encounter with the harsh realities of Russian life; Chekhov's conclusion is that freedom and happiness are inseparable.

8 -----. "Krest'ianskaia tema v tvorchestve Chekhova vos'midesiatykh godov" [The peasant theme in Chekhov's work of the 1880s]. In O russkom realizme XIX veka i voprosakh narodnosti literatury: sbornik statei [On Russian realism of the 19th century and questions of its national character: an anthology]. Edited by P.P. Gromov, I.S. Eventov, and B.M. Eikhenbaum. Moscow-Leningrad: Khudozhestvannaia literatura, pp. 357-401.

Notes that Chekhov was free from both the populist and the Tolstoyan idealization of peasant life; however the thirty or more of his stories of the 1880s that touch on rural life show the influence both of Turgenev and the "plebeian" writers of the 1860s and 70s. Unlike the plebeians, however, Chekhov approaches peasant life not in terms of class or economics but seeks broader, more universally human factors to explain peasant psychology.

9 BERKOVSKII, N.Ia. "Chekhov, povestvovatel' i dramaturg" [Chekhov: storyteller and dramatist].

Teatr, no. 1, pp. 87-99.

Characterizes Chekhov's work as a whole, noting the accuracy and scope of his depiction of the Russia of his day and commenting on specific features of his art: he shows the interaction of his characters with their environment and with one another; he uses minor details to convey meaning; many of his stories show the "plotlessness" of life. Like his stories, his plays show people crushed by life's daily routine. The Three Sisters reveals the secret of all of Chekhov's works: that it is not his characters who are ill but "the interests represented through those characters." Several reprints, including 1962.1.

10 BOGOSLOVSKII, N.V. "Rannii Chekhov" [The early Chekhov]. Okt, no. 1, pp. 160-75.

Surveys Chekhov's first seven years as a writer, emphasizing his links with other writers and publishers. During these years he perfected his realistic manner and mastered the small form.

11 BRANDON, JAMES R. "Toward a Middle-View of Chekhov." Educational Theatre Journal 11:270-75.

Takes issue with Jacqueline Latham's view of The Cherry Orchard as a comedy (see 1958.13) and attempts to find a middle ground between the interpretations of Chekhov as a melancholy writer or as an absurdist. The 1959 MAT production of The Cherry Orchard offers such a middle view. Chekhov's plays are both comic and tragic and his characters "essentially normal, if exceedingly complex."

12 CANNAC, EVGENIJ. "Rannie povesti Chekhova" [Chekhov's early tales]. In Anton Čechov: 1860-1960. Some Essays. Edited by Thomas Eekman. Leiden: E.J. Brill, pp. 1-7.

Examines four of Chekhov's early long works and points out a number of themes, images, and ideas that reappear in later writings. The prevailing mood in these, however, is thoroughly pessimistic.

13 CHEKHOVA, M.P. Iz dalekogo proshlogo [From the distant past]. Transcribed by N.A. Sysoev. Moscow: Khudozhestvennaia literatura, 272 pp.

The autobiography of Chekhov's sister, this contains information on his family and personal life, his close friends, and his views on a variety of topics. Details of his acquaintance with Lika Mizinova and with Lidia Avilova are also included, as is information on a number of prototypes of his literary characters. Illustrated.

14 CHIZHEVSKII, DMITRIY [Tschizewskij]. "Über die Stellung Čechovs innerhalb der russischen Literaturentwicklung." In Anton Čechov: 1860-1960. Some Essays. Edited by Thomas Eekman. Leiden: E.J. Brill, pp. 293-310.

Chekhov's style eschews detailed motivation in favor of blind chance, avoids objective narration in favor of viewing events through the mind of a characters, and stresses the process of change in his characters' moods and sensations. He thus transforms "reality" and places the portrayal of human spiritual life at the center of his art. Chekhov is not a realist but an impressionist, and his writings prepared the way for symbolism. Translated in part: 1967.9.

15 CHUDAKOV, A.P. "Iazyk i stil' rasskaza A.P. Chekhova 'Tolstyi i tonkii'" [The language and style of Chekhov's story "The Fat Man and the Thin Man"]. RJŠ, no. 1, pp. 18-21.

Examines the story as a typical example of Chekhov's work in the humor magazines. After a brief exposition the characters develop through dialogue with only minimal interruption from the narrator.

16 COLE, TOBY. "Anton Chekhov: Advice to Playwrights." In Playwrights on Playwriting: The Meaning and Making of Modern Drama from Ibsen to Ionesco. Introduction by John Gassner. New York: Hill & Wang, pp. 23-29.

Contains excerpts from twelve of Chekhov's letters in which he outlines his views on the drama and gives advice to fellow dramatists.

17 DICK, GERHARD. "Anton Čechov und Gerhart Hauptmann." In Anton Čechov: 1860-1960. Some Essays. Edited by Thomas Eekman. Leiden: E.J. Brill, pp. 8-12.

Reviews the historical evidence for the two dramatists' reactions to one another's work and argues that Hauptmann's Einsame Menschen had some influence on Chekhov's later plays. Chekhov also influenced Hauptmann's later work.

18 EEKMAN, THOMAS, ed. Anton Čechov: 1860-1960. Some Essays. Edited by Thomas Eekman. Leiden: E.J. Brill, 335 pp.

Contains twenty original esays in English, French, German, and Russian on a variety of aspects of Chekhov's work. Includes 1960.12, 1960.14, 1960.17, 1960.19, 1960.20, 1960.21, 1960.28, 1960.29, 1960.30,

1960.31, 1960.35, 1960.41, 1960.47, 1960.48, 1960.64, 1960.66, 1960.68, 1960.70, 1960.76, and 1960.78.

19 -----. "Čechov and the Europe of his Day." In Anton Čechov: 1860-1960. Some Essays. Edited by Thomas Eekman. Leiden: E.J. Brill, pp. 13-38.

Examines Chekhov's attitude to Western Europe as expressed in his fiction and letters and concludes that he had a deep admiration for European life and culture. Chekhov was a Westernizer, but also remained a real Russian.

20 ESIN, B.I. Chekhov-zhurnalist: lektsiia [Chekhov the journalist: a lecture]. Moscow: Izdatel'stvo Moskovskogo universiteta, 18 pp.

Surveys briefly Chekhov's journalism, including his work in the humor magazines, his later articles in Novoe vremia, and his studies of Siberia and Sakhalin. Esin treats the topic in more detail in 1977.16.

21 FEDIN, KONSTANTIN. "Slovo o Chekhove" [Speech on Chekhov]. In Literaturnoe nasledstvo [Literary legacy] Vol. 68, Chekhov. By Akademiia nauk SSSR. Moscow: Akademiia nauk, pp. v-vii.

In this opening speech at an official ceremony marking Chekhov's one-hundred-year jubilee, Fedin stresses Chekhov's world-wide importance and influence and argues that his works are not gloomy or defeatist but life-affirming calls to a better life through work.

22 FILOLOGICHESKIE NAUKI, no. 4, pp. 58-95.

Contains a special section on Chekhov consisting of five articles. G.N. Pospelov deals with plot construction in Chekhov's longer stories, noting that their episodes are commonly linked by the mood and thoughts of the hero. M.P. Gromov considers the genre of The Cherry Orchard, arguing that it is a comedy with lyrical touches; S.A. Koporskii discusses the style of "The Steppe." Two other articles deal with Chekhov's reception in Germany and in Turkey.

23 GERHARDI, WILLIAM. "The Unpassing Moment." Listener 63 (January 21):121-22.

Characterizes Chekhov generally and comments on his image among critics and readers. His works transform common life into "the unpassing moment," removing it from the consecutive order of time. "The undercurrent of the space-time continuum--duration, not sequence--in Chekhov's work is, when all is said, his most distinguishing achievement."

24 GITOVICH, N.I. "Chekhov v neizdannoi perepiske sovremennikov" [Chekhov in the unpublished correspondence of his contemporaries]. VLit, no. 1, pp. 97-111.

Contains excerpts from twenty-seven letters of Chekhov's contemporaries dating from 1884 to 1905 in which he is discussed. The material includes comments about him, his views on literature, his work in progress, and about a number of projects which remained unrealized. Annotated.

25 -----. "Belovaia rukopis' rasskaza 'Poprygun'ia'" [The fair copy of the story "The Grasshopper"]. In Literaturnoe nasledstvo [Literary legacy] Vol. 68, Chekhov. By Akademiia nauk SSSR. Moscow: Akademiia Nauk, pp. 130-32.

Describes the genesis of the story and lists the corrections made by Chekhov.

26 GITOVICH, N.I. and FEDOROV, I.V. A.P. Chekhov v vospominaniiakh sovremennikov. Seriia literaturnykh memuarov [Chekhov in reminiscences of his contemporaries. Literary memoirs series]. Edited by S.N. Golubov, V.V. Grigorenko, N.K. Gudzii, S.A. Makashin, and Iu.G. Oksman. Moscow: Khudozhestvennaia literatura, 834 pp.

A revised version of 1954.23, it contains thirty-four reminiscences of Chekhov by family members, friends, acquaintances and fellow writers. Included are seven new items and expanded version of six items published in the previous edition; five items frequently reprinted elsewhere are deleted. Includes 1904.10, 1905.4, 1923.7, and 1943.3. (Other contributors are listed individually in the Index section below).

27 GORBACHEVICH, K.S. "Rabota A.P. Chekhova nad iazykom prozy" [Chekhov's work on the language of his prose]. RJŠ, no. 1, pp. 24-28.

Through a study of manuscripts of Chekhov's early works, attempts to work out his principles of selecting one of several synonyms. Chekhov chose words to keep the narration stylistically neutral, to achieve greater precision, to conform to more accepted usage, and to achieve better rhythym.

28 GOURFINKEL, NINA. "Čechov chroniquer de la vie théâtrale." In Anton Čechov: 1860-1960. Some Essays. Edited by Thomas Eekman. Leiden: E.J. Brill, pp. 39-58.

Examines Chekhov's youthful theatrical reviews, letters, and early stories set in the theatrical world.

His remarks on the theatre here are generally very critical and prove that from the beginning of his career Chekhov set very high standards for the theatre.

29 HARDER, HANS-BERND. "Zur Entwicklung der Poetik Čechovs: 1886 bis 1890." In Anton Čechov: 1860-1960. Some Essays. Edited by Thomas Eekman. Leiden: E.J. Brill, pp. 59-82.

Examines remarks on literature made in Chekhov's letters of his middle period, a time when, Harder argues, he was seeking new directions in his work. His attempts at larger forms revealed to him how crucial were his qualities of brevity and objectivity, two features that clash with the traditional poetics of the novel. Thus in 1890 he renounced the traditional forms and gave birth to a new literature.

30 IVASK, GEORGE. "Chekhov and the Russian Clergy." In Anton Čechov: 1860-1960. Some Essays. Edited by Thomas Eekman. Leiden: E.J. Brill, pp. 83-92.

Comments on Chekhov's attitude to the church and religion generally and surveys the portraits of clergymen found in his writings.

31 JACOBSSON, GUNNAR. "Die Novelle 'Der Student': Versuch einer Analyse." In Anton Čechov: 1860-1960. Some Essays. Edited by Thomas Eekman. Leiden: E.J. Brill, pp. 93-102.

Argues that "The Student" gives an accurate expression of Chekhov's own view of life. The story's central character is brought from pessimism to optimism by his perception that the permanence of truth and beauty give human life significance.

32 KATAEV, VALENTIN. "Dobroe, bol'shoe serdtse" [A good, great heart]. Literaturnaia gazeta, no. 13 (30 January), pp. 1, 3.

The keynote speech at a session commemorating Chekhov's one-hundred-year jubilee held on January 29, it describes his personality, his literary innovations and influence, and notes the universal significance of his work. Several reprints.

33 KONSHINA, E.N., ed. "Belovaia rukopis' rasskaza 'Nevesta'" [The fair copy of the story "Betrothed"]. In Literaturnoe nasledstvo [Literary Legacy] Vol. 68, Chekhov. By Akademiia nauk SSSR. Moscow: Akademiia nauk, pp. 87-108.

Contains the fair copy of the story as produced by Chekhov in February 1903. An introductory section outlines the changes Chekhov made in each of the various stages in creating the story.

34 KORETSKAIA, I.V. and GITOVICH, N.I. "Chekhov i Kuprin" [Chekhov and Kuprin]. In Literaturnoe nasledstvo [Literary legacy] Vol. 68, Chekhov. By Akademiia nauk SSSR. Moscow: Akademiia nauk, pp. 363-94.

Describes the relationship of the two writers; outlines Chekhov's influence on Kuprin and comments on the latter's reminiscences of Chekhov. Also includes seventeen of Kuprin's letters to Chekhov.

35 LAFFITTE, SOPHIE. "Čechov et Tolstoj." In Anton Čechov: 1860-1960. Some Essays. Edited by Thomas Eekman. Leiden: E.J. Brill, pp. 109-135.

Chronicles the historical relationship of the two writers and discusses their reactions to each other's works and personalities. Although Tolstoy's ideas exerted strong influence on Chekhov for a time, the two were of fundamentally different temperaments. Their differences can be seen in works such as "A Dreary Story" and "Ward Six," as well as in their pronouncements on death, love, women, and other matters.

36 -----. "Chekhov vo Frantsii" [Chekhov in France]. In Literaturnoe nasledstvo [Literary Legacy] Vol. 68, Chekhov. By Akademiia nauk SSSR. Moscow: Akademiia nauk, pp. 705-746.

Traces Chekhov's reception in France to 1958. Includes a list of French translations of his work and a brief bibliography of French criticism plus a chronology of performances of his plays in France.

37 LAKSHIN, V. Ia. "Khudozhestvennoe nasledie Chekhova segodnia" [Chekhov's artistic legacy today]. VLit, no. 1, pp. 60-79.

Discusses Chekhov's place in the history of Russian realism and the significance of his work for contemporary literature. His stories are characterized by their expressive use of detail and their objective narration that still manages to express the author's point of view.

38 LITERATURNAIA GAZETA, no. 12 (28 January).

Special issue marking the one-hundreth anniversary of Chekhov's birth, it contains tributes by Soviet writers and assessments of his influence on Soviet and world literature.

39 LITERATURNYI MUZEI A.P. CHEKHOVA. A.P. Chekhov: sbornik statei i materialov [A.P. Chekhov: a

collection of articles and materials]. No. 2. Rostov-na-Donu: Rostovskoe knizhnoe izdatel'stvo, 309 pp.

Contains eleven articles on Chekhov's works including studies of individual stories, influences on his work, style, the theatre, and biographical studies. Also contains three articles on Chekhov's reception abroad and two reminiscences of him.

40 MALIUGIN, L.A. "Dramaturgiia Chekhova i ee issledovateli" [Chekhov's drama and its students]. Okt, no. 1, pp. 176-92.

Takes issue with Ermilov's Dramaturgiia Chekhova (1948.4), arguing that it underestimates the importance of Ivanov in the development of Chekhov's drama; that it overestimates Dorn in The Seagull; minimizes the social content of Uncle Vanya; simplifies The Three Sisters; and distorts The Cherry Orchard. Reprinted: 1967.17.

41 MATLAW, RALPH E. "Čechov and the Novel." In Anton Čechov: 1860-1960. Some Essays. Edited by Thomas Eekman. Leiden: E.J. Brill, pp. 148-67.

Examines Chekhov's attempts to write a novel, beginning with his early parodies of the novel form through his "Unnecessary Victory", "Belated Flowers", and The Shooting Party, and concluding with a discussion of "The Duel," "the last of Čechov's extended works to assume the traditional form of the novel." Matlaw concludes that the novel form was uncongenial to Chekhov's "essentially miniaturist skills."

42 MAUROIS, ANDRÉ. "The Art and Philosophy of Anton Tchekov." In The Art of Writing. Translated by Gerard Hopkins. London: The Bodley Head, pp. 224-64.

Surveys Chekhov's biography; quotes from his letters and reminiscences of contemporaries to provide a sketch of his personality; discusses his drama generally. The purpose of his art was, as he said, "to help liberate humans from brute force and lies, no matter what form they take."

43 MIKHAILOVSKII, B.V. "Chekhov i ego mesto v razvitii realizma: k 100-letiiu so dnia rozhdeniia A.P. Chekhova" [Chekhov and his place in the development of realism: on the hundreth anniversary of his birth]. VAN, no. 1, pp. 41-47.

Argues that two strains of realism are present in Chekhov's work: one, a satirical, is in the tradition of the "revolutionary democrats" such as

Saltykov-Shchedrin; a second and more important one is the psychological realism of the Tolstoy tradition. Mikhailovsky surveys Chekhov's influence on foreign and Russian writers.

44 NECHAEV, V.P. and MIRKINA, Iu.M., eds. A.P. Chekhov: Rukopisi. Pis'ma. Biograficheskie dokumenty. Vospominaniia. Teatral'nye postanovki. Risunki. Fotografii. Opisanie materialov tsentral'nogo gosudarstvennogo arkhiva literatury i iskusstva SSSR [A.P. Chekhov: Manuscripts. Letters. Biographical documents. Reminiscences. Theatrical performances. Drawings. Photographs. A description of materials from the Central State Archives of Literature and Art of the USSR]. Moscow: Sovetskaia Rossiia, 272 pp.

Lists manuscripts, letters, photographs, and other materials held in the Chekhov "fund" of the State Archives (TsGALI). Unannotated. Index.

45 NEMIROVICH-DANCHENKO, Vl.I. "Iz rezhisserskogo ekzempliara Ivanova" [From the director's copy of Ivanov]. Teatr, no. 1, pp. 148-51.

Nemirovich-Danchenko's lecture to the cast of the MAT's 1904 production of Ivanov, it sketches in the play's historical background. The play's era is characterized as one of disillusionment after the perceived failure of the reforms of the 1860s. Ivanov himself has been broken in the struggle.

46 NIKULIN, LEV. "Khudozhnik zhizni" [An artist of life]. In Chekhov--Bunin--Kuprin: literaturnye portrety [Chekhov, Bunin, Kuprin: Literary portraits]. Moscow: Sovetskii pisatel', pp. 3-170.

An expanded version of 1959.22, it consists of a general appreciation of Chekhov and an assessment of his significance that comments on his evaluation by a variety of critics, largely English or emigre Russians.

47 NILSSON, NILS ÅKE. "Intonation and Rhythm in Čechov's Plays." In Anton Čechov: 1860-1960. Some Essays. Edited by Thomas Eekman. Leiden: E.J. Brill, pp. 168-80.

Argues that Chekhov and several other dramatists of his time opposed the prevailing theatrical conventions of their day. Like Tolstoy Chekhov sought to express emotions in ways that went beyond words. One such means is intonation, which is used to express varying emotional keys. The shifts in emotional key create a rhythm that producers of Chekhov's plays should express. Reprinted:

1967.9.

48 PAPERNYI, Z.S. "Pravda i vera Chekhova" [Chekhov's truth and faith]. In Anton Čechov: 1860-1960. Some Essays. Edited by Thomas Eekman. Leiden: E.J. Brill, pp. 181-86.

Argues that Chekhov's works portray the "truth" of life as it actually is, but also convey his "faith" that it should be and will be better. His use of lyrical details plays a key role in suggesting that the actual can be brought closer to the ideal.

49 -----. A.P. Chekhov: ocherk tvorchestva [Chekhov: an outline of his work]. Moscow: Khudozhestvennaia literatura, 303 pp.

A revised and considerably expanded version of 1954.25. This edition has new chapters on Chekhov's humor and his early works; on the stories of 1886-87; on "Ionych;" and on Uncle Vanya. Some material on the drama is included. More emphasis is placed on tracing the psychological process whereby Chekhov's characters are awakened to life's difficulties or become indifferent to them.

50 -----. "Probuzhdenie geroia" [The awakening of a character]. VLit, no. 1, pp. 80-96.

Argues that a central theme in Chekhov's work is human indifference and that his stories work to rouse people from their torpor. His stories show characters worn down by the coarseness of life as, for example, in "Ionych;" but a second, "hidden" plot reveals Chekhov's scorn for those who allow themselves to be defeated by circumstances.

51 POLOTSKAIA, E.A. "Bibliografiia vospominanii o Chekhove" [A bibliography of reminiscences of Chekhov]. In Literaturnoe nasledstvo [Literary legacy] Vol. 68, Chekhov. By Akademiia nauk SSSR. Moscow: Akademiia nauk, pp. 891-928.

Lists 186 published and eighteen unpublished reminiscences of Chekhov. Supplements and brings up to date Fridkes (1930.2). Detailed annotations.

52 POLOTSKAIA, E.A., and GITOVICH, N.I. "Chekhov i Meierkhol'd" [Chekhov and Meyerhold]. In Literaturnoe nasledstvo [Literary legacy] Vol. 68, Chekhov. By Akademiia nauk SSSR. Moscow: Akademiia nauk, pp. 417-48.

Describes Meyerhold's acquaintance with Chekhov and discusses Chekhov's influence on him, his roles in Chekhov's plays, and his reaction to Chekhov's drama generally. Also includes eighteen of Meyerhold's letters to Chekhov.

53 PRIESTLY, J.B. Literature and Western Man. London: Heinemann, pp. 293-97.

Surveys Chekhov's plays within the context of a general discussion of modern western drama. Argues that Chekhov belongs to the nineteenth century and is "perhaps the most startlingly original dramatist of the whole age." His drama is essentially poetic and suggests the complexity and vividness of life.

54 PUSTIL'NIK, L.S. "Chekhov i Pleshcheev" [Chekhov and Pleshcheev]. In Literaturnoe nasledstvo [Literary legacy] Vol. 68, Chekhov. By Akademiia nauk SSSR. Moscow: Akademiia nauk, pp. 293-362.

Describes the acquaintance of Chekhov with the poet Pleshcheev and argues that Pleshcheev played a considerable role in Chekhov's move into the mainstream of Russian literature in the late 1880s. Thirty-six letter of Pleshcheev to Chekhov are included.

55 RADIAN'SKE LITERATUROZNAVSTVO, no. 1, pp. 47-86.

Contains five articles: Chekhov's views on tendentiousness in literature; his literary craftsmanship; his relations with the dramatist Stepan Vasilchenko; his problems with censorship; and on the activities of the Chekhov Museum in Yalta.

56 REVIAKIN, A.I. "Vishnevyi sad" A.P. Chekhova: posobie dlia uchitelei [Chekhov's Cherry Orchard: an aid for teachers]. Moscow: Uchpedgiz, 256 pp.

Contains chapters on the historical setting of the play, Chekhov's attitudes to the political situation of his day; the history of the play's writing; analyses of its theme, conflict, characters, structure, genre, and dialogue; its place in Russian criticism and general significance.

57 ROSKIN, A.I. "Opasnosti i soblazny" [Dangers and temptations]. Teatr, no. 1, pp. 110-16.

Argues that Chekhov's plays were slow to be accepted in the post-revolutionary era because they appeared overly "domestic" and subjective (in the sense that Chekhov projects himself through his characters). Reviews a number of Soviet productions of Chekhov's plays, arguing that he must be performed without sentimentality and without distortions of his own ideas as expressed by his characters. His plays should be "majestic."

58 RUDNITSKII, K.A. "O poetike chekhovskoi dramy:

zametki" [On the poetics of Chekhov's drama: some remarks]. Teatr, no. 1, pp. 117-27.

Argues that Chekhov's plays are characterized by their "monologic" nature: his characters speak principally of themselves and to themselves or to the audience. This gives his drama its lyrical flavor. He does not make heroes out of any of his characters, yet is able to convey the spiritual beauty and nobility of ordinary people.

59 RUSSKII IAZYK V SHKOLE. No. 1, pp. 2-51.

Special issue on Chekhov. Contains eleven articles on style and language. Includes 1960.5 and 1960.15.

60 SHERESHEVSKAIA, M.A. "Angliiskie pisateli i kritiki o Chekhove" [English writers and critics on Chekhov]. In Literaturnoe nasledstvo Vol. 68, Chekhov. By Akademiia nauk SSSR. Moscow: Akademiia nauk, pp. 801-832.

Outlines Chekhov's reception in England and summarizes critical opinion of his work. Excerpts from the writings of sixteen English writers and critics are included.

61 SHKLOVSKII, VIKTOR. "Vperedi vremeni" [Ahead of his time]. Znamia, no. 1, pp. 171-85.

A slightly expanded version of 1959.28. Reprinted: 1966.18.

62 SIMONOV, RUBEN. "Chekhov u Vakhtangovtsev" [Chekhov among the Vakhtangovites]. Teatr, no. 1, pp. 104-07.

Discusses Vakhtangov's 1921 production of Chekhov's The Wedding.

63 STANISLAVSKII, K.S. "Iz rezhisserskogo ekzempliara 'Trekh sester'" [From the director's copy of The Three Sisters]. Teatr, no. 1, pp. 139-47.

Contains excerpts from Stanislavsky's copy of the play with his notes for its production. These show, among other things, that he tried to make the play's ending more optimistic.

64 STENDER-PETERSEN, A.D. "Zur Technik der Pause bei Čechov." In Anton Čechov, 1860-1960: Some Essays. Edited by Thomas Eekman. Leiden: E.J. Brill, pp. 187-206.

Examines the use of the pause in Chekhov's five major plays. Pauses are used to indicate psychological undercurrents and to show the lack of communication between characters; they also have structural functions in monologues and within individual scenes. Chekhov's use of the pause increased until The Three Sisters, then dropped with The Cherry Orchard.

65 STROEVA, M.N. "Chekhov i sovetskaia drama: k postanovke voprosa" [Chekhov and Soviet drama: toward a formulation of the question]. Teatr, no. 1, pp. 69-82.

Argues that Chekhov had a deep influence on Soviet playwrights--in spite of the many apparent differences between his plays and theirs--because he "discovered the laws of twentieth-century drama." Traces Chekhov's influence on Pogodin, Afinogenov, Leonov, Arbuzov, Rozov, and others.

66 STRUVE, GLEB. "Chekhov i Grigorovich: ikh lichnye i literaturnye otnosheniia" [Chekhov and Grigorovich: their personal and literary relations]. In Anton Čechov, 1860-1960: Some Essays. Edited by Thomas Winner. Leiden: E.J. Brill, pp. 207-66.

Outlines the history of the two writers' acquaintance on the basis of their letters and memoir material; argues that his relations with Grigorovich illustrate Chekhov's essential coldness to people and incapacity for close, sustained friendships. Grigorovich exerted no direct influence on Chekhov's work, but his "Sleepy" was probably inspired by Grigorovich's "Karelin's Dream."

67 STYAN, J.L. "Shifting Impressions: The Cherry Orchard." In The Elements of Drama. Cambridge: Cambridge University Press, pp. 64-85. Several reprints.

Discusses the play, specifically the last scene between Varya and Lopakhin, in therms of the impressions it creates on its audience. Chekhov does not put the usual theatrical emphasis on character. His plays concern relationships between characters rather than the characters themselves; understanding these relationships involves much shifting of impressions by the audience and a keen sense for the significance of the trivialities that the characters express.

68 SVATOŇOVÁ, ILJA. "O lirizme Chekhova: neskol'ko zametok" [On Chekhov's lyricism: a few observations]. In Anton Čechov, 1860-1960: Some Essays. Edited by Thomas Eekman. Leiden: E.J. Brill, pp. 267-76.

Discusses the prose of Chekhov's last decade and

argues that these lyrical "intimate miniatures" best express his realism. His lyrical stories focus on the awakening within a character of his awareness of his past errors.

69 TEATR, no. 1, pp. 1-169.
Special issue on Chekhov and his drama. Contains appreciations of his art by Soviet and foreign theatrical figures, nine critical articles, material from archives, and six brief notices on various aspects of his dramatic work. Illustrated. Includes 1960.9, 1960.45, 1960.57, 1960.58, 1960.62, 1960.63, 1960.65, 1960.72, and 1960.81.

70 TIMMER, CHARLES B. "The Bizarre Element in Čechov's Art." In Anton Čechov, 1860-1969: Some Essays. Edited by Thomas Eekman. Leiden: E.J. Brill, pp. 277-92.
Outlines Chekhov's use of bewildering irrelevancies in his early fiction, where it creates an effect close to the grotesque, and in his mature art, where it approaches the absurd. Aside from its philosophical significance, the bizarre is used to retard the action, to restrain emotion, to communicate hidden meaning, and to reveal character. Reprinted in part: 1977.3.

71 TRACY, ROBERT. "A Čexov Anniversary." SEEJ 4:25-34.
Discusses George Calderon's 1909 production, in Glasgow, of The Seagull, the first of Chekhov's plays to be staged in English. Calderon took care to introduce his play to an audience unfamiliar with Chekhov's new techniques by lecturing them (see 1912.2). Critical response to the play was generally favorable, but not until later London productions did Chekhov's British reputation as a dramatist begin to take shape.

72 TUROVSKAIA, M.I. "Na razlome epokh" [At the break between eras]. Teatr, no. 1, pp. 17-38.
Argues that Chekhov's plays cannot be judged by traditional criteria: his characters are engaged in a struggle not with Fate or with Evil but with life itself. He created a new era in the drama, and the endings of his plays--which avoid the traditional finality of a marriage or a death--are but one indicator of his innovative techniques.

73 VINOGRADOVA, K.M. "Stranitsa iz chernovoi rukopisi rasskaza 'Dama s sobachkoi'" [A page from the rough copy of the story "Lady With the Little Dog"]. In

Literaturnoe nasledstvo [Literary legacy] Vol. 68, Chekhov. By Akademiia nauk SSSR, Moscow: Akademiia nauk, pp. 133-40.

Discusses the changes Chekhov made in the first published version of the story (1899) for his Collected works (1903) and reproduces the text of the final page of the rough copy of Chapter Four. The manuscript shows the care with which Chekhov characterized Gurov and reveals his attempts to underline Gurov's regeneration.

74 VLADIMIRSKAIA, A.R. "Avtograf dobavlenii ko vtoromu aktu Vishnegogo sada" [A manuscript copy of additions to Act 2 of The Cherry Orchard]. In Literaturnoe nasledstvo [Literary legacy] Vol. 68, Chekhov. By Akademiia nauk SSSR. Moscow: Akademiia nauk, pp. 141-46.

Describes the changes made to the original version of Act 2 by Chekhov during rehersals of the play in Moscow during December 1903 and January 1904.

75 -----, ed. "Dve rannie redaktsii p'esy Tri sestry" [Two early editions of the play The Three Sisters]. In Literaturnoe nasledstvo [Literary legacy]. Vol. 68, Chekhov. By Akademiia nauk SSSR. Moscow: Akademiia nauk, pp. 1-86.

Contains the texts of the first "Yalta" edition of the play together with the corrections and changes Chekhov introduced while revising the play in Nice in December 1900. An introductory article outlines the genesis of the play and comments on Chekhov's editorial work.

76 WILCZKOWSKI, C. "Un amour de Čechov." In Anton Čechov, 1860-1960: Some Essays. Edited by Thomas Eekman. Leiden: E.J. Brill, pp. 311-24.

Examines links between Chekhov's biography and some of the love stories in his works. Argues that Lydia Avilova (see 1947.1) was in fact one of Chekhov's secret loves. The love affairs in his fiction between 1887 and 1892 fail because of masculine egotism, not because of external obstacles. After 1892 the agressive female appears in his works, possible a result of his relationship with the actress Iavorskaia.

77 WINNER, THOMAS G. "Chekhov v Soedinennykh shtatakh Ameriki" [Chekhov in the U.S.A.]. In Literaturnoe nasledstvo [Literary legacy] Vol. 68, Chekhov. By Akademiia nauk SSSR. Moscow: Akademiia nauk, pp. 777-800.

Chronicles the translations of Chekhov, the performances of his plays, and Chekhov's critical reception in the United States from 1891 to 1958.

78 -----. "Čechov and Scientism: Observations on the Searching Stories." In Anton Čechov, 1860-1960: Some Essays. Edited by Thomas Eekman. Leiden: E.J. Brill, pp. 325-335.

Discusses five stories from the period 1889 to 1893 which reflect Chekhov's search for a world view. Here he rejects the narrowly scientific approach to life: "A Dreary Story" deals with the psychological collapse of a scientist; "Gusev" and "The Duel" deflate the self-importance of intellectuals. In "Ward Six" intellectualism prevents contact with genuine and pressing problems of life. "The Black Monk" deals with a character's delusions of intellectual greatness.

79 WORLD THEATER 9:99-148.

Special issue on Chekhov. Contains an article by Pavel Markov discussing changes in the interpretation of Chekhov's plays in the USSR over the past fifty years and comments by twenty-three European producers and stage designers on the question "In what style should Chekhov be staged?"

80 YACHNIN, RISSA. Chekhov in English: A Selective List of Works By and About Him 1949-1960. New York: New York Public Library, 11 pp.

Continues Heifetz (1949.4) to 1960. Unannotated.

81 ZAMANSKII, S. "Sila chekhovskogo podtektsa" [The strength of Chekhov's subtext]. Teatr, no. 1, pp. 101-06.

Argues that the "subtext" or undercurrent in Chekhov's plays conveys those feelings which characters are unable to express openly themselves. The subtext may be expressed in some seemingly trivial remark, a gesture, a pause, or in the sharp contrast created by two character's successive but unrelated lines of dialogue. Another type of subtext, not linked to any single character's feelings, reflects the force of the daily routine of life.

1961

1 AKIMOV, Iu.L. "Velikii pisatel' russkogo naroda" [A great writer of the Russian people]. In Stat'i o russkikh pisateliakh [Articles on Russian writers]. Moscow: Khudozhestvennaia literatura, pp. 59-79.

A brief general survey of Chekhov's life and work that argues that he was by no means "indifferent;" he was a thoroughly national writer, deeply concerned with problems of his society. The main theme of his writings is the attempt to define a free personality.

2 BERDNIKOV, G.P. A.P. Chekhov: ideinye i tvorcheskie iskaniia [Chekhov: his ideological and creative quest]. Moscow-Leningrad: Khudozhestvannaia literatura, 506 pp.

Examines the evolution of the ideas expressed in Chekhov's stories and letters (but only marginally those expressed in his plays). Chekhov's work is examined in the context of the literary currents of his day, and many comparisons are made between it and the writings of contemporaries such as Garshin, Korolenko, and Tolstoy. Considerable attention is paid to the impact of Chekhov's Sakhalin journey on his work. His major theme--the conflict of the thoughtful man with his environment--was a legacy from his predecessors, but his treatment of it is entirely original.

3 BURSOV, B.I. "Chekhov i russkii roman" [Chekhov and the Russian novel]. In Problemy realizma russkoi literatury XIX veka [Problems of realism in nineteenth-century Russian literature]. Edited by B.I. Bursov and I.Z. Serman. Moscow and Leningrad: AN SSSR, pp. 281-306.

Examines the question of why Chekhov wrote no novels. The answer lies in the historical conditions under which he lived and in his characters, who are formed by those conditions. He in fact could find no hero, and without a hero a novel was impossible. His characters can reveal their essence within the small form which, in his hands, played the same role as did the novel in the preceding age.

4 DÜWEL, WOLF. Anton Tschechow: Dichter der Morgendämmerung. Wege zur Literatur. Beiträge zur russischen und sowjetischen Literatur. Halle: Verlag Sprache und Literatur, 187 pp.

A critico-biographical study. Chekhov's career is divided into three periods: 1880 to 1887; 1888 to 1897; and 1897 to 1904. The second period is marked by works of social criticism, the last by its focus on the drama. A few representative writings from each period are discussed.

5 ERMILOV, V.V. "Polemicheskie zametki" [Polemical remarks]. VLit, no. 5, pp. 116-19.

Replies to L. Maliugin's criticisms (1961.12),

arguing that Chekhov explained and condemned his character Ivanov and reaffirming that the play is much weaker than his later ones.

6 FEDIN, KONSTANTIN. "Chekhov." In Pisatel', iskusstvo, vremia [The writer, art, time]. Moscow: Sovetskii pisatel', pp. 26-37.

Describes Chekhov as a writer with an amazing breadth of vision whose writings have forever characterized the last quarter of the nineteenth century. His works and influence have spread over the whole world. Sev ral reprints.

7 GOL'DINER, V.D. and KHALIZEV, V.E. "Rabota Chekhova nad rasskazom 'Nevesta'" [Chekhov's work on the story "Betrothed"]. VLit, no. 9, pp. 167-83.

Examines the genesis of the story and argues that it, together with The Cherry Orchard, represents the beginnings of a new stage in Chekhov's work. In successive drafts Chekhov shifted the story's conflict from the external to the internal, intensified its emotional currents, and relied more on expressive details to convey his meaning. He also removed a reference to his heroine's intentions to join the revolutionaries.

8 HARRISON, JOHN Wm. "Symbolic Action in Chekhov's 'Peasants' and 'In the Ravine'." MFS 7:369-72.

Argues that the symbolic action of each story is different: in "Peasants" it is one of "stripping bare;" in "In the Ravine" it is counterfeiting. The symbolic action of the first story holds together its loosely related series of events; that of the second story works at a deeper level and links plot and social criticism by its symbolizing hypocrisy. The stripping bare of "Peasants" reveals the spiritual and moral poverty of the village.

9 KATZER, JULIUS, ed. A.P. Chekhov: 1860-1960. Moscow: Foreign Languages Publishing House, 166 pp.

Contains translations of previously published material, including 1905.4 and 1923.7, two chapters of a study by Kornei Chukovsky (included in 1967.1), three essays by V.V. Ermilov (1959.9, 1959.10, and 1959.11), and the reminiscences of Chekhov's wife (see 1960.27).

10 KOMINA, R.V.; MALAFEEVA, I.A.; FRADKINA, S.Ia.; and GENKEL', M.A., eds. Tvorchestvo A.P. Chekhova. Iubileinyi vypusk "uchenykh zapisok" filologicheskogo fakul'teta [Chekhov's work: a jubilee edition of scholarly papers of the Faculty of Philology]. Perm: Permskii gos. universitet, 183 pp.

Contains four articles on Chekhov's outlook and works, two comparative studies (Saltykov-Shchedrin and Ostrovsky), and a study of his influence on English literature.

11 LAFFITTE, SOPHIE. "L'art de Čechov." Revue des Études Slaves 39:107-23.

Examines some of the innovative features of Chekhov's art. He achieved amazing brevity in his plotless short stories and created masterpieces of drama without action. Simplicity, brevity, and grace are hallmarks of his art.

12 MALIUGIN, L.A. "Chekhov nachinaetsia s Ivanova" [Chekhov begins with Ivanov]. VLit, no. 5, pp. 94-108.

Surveys the critical debate over the significance of the play in Chekhov's dramatic career, arguing that although it is not on a level with his later masterpieces it is a worthy play, "the first chapter in Chekhov's dramatic work," and deserves to be staged more often. Takes issue with Ermilov's (1948.4) and Berdnikov's (1957.2) criticisms of the play's weaknesses. Ermilov replies in 1961.5; the debate continues in 1964.11. Reprinted: 1967.17 as "Pervaia glava" [The first chapter].

13 MEVE, E.B. Meditsina v tvorchestve i zhizni A.P. Chekhova [Medicine in Chekhov's works and life]. Kiev: Gosudarstvennaia meditsinskoe izdatel'stvo USSR, 288 pp.

Examines Chekhov's career as a doctor and argues that his medical training enabled him to elaborate an approach to writing that combined scientific precision with artistic feeling. Chapters are devoted to Chekhov's portrayal of abnormal psychic states and mental illness and to his depiction of physical illnesses. Included also is a section on Chekhov's activities as a doctor. Detailed bibliography.

14 NAZARENKO, VADIM. "Slovo i obraz" [Word and image]. In Iazyk iskusstva: o masterstve poeta i prozaika [The language of art: on the craftsmanship of the poet and the prose writer]. Leningrad: Sovetskii pisatel', pp. 69-82.

Examines the purpose of the opening and closing "frame" in "The Man in the Case;" argues that this provides an important link in the story's chain of imagery and gives the story a much broader significance than it otherwise would have. Translated in part: 1976.15.

15 SLONIM, MARC. Russian Theater from the Empire to the Soviets. Cleveland and New York: World, pp. 118-32.

Discusses the production of Chekhov's plays by Russian theaters generally and by the MAT specifically.

16 STRUVE, GLEB. "On Chekhov's Craftsmanship: The Anatomy of a Story." SlavR 20:465-76.

The economy of means and the use of compositional and stylistic devices in "Sleepy" show Chekhov's mastery of the short story form. Chekhov manages vividly to evoke the state between sleep and waking. The story is structured like a piece of music with recurring images and impressionistic details. Reprinted: 1979.14.

17 WINNER, THOMAS G. "The Čexov Centennial Productions in the Moscow Theaters." SEEJ 5:255-62.

Reviews briefly the Soviet reception of Chekhov's plays, noting that their true revival did not occur until Nemirovich-Danchenko's 1940 production of The Three Sisters. Reviews the 1960 productions of Platonov, Ivanov, The Wood Demon, The Seagull, and The Cherry Orchard. Argues that the production of The Wood Demon revealed that the play has been underestimated. Most theaters continue to be heavily influenced by Stanislavsky's productions, although the Maly Theater's Ivanov was original and effective.

1962

1 BERKOVSKII, N.Ia. "Chekhov, povestvovatel' i dramaturg" [Chekhov, narrator and dramatist]. In Stat'i o literature [Articles about literature]. Moscow and Leningrad: Khudozhestvennaia literatura, pp. 404-51.

Reprinted from 1960.9

2 BLOK, ALEKSANDR. "O drame" [On the drama]. Sobranie sochinenii [Collected works]. Vol. 5. Moscow-Leningrad: Khudozhestvannaia literatura, p. 169.

Reprinted from 1907.1.

3 BRAGIN, S.G., ed. A.P. Chekhov: sbornik statei i materialov [Chekhov: a collection of articles and material]. Simferopol': Krymizdat, 127 pp.

Contains eight articles dealing with aspects of Chekhov's biography, his correspondence with Bunin, his reception in Poland and Rumania, his vaudeville The Anniversary, and problems of translation. Also included are twenty-eight letters of Chekhov's sister to Olga Knipper and a description of the Chekhov museum in Yalta. Illustrated.

4 CORRIGAN, ROBERT. Introduction to Six Plays by Chekhov. New York: Holt, Reinhart and Winston, pp. xii-xlii. Reprint. New York: Drama Book Specialists, 1979. Several other reprints, including 1964.4.

Characterizes Chekhov's plays generally, arguing that their contemporaneity is a result of their reflection of "the mood of spiritual discouragement which permeates the anxieties of the mid-twentieth century." A leitmotiv of all his work is a despair over the inability to solve life's most important problems. Yet his plays are not unrelieved gloom, since they continue the quest for solutions. The plays are not imitations of actions; rather they show life as it is. They are "dramas of indirection" that reveal the inner lives of their characters through a whole range of ironic devices. The plays are comedies in the sense that they deal with man's capacity to endure.

5 DOBIN, E.S. Geroi. Siuzhet. Detal' [The hero. The plot. The detail]. Leningrad: Sovetskii pisatel', pp. 345-73.

Examines Chekhov's use of detail as a means of creating a character or an object with great vividness and economy. The detail [detal'] is distinguished from the particular [podrobnost']; a single detail, if expressive enough, can replace a mass of particulars. Translated: 1976.15.

6 EEKMAN, THOMAS. "A Recurrent Theme in Chekhov's Works." SSl 8:3-25.

Discusses the impact of his father's bankruptcy (1876) on Chekhov, arguing that the resulting poverty and homelessness are frequently reflected in his writings. Homelessness or expulsion from a family home are themes repeated throughout his works. Linked with this, especially in the later works, is the countermotif of moving away from the old to begin a new life.

7 FREEDMAN, MORRIS. "Chekhov's Morality of Work." MD 5:83-92.

Examines the themes of illusion and reality and work as means of escape from futility. Reprinted: 1967.2.

8 HAUSER, ARNOLD. The Social History of Art. Vol. 4, Naturalism, Impressionism, The Film Age. London: Routledge & Kegan Paul, pp. 195-98 and passim.

Discusses Chekhov within the context of impressionism in European literature and argues that he is "the purest representative of the whole movement." The philosophy of his works is based on the mutual isolation of human beings and on passivity and indolence. This gives rise to the episodic nature of his stories and to the absence of conflict in his plays.

9 KHALIZEV, V.E. "Uroki Chekhova-dramaturga" [Lessons of Chekhov the dramatist]. VLit, no. 12, pp. 78-94.

Examines some traditional features of the drama and shows how Chekhov changed these in his plays, which represent a turning point in the history of the drama. He used a new form of dramatic conflict which no longer involved conflicts between characters; his characters reveal themselves not in their efforts to achieve some goal but in the development of their feelings; he abandons the traditional "unity of action." Thus he liberated his plays from the restrictions of traditonal dramatic poetics.

10 KRUTCH, JOSEPH WOOD. "Modernism" in Modern Drama. New York: Russell & Russel, pp. 66-77.

Examines Chekhov's drama within the context of European modernism. Unlike traditional drama, his plays rarely present the great passionate moments on stage; he believes that the most typical aspects of life are not its heightened moments but its featurelessness and lack of passion.

11 LAFFITTE, SOPHIE. "Deux amis: Čechov et Levitan." Revue des Études Slaves 41:135-49.

Describes Chekhov's friendship with the painter Isaac Levitan, noting each one's views on the other's work and pointing out Levitan's influence on a number of Chekhov's writings. Many of Chekhov's descriptions of landscape are reminiscent of Levitan's paintings.

12 LEWIS, ALLAN. "The Comedy of Frustration: Chekhov." In The Contemporary Theatre: The Significant Playwrights of Our Time. Foreword by John Gassner. New York: Crown, pp. 59-80.

Discusses Chekhov's plays within the context of the development of modern drama; analyzes The Cherry Orchard, arguing that it represents the fullest possible development of his attempt to depict "life as it is." The play is a comedy, but a difficult one to perform since the characters are full of complexities and not one-sided as comic characters usually are.

13 MURATOVA, K.D., ed. Istoriia russkoi literatury XIX veka: bibliograficheskii ukazatel' [The history of Russian literature of the nineteenth century: a bibliographical guide]. Moscow: Akademiia nauk, pp. 791-806.

Lists editions of Chekhov's own writings, biographical works, and Russian criticism of his prose and drama. Unannotated, but notes contents of collections. Contains 411 items.

14 O'CONNOR, FRANK. "The Slave's Son." In The Lonely Voice: A Study of the Short Story. Cleveland and New York: World, pp. 78-98.

Chekhov began writing under the influence of Maupassant. But in writing of his two obsessions--human loneliness and venial, as opposed to mortal sin--he gradually found his own voice. His later work is dominated by the theme of the false personality. Several reprints.

15 ROMANENKO, V.T. Chekhov i nauka [Chekhov and science]. Khar'kov: Khar'kovskoe knizhnoe izdatel'stvo, 208 pp.

Argues that Chekhov gradually developed a thoroughly scientific view of life grounded in materialism and atheism. This view is reflected specifically in his aesthetics, where he insisted that the writer must work not only through his artistic instincts but must also base his writing solidly on scientific fact. The influence of his medical studies and of various contemporary scientists is assessed; his portrayal of scientists and the application of his scientific method in a number of stories are analyzed.

16 SHTEIN, A.P. Kriticheskii realism i russkaia drama XIX veka [Critical realism and nineteenth-century Russian drama]. Moscow: Khudozhestvennaia literatura, pp. 322-68.

Examines Chekhov's dramatic work within the context of nineteenth-century Russian drama. The source of his characters' sufferings in The Seagull and Uncle Vanya lies in external reality rather than in the actions of other characters, and it is this conflict of their inner strivings with the external world that interests him. The Cherry Orchard, with its anticipation of happiness in the future, is very much in the tradition of Russian drama. Chekhov's plays, like Tolstoy's, contain many features similar to those of western drama of the period.

17 SIMMONS, ERNEST J. Chekhov: A Biography. An Atlantic Monthly Press Book. Boston and Toronto: Little, Brown, 669 pp.

A detailed biography that takes into account new material appearing in the USSR in connection with the Chekhov centenary of 1960. It aims to give a complete picture of Chekhov's personality and outlook; his writings are not discussed at length. Restlessness is an essential character trait, and his inherent joy of life alternated with an equally inherent revulsion to it since beneath his outward optimism and affability lay a profound melancholy whose sources are unknown. Reviewed: 1963.16.

18 SLONIM, MARC. From Chekhov to the Revolution: Russian Literature 1900-1917. A Galaxy Book. New York: Oxford University Press, pp. 55-78.

Suggests that Chekhov created the "moody man," the passive and lonely character whose life is entangled with lies. Chekhov's literary method is to strip away falsity and illusion and only indirectly to suggest his characters' real concerns. While his works convey feelings of doom and futility they are not without elements of hope and humor.

19 STYAN, J.L. The Dark Comedy: The Development of Modern Comic Tragedy. Cambridge: Cambridge University Press, pp. 82-119 and passim. Reprint. 1968.27.

Examines Chekhov's drama within the tradition of European naturalism and argues that he is "the first truly dark comedian." A detailed analysis of Act 4 of The Cherry Orchard shows how carefully Chekhov balances comedy and pathos to control the sympathies of his audience.

20 SURKOV, E.D. "Chekhov i teatr" [Chekhov and the theater]. In Na dramaticheskie temy: stat'i [On aspects of the drama: articles]. Moscow: Sovetskii pisatel', pp. 316-43.

Describes Chekhov's relationship with the Russian theater before his involvement with the MAT.

1963

1 BUGROV, B.S. "Sud'by chekhovskikh traditsii v russkoi dramaturgii 1910-kh godov" [The fate of the Chekhov tradition in Russian drama, 1900-1910]. VMU, no. 6, pp. 30-43.

Examines Chekhov's influence on Russian drama

from 1900 to 1910. His plays were regarded as impressionistic at this time, largely because of a perceived crisis in realistic drama. Those dramatists who imitated Chekhov tried only to use his dramatic devices but failed to continue his attempts at a full and faithful portrayal of real life.

2 CHUDAKOVA, M.O. and CHUDAKOV, A.P. "Iskusstvo tselogo: zametki o sovremennom rasskaze" [The art of the whole: remarks on the contemporary short story]. NovM, no. 2, pp. 239-52.

Discusses some contemporary Soviet short stories with reference to Chekhov's technique, arguing that his stories provide a model of harmony and wholeness for contemporary writers.

3 ERENBURG, ILYA. [Ehrenburg]. "On Re-reading Chekhov." In Chekhov, Stendhal, and Other Essays. Translated by Anna Bostock, Yvonne Kapp, and Tatiana Shebunina. New York: Alfred A. Knopf, pp. 3-79.

Translation of 1959.7.

4 ERLICH, VICTOR, ed. "Chekhov and West European Drama." YCGL 12:56-60.

A discussion by eleven critics on the influence and reception of Chekhov's plays in the West. Thomas Winner defines the topic by noting the changes that were occurring in western drama during Chekhov's lifetime, his relationship to naturalism, impressionsim, and symbolism. Others discuss his reception in France, influences on his work, the nature of his comedy, and interpretations of his plays.

5 ERMILOV, V.V. "Nechto nepopravimo komicheskoe... : ob antimire kritika V. Nazarenko" [Something irreparably comic: on the antiworld of the critic V. Nazarenko]. VLit, no. 11, pp. 142-51.

Takes issue with Nazarenko's interpretation of "The Artist's Story" (1963.14), arguing that it utterly distorts the meaning of the story. Lida's activities are only attempts to remedy the symptoms of social injustice; the artist wishes to remedy the problem itself.

6 GURBANOV, V.V. "O leksike rasskazov A.P. Chekhova" [On the vocabulary of Chekhov's stories]. In Iz istorii slov i slovarei: ocherki po leksigologii i leksikografii [From the history of words and dictionaries: lexicological and lexicographical sketches]. Edited by B.A. Larin. Leningrad: Leningradskii Universitet, pp. 37-46.

Argues that Chekhov often uses abstractions such

as "ideal," "progress," and "principles" ironically to expose their lack of meaning when uttered by thoughtless characters. Similarly he attacks the use of cliche's and sentimental expressions. His critical attitude to diction helped purify the language.

7 ISSERLIN, E.M. "Zametki o iazyke rasskazov A.P. Chekhova" [Remarks on the language of Chekhov's stories]. In _Iz istorii slov i slovarei: ocherki po leksikologii i leksikografii_ [From the history of words and dictionaries: lexicological and lexicographical sketches]. Edited by B.A. Larin. Leningrad: Leningradskii universitet, pp. 53-58.

Argues that each great writer must have "his own" language and examines some features of Chekhov's. He often uses gender in ways that make grammatical but not strictly logical sense, or associates gramatically similar but logically disparate words. This is done for satirical purposes.

8 KLEINE, DON W. "The Chekhovian Source of 'Marriage à la Mode'." _PQ_ 42:284-88.

Argues that "The Grasshopper" was a source, perhaps an unconscious one, for Katherine Mansfield's "Marriage à la Mode." Chekhov's story is predominantly a character study; Mansfield's is a satire.

9 KOZHEVNIKOVA, N.A. "Ob osobennostiakh stilia Chekhova: nesobstvenno priamaia rech'" [On the features of Chekhov's style: _erlebte Rede_]. _VMU_, no. 2, pp. 51-62.

Examines the development of Chekhov's technique of conducting the narrative in the words of a character or from that character's point of view. In this respect his work can be divided into three periods; in the middle period (1888-1892) his stories become increasingly objective and _erlebte Rede_ is used to convey a character's thoughts. As Chekhov's stories become increasingly psychologically-oriented the role of this type of narrative becomes more pronounced and serves not only as a means of a character's self-revelation but also allows Chekhov to express his own attitude to his characters.

10 LAKSHIN, V.Ia. _Tolstoy i Chekhov_ [Tolstoy and Chekhov]. Moscow: Sovetskii pisatel', 570 pp.

Describes the personal relations of the two writers, their meetings, discussions, their views of one another, and the differences in their outlooks. A detailed comparison/contrast is made of _Uncle Vanya_ and _A Living Corpse_. Although the personalities of the two writers were very different, Lakshin argues that they shared a desire to answer the same fundamental questions about life. Revised: 1975.10. Translated in part: 1976.15.

11 LUCAS, F.L. The Drama of Chekhov, Synge, Yeats and Pirandello. London: Cassell, pp. 1-146.

Includes a biographical sketch, a brief essay on Chekhov's drama generally, studies of each act of his five major plays, and a concluding section on how Chekhov's style and ideas derive from his personality. Brevity, simplicity, and scientific truthfulness are his fundamental qualities as a writer. His view of life has room for both optimism and pessimism, just as his attitude can be detached or sympathetic.

12 MARSHALL, RICHARD H., Jr. "Čexov and the Russian Orthodox Clergy." SEEJ 7:375-91.

Examines the role of religion in Chekhov's upbringing and notes that he retained no permanent antipathy toward the clergy. Although he was an agnostic, "his humanistic philosophy was to a large extent a secular version of the traditional Judaeo-Christian ethic." A survey of the portrayal of clergy in his stories shows that his treatment is sympathetic even when pointing out the failings of his priests; the best among them, however, "come close to Chekhov's ideal of character fulfillment."

13 MENDELSOHN, MICHAEL J. "The Heartbreak Houses of Shaw and Chekhov." The Shaw Review 6:89-95.

Argues that the influence of The Cherry Orchard on Shaw's Heartbreak House lies in the apparent plotlessness, the peculiarities of dialogue in which the characters talk but seldom listen, the overall dreamlike tone, the characters themselves, and the theme of the failure of a way of life.

14 NAZARENKO, V.A. "Lida, Zhenia i Chekhovedy...: o meste literaturoveda v rabochem stroiu" [Lida, Zhenia, and the Chekhovists: on the literary scholar's place in the ranks of the workers]. VLit, no. 11, pp. 124-41.

Examines various interpretations of "The Artist's Story" and argues that its point is not in the ideological debate between the artist and Lida. He in fact loves Lida but declines to find happiness with her so that he can dedicate himself to his art. Chekhov thus uses his hero as an example of how seriously artists should take their calling. Ermilov rebuts this interpretation in 1963.5.

15 SAINT-DENIS, MICHEL. "Chekhov and the Modern

Stage." Translated by Phillipe Poisson. Drama Survey 3:77-81.

Discusses Laurence Olivier's 1962 production of Uncle Vanya, noting that the anti-naturalist staging "gave a more intense reality to the expression of the characters and thus to the meaning of the play." Yet this approach also eliminated "the life of things" which is so important in a Chekhov play. The MAT's productions simplify Chekhov and "make a bourgeois" of him.

16 STRUVE, GLEB. "Ernest J. Simmons, Chekhov: A Biography." Slav R 22:591-95.

A review article on Simmons' study (1962.17) which it describes as "to date the most detailed biography of Chekhov in any language." Simmons is criticized for an overabundance of detail that sometimes obscures his subject and for failing to provide an adequate picture of Russian life of the period. Although the book is valuable it does not sufficiently illuminate some aspects of his personality (his vulgarity [poshlost'] and his indifference to people) and does not resolve the enigma of Chekhov.

17 SVETOV, F.G. "Rozhdenie kharaktera" [The birth of a character]. VLit, no. 10, pp. 171-88.

Examines the origins of two Chekhov stories, "Anna Round the Neck" and "Gooseberries," tracing the gradual "crystallization" of their main characters and how each one embodies the main idea of each story.

18 VINOGRADOV, V.V. Stilistika. Teoriia poeticheskoi rechi. Poetika [Stylistics. The theory of poetic speech. Poetics]. Moscow: Akademiia nauk SSSR, pp. 46-51, 54-61, 80-89, and 194-96.

Discusses examples of Chekhov's use of dialogue to typify the social or professional status of the speaker and shows how he uses stylistic nuances as a means of characterization. Stylistic changes made in later revisions of his stories such "The Investigator" reveal how the "nucleus" of his style changes with his subject. Translated in part: 1976.15.

19 WINNER, THOMAS G. "Theme and Structure in Čexov's 'The Betrothed'." ISS 3:163-72.

Argues that the theme of the story--Nadia's growing emancipation--harmonizes with the story's structure. Its three parts trace the phases of her growing awareness of the limitations and inadequacies of her environment. The interplay of beauty and vulgarity helps realize the theme.

20 ----- "Myth as a Device in the Works of Chekhov." In Myth and Symbol: Critical Approaches and Applications. Edited by Bernice Slote. Lincoln, Neb.: University of Nebraska Press, pp. 71-78.

Examines Chekhov's use of archetypal patterns from literature and classical mythology. One of his commonest literary archetypes is Anna Karenina, and Winner discusses two stories where this archetype is particularly important, "Anna Round the Neck" and "The Lady With the Little Dog."

1964

1 ALEKSANDROV, B.I. A.P. Chekhov: Seminarii [Chekhov: a seminar]. 2d ed., rev. and expanded. Moscow-Leningrad: Prosveshchenie, 214 pp.

An updated version of 1957.1, it includes essays on the publication of Chekhov's works, his critical reception in Russia (1957.1 has more material on pre-revolutionary criticism), and a list of topics for the study of his work together with relevant bibliographical references. Includes only Russian-language sources. Unannotated.

2 BRUSTEIN, ROBERT. "Anton Chekhov." In The Theatre of Revolt. An Atlantic Monthly Press Book. Boston-Toronto: Little, Brown & Co., pp. 137-79.

This expanded version of 1964.3 devotes more space to general characteristics of Chekhov's art, which is seen as a revolt against the indolence and moral inertia of his characters and against the force of their environment which drags them down. This version also has an analysis of The Cherry Orchard, a play which, like The Three Sisters, deals with the collapse of a cultural elite but does so from a comic-ironic point of view.

3 -----. Foreword to Chekhov: The Major Plays. Translated by Ann Dunnigan. New York: New American Library, pp. vii-xxii. Reprinted and expanded in 1964.2.

Argues that "culture"--meaning humanity, decency, intelligence, accomplishment, and will--was Chekhov's principal ideal and that his plays turn on the conflict between culture and its enemies. The Three Sisters, "the most stunning example of his dramatic approach," provides excellent illustrations of his technique as a dramatist. Reprinted: 1977.3.

4 CORRIGAN, ROBERT W. "The Plays of Chekhov." In The

Context and Craft of Drama. Edited by Robert W. Corrigan and James L. Rosenberg. San Francisco: Chandler, pp. 139-67.
Reprinted from 1962.4.

5 FREEDMAN, MORRIS. Essays in the Modern Drama. Boston: D.C. Heath, 374 pp.
Contains 1949.2, an excerpt from 1952.5, and reviews by Stark Young (1948.8).

6 GIFFORD, HENRY. "Chekhov the Humanist." In The Novel in Russia: From Pushkin to Pasternak. Modern Languages and Literature, edited by J.M. Cohen. London: Hutchinson, pp. 125-34.
Argues that Chekhov's long effort of self-improvement left him a humanist. His values of restraint, lucidity, and balance are essentially classical. He has no doctrine, only his humanity.

7 HINGLEY, RONALD. Preface, Introduction, Appendices, and Notes to The Oxford Chekhov. Vol. 3. Edited and translated by Ronald Hingley. London: Oxford University Press, pp. ix-xix, 1-14, and 273-336.
Discusses problems of translating Chekhov's plays; points out the links between The Wood Demon and Uncle Vanya, noting that in the latter Chekhov discovered that his true element as a dramatist was inconclusiveness. Comments on the texts, composition, contemporary reception and variants to The Wood Demon, Uncle Vanya, The Three Sisters, and The Cherry Orchard. Chekhov's comments on the three latter plays are included. Explanatory notes to the plays are also provided.

8 HOY, CYRUS. The Hyacinth Room: An Investigation Into the Nature of Comedy, Tragedy, and Tragicomedy. New York: Alfred A. Knopf, pp. 303-07.
Discusses Chekhov's plays in the context of modern tragicomedy, arguing that they fuse comic and tragic elements because their author focuses on the tragicomic nature of life itself.

9 IL'IN, V.N. "Glubinnye motivy Chekhova" [Chekhov's most fundamental motifs]. Voz 148:76-92.
Examines a series of stories and The Seagull which, Il'in argues, express the essence of Chekhov's own views. He was one of the greatest poets of the "tragedy of existence." He portrays many people who have become lost in their world; but he also creates characters who find their salvation. His works present an "irrefutable" Christian argument in favor of the existence of God.

10 KALACHEVA, S.V. "K tvorcheskoi istorii 'Dueli' A.P. Chekhova" [On the creative history of Chekhov's "Duel"]. VMU, no. 3, pp. 35-46.

Examines the place of "The Duel" in Chekhov's creative biography, arguing that when one compares it to Ivanov and other writings of the late 1880s and early 1890s one can see how much his views changed after his journey to Sakhalin. A comparison of von Koren with Dr. Lvov shows the evolution of Chekhov's treatment of a similar character. "The Duel" also shows, for the first time, a character who manages to rise above the banality of life.

11 KHALIZEV, V.E. "Drama A.P. Chekhova Ivanov" [Chekhov's drama Ivanov]. RLit, no. 1, pp. 65-83.

Enters the debate between Maliugin (1961.12) and Ermilov (1961.5) on the significance of Ivanov, supporting and refining the latter's view that Ivanov lacks a solid ideological foundation. Argues that the play is Chekhov's warning about the dangers of reconciling oneself to injustice and shows the ineffectiveness of purely "romantic" protests against such injustice.

12 KOVALEV, Vl.A. "Formy publitsiticheskoi rechi v khudozhestvennykh proizvedeniiakh A.P. Chekhova" [Forms of journalistic discourse in Chekhov's literary works]. In Iz istorii russkoi zhurnalistiki vtoroi poloviny XIX veka: stat'i, materialy i bibliografiia [From the history of Russian journalism of the second half of the nineteenth century: articles, materials and bibliography]. Edited by A.V. Zapadov. Moscow: Izdatel'stvo MGU, pp. 137-58.

Argues that Chekhov's works are not only objective depictions of reality but also have deliberately ideological and "pedagogical" elements. Chekhov's own pronouncements on the purpose of literature bear this out. Chekhov communicates ideas through the ideological debates of characters, in the monologues or thoughts of a single character, and even in the descriptions of nature in his stories.

13 MAGARSHACK, DAVID. Introduction to Platonov: A Play in Four Acts and Five Scenes. By Anton Chekhov. Translated by David Magarshack. London: Faber & Faber, pp. 9-13.

Discusses the origins of the play and notes that it contains most of the principal themes of Chekhov's later drama and employs a number of dramatic techniques that he later refined in subsequent plays.

14 MALIUGIN, L.A. "Sud'ba Chaiki" [The fate of The Seagull]. Teatr, no. 9, pp. 60-68.

Discusses the plays reception among its contemporary Russian critics; points out some historical prototypes of its principal characters; describes its failure when staged in St. Petersburg and its success when staged by the MAT. Reprinted: 1967.17.

15 MILLER, JIM WAYNE. "Stark Young, Chekhov and the Method of Indirect Action." GaR 18:98-115.

Argues that Chekhov's plays influenced the novels of Stark Young. This influence is seen specifically in their use of undercurrent and indirect action. There are also parallels between the culture of Imperial Russia in Chekhov and that of the Old South in Young.

16 NAG, MARTIN. "Ibsen, Čechov und Blok." SSl 10:30-48.

Examines Chekhov's mixed feelings toward Ibsen and argues that The Wild Duck did influence The Seagull at least technically in the use of the central symbol.

17 PAPERNYI, Z.S. "Smekh Chekhova" [Chekhov's laughter]. NovM, no. 7, pp. 224-32.

Argues that Chekhov did not change from a comic writer to a serious one; rather he matured and his humor matured with him. The ironic humor of his later works conveys his sense of life's complexity.

18 SUBBOTINA, K. "Tvorchestvo A.P. Chekhova v otsenke angliiskoi kritiki 1910-1920-kh godov" [Chekhov's work as appraised by English critics in the 1910s and 1920s]. RLit, no. 2, pp. 139-48.

Surveys the main topics in English criticism of Chekhov to 1929: the absence of plot in his stories, his impressionism and symbolism, the "philosophy" of his writings, the comparison of his writings with music, and his technique of psychological analysis.

1965

1 BERKOVSKII, N.Ia. "Chekhov: ot rasskazov i povestei k dramaturgii" [Chekhov: from short stories and tales to the drama]. RLit, no. 4, pp. 21-63. Continued in 1966.1.

Discusses the evolution of Chekhov's short story and his changing attitude to plot. He commonly writes a "story of juxtaposition" with unity of meaning rather than unity of plot. He shows how humans can influence one another simply by their presence: even a glance can be an event, a part of the "action" of the story.

2 DAVIE, DONALD. Russian Literature and Modern English Fiction: A Collection of Critical Essays. Patterns of Literary Criticism, edited by Marshall McLuhan, R.J. Schoek, and Ernest Sirluck. Chicago and London: The University of Chicago Press, pp. 203-35.

Contains 1927.4 and 1954.24.

3 DUPEE, F.W. "To Moscow Again." In "The King of the Cats" and Other Remarks on Writers and Writing. New York: Farrar, Straus & Giroux, pp. 90-96.

Reviews a 1964 New York production of The Three Sisters, noting that none of the play's characters with any sensibility can live in the present. The play belongs to the end of the age of realism and anticipates the theater of the absurd.

4 EDWARDS, CHRISTINE. The Stanislavsky Heritage: Its Contribution to The Russian and American Theatre. New York: New York University Press, pp. 72-79 and passim.

Discusses the MAT's production of The Sea Gull and Chekhov's contribution to the theater's treatment of his plays.

5 HAGAN, JOHN. "The Shooting Party, Čexov's Early Novel: Its Place in His Development." SEEJ 9:123-40.

Notes that although the novel has many structural weaknesses it shows an impressive mastery of the technique of the melodramatic thriller. Chekhov was probably attempting simultaneously to write a "serio-comic detective story" and to poke fun at such thrillers. He uses narrative techniques and treats themes that he refined in his later work. The Shooting Party is also an early attempt to paint a comprehensive picture of Russian society.

6 -----. "The Tragic Sense in Chekhov's Earliest Stories." Criticism 7:52-80.

Examines a selection of "serious" stories from Chekhov's pre-1885 output which, Hagan argues, is by no means all buffoonery. Here one can find tragedies of character, of social circumstance, and of natural circumstance.

7 HINGLEY, RONALD. Preface, Introduction, Appendices,

and Notes to The Oxford Chekhov. Vol. 8. Edited and translated by Ronald Hingley. London: Oxford University Press, pp. ix-xiv, 1-11, and 269-321.

Comments on problems of translating Chekhov's stories of 1895 to 1897; surveys the social and cultural background to "His Wife," "Whitebrow," "Anna Round the Neck," "Murder," "Ariadne," "The Artist's Story," "My Life," "Peasants," "The Savage," "Home," and "In the Cart;" discusses their texts, composition, and variants. Explanatory notes to the stories are also provided.

8 MALIUGIN, L.A. "Zhizn' p'esy" [The life of a play]. Neva, no. 6, pp. 196-204.

Comments on the continuing interest in The Three Sisters in the USSR and abroad; discusses the 1964 Soviet film version of the play and the production by Tovstonogov. Argues that the play is, in fact, the "little novel" Chekhov reported he was writing in 1899. It has the complexity and scope of a long novel. Reprinted: 1967.17.

9 MATHEWSON, RUFUS W. Afterword to Ward Six and Other Stories by Anton Chekhov. A Signet Classic. Translated by Ann Dunnigan. New York: New American Library, pp. 379-95.

Comments on six stories ("The Name-Day Party," "A Dreary Story," "The Duel," "Ward Six," "My Life," "In the Ravine"), each of which deals in some way with individuals corrupted by their society.

10 RAHV, PHILIP. "The Education of Anton Chekhov." In The Myth and the Powerhouse. New York: Farrar, Straus & Giroux, pp. 175-81.

Reprinted from 1955.11.

11 ROSSBACHER, PETER. "Nature and the Quest for Meaning in Chekhov's Stories." RusR 24:387-92.

Argues that Chekhov can be called a religious man; but he could not satisfy his religious quest through Christianity. His typical characters also seek meaning but rarely find it; recognizing the element of mystery in nature leads them to an awareness of their loneliness and the futility of their existence.

12 SCHRÖDER, J. "Zur Wandlung des Čechov-Bildes in England." ZS 10:519-26.

Discusses Chekhov's reception in England, arguing that his popularity after World War I was a result of interpreting him as a pessimist, a view that was much in tune with the mood of the era. Russian emigré critics also supported this view. Only in the 1960s has the image of an optimistic Chekhov begun to emerge.

13 SEYLER, DOROTHY U. "The Sea Gull and The Wild Duck: Birds of a Feather?" MD 8:167-73.
Examines Chekhov's comment on dramatic theory in The Sea Gull and the role that the gull plays in that comment. Seyler argues that Chekhov was satirizing symbolism and "Ibsenism" generally and The Wild Duck in particular. Chekhov believed Ibsen's plays to be too intellectualized and his characters unconvincing.

14 SIMMONS, ERNEST J. "Chekhov: It is Impossible to Deceive in Art." In Introduction to Russian Realism: Gogol, Dostoevsky, Tolstoy, Chekhov, Sholokhov. Bloomington, Ind.: Indiana University Press, pp. 181-224.
Surveys Chekhov's career against a background of the history and culture of his era. He insisted that the artist depict life objectively without becoming emotionally involved; yet this lack of involvement provoked a spiritual crisis. His post-Sakhalin writings do show a new social emphasis, yet he maintains the degree of objectivity that is the special mark of his realism.

15 SOËP, CAROLINE. "Tchékhov et l'institutrice du village." RBPH, no. 43, pp. 970-82.
Surveys Chekhov's answers to letters from his readers, focusing on those from women teachers in country schools and discussing his views on schooling generally. Elements of this correspondence found their way into his story "In the Cart."

16 VOLKOV, NICOLAS. "Thèmes hamletiens dans La Mouette de Tchekhov." RHT 17:408-12.
Discusses the importance of Hamlet generally in Chekhov's writings and surveys some specific parallels between that play and The Seagull. The basic cast of characters is similar and several scenes in each play show an obvious kinship.

17 WILLIAMS, RAYMOND. "Anton Chekhov." In Drama From Ibsen to Eliot. London: Chatto & Windus, pp. 126-37.
Argues that Chekhov, faced with the problem of representing faithfully a life which had few characters who could articulate their problems, resorted to symbols such as the seagull and the cherry orchard. These are unsatisfactory and signify the crisis of naturalism. Chekhov's drama contains all the virtues and all the limitations of the naturalist theater; he is "highly placed among the questionable deities" of "sacred art."

Revised and expanded: 1968.29.

1966

1 BERKOVSKII, N.Ia. "Chekhov: ot rasskazov i povestei k dramaturgii" [Chekhov: from short stories and tales to the drama]. RLit, no 1, pp. 15-42.

A continuation of 1965.1, it surveys Chekhov's drama from Platonov to The Cherry Orchard. Platonov grew out of the stories "A Lady", "An Unnecessary Victory," and the novel The Shooting Party, but is also linked with all his later plays. His last three plays convey the sense of an oncoming cataclysmic social upheaval. His drama is imbued with the spirit of the everyday. He mastered the technique of "micro-expressiveness"--the use of tiny details to involve the spectator and convey to him his sense of life.

2 BITSILLI, PETR M. [Bicilli]. Anton P. Čechov: Das Werk und sein Stil. Forum Slavicum, vol. 7. Edited by Dmitrij Tschižewskij. Translated by Vincent Sieveking. Munich: Wilhelm Fink, 252 pp.

German translation of 1942.1. Contains bibliographies of Chekhov criticism and of Bitsilli's writings. Indexed.

3 CONRAD, JOSEPH L. "Čexov's 'The Man in a Shell': Freedom and Responsibility." SEEJ 10:400-10.

Argues that the story superbly presents two themes that run through much of Chekhov's mature work: a concern for personal, inner freedom and a equal concern for moral responsibility.

4 GANZ, ARTHUR. "Arrivals and Departures: The Meaning of the Journey in the Major Plays of Chekhov." DramS, no. 5, pp. 5-23.

Examines the theme of realization of the self in Chekhov's plays. His last plays involve symbolic journeys: characters are confronted not only by the vastness of their country but by a journey to self-realization and happiness in the "immeasurably distant" future. Reprinted: 1980.12.

5 GOURFINKEL, NINA. Anton Tchékhov. Textes de Tchékhov, documents, chronologie, repertoire des oeuvres, bibliographie, illustrations. Théâtre de tous les temps, no. 4. Paris: Seghers, 191 pp.

A biography of Chekhov the dramatist composed

largely of excerpts from his letters. Also includes a selection of letters in which he comments on the theater generally and a selection of remarks of contemporaries on Chekhov's plays. Some excerpts from The Wood Demon are compared with its later reworking as Uncle Vanya. A chronology of Chekhov's life, a list of performances of his plays in Russia and in France (1898-1950), notes on theatrical figures who played some role in Chekhov's life, and a brief bibliography of Russian and French works on Chekhov are also provided.

6 GURVICH, I.A. "Svoeobrazie Chekhovskogo realizma" [The originality of Chekhov's realism]. VLit, no. 9, pp. 149-65.

Examines Chekhov's own evaluation of his characters, arguing that he judges most harshly those who appear in his early works; in his later writings he expresses his sadness that they do not always live up to their potential. Here he also develops the notion of "involuntary guilt;" i.e., he creates a character who is clearly wrong but who is unable to be anything else.

7 HAGAN, JOHN. "Chekhov's Fiction and the Ideal of 'Objectivity'." PMLA 81:409-17.

Argues that the term "objectivity" (in the sense of moral indifference or reluctance to condemn) cannot be applied to Chekhov's fiction. But "objectivity" is very much a feature of his work when the term is understood as his dispassionate attitude while writing; as his impartiality and disinterestedness; as his practice of offering a diagnosis but not a cure for social ills; and as his technique of allowing characters and events to convey their meaning by implication rather than through authorial comment.

8 HYMAN, STANLEY EDGAR. "Dr. Chekhov's Diagnosis." In Standards: A Chronicle of Books for Our Time. A New Leader Book. New York: Horizon Press, pp. 153-57.

Reviews Seven Short Novels by Chekhov (New York: Bantam Books, 1963), noting that these seven works represent Chekhov at the height of his fictional powers and show his command of the whole range of Russian life. His stories make up his diagnosis of the human condition; he offers us no prescription since he knew that the malady was incurable.

9 KALMANOVSKII, E.S. "Sestry Prozorovy vchera, segodnia i zavtra" [The Prozorov sisters yesterday, today and tomorrow]. Zvezda, no. 1, pp. 204-12.

Discusses recent Soviet critical evaluations of

The Three Sisters and comments generally on the play's relevance to the contemporary world. Its characters, and Chekhov's characters as a group, refuse to hide their flaws and weaknesses. They are also "creative" and long to remold life according to their dreams.

10 KRAMER, KARL D. "Chekhov at the End of the Eighties: The Question of Identity." ÉSl 11:3-18.

Argues that Chekhov's literary crisis of the late 1880s is reflected in the stories of the period. These concern characters whose values are not shared by others around them and who are pressed to conform. In the five stories of the period Chekhov comes to grips with the problem of identity.

11 LEMAN-ABRIKOSOV, G. "Veroiatnyi istochink Vishnegogo sada A.P.Chekhova" [A probable source of Chekhov's Cherry Orchard]. RLit, no. 1, pp. 186-89.

Argues that a work by I.P. Belokonskii, Derevenskie vpechatleniia [Rural impressions], provided a source for Chekhov's play. The basic situation in Belokonskii's story, as well as its principal characters, parallel those of The Cherry Orchard.

12 PACHMUSS, TEMIRA. "Anton Chekhov in the Criticism of Zinaida Gippius." ÉSl 11:35-48.

Surveys Gippius' remarks on Chekhov (see 1904.7, 1904.8, 1925.4) and notes that she regarded his plays as monotonous and pessimistic. According to Gippius, his writings numb his readers' sensibilities and create indifference toward life. Still he is able to present life's trivial details with artistry and subtlety; he has a love-hate attitude toward life.

13 REEVE, F.D. "Three Years." In The Russian Novel. New York: McGraw-Hill, pp. 274-301.

Maintains that "Three Years" is "Chekhov's novel about 'family happiness'." It is a comic tragedy whose irony encompasses the ironies of life; it speaks directly to our century.

14 SEMANOVA, M.L. Chekhov i sovetskaia literatura: 1917-1935. [Chekhov and Soviet literature: 1917-1935]. Moscow-Leningrad: Sovetskii pisatel', 311 pp.

Traces the changing attitudes to Chekhov during the first eighteen years of the Soviet regime. Semanova surveys attitudes of critics, scholars, and political figures toward Chekhov and attempts to assess his influence on Soviet prose and drama.

15 SHAKH-AZIZOVA, T.K. Chekhov i zapadno-evropeiskaia drama ego vremeni [Chekhov and West-European drama of his time]. Moscow: Nauka, 151 pp.

Investigates Chekhov's links with the "new drama" of Zola, Ibsen, Hauptmann, Strindberg, Maeterlinck, Shaw, and others. The main traits of this drama were a deep-seated sense of malaise, loneliness as a fact of life, and a sense of frustration.

16 SHARYPKIN, D. "Chekhov o Strindberge" [Chekhov on Strindberg]. RLit, no. 3, pp. 162-66.

Discusses Chekhov's pronouncements on Strindberg, arguing that he was "an integral element of that literary atmosphere in which Chekhov lived." Interest in the problem of women's role in society was one common feature of both writers.

17 SHESTOV, LEV. "Anton Tchekhov: Creation from the Void." In Chekhov and Other Essays. New introduction by Sidney Monas. Ann Arbor: University of Michigan Press, pp. 3-60.

Translation of 1905.9.

18 SHKLOVSKII, VIKTOR. "A.P. Chekhov." In Povesti o proze: razmyshleniia i razbory [Tales about prose: reflections and critiques]. Vol. 2. Moscow: Khudozhestvennaia literatura, pp. 333-70.

An expanded version of 1959.28, it argues that Chekhov considered the cognition and the portrayal of some element of the external world as sufficient in itself to provide a plot for a story. "Sleepy" is constructed around several systems of repeated details; these sum up the situation of the heroine. Translated in part: 1976.15.

19 SMITH, J. OATES. "Chekhov and the 'Theater of the Absurd'." BuR, no. 3, pp. 44-58.

Argues that Chekhov's plays anticipate the modern theater of the absurd and compares them to the drama of Beckett and Ionesco. "The point at which Chekhov's meticulous symbolic naturalism touches the inexplicable, the ludicrous, the paradoxical, is the point at which his relationship to our contemporary 'theater of the absurd' is most clear."

20 STROEVA, M.N. [Stroyeva]. "The Three Sisters at the M.A.T." Translated by Elizabeth Hapgood. In Stanislavski and America: An Anthology from the Tulane Drama Review. Edited by Erica Munk. Introduction by Richard Schechner. New York: Hill & Wang, pp. 45-59.

Translation of a portion of 1955.16.

21 USMANOV, L.D. "Iz nabliudenii nad stilem pozdnego Chekhova" [Some observations on the style of the late Chekhov]. VLU, no. 2, pp. 95-98.

Examines Chekhov's technique, in his later stories, of modifying the author's words (his "voice") to reflect the speech habits, intonations, and mentality of a specific character. This new narrative technique is one of Chekhov's contributions to the short story.

22 VALENCY, MAURICE. The Breaking String: The Plays of Anton Chekhov. New York: Oxford University Press, 324 pp. Reprint. 1983.22.

Contains studies of Chekhov's major plays, their writing and production within the context of the Russian theater of his day; the links between his plays and his short stories and the influence of European drama of the day are also examined. Chekhov was "primarily an ironist and his plays were, on the whole, comedically conceived... His plays are full of laughter, but in each we hear the sound of the breaking string..." The plays focus on the breaking of "the golden string that connected man with his father on earth and his father in heaven, the age-old bond that tied the present to the past."

23 VIDUETSKAIA, I.P. "Mesto Chekhova v istorii russkogo realizma: k postanovke problemy" [Chekhov's place in the history of Russian realism: toward a formulation of the problem]. IAN, no. 1, pp. 31-42.

Argues that Chekhov's age was one of a "crisis of realism" in which the larger genres were unable to capture the new complexities of life. Chekhov's small forms manage to do this, however. Critics who wish to establish Chekhov's place in literature should determine precisely how his new techniques altered the concept of realism.

24 WILLIAMS, RAYMOND. Modern Tragedy. London: Chatto & Windus, pp. 139-46.

Argues that Chekhov is a "realist of breakdown;" the disintegration of his characters' society becomes their personal disintegration.

25 WINNER, THOMAS. Chekhov and his Prose. New York: Holt, Rinehart & Winston, 263 pp.

Surveys the evolution of Chekhov's prose from his earliest comic stories to "Betrothed," examining major themes, technical devices, and stylistic features. Midway through his career he produced a series of "searching stories" concerned with the quest for a "guiding idea." The fullest expression of his concern with vulgarity (poshlost') came with his trilogy and "Ionych;" subsequently a more optimistic tone enters his work.

1967

1 CHUKOVSKII, KORNEI. O Chekhove [About Chekhov]. Moscow: Khudozhestvennaia literatura, 205 pp.

Attempts to clarify various misconceptions about Chekhov's work and character and also includes material characterizing his artistic technique; argues that he was a master of expressive detail and could see the unique qualities of each of the innumerable forms of life. There is a striking disharmony between his sunny personality and his sombre works. Also reviews Thomas Winner's Chekhov and his Prose (1966.25) and discusses Chekhov's vocabulary and problems of translation, specifically in Hingley's The Oxford Chekhov (1965.7). Several reprints.

2 FREEDMAN, MORRIS. "Chekhov's Morality of Work." In The Moral Impulse: Modern Drama from Ibsen to the Present. Crosscurrents. Edited by Harry T. Moore. Preface by Harry T. Moore. Carbondale and Edwardsville: Southern Illinois University Press, pp. 31-44.

Reprinted from 1962.7.

3 GASSNER, JOHN. "The Duality of Chekhov." In Chekhov: A Collection of Critical Essays. Edited by Robert Louis Jackson. Twentieth Century Views, edited by Maynard Mack. Englewood Cliffs, N.J.: Prentice-Hall, pp. 175-83.

Attempts to reconcile the view of Chekhov as a cheerful writer of comedy with that of Chekhov the gloomy tragedian. His plays belong to the mixed, modern genre of tragicomedy or drama. He "transcends the superficiality that often adheres to optimistic literature and at the same time escaped the morbidity that besets pessimistic profundity." Reprinted: 1977.3.

4 -----. "The Modernity of Chekhov." In Dramatic Soundings: Evaluations and Retractions Culled from 30 Years of Dramatic Criticism. New York: Crown, pp. 69-75.

Characterizes Chekhov's drama generally, noting that he shifts its focus from external to internal action. His interests in science and social reform had profound influence on his writing. His modernism is progressive, active, and hopeful, "the modernism of health rather than disease;" it is thus a true classicism.

5 GILLÈS, DANIEL. Tchékhov, ou le spectateur désenchanté. Paris: Juillard, 505 pp.

A biographical study with critical discussion of selected stories and major plays. Gillès views Chekhov as a melancholy man, cordial to those around him yet essentially indifferent and insensitive to their problems. He avoided serious attachments with women and when he married he ensured that he maintained his freedom. As an artist he was essentially an impressionist. Translated: 1968.7.

6 -----. "Tchékov, poète invisible." RdP, September, pp. 81-94.

A general appreciation of Chekhov's work that regards him as an "invisible" poet who masked himself behind his realism. Chekhov in fact abandoned traditional realism. He poeticizes the everyday and the ordinary. The qualities of his works are the qualities of the man himself.

7 GROSSMAN, L.P. "Roman Nina Zarechnoi" [The romance of Nina Zarechnaya]. Prometei 2:218-89.

An account of the life of the actress Lidia (Lika) Mizinova and her relations with Chekhov and the writer I.N. Potapenko. Grossman traces the links of this relationship with the romantic triangle of Nina-Treplyov-Trigorin in The Seagull.

8 HINGLEY, RONALD. Preface, Introduction, Appendices, and Notes to The Oxford Chekhov. Vol. 2. Edited and translated by Ronald Hingley. London: Oxford University Press, pp. ix-xiii, 1-8, and 282-356.

Comments on problems of translating Platonov, Ivanov, and The Seagull; discusses their place in Chekhov's dramatic work; discusses the genesis of Platonov and the composition, texts, and variants of Ivanov and The Seagull. The first stagings of the latter two plays, their critical reception, and Chekhov's comments about them are summarized. Explanatory notes are also provided.

9 JACKSON, ROBERT LOUIS, ed. Chekhov: A Collection of Critical Essays. Twentieth Century Views, edited by Maynard Mack. Englewood Cliffs, N.J.: Prentice-Hall, 213 pp.

Contains articles on Chekhov generally, general studies of his drama, individual studies of his major plays, and an introduction by Jackson (see 1967.11). Includes a bibliography and 1905.4, 1908.5, 1914.5,

1927.2, 1944.2, 1946.2, 1948.4, 1949.2, 1955.18, 1957.2, 1958.20, 1960.14, 1960.47, 1967.3, and 1967.10.

10 -----. "Chekhov's Seagull: The Empty Well, the Dry Lake, and the Cold Cave." In Chekhov: A Collection of Critical Essays. Edited by Robert Louis Jackson. Twentieth Century Views, edited by Maynard Mack. Englewood Cliffs, N.J.: Prentice-Hall, pp. 99-111.

Chekhov uses the Oedipus myth and the myth of creation to express his concerns about illusion and reality in art and life and to convey the play's fundamental theme, the problem of talent. Konstantin's play expresses his personal hopes and fears and also reveals his weakness. Like so many of Chekhov's characters, he passively accepts the notion that his life is governed by fate and so fails in self-realization. Konstantin is trapped in an oedipal situation from which he lacks the courage to free himself. The Seagull also has the basic elements of the myth of Plato's cave: Nina leaves the world of illusions to make the difficult journey to reality; Konstantin prefers to remain in the world of shadows. Reprinted: 1981.1.

11 -----. "Perspectives on Chekhov." In Chekhov: A Collection of Critical Essays. Edited by Robert Louis Jackson. Twentieth Century Views, edited by Maynard Mack. Englewood Cliffs, N.J.: Prentice-Hall, pp. 1-20.

Attempts to establish a unified image of Chekhov. Reviews Chekhov's changing image in Russian criticism and argues that in the resolution of his main philosophical interest--"the relationship, most often tragic, between will and environment, freedom and necessity, man's character and his fate"--the split between Chekhov as optimist and Chekhov as pessimist can be reconciled.

12 KATAEV, V.B. "Povest' Chekhova Duel': k probleme obraza avtora" [Chekhov's tale "The Duel:" on the problem of the image of the author]. IAN 26:522-32.

Argues that Chekhov is not attempting to support or reflect the views of any of his characters in "The Duel;" the only expression of his own views comes in the phrase "no one knows the real truth." This is not an admission of his pessimism or confusion, however; it should be seen an an expression of his faith in the value of humanity's continuing quest for something better and a denial that any single person or theory has a monopoly on truth.

13 KERR, WALTER. Tragedy and Comedy. New York: Simon

& Schuster, pp. 234-40.

Notes that Chekhov's major plays have been most commonly produced as tragedies or near tragedies even though their author insisted they were comedies. This is because his are "comedies of the mind", and we are reluctant to see our own seriousness and intellectuality parodied.

14 LAU, JOSEPH S.M. "Ts'ao Yü, The Reluctant Disciple of Chekhov: A Comparative Study of Sunrise and The Cherry Orchard." MD 9:358-72.

Argues that Chekhov's "dramatic inconclusiveness" was his chief attraction for Ts'ao Yü. The latter's 1936 play Sunrise was modelled on Chekhov, but it fails because it misunderstands Chekhov's methods. Chekhov prefers to "show;" Ts'ao Yü to "tell."

15 LITERATURNYI MUZEI A.P. CHEKHOVA. Sbornik statei i materialov, no. 4 [An anthology of articles and materials]. Rostov-on-the-Don: Rostovskoe knizhnoe izdatel'stvo, 299 pp.

Contains nineteen articles, both specific and general, on Chekhov's works, romanticism, realism, comparisons with other writers, his language, and biographical material.

16 McCONKEY, JAMES. "In Praise of Chekhov." HudR 20:417-28.

Describes the author's very personal reaction to Chekhov's works, particularly to those stories that involve two antithetical characters. His writings convey the notion of the personality as a bulwark against the incomprehensibility of infinity and a sense of universal brotherhood.

17 MALIUGIN, L.A. Teatr nachinaetsia s literatury: stat'i [The theater begins with literature: articles]. Moscow: Iskusstvo, pp. 147-242.

Contains five essays on Chekhov's drama and its interpretation by Soviet critics including 1960.40, 1961.11, 1964.14, and 1965.8.

18 MORAVČEVICH, NICHOLAS. "The Dark Side of the Chekhovian Smile." Drama Survey 5:237-51.

Examines the two main interpretations of Chekhov's plays--as essentially optimistic and essentially pessimistic--and argues that the recent swing toward the optimistic interpretation derives from post-war Soviet re-evaluations of Chekhov's drama. There is a significant pessimistic dimension in Chekhov's plays, and if they are to be called comedies the term should be understood in its broadest sense, as used in Balzac's Comédie Humaine or Dante's Divina Commedia.

19 MROSIK, JULIUS. "Vom Symbolmotiv der Möwe in Čechovs 'Čajka' und seiner Herkunft: ein Beitrag zur vergleichenden Literaturwissenschaft." WSl 12:22-58.

Examines the function of the seagull as a recurring symbol in the play and discusses various sources that have influenced it, including Ibsen's Wild Duck and Pushkin's "Rusalka," as well as incidents from the life of the painter Levitan. Argues that Chekhov was influenced by Ibsen's dramatic technique, specifically by the latter's use of the symbol.

21 MYSHKOVSKAIA, L.M. "Tvorcheskie osobennosti Chekhova" [Distinctive features of Chekhov's art]. In O masterstve pisatelia: stat'i 1932-1959 gg. [On the writer's craft: articles, 1932-1959]. Compiled by K.N. Polonskaia. Moscow: Sovetskii pisatel', pp. 302-46.

An expanded version of 1959.20, it devotes more attention to his new approach to plot, the compactness and economy of his stories, the restraint and objectivity of his manner, his mastery of language and dialogue, and to the lyricism of his prose.

21 -----. "Tvorchestvo Chekhova: k 75-letiiu so dnia rozhdeniia A.P. Chekhova)" [Chekhov's work: for the 75th anniversary of his birth]. In O masterstve pisatelia: stat'i 1932-1959 gg. [On the writer's craft: articles, 1932-1959]. Compiled by K.N. Polonskaia. Moscow: Sovetskii pisatel', pp. 280-301.

Discusses Chekhov's significance as a master of the short story form and analyzes specific features of his stories. These contribute to his strict economy of means, the maximum exploitation of every element of the work. An examination of his revisions to his works shows that his economy and simplicity were achieved at great effort.

22 OFROSIMOV, Iu. "Tri sestry--segodnia" [The Three Sisters today]. NovŽ 89:269-72.

Surveys western productions of the play, arguing that they are all more or less reworkings of the MAT staging. But the Prague production by Otomar Krejča is original; it stresses Chekhov's contemporaneity and shows how he links today's theater with the theater of the past.

23 RUKALSKI, ZYGMUNT. "Fin-de-siècle in France and Russia." ÉSl 12:124-27.

Argues that the works of both Chekhov and Maupassant are filled with the anxiety, gloom, and spiritual malaise prevalent at the end of the nineteenth century. The climate of the fin-de-siècle was responsible for much of the despair of both writers.

24 SMOLKIN, M. "Shekspir v zhizni i tvorchestve Chekhova" [Shakespeare in Chekhov's life and works]. In Shekspirovskii sbornik [A collection of articles on Shakespeare]. Edited by A. Ankist. Moscow: Vserossiiskoe teatral'noe obshchestvo, pp. 72-84.

Chronicles Chekhov's lifelong interest in Shakespeare and argues that it was the total image of Shakespeare as an artist rather than specific themes or motifs that attracted him. The figure of Hamlet, however, was a powerful influence, and many of Chekhov's works deal with Russian "Hamletism."

25 STANISLAVLEVA, V.N. "Golos geroia i pozitsii pisatelia: o publitsisichnosti proizvedenii Chekhova 90-kh godov" [The character's voice and the author's position: on the publicistic element in Chekhov's work]. FN, no. 6, pp. 3-15.

Examines Chekhov's techniques of evaluating his characters and the major problems of his age. He does this covertly, "so that the reader does not notice," and so creates a new method of analyzing real life: social evils are revealed in the apparently most trivial aspects of life, and the most ordinary facts become the basis for a work of art. His approach is objective but still conveys his evaluations. In this way he awakens a sense of human dignity in his readers.

26 STATES, BERT O. "Chekhov's Dramatic Strategy." YR 61:212-24.

Notes that the basic structural pattern of Chekhov's plays is the visit of a group of outsiders to a family estate. His achievement was to give order and expression to the real but normally unseen pressures of existence without compromising their complexity. Reprinted in slightly revised form: 1971.30.

27 TRILLING, LIONEL. "Commentary to 'Enemies'." In The Experience of Literature: A Reader With Commentaries. Garden City, N.Y.: Doubleday, pp. 556-59.

Notes Chekhov's characteristic trait of modesty and the absence of the heroic in his work. In "Enemies" Dr. Kirilov asserts his right to be thought heroic because of his suffering, but in trying thus to assert his moral superiority over Abogin he diminishes his stature.

28 -----. "Commentary to The Three Sisters." In The Experience of Literature: A Reader With Commentaries. Garden City, N.Y: Doubleday, pp. 250-55.

Argues that the play presents characters who are very close to us, partly because Chekhov shows clearly the role of environment in their lives. Chekhov's statement that the play was a "gay comedy" was directed to the actors; when played briskly in comic style the play will lead the audience to greater detachment and thought.

29 ZOSHCHENKO, MIKHAIL. "O komicheskom v proizvedeniiakh Chekhova" [On the comic element in Chekhov's works]. VLit, no. 2, pp. 150-55.

Argues that Chekhov's humor is not "all-forgiving" but satirical, and his satire is directed against "lies, stupidity, hypocrisy, servility, arrogance, callousness." The satirist is one who sees and describes life's negative aspects while being aware that life offers other features as well. In creating weak, despondent, and divided people Chekhov was creating satire.

1968

1 AL'TSHULLER, A. Ia. "Chekhov i Aleksandrinskii teatr ego vremeni" [Chekhov and the Alexander Theater of his time]. RLit, no. 3, pp. 164-75.

Makes a detailed study, based on new materials, of Chekhov's relationship with the Alexander Theater where his Ivanov and The Seagull were first staged.

2 ATCHITY, KENNETH JOHN. "Chekhov's Infernal Island." RS 36:335-40.

The Island of Sakhalin should not be considered simply a social document; it is "literature-in-the-making, the raw material of Chekhov's realism." The book's effect is like that of Dante's trip through Hell.

3 BIALYI, G.A. "Zametki o khudozhestvennoi manere A.P. Chekhova" [Remarks on Chekhov's artistic manner]. Uchenye zapiski Leningradskogo gos. universiteta im. A.A. Zhdanova, no. 339. Seriia filologicheskikh nauk. No. 72, Russkaia literatura, pp. 126-46.

Surveys remarks about Chekhov's work made by his contemporaries, generally those who were readers rather than critics. Most comments concern the newness and freshness of Chekhov's manner. His objectivity and apparent lack of tendency troubled his contemporaries. Bialyi also discusses comparisons made by readers between Chekhov and contemporary writers. Reprinted: 1973.7.

4 BRERETON, GEOFFREY. "The Tragic in Comedy: Chekhov." In Principles of Tragedy: A Rational Examination of the Tragic Concept in Life and Literature. London: Routledge & Kegan Paul, pp. 214-22.

Argues that Chekhov's great plays are comedies. His characters are not tragic because even though we may sympathize with them we cannot respect or admire them to any great degree.

5 CHICHERIN, A.V. "Rol' protivitel'noi intonatsii v proze Chekhova" [The role of adversative intonation in Chekhov's prose]. In Idei i stil': o prirode poeticheskogo slova [Idea and style: on the nature of poetic language]. 2d ed. Moscow: Sovetskii pisatel', pp. 314-20.

Examines Chekhov's use of indirect expressions of thought in which affirmations are presented indecisively or partially refuted within the same statement. Chekhov's style is by no means simple but reflects the compexity and confusion of life as he saw it. Translated: 1976.15.

6 CROYDEN, MARGARET. "'People Just Eat Their Dinner': The absurdity of Chekhov's Doctors." TQ, no. 3, pp. 130-37.

Argues that the essence of Chekhov's creativity lies not in naturalism but in the Absurd. The doctors in his plays reflect his own philosophical and social observations; his doctors are very much aware of the meaninglessness of existence.

7 GILLÈS, DANIEL. Chekhov: Observer Without Illusion. Translated by Charles Lam Markmann. New York: Funk & Wagnalls, 436 pp.

Translation of 1967.5.

8 HAMBURGER, H. "The Function of the Verbum Dicendi in Čexov's Smert' cinovnika." In Dutch Contributions to the Sixth International Congress of Slavicists. Slavistic Printings and Reprintings, no. 86. Edited by A.G.F. van Holk. The Hague: Mouton, pp. 98-121.

Makes a linguistic analysis of "The Death of a Clerk."

9 HINGLEY, RONALD. Preface, Introduction, Appendices,

and Notes to The Oxford Chekhov. Vol. 1. Edited and translated by Ronald Hingley. London: Oxford University Press, pp. ix-xii, 1-7, and 171-203.

Comments on problems of translating Chekhov's short plays; discusses their place within his literary career as a whole; discusses the composition and the texts of "On the Highway," "Swan Song," "The Bear," "The Proposal," "Tatyana Repin," "A Tragedian in Spite of Himself," "The Wedding," "The Anniversary," "Smoking is Bad For You," and "The Night Before the Trial." Explanatory notes for the plays are also provided.

10 KATAEV, V.B. "Geroi i ideia v proizvedeniiakh Chekhova 90-kh godov" [Character and idea in Chekhov's works of the 1890s]. VMU, no. 6, pp. 35-47.

Examines the relationship between the ideas expressed by Chekhov's characters and the author's own ideas. Unlike most of the writers of his age Chekhov does not seek to express specific ideas in his stories; rather he shows how every idea or opinion is dependent on circumstances. "Truths" uttered by characters are relative and not absolute. Chekhov's sense of the complexity of life is expressed not by any one character but by the entire structure of the work.

11 -----. "O roli shkoly G.A. Zakhar'ina v tvorchestve Chekhova" [On the role of the school of G.A. Zakhar'in in Chekhov's work]. FN, no. 6, pp. 104-07.

Argues that the principles taught by one of Chekhov's professor's of medicine, G.A. Zakharin, had a profound influence on his methods of portraying characters. Zakharin insisted that the doctor should not treat some abstract disease but concern himself with the specific complaints of his patient. "The individualization of each case" was Zakharin's principle in medicine and Chekhov's in literature. Thus the "ideas" in Chekhov's work do not exist in the abstract but are "symptoms" arising from the experience of the individual who expresses them.

12 KUZNETSOVA, M.V. A.P. Chekhov: voprosy masterstva [Chekhov: questions of craftsmanship]. Part 1. Sverdlovsk: Sredne-Ural'skoe knizhnoe izdatel'stvo, 236 pp.

Examines the evolution of Chekhov's prose technique. The main themes of his early work are discussed, and the particular qualities of his humor are outlined. Chekhov's narrative techniques in his later works are compared with his earlier ones; his techniques of conveying the psychology of his characters and his methods of composing his stories are also discussed.

13 LAHR, JOHN. "Pinter and Chekhov: the Bond of Naturalism." TDR, no. 2, pp. 137-145.

Pinter and Chekhov show a "passion for objectivity and clinical analysis of the human animal." In Chekhov, however, the world of nature and of objects still has a human measure; Pinter's characters are abstracted from their environment.

14 LELCHUK, ALAN. "An Analysis of Technique in Chekhov's 'Anyuta'." SSF 6:609-18.

Makes a close analysis of the story, arguing that it is a good example of Chekhov's craftsmanship and reveals how he mastered the art of the short story form. His material here is modest, but his technical skill makes it memorable. Chekhov breaks up the time sequence into five blocks of action; this allows him to convey insights into his characters and to control the reader's reactions.

15 LETTENBAUER, WILHELM. "Die Funktion idiomatischer Ausdrücke in der stilistischen Struktur von Werken A.P. Čechovs." Slavistischer Studien zum vi. Internationalen Slavistenkongress in Prag 1968. Edited by Erwin Koschmieder and Maximilian Braun. Munich: Rudolf Trofenik, pp. 496-509.

Discusses the concept of idiomatic expressions generally and examines their use in Chekhov's works, principally in his plays. Such expressions help convey the effect of everyday speech. Chekhov also uses many literary quotations which enrich the texture of his dialogue.

16 McLEAN, HUGH. "Čexov's 'V ovrage': Six Antipodes." In American Contributions to the Sixth International Congress of Slavists. Vol. 2, Literary Contributions. Edited by William E. Harkins. The Hague and Paris: Mouton, 285-305.

Examines fundamental polarities in the story: its specific, concrete world and its general significance; the use of metonymy and the use of metaphor; the tendency toward objective, "scientific" description and the tendency toward emotional appeals to the reader. The story's impact derives from the skill with which these polarities are kept in balance.

17 MATHEWSON, RUFUS W. Jr. "Intimations of Mortality in Four Čexov Stories." In American Contributions to the Sixth International Congress of Slavists. Vol. 2, Literary Contributions. Edited by William

E. Harkins. The Hague and Paris: Mouton, pp. 261-83.

Analyzes scenes from four stories in which the central character confronts the larger natural world and ponders his place within it. In "The Kiss" Ryabovich contemplates the river and discovers his own mortality, losing his attachment to life. Gusev's ordered peasant world is shattered as he stares at the raging sea. In the cemetery Ionych is offered a choice between life and death. Gurov's aesthetic response to the sea ("The Lady With the Little Dog") is transformed into an ethical insight and he is liberated from the empty forms of his public life. In each scene the response to the beauty of nature is linked with death.

18 MELCHINGER, SIEGFRIED. Anton Tschechow. Friedrichs Dramatiker des Welttheaters. Vol. 57. Velber, Germany: Friedrich Verlag, 150 pp.

Includes a chronology, a biographical essay, an essay on Chekhov's views on the theater, brief studies of his plays, and an account of stage productions in Europe. Selected bibliography. Illustrated. Translated: 1972.20.

19 MILLER, J. WILLIAM. "Anton Chekhov." In Modern Playwrights at Work. Vol. 1. New York: Samuel French, pp. 114-59.

Examines in detail Chekhov's technique as a playwright, discussing his relations with the Russian theater of his day and his aesthetic credo as a dramatist. Miller follows Chekhov's working methods in detail, including descriptions of the genesis of his plays, their gradual development, the evolution of their characters, and his reworking and rewriting.

20 MULLER, HERBERT J. "The Realism of Chekhov." In The Spirit of Tragedy. New York: Alfred A. Knopf, pp. 283-93.

Argues that The Three Sisters is a tragedy even though it fits none of the usual definitions of the genre. The play is not high tragedy, but it enriches the art of the drama; it is a realistic tragedy which has no catastrophe and which is played out at the level of everyman.

21 NILSSON, NILS ÅKE. "Leksika i stilistika pisem Chekhova" [The vocabulary and stylistics of Chekhov's letters]. SSl 14:33-58.

Examines Chekhov's letters as examples of a literary genre, focusing on their style rather than on their content. The style of his letters displays a whole range of features that depart from the literary norm: increased use of Biblical and Church Slavonic expressions; "bureaucratic" language; "barbarisms", including Greek, Latin, French, and German expressions; dialects such as Ukrainianisms and South Russian features; colloquialisms and slang; and neologisms, both his own original ones and those typical of his era. His letters display great lexical richness and are the "linguistic laboratory" for his prose.

22 -----. Studies in Čechov's Narrative Technique: "The Steppe" and "The Bishop." Stockholm Slavic Studies, no. 2. Stockholm: Almqvist & Wiksell, 110 pp.

"The Steppe" and "The Bishop" respectively begin and end Chekhov's mature period as a writer. "The Steppe" reveals some inconsistency in narrative technique, shifting between Egoroshka's perceptions and those of the narrator or blending the two. "The Bishop," "a perfect story," shows full mastery of technique. It also contains a resolution of the problem of "Nature's indifference" posed in earlier stories.

23 RÉV, MARIJA. "Chekhov i nekotorye problemy russkoi literatury kontsa 19 v." [Chekhov and some problems of Russian literature at the end of the nineteenth century]. SSASH 14:341-52.

Discusses the "crisis" in Russian literature in the 1880s and examines the responses of the "young writers"--Chekhov, Garshin, and Korolenko--to it. Chekhov helped renew Russian realism through his prose innovations: the use of deeply significant detail, the blending of author's and character's speech, and, generally, the practice of basing his works solidly on concrete facts of everyday life.

24 ROSSBACHER, PETER. "Čexov's Fragment 'Solomon'." SEEJ 12:27-34.

Discusses the fragment for a play about Solomon found in Chekhov's notebook, arguing that it should be seen in the context of his spiritual quest. Chekhov was deeply disturbed by life's inexplicability. His Solomon experiences life as full of despair and terror because he can find no meaning in it. Chekhov's artistic vision had distinct affinities with the book of Ecclesiates, but his heroes are unable to follow Solomon's advice: "seize the day."

25 SIMMONS, ERNEST J. "Tolstoy and Chekhov." Midway, no. 4, pp. 91-104.

Discusses Tolstoy's attitude to Chekhov and

comments on the role of Tolstoyism in Chekhov's work. Chekhov's skeptical mind and his medical training were the main causes of his rejection of Tolstoyism even though he continued to admire Tolstoy the artist. But the two writers' approaches to fiction were fundamentally different.

26 SPEIRS, LOGAN. "Tolstoy and Chekhov: 'The Death of Ivan Ilych' and 'A Dreary Story.'" OR, no. 8, pp. 81-93.

Argues that Chekhov's story "reveals the unsatisfactoriness of 'The Death of Ivan Ilych' perfectly." Tolstoy's work was written to a preconceived scheme; Chekhov explores the same theme but does so without a predetermined ideological framework and so discovers somethin new. His hero is more interesting and more alive than Ivan Ilych. Tolstoy's story expresses his own terror of death; Chekhov's expresses only his hero's despair.

27 STYAN, J.L. The Dark Comedy: The Development of Modern Comic Tragedy. 2d ed. Cambridge: Cambridge University Press, pp. 57-64; 74-106, and passim.

Reprinted from 1962.19.

28 TOVSTONOGOV, GEORGII. "Chekhov's Three Sisters at the Gorky Theatre." Translated by Joyce Vining. TDR, no. 2, pp. 146-55.

Describes two extremes in the traditional Russian interpretation of Chekhov's plays: the melancholy pessimism of the MAT, and the relentless optimism of the Stalin era. Tovstonogov's own 1965 production of The Three Sisters attempted to modernize Chekhov by stressing the complexity of the characters and underlining the fact that they themselves bear most of the responsibility for their failures. Reprinted: 1977.3.

29 WILLIAMS, RAYMOND. "Anton Chekhov." In Drama from Ibsen to Brecht. London: Chatto & Windus, pp. 101-111.

A revised version of 1965.17. More emphasis is placed on examining Chekhov's alterations to dramatic conventions. His last plays do not revolve around an isolated figure battling stagnating forms of social life; rather a whole group of characters wants liberation but are defeated before the struggle can begin. Chekhov develops a new kind of dialogue to express this mood of questioning and defeat. His art represents both the triumph and the crisis of naturalist drama and theater.

30 -----. "The Seagull, by Chekhov." In Drama in

Performance. The New Thinkers' Library. Edited by Raymond Williams. London: C.A. Watts, pp. 107-33.

Describes the first performance of the play by the MAT and analyzes three scenes from the point of view of their performance on stage. The Seagull illustrates a contradiction: high naturalist drama seems to make the externals of life real in theatrical terms, but in fact it seeks to show that these are only a limited reality in theatrical terms.

1969

1 CONRAD, JOSEPH L. "Čexov's 'An Attack of Nerves'." SEEJ 13:429-43.

Examines the structure of the story generally and argues that Chekhov uses many stylistic devices and details reminiscent of Garshin's work. Chekhov's attitude to Garshin is complex and difficult to determine; he remains strictly objective toward his material, however. The story marks the end of Chekhov's "transitional period" and signifies his emergence as a major writer.

2 CROSS, A.G. "The Breaking Strings of Chekhov and Turgenev." SEER 47:510-13.

Comments on Valency's interpretation of the sound of the breaking string in The Cherry Orchard (see 1966.22) and notes that Turgenev's "Bezhin Meadow" and his prose poem "The Nymphs" contain similar sounds.

3 CURTIN, CONSTANCE. "Bridging Devices in Chekhov's 'The Bishop'." CSS 3:705-11.

Argues that Chekhov uses bridging devices such as the repetition of a particular word or various sound effects to link elements of his stories together. "The Bishop" provides a case study; its use of sounds and details unite diverse structural elements and help convey the story's meaning.

4 De BEAR NICOL, BERNARD, ed. "Anton Chekhov--Naturalist or 'Absurdist'?" In Varieties of Dramatic Experience: Discussions on Dramatic Forms and Themes Between Stanley Evernden, Roger Hubank, Thora Burnley Jones, and Bertrand de Bear Nicol. London: University of London Press, pp. 173-92.

Consists of a discussion about naturalist and absurdist elements in The Three Sisters and The Cherry Orchard. One view sees Chekhov escaping from naturalism by becoming the most extreme of the naturalists; his plays progressively represent his growing awareness of the absurdity of life. A second view focuses on defining terms and on dramatic technique, arguing that labelling him an absurdist reduces the depth of his observations on people and "weakens the potential of his poetic achievement."

5 JARRELL, RANDALL. Notes on The Three Sisters by Anton Chekhov. Translated and with notes by Randall Jarrell. New York: Macmillan, pp. 101-160.

Contains Jarrell's uncompleted notes on the play as edited by his wife. Discusses the play generally, arguing that its inconsistencies and ambiguities reflect the "randomness" of real life. The play's themes and its setting are examined, each of the characters is discussed, and the specific qualities of each act are enumerated. "An essential part of the play is the meaning of life as opposed to the meaninglessness of life."

6 -----. "Six Russian Short Novels." In The Third Book of Criticism. New York: Farrar, Straus & Giroux, pp. 267-75.

Argues that Chekhov's "Ward Six" "forcibly contradicts" Tolstoy's analysis of human experience. For Chekhov the immediacy of pure experience is ultimate; one must simply do one's duty in day-to-day living. The story suggests that Tolstoy's teaching of non-resistance implies taking evil for granted.

7 KARLINSKY, SIMON. "Chekhov, Beloved and Betrayed." Delos, no. 3, pp. 192-97.

Criticizes two translations of Chekhov's non-fiction. The Hellman-Lederer edition of his letters (1955.4) misses many of his idioms, is inaccurate, and has a number of omissions. The translation of The Island of Sakhalin by Luba and Michael Terpak (New York: Washington Square Press, 1967) is even worse.

8 KERR, WALTER. "Chekhov and Others." In Thirty Plays Hath November: Pain and Pleasure in the Contemporary Theater. New York: Simon & Schuster, pp. 146-59.

Comments on Chekhov's last four plays and on the nature of his comedy generally. American productions of his plays have ignored their comedy and made them too tearful. The MAT's production does allow some of the comedy of The Cherry Orchard to emerge, but still treats the play more seriously than Chekhov would have liked. The Cherry Orchard shows the delicacy and control of his comedy.

9 KHALIZEV, V.E. "A.P. Chekhov i meditsinskaia obshchestvennost' moskovskoi gubernii" [Chekhov and the medical community of Moscow Province]. IAN 28:66-70.

Examines Chekhov's contacts with zemstvo doctors in the Moscow area, arguing that these show he was very much involved with the new social and ideological currents of his day. Khalizev surveys Chekhov's correspondence with various zemstvo doctors, arguing on the basis of his and their letters that he generally shared their "progressive" views.

10 -----. "P'esa A.P. Chekhova Vishnevyi sad" [Chekhov's play The Cherry Orchard]. In Russkaia klassicheskaia literatura: razbory i analizy [Russian classical literature: critiques and analyses]. Edited by D. Ustiuzhanin. Moscow: Prosveshchenie, pp. 358-88.

Re-examines the play, arguing that its central figures are not portrayed as schematically as many Soviet critics have suggested. Gaev and Ranevskaya are not exploiters but sensitive people who personify aristocratic culture; but at the same time they are frivolous and irresponsible landowners. Lopakhin, a paradoxical character, also does not know how to care for the orchard. Trofimov is portrayed sympathetically but is naive and narrow-minded. None of the major characters is thus worthy of inheriting the material and spiritual wealth symbolized by the cherry orchard.

11 LAFFITTE, SOPHIE. "La personnalité de Tchékhov." CSP 11:251-60.

Notes that Chekhov's essential personality remains a mystery even though we know the external facts of his life in great detail. His dislike of preaching and his avoidance of subjectivity have meant that he left few clues about his outlook on life. But a careful and thoughtful analysis of his works reveals his detachment, moral stoicism, rationality, and essentially tragic view of life.

12 LAU, JOSEPH S.M. "The Peking Man and Ivanov: Portraits of Two Superfluous Men." ConL 10:85-102.

Compares Chekhov's Ivanov with Ts'ao Yü's play Peking Man (1940) which employs a number of Chekhovian dramatic techniques. Chekhov, and Russian literature generally, had appeal to the Chinese because early twentieth-century China had much in common with late nineteenth-century Russia. The "superfluous man" was a feature of both societies.

13 LINKOV, V.Ia. "K probleme ideinogo obobshcheniia v proze A.P. Chekhova" [On the problem of ideological generalization in Chekhov's prose]. FN, no. 6, pp. 49-57.

Investigates the problem of drawing general conclusions from the specific events and characters presented in Chekhov's works. One can generalize on the basis of utterances of characters, but only after taking into account the full circumstances and the context in which the utterance was made.

14 LITERATURNYI MUZEI A.P. CHEKHOVA. Sbornik statei i materialov [A collection of articles and materials]. No. 5. Rostov-on-the Don: Rostovskoe knizhnoe izdatel'stvo, 177 pp.

Contains fourteen articles on various aspects of Chekhov's works, his relationship with other writers, and his reception in Russia.

15 MEILAKH, B.S. "Problemnaia situatsiia, tvorchestvo i chitatel': Chekhov" [The problematic situation, the work, and the reader: Chekhov]. In Talant pisatelia i protsessy tvorchestva [The writer's talent and the processes of creation]. Leningrad: Sovetskii pisatel', pp. 305-435.

Attempts to describe Chekhov's approach to literature and his creative process generally by analyzing his diaries and pronouncements made about his art in letters and to contemporaries. Chekhov wanted to depict the inner worlds of ordinary people. His method of doing this combines artistic talent with scientific analysis. His later work is less stricly objective and more prone to making judgements, albeit implicit ones, about his subjects. His notebooks allow us to follow his creative process and to see the close attention he paid to the "architecture" of his works.

16 MEIERKHOL'D, VSEVOLOD. "The Naturalistic Theater and the Theater of Mood." In Meyerhold on Theatre. Translated and edited with commentary by Edward Braun. New York: Hill & Wang, pp. 23-34.

Translation of 1908.5.

17 PAPERNYI, Z.S. "Ispytanie geroia: o povesti A.P. Chekhova 'Ionych'" [The trial of a character: on Chekhov's "Ionych"]. In Russkaia klassicheskaia literatura: razbory i analizy [Russian classical literature: critiques and analyses]. Edited by D. Ustiuzhanin. Moscow: Prosveshchenie, pp. 389-405.

Argues that interpretations of Chekhov's works must not be categorical or final. Examines the genesis of

"Ionych" and makes a close reading of the text. Ionych is a divided character, both an idealist and a gross materialist. He is tested by life and fails the test.

18 POKUSAEV, E.I. "Ob ideino-khudozhestvennoi kontseptsii rasskaza A.P. Chekhova 'Vragi'" [On the ideological and artistic conception of Chekhov's story "Enemies"]. In _Ot "Slovo o polku Igoreve" do "Tikhogo Dona:" Sbornik statei k 90-letiiu N.K. Piksanova_ [From _The Tale of the Host of Igor_ to _The Quiet Don_: a collection of articles for the ninetieth birthday of N.K. Piksanov]. Edited by K.D. Muratova, F. Ia. Priima, N.I. Prutskov, and N.N. Monakhov. Leningrad: Nauka, pp. 183-90.

Takes issue with Ermilov's interpretation of the story (1951.1), arguing that Chekhov's sympathies are not reserved for only one character but are given to both. Both characters are deceived, both suffer, and both are wrong to be angry at one another.

19 POLOTSKAIA, E.A. "Vnutrenniaia ironiia v rasskazakh i povestiakh Chekhova" [Internal irony in Chekhov's short stories and tales]. In _Masterstvo russkikh klassikov: sbornik_ [The craftsmanship of the Russian classics: a collection]. Moscow: Sovetskii pisatel', pp. 438-93.

Chekhov's early works frequently use direct and open irony. After 1886 the irony becomes hidden and "internal," expressed not by the author's words but by the entire context of the work itself; the work still appears to be wholly objective, however. Internal irony is "dynamic" in that it reveals itself gradually through the movement of the narrative.

20 RÉV, MARIJA. "Ob ideino-khudozhestvennom svoeobrazii rasskaza A.P. Chekhova 'Vragi'" [On the ideological-artistic distinctiveness of Chekhov's story "Enemies"]. _Annales universitatis scientiarum Budapestiensis_. Sectio philologica moderna. Vol. 1. Pp. 161-70.

Analyzes the structure of the story, arguing that it displays remarkable economy of means. This economy arises from Chekhov's skillful use of dialogue, from his use of parallels and antitheses, and from his own laconic comments.

21 ROSSBACHER, PETER. "The Function of Insanity in Čexov's 'The Black Monk' and Gogol's 'Notes of a Madman'." _SEEJ_ 13:191-99.

Argues that Chekhov's works contain a definable literary type, a despondent, bored, and suffering hero.

Kovrin, sane, is a typical Chekhovian character; the insane Kovrin is an antitype. He no longer suffers because he can go beyond the point where the literary type became stuck. He reveals Chekhov's longing for a better life where happiness is the norm.

22 RUDNITSKII, KONSTANTIN. Rezhisser Meierkhol'd [Meyerhold the director]. Moscow: Nauka, pp. 13-21, 24-26, 33-39, 474-78, and passim.

Discusses the MAT's production of The Seagull and comments on Chekhov's relationship with the company. Meyerhold's productions of The Cherry Orchard and of Chekhov's one-act plays are also described. Translated: 1981.37.

23 RUKALSKI, ZYGMUNT. "Maupassant and Chekhov: Similarities." CSP 11:346-58.

Discusses a number of points of similarity in their techniques: both writers are objective and both use the settings of their works expressively. Both deal with themes of selfish love, selfless love, and the vanity of existence. The two writers' differences are examined in 1971.26.

24 YARMOLINSKY, AVRAHM. "Anton Chekhov--Humane to the Tips of His Fingers." In The Russian Literary Imagination. New York: Funk & Wagnalls, pp. 83-110.

Reprinted, slightly revised and abbreviated, from 1947.7.

25 ZALYGIN, SERGEI. "Moi poet" [My poet]. Moskva, no. 5, pp. 88-131. Several reprints.

A personal response to Chekhov's work and personality that stresses his qualities of rationality, restraint, and compassion. He sought solitude and detachment as a means of dedicating himself to creative work. His tact is expressed in his refusal to allow his genius to be exempt from the most ordinary human demands. His works convey a notion of a human norm or ideal which does not exist in nature but which ought to. His new method of diagnosis of human dilemmas uncovered new qualities and complexities in human beings. Translated: 1972.29.

1970

1 ADLER, JACOB H. "Two Hamlet Plays: The Wild Duck and The Sea Gull." JML 1:226-48.

Examines the relationship between the three plays, arguing that the first and second provided sources for the third, and that The Wild Duck provides a critique of Hamlet as The Seagull does of The Wild Duck. Chekhov's play has many parallels with both Ibsen's and Shakespeare's; although his attitude to Ibsen is ambiguous, he probably borrowed the notion of a "Hamlet play" from him.

2 BALABANOVICH, E.Z. Chekhov i Chaikovskii [Chekhov and Tchaikovsky]. Moscow: Moskovskii rabochii, 184 pp.

Outlines the acquaintance of the two artists, discussing their views on each other's art and Chekhov's attitude to music generally. Balabanovich argues that Chekhov's works are profoundly musical--in their language, their stress on sound, their structure, and their lyrical intonation. Chekhov's and Tchaikovsky's works share a common artistic make-up and their fundamental aesthetic principles are similar.

3 CONRAD, JOSEPH L. "Čexov's 'Veročka': A Polemical Parody." SEEJ 14:465-74.

Argues that "Verochka" parodies Turgenev's "Asya" in particular and aspects of Turgenev's style generally. Chekhov's Ognev is a descendant of the superfluous man; the plot of "Verochka" captures the essence of Turgenev's love plots.

4 DRIVER, TOM F. "Anton Chekhov." In Modern Query: A History of the Modern Theatre. New York: Delacorte Press, pp. 217-48.

Notes that Chekhov's importance as a dramatist lies not in the quantity of his playwriting nor in its excellence but in its originality and depth. His transformation of the "Aristotelian tradition" of western drama is radical: his plays are constructed in a new manner so that their meaning emerges not from the traditional pattern of action but from the expression of a sensibility. Chekhov's drama imitates "the texture of certain selected moments in life."

5 GROMOV, PAVEL. "Stanislavskii, Chekhov, Meierkhol'd" [Stanislavksy, Chekhov, Meyerhold]. Teatr, no. 1, pp. 83-89.

Examines Chekhov's influences on Meyerhold and Stanislavsky. Argues that Treplyov's play in The Seagull is not intended as an attack on literary modernism; it is, rather, a restatement of some philosophical ideas of the age, notably those of Vladimir Solovyov, and of problems of aesthetics that concerned both Chekhov and the young

Meyerhold. All three sought new directions for the drama and theater.

6 GURVICH, I.A. <u>Proza Chekhova: chelovek i deistvitel'nost'</u> [Chekhov's prose: man and reality]. Moscow: Khudozhestvennaia literatura, 183 pp.

Examines a selection of Chekhov's stories to show how he portrays his characters' relationship to their surroundings, their daily routine, and their own ideas. Argues that Chekhov's writings form a single, seamless whole with a single "general idea," that of "universal uneasiness." The ideas expressed in his works are important not so much for their content as for what they reveal about the one who expresses them. His characters are often unintentionally guilty; they are pushed by circumstances into living lives they know are wrong.

7 -----. "'Skuchnaia istoriia': rasskaz i rasskazchik u Chekhova" ["A Dreary Story:" story and narrator in Chekhov]. <u>RLit</u>, no. 3, pp. 125-30.

Argues that the narrator's conclusion about the absence of a "general idea" in his life should not be taken at face value. He is too critical of himself and tends to take temporary phenomena for permanent ones.

8 HINGLEY, RONALD. Preface, Introduction, Appendices, Notes, and Bibliography to <u>The Oxford Chekhov</u>. Vol. 5. Translated and edited by Ronald Hingley. London: Oxford University Press, pp. ix-xi, 1-15, and 225-57.

Discusses problems of translating Chekhov's stories of 1899 to 1891; describes Chekhov's literary career during that period, including his journey to Sakhalin and its influence on his writing. Historical and cultural background to "The Princess," "A Dreary Story," "Horse Thieves," "Gusev," "Peasant Women," and "The Duel" are included. Discusses individually the writing, the texts, and the variants of these stories. Explanatory notes for the stories and a bibliogrpahy of English-language translations and critical works are included.

9 KARLINSKY, SIMON. "Nabokov and Chekhov: The Lesser Russian Tradition." <u>TriQ</u> 17:7-16.

Compares the reception of Chekhov and Nabokov, noting that both were criticized for supposedly disregarding the humanitarian tradition of Russian literature. The two writers share concerns such as a deep respect for their chosen art form independent of its ideology, and an interest in science and the natural world that contributes to a precision of observation.

10 KENDLE, BURTON. "The Elusive Horses in The Sea Gull." MD 13:63-66.

Sees the repeated motif of the request for horses as an expression of the characters' desire to escape from the boredom and "spiritual imprisonment" of the Sorin estate. Nina, however, is the only one who manages to use her horses.

11 KRAMER, KARL D. The Chameleon and the Dream: The Image of Reality in Čexov's Stories. Slavistic Printings and Reprintings, no. 78. The Hague and Paris: Mouton, 182 pp.

Focuses on two aspects of Chekhov's vision of life: the sense of personal identity, and his characters' concept of external reality. Chekhov's characters in fact have no sense of personal identity; they are chameleons whose personalities alter with circumstances. In later stories Chekhov shifts his emphasis to "the dream:" he depicts a character's feelings about reality rather than the reality itself. The post-1893 stories show a resigned and even cheerful attitude: man's relationship to himself and to external reality is unstable, and all values are relative. The result is the "story of ambiguity" in which the chameleon triumphs over the dream.

12 Le FLEMING, L.S.K. "The Structural Role of Language in Chekhov's Later Stories." SEER 48:323-40.

Examines Chekhov's revisions of three stories ("An Unpleasantness," "The Princess," "The Name-Day Party") and argues that he chose his language to be as comprehensible and unobtrusive as possible. Thus he deleted words that might draw attention to themselves, thereby allowing the reader to focus his attention on the content of his language rather than on the language itself.

13 MATEŠIĆ, JOSIP. "Wiederholung als Stilmittel in der Erzählprosa Čechovs." WSl 15:17-25.

Examines Chekhov's repetition of words, phrases, or sentences and how these contribute to his economy of means and to the rhythm of his prose.

14 MORAVČEVICH, NICHOLAS. "Chekhov and Naturalism: From Affinity to Divergence." CompD, no. 4, pp. 219-40.

Chekhov's early writings show a distinct affinity for naturalism, but in the early 1890s he began developing his own new and revolutionary impressionist techniques in the drama. Reprinted: 1977.3.

15 NAG, MARTIN. "On the Aspects of Time and Place in Chekhov's Dramaturgy." SSl 16:23-33.

Analyzes the relationship between the actual time and place plan and the writer's time and place plan in Chekhov's last four plays. He both uses and criticizes Ibsen's technique in that he attempts to convey the "real" sense of time and place on the stage, yet to do so "anti-dramatically."

16 POSPELOV, G.N. "Stil' povestei Chekhova" [The style of Chekhov's tales]. In Problemy literaturnogo stilia [Problems of literary style]. Moscow: Izdatel'stvo Moskovskogo universiteta, pp. 283-329.

Describes Chekhov's new principles of plot construction in his tales of the 1890s and 1900s. He tends here to avoid conflicts based on antitheses of characters and to develop a whole series of narrative techniques that shift the emphasis of the plot to the character's thoughts about his surroundings. Translated in part: 1976.15.

17 PRIESTLY, J.B. Anton Chekhov. International Profiles, edited by Edward Storer. London: International Textbook Company, 87 pp.

Takes a very personal view of Chekhov's life and art, arguing that he was at his best in the drama rather than in the short story, where he tends to overemphasize gloom and despair and where the limitations of the form itself sometimes compel him to distort human experience. Includes biographical chronology. Illustrated.

18 RHYS, BRINLEY. "Chekhov." SR 78:163-75.

Reviews Daniel Gillès' biography (1967.5) and Randall Jarrell's translation of The Three Sisters (New York: Macmillan, 1969) and comments on translations generally. Notes that Chekhov is a most elusive writer, especially as a playwright. Gillès fails to capture Chekhov's sense of poetry; Jarrell's notes are incomplete and erratic and his translation has many peculiarities.

19 SCHRAMM, GODEHARD. "Wiederholung als Konstruktionselement in Čechovs 'Tolstyi i tonkii'." WSl 15:235-52.

Makes a close reading of "The Fat Man and the Thin Man," dividing the story into units of narrative and examining the various functions of the repetitions of words and phrases.

20 SELGE, GABRIELE. Anton Čechovs Menschenbild: Materialen zu einer poetischen Anthropologie. Forum

Slavicum. Vol. 15. Edited by Dmitrij Tschižewskij. Munich: Wilhelm Fink, 130 pp.

Argues that Chekhov's mature stories and plays, taken together, make up an "anthropology," i.e., a picture of human beings generally, apart from any specific historical context. This anthropology is grounded in the notions of daily life, from which the characters cannot escape, and in the endlessness of the life process itself. Loneliness, restlessness, and rootlessness are basic conditions of his human beings. The functions of time and work are also examined, as is the role of Chekhov's anthropology in determining his narrative technique.

21 STYAN, J.L. "The Idea of a Definitive Production: Chekhov In and Out of Period." CompD 4:177-96.

Examines some of the factors that create a sense of discordance and ambiguity in Chekhov's plays and argues that there will never be a definitive production. Great directors always find new things in the plays as they adjust them to new audiences.

22 UL'IANOV, N. "Mistitsizm Chekhova" [Chekhov's mysticism]. NovŽ 98:91-103.

Argues that Chekhov was "a mystic by nature" since elements of the supernatural are present throughout his writings. Many of his stories deal with the mysterious forces that seem to govern life. The mystical ideas expressed in Treplyov's play in The Seagull are Chekhov's own.

23 ZAMIATIN, EVGENYI. "Chekhov." In A Soviet Heretic: Essays by Yevgeny Zamyatin. Edited and translated by Mirra Ginsburg. Chicago-London: University of Chicago Press, pp. 224-30.

Translation of 1955.20.

1971

1 ALEXANDRE, AIMÉE. A la recherche de Tchékhov: essai de biographie intérieure. Paris: Buchet-Chastel, 264 pp.

An intimate examination of Chekhov's personality derived from a close reading of his works and letters that seeks to uncover aspects of his personality that he kept hidden from his readers and even from his closest friends. Chekhov "est la pudeur incarnee;" reserve is a leitmotiv of his life and his works. He did not really "squeeze the slave" out of himself as bury his inherited personality beneath a veneer of joviality, consideration, and philanthropic activity. Essentially he was a lonely, despairing man who found no sense in life.

2 BECKERMAN, BERNARD. "Dramatic Analysis and Literary Interpretation: The Cherry Orchard as Exemplum." NLH 2:391-406.

Attempts to define the structural pattern of the play's action, arguing that critical method should describe what is happening among the characters and not seek to recreate the stage performance by showing the effect the drama can have on a spectator. Dramatic analysis is fundamentally different from literary interpretation since the dramatic text is perceived in a vastly different manner from the literary one. The Cherry Orchard shows the mark of a major dramatist in its manner of "shaping human relationships into provocative, unresolved actions."

3 BIRKENMAIER, WILLY. Die Darstellung des Christentums im Werke Čechovs. Tubingen: n.p., 152 pp.

Describes the influence of religion in Chekhov's life and surveys his presentation of the clergy and the Orthodox liturgy in his writings; argues that the expression of his loss of faith in his letters referred specifically to dogmatic religion. "Das Wesen des Christentums, wie Čechov es an den Gestalten von Lipa, Sonja und dem Bischof darstellt, besteht in jener besonderen Fähigkeit, ins Leben einzudringen, das heisst, daran zu glauben, dass auch des unglücklichste Leben auf eine höhere Realität hinweist."

4 BRESHCHINSKII, D. "'Na podvode' A.P Chekhova: opyt vremennoi kritiki" [Chekhov's "In the Cart:" a temporal analysis]. RLJ, no. 92, pp. 9-22.

Time is a major theme in the story. The heroine tries to find herself and her roots, to make a connection between her past and her future and so to regain her sense of the unity of the temporal flow. Her inability to do so reflects Chekhov's pessimism. The story has three "layers" of time: the heroine's actual present while on her journey; the larger present of her unchanging everyday life; and her past and future.

5 BROIDE, EDGARD. "K probleme chekhovskogo komizma" [On the problem of Chekhov's comedy]. In Stranitsy istorii russkoi literatury: k 80-letiiu chlena-korrespondent AN SSSR N.F. Bel'chikova [Pages from the history of Russian literature: for the eightieth birthday of N.F. Bel'chikov, Corresponding Member of the USSR Academy of Sciences]. Edited by

D.F. Markov. Moscow: Nauka, pp. 76-80.

Discusses the nature of Chekhov's humor, arguing that it was one means whereby he defined his attitude to life.

6 CHUDAKOV, A.P. Poetika Chekhova [Chekhov's poetics]. Moscow: Nauka, 291 pp.

Makes a chronological survey of Chekhov's narrative, dividing it, on the basis of a statistical study, into three distinct periods: 1880-87; 1888-94; 1895-1904. The first period is marked by "subjective" narrative technique in the sense that the narrator expresses value judgements and intervenes in the story. In the middle period the narration becomes "objective," i.e., limited only to the characters' perspectives. The last period gives a central role to the narrative voice, a voice that is close to the author's but is not identified with him and is able to shift from character to character. Part 2 of the study examines the other elements of the world depicted in Chekhov's writings: the material world; the interconnected levels of story and plot (fabula and siuzhet); and ideas. These levels are all structured in accordance with the same principle of randomness (sluchainost') whereby the essential and significant are thrown together with the secondary and irrelevant. This principle explains the uniqueness of Chekhov's non-hierarchical, "adogmatic" world. Translated: 1983.5.

7 EEKMAN, THOMAS. "Anton Čechov and the Classical Languages." Slavia 40:48-60.

Surveys Chekhov's use of Latin and Greek and of the classics generally. He had a solid classical education and frequently used Latin phrases and cited Latin and Greek writers in his letters and fiction. His works also portray a number of teachers of classical languages. Marcus Aurelius impressed him but did not influence his outlook. Chekhov made wide use of his classical education although it did not inspire any of his subjects or heroes.

8 FODOR, A. "A la découverte d'un Tchékhov soviétique." ÉSl 15:3-15.

Surveys the changing Soviet attitudes to Chekhov from the near indifference of the 1920s to his gradual elevation to the status of a full-fledged classic. Opinion about Chekhov's acceptability in Soviet Russia was sharply divided in the 1920s. Soviet scholars attempted to show that Chekhov became concerned with politics toward the end of his life.

9 GOODLIFFE, JOHN D. "Time in Chekhov's Plays."

NZSJ, no. 7, pp. 32-41.

Argues that time is one of the most important preoccupations of the characters in Chekhov's last four plays. They are placed in situations where time is a critical factor; the plays themselves contain many reminders ("markers") of the passage of time. His characters may try to escape from time but few manage to do so for more than a few moments.

10 HINGLEY, RONALD. Preface, Introduction, Appendices, Notes, and Bibliography to The Oxford Chekhov. Vol. 6. Translated and edited by Ronald Hingley. London: Oxford University Press, pp. ix-xii, 1-17, and 263-316.

Discusses problems of translating Chekhov, specifically the stories of 1892 and 1893; surveys Chekhov's literary career during 1892 and 1893 and provides historical and cultural background to the stories of the period; discusses individually the writing, the texts, and the variants of eight stories published in 1892 and 1893. Explanatory notes for the stories and a bibliography of English-language translations and critical works are included.

11 HÜBNER, FRIEDRICH. Die Personendarstellung in den Dramen Anton P. Čechovs. Biblioteca Slavonica, vol. 4. Edited by C.A. v.d. Berk and D. Gerhardt. Amsterdam: Adolf M. Hakkert, 350 pp.

Examines Chekhov's technique of characterization and the structural function of the characters in his last five plays. Seven categories of characterization are elaborated (eight for three plays) and each play examined in detail. Hubner concludes that the characters in each play live in a state of alienation; they are unable to reconcile their ideal of life with their actuality. In The Seagull, The Three Sisters, and The Cherry Orchard the characters' alienation is more existential than social, more symbolic than concrete. Includes a bibliography.

12 KOŚNY, WITOLD. "Bedeutung und Funktion der literaturischen zitate in A.P. Čechovs Tri sestry." WSl 16:126-50.

Surveys the literary quotations in the play and argues that they serve a variety of functions: as characterization generally; as a means of conveying a character's inner state; as a link with a larger reality outside the play; as a means of showing the breakdown of communication.

13 KOVARSKII, N.A. "Geroi Chaiki" [The characters of The Seagull]. In Stranitsy istorii russkoi

literatury: k 80-letiiu chlena-korrespondenta AN SSSR N.F. Bel'chikova [Pages from the history of Russian literature: for the eightieth birthday of N.F. Bel'chikov, Corresponding Member of the USSR Academy of Sciences]. Edited by D.F. Markov. Moscow: Nauka, pp. 185-98.

Examines some of the literary and autobiographical sources that influenced the play and its characters. The wide range of influences that played roles in creating the characters suggests that they belong to different genres: Trigorin is a comic hero, Treplyov a tragic one.

14 LAFFITTE, SOPHIE. Tchékhov: 1860-1904. Paris: Librairie Hachette, 272 pp.

A biography that deals at length with Chekhov's friendships with Suvorin and Levitan, his attitudes toward the West, and his marriage. An introductory essay discusses Chekhov's poetics generally and stresses the contradiction between his tragic view of life and his illogical faith in future happinesss. Illustrated. Translated: 1974.27.

15 LINKOV, V.Ia. "Povest' A.P. Chekhova 'Duel'' i russkii sotsial'no-psikhologicheskii roman pervoi poloviny XIX veka" [Chekhov's tale "The Duel" and the Russian socio-psychological novel of the first half of the nineteenth century]. In Problemy teorii i istorii literatury: sbornik statei posviashchennyi pamiati professora A.N. Sokolova [Problems of the theory and history of literarture: a collection of articles in memory of Professor A.N. Sokolov]. Edited by V.I. Kuleshov, R.M. Samarin, and A.G. Sokolov. Moscow: Izdatel'stvo Moskovskogo universiteta, pp. 377-92.

Argues that "The Duel" shows clearly how much Chekhov's realism differs from that of his predecessors. Laevsky is Chekhov's version of the traditional Onegin-Rudin-Oblomov social type. But unlike his predecessors Chekhov is not interested in assessing the social significance of his hero; his concern is how people live in their world. Chekhov stresses not the effects of environment on Laevsky but his personal responsibility for his fate.

16 -----. "Znachenie rasskaza 'Ogni' v razvitii povestvovatel'nykh priemov Chekhova" [The significance of the story "Lights" in the development of Chekhov's narrative devices]. VMU, no. 2, pp. 16-24.

"Lights" [1888] was written at the critical

moment in Chekhov's career, a time when he began working out a deeper and more serious approach to literature. The story does not aim to solve the philosophical problem of pessimism; rather it explores the role ideas play in determining personality and behavior. The story as a whole illustrates the danger of formulating a world view on the basis of ready-made ideas and suggests that only those ideas that have been tested through personal experience have validity for the individual. As in the rest of Chekhov's post-1888 work the reader must not necessarily accept a character's ideas at face value but evalutate them critically within the context of the work.

17 MUCHNIC, HELEN. "Poet of Hopelessness: Chekhov." In Russian Writers: Notes and Essays. New York: Random House, pp. 204-11.

Reviews four books on or by Chekhov. His play Platonov (as translated by David Magarshack in 1964.13) is an "intellectual farce" that parodies the superfluous man. Hingley's biography (1950.3) takes issue with Shestov's view of Chekhov (1905.9) but goes too far. Chekhov's "hopelessness" is not maudlin but is a mark of strength and courage; his pessimism arises not from humans themselves but from their delusions. Winner's study (1966.25) deals with Chekhov's craftsmanship with insight and precision.

18 NIKIPELOVA, N.A. "O p'ese Chekhova Tat'iana Repina" [On Chekhov's play Tatyana Repina]. VRL, no. 2, pp. 54-59.

Compares Chekhov's play with Suvorin's play of the same name, arguing that Chekhov's places more emphasis on psychology and avoids clichés. The play anticipates some of the methods of his later drama.

19 O'TOOLE, L.M. "Structure and Style in the Short Story: Chekhov's 'Student'." SEER 49:45-67.

Uses "The Student" to illustrate a method of structural analysis of the short story. O'Toole argues that the fable, plot, narrative structure, setting, point of view, characterization, and language all combine around a central axis or theme, which here is catharsis or "the power of tragedy to move and inspire."

20 PAUL, BARBARA. "Chekhov's 'Five Sisters'." MD 14:436-40.

Argues that both Andrei and Dr. Chebutykin should be considered "sisters" since all five characters are needed to complete the pattern of experience revealed in the play. Irina's story is central, however, and is the only one revealed in its entirety.

21 POLIAK, L.M. "Traditsii Chekhova v sovremennoi novellistike" [The Chekhov tradition in the contemporary short story]. In Zhanro-stilevye iskaniia sovremennoi sovetskoi prozy [Generic and stylistic quests in Soviet prose]. Edited by L.M. Poliak and V.E. Kovskii. Moscow: Nauka, pp. 232-65.

Traces Chekhov's influence on the prose of Yury Kazakov, Boris Zubavin, Sergei Antonov, Sergei Nikitin, Boris Bedny, Iuryi Nagibin, and others. His influence is revealed in these writers' concerns with everyday subjects and simple plots, their use of understatement, unresolved endings, muted conflicts, a sub-text, and a generally lyrical mood.

22 POLOTSKAIA, E.A. "Chelovek v khudozhestvennom mire Dostoevskogo i Chekhova" [Man in the artistic world of Dostoevsky and Chekhov]. In Dostoevskii i russkie pisateli: traditsii, novatorstvo, masterstvo [Dostoevsky and Russian writers: traditions, innovation, craftsmanship]. Edited by V.Ia. Kirpotin. Moscow: Sovetskii pisatel' pp. 184-245.

Argues that even though Chekhov's art seems utterly different from Dostoevsky's, there are important links between the two writers, both in their general aesthetic aims and in specific individual works. They both attempt to reveal the depths and the complexity of human nature, although they do so by different means. Chekhov's treatment of human nature would have been impossible without the discoveries made by Dostoevsky.

23 -----. "Razvitie deistviia v proze i dramaturgii Chekhova" [The development of the action in Chekhov's prose and drama]. In Stranitsy istorii russkoi literatury: k 80-letiiu chlena-korrespondenta AN SSSR N.F. Bel'chikova [Pages from the history of Russian literature: for the eightieth birthday of N.F. Bel'chikov, Corresponding Member of the USSR Academy of Sciences]. Edited by D.F. Markov. Moscow: Nauka, pp. 330-38.

Argues that there is a common principle of composition at work in both Chekhov's narrative prose and his plays, a principle that can be seen if one examines the development of the action in his works. The action in his stories develops through four phases: the opening; the everyday flow of events; a culmination, revealing the inner anxiety of the characters; a closing, which restores a certain equilibrium. The same four stages can be seen in his plays; usually each act represents a distinct stage.

24 PRUTSKOV, N.I. "Ob odnoi paralleli: Anna Karenina Tolstogo i 'Dama s sobachkoi' Chekhova)" [On one parallel: Tolstoy's Anna Karenina and Chekhov's "The Lady With the Little Dog"] In Poetika i stilistika russkoi literatury. Pamiati Viktora Vladimirovicha Vinogradova [The poetics and stylistics of Russian literature: In memory of V.V. Vinogradov]. Edited by M.P. Alekseev, P.N. Berkov, A.S. Bushmin, D.S. Likhachev, and V.I. Malyshev. Leningrad: Nauka, pp. 236-46.

Takes issue with B. Meilakh's interpretation of the relationship between Anna Karenina and "The Lady With the Little Dog" (1956.4). With Chekhov love does not destroy but regenerates; it leads his characters to reassess their lives and to change them for the better.

25 ROSEN, NATHAN. "The Unconscious in Čexov's 'Van'ka' (With a Note on 'Sleepy')." SEEJ 15:441-54.

Argues that the ending of "Vanka" should not be seen as its culminating point but only another among many important details. When all these details are considered the meaning of the story can be discerned in Vanka's unconscious movement to find the strength to survive in a hostile world. "Sleepy" deals with a similar theme and uses similar techniques.

26 RUKALSKI, ZYGMUNT. "Maupassant and Chekhov: Differences." CSP 13:374-402.

A companion article to 1969.23, it discusses six significant aspects in which the work of the two authors differs: their portrayal of various social groups (peasants, prostitutes, civil servants, clergy, gentry); their portrayal of different temperamental types; the situations in which they are placed; their portrayal of sense perceptions; their descriptions of nature; and their use of color. These suggest that their world views were substantially different.

27 SPEIRS, LOGAN. "Chekhov's 'Ideas'." In Tolstoy and Chekhov. Cambridge: Cambridge University Press, pp. 154-61.

Argues that Chekhov's view of life offers no permanent solutions; his art challenges his audience to find their own answers. Thus his art never fully satisfies even though it speaks directly to us.

28 -----. Tolstoy and Chekhov. Cambridge: Cambridge University Press, 237 pp.

Contains eight essays on Chekhov which examine Tolstoy's influence on his work or compare the two writers' handling of similar themes. Included are 1971.27, studies of "The Name-Day Party," "A Dreary Story," "Peasants," "In the Ravine," and of Chekhov's last four plays. Argues that both writers share a passionate devotion to telling the truth about life and a certain suspicion of "literariness" in the practice of their art. But Chekhov's honesty prevented him from making connections between the unrelated events of which life, in his view, consisted.

29 SPERBER, MICHAEL A. "The 'As If' Personality and Chekhov's 'The Darling'." PsyR 58:14-21.

Argues that Chekhov's Olenka can be considered as manifesting an emotional disturbance in which the individual's relationship to life lacks genuineness but outwardly functions "as if" if were complete. She has no sense of self and so becomes dependent on a series of men whose behavior she imitates.

30 STATES, BERT O. "The Ironic Drama: Chekhov." In Irony and Drama: A Poetics. Ithaca, N.Y. and London: Cornell University Press, pp. 85-108.

A revised verion of 1967.26, it examines Chekhov's dramas within a framework of Northrop Frye's literary modes.

31 STYAN, J.L. Chekhov in Performance: A Commentary on the Major Plays. Cambridge: Cambridge University Press, 341 pp.

Makes a close scene-by-scene analysis of Chekhov's last four plays, focusing on his use of details and explaining how these details work together to produce his effects. The "submerged life of the text" is examined in detail. The origins and the early productions of each play are also described within the context of Russian theatrical history. Chekhov is a great dramatist because of his stage technique.

32 USMANOV, L.D. "Printsip 'szhatosti' v poetike pozdnego Chekhova-belletrista i russkii realizm kontsa XIX veka" [The principle of conciseness in the poetics of Chekhov's later literary works and Russian realism of the end of the nineteenth century]. In Poetika i stilistika russkoi literatury. Pamiati Akademika Viktora Vladimirovicha Vinogradova. [Poetics and Stylistics of Russian literature: In memory of Academician V.V. Vinogradov]. Edited by M.P. Alekseev, P.N. Berkov, A.S. Bushmin, D.S. Likhachev, and V.I.

Malyshev. Leningrad: Nauka, pp. 246-53.

Examines some of the stylistic techniques Chekhov used to achieve his economy of means, including the combining of author's and character's speech ("polyphonic layering"), portrayal of several characters simultaneously, and the combining of description with narration.

1972

1 BERDNIKOV, G.P. Chekhov-dramaturg: traditsii i novatorstvo v dramaturgii Chekhova [Chekhov the dramatist: traditional features and innovation in Chekhov's drama]. 2d ed., rev. Moscow: Iskusstvo, 318 pp.

Maintains the format of the first edition (1957.2) but expands most chapters and particularly its treatment of The Seagull. New material is also included on Chekhov's response to social and cultural issues of his day.

2 -----. "O poetike Chekhova i printsipakh ee issledovaniia" [On Chekhov's poetics and principles for studying them]. VLit, no. 5, pp. 124-41.

Reviews Chudakov's Poetika Chekhova (1971.6), taking issue with, among other things, the "principle of randomness" that Chudakov finds in Chekhov's works, arguing that Chekhov viewed life as neither chaotic nor "accidental." Chudakov's methodology is simply wrong.

3 BESSONOV, B.L. "A.I. Ertel' i A.P. Chekhov: istoriia literaturnykh otnoshenii i lichnogo znakomstva" [A.I. Ertel' and Chekhov: the history of their literary relationship and personal acquaintance]. RLit, no. 3, pp. 150-63.

Surveys the acquaintance of the two writers and discusses their views of each others' work.

4 BRODSKAIA, G. "Briusov i Chekhov" [Briusov and Chekhov]. Teatr, no. 2, pp. 97-100.

Discusses Briusov's unpublished article on The Cherry Orchard (see 1976.4), arguing that his aesthetic system was fundamentally different from Chekhov's.

5 CONRAD, JOSEPH L. "Unresolved Tension in Čexov's Stories, 1886-88." SEEJ 16:55-64.

Examines the theme of tension resulting from a character's isolation and alienation, arguing that Chekhov's portrayal of that tension deepened and intensified in the years 1886 to 1888.

6 CURTIS, JAMES M. "Spatial Form in Drama: The Seagull." CASS 6:13-37.

Makes a close reading of the play, stressing Chekhov's use of juxtaposition and arguing that this is a basic trait of modernist art. Joseph Frank's notion of spatial form and T.S. Eliot's concept of the "simultaneous order" of all literature are applied to derive a method for analyzing the play. Chekhov's technique of juxtaposing both themes and motifs shows his affinity with modernism.

7 CURTIS, PENELOPE. "Chekhov." Quadrant, no. 3, pp. 13-22.

Discusses Chekhov's plays generally and argues that The Three Sisters is his greatest. This play deals with "the mystery of personal and psychic freedom" and "the communal nature of the human reality." Continued: 1972.8.

8 -----. "Meditations on Chekhov." Quadrant, no. 4, pp. 31-45.

Continuation of 1972.7. Discusses The Cherry Orchard and argues that it deals with the failure to articulate communication. It is "the most determinist of Chekhov's plays" because its characters refuse to acknowledge the passing of time.

9 EBANOIDZE, N.E. "Opyt stilisticheskogo analiza novelly A.P. Chekhova 'Eger''" [A Stylistic analysis of Chekhov's story "The Huntsman"]. FN, no. 4, pp. 31-37.

Makes a close reading of the story, arguing that it is a fine example of Chekhov's craftsmanship and shows the care and precision with which he uses language.

10 GASKELL, RONALD. "Chekhov. The Cherry Orchard." In Drama and Reality: The European Theatre Since Ibsen. London: Routledge & Kegan Paul, pp. 94-98.

Contrasts Chekhov's view of life with Ibsen's and argues that Chekhov sees life in terms of sensibility. He feels his characters intuitively as we feel ourselves. His plays, The Cherry Orchard specifically, are marked by a feeling for the reality of time.

11 GOTMAN, SONIA. "The Role of Irony in Čexov's Fiction." SEEJ 16:297-306.

Discusses the concept of irony and argues that Chekhov uses it to eliminate ignorance and help him make his points. "A Fit of Nerves" is taken as a case study. Chekhov expects his reader to see what his hero does not see: that he, Vasilev, as a law student, should be able to apply his training to help solve the social problems that cause him so much pain.

12 GROMOV, L.P.; MILYKH, M.K.; and CHESNOKOVA, P.V., eds. Stat'i o Chekhove [Articles on Chekhov]. Rostov-on-the-Don: Rostovskii-na-Donu pedagogicheskii institut, 109 pp.

Contains eleven articles on a variety of aspects of Chekhov's prose and drama.

13 HAHN, BEVERLY. "Chekhov: The Three Sisters." CR, no. 15, pp. 3-22.

Argues that The Three Sisters, the "finest of modern plays," has a "deep organic and poetic unity" and conveys a sense of life that is by no means absurd. It is a play about striving. Its dominant mood is one of lyrical sadness, and its ending, although bleak, is not without hope.

14 HAMBURGER, H. "The Function of Viewpont in Čechov's 'Griša'." RusL 3:5-15.

A structural study that elaborates a theory of point of view by analogy with a movie camera; applies this theory to Chekhov's "Grisha."

15 HODGSON, PETER. "Metaliterature: An Excerpt from the Anatomy of a Chekhovian Narrator." PCP 7:36-42.

Approaches "A Dreary Story" as a work of "metaliterature" (literature about literature). Chekhov undermines his narrator very gradually and subtly by exposing his rhetoric. We learn of his pride in his "performance" as a lecturer, thus coming to suspect his reliability.

16 KNIPPER-CHEKHOVA, O.L. Vospominaniia i stat'i. Perepiska s A.P. Chekhovym (1902-04) [Memoirs and articles. Correspondence with Chekhov]. Edited by V.Ia. Vilenkin. 2 vols. Moscow: Iskusstvo, 448 + 432 pp.

Vol. 1 contains Olga Knipper's reminsicences of Chekhov (included in 1960.27) and various other figures from the MAT and theatrical world generally as well as the whole of the correspondence between her and her husband (forty-five letters in all). Vol. 2 contains her letters to literary and theatrical figures as well as reminsicences of her. Illustrated and annotated. Index.

17 MAGARSHACK, DAVID. The Real Chekhov: An Introduction to Chekhov's Last Plays. London: George Allen & Unwin, 249 pp.

Takes issue with directors who ignore Chekhov's own intentions in his plays and so distort their meaning. Detailed scene-by-scene analyses of his four last plays are provided; these include summations of Chekhov's attitude to each work and to the issues raised in it. The Seagull deals with the nature of creative art; Uncle Vanya, "an old-fashioned" play, involves a selfish idealist (Vanya) and an unselfish one (Astrov). His last two plays are more bound up with social concerns: The Three Sisters reveals Chekhov's awareness of the growth of the revolutionary movement; The Cherry Orchard condenses not only Russian but western social history.

18 MATLEY, IAN M. "Chekhov and Geography." RusR 31:376-82.
Discusses Chekhov's concerns with geography, cartography, and conservation in The Wood Demon and Uncle Vanya and describes a number of contemporary scientists and historians who probably influenced his environmentalism.

19 MAYS, MILTON. A. "'Gooseberries' and Chekhov's Concreteness." SHR 6:63-67.
Argues that the point of the story is by no means expressed in the moral which Ivan draws from it; like his brother he is "excessive" and tries to reduce the complexity of experience to a single maxim. The bad smell from his pipe that lingers after he has gone to sleep helps make readers aware of his insensitivity.

20 MELCHINGER, SIEGFRIED. Anton Chekhov. World Dramatists. Translated by Edith Tarcov. New York: Frederick Ungar, 184 pp.
Translation of 1968.18. Also includes a list of American stage productions of Chekhov's plays.

21 OATES, JOYCE CAROL. "Chekhov and the Theater of the Absurd." In The Edge of Impossibility: Tragic Forms in Literature. New York: Vanguard, pp. 115-37.
Discusses The Cherry Orchard and The Three Sisters in the context of the modern absurdist theater and argues that Chekhov's plays antcipate most of the features of today's avant-garde. His technique is naturalistic only in appearance; fundamentally it is symbolic. The absurd in Chekhov's plays resides in both their content and their language.

22 POLOTSKAIA, E.A. "K istochnikam rasskaza Chekhova 'Ariadna:' zhiznennye vpechatleniia" [On the sources of Chekhov's story "Ariadne:" impressions

from life]. IAN 31, no. 1:55-61.

Examines the biographical sources of the story, arguing that they go back to Chekhov's childhood; events from the life of Lika Mizinova and traits borrowed from the actress Lidiia Iavorskaia are also reflected in the work.

23 ROMANENKO, V.T. "'Chernyi monakh' A.P. Chekhova i ego kritiki" [Chekhov's "Black Monk" and its critics]. In Zhurnalistika i literatura [Journalism and literature]. Edited by E.A. Lazarevich. Moscow: Izdatel'stvo Moskovskogo universiteta, pp. 203-20.

Surveys the reception of the story among critics of Chekhov's own time, arguing that their comments obscured the fact that the story was built around a common Chekhovian theme, the moral responsibility of a person for his actions and ideas.

24 SCHEIBITZ, CHRISTINA. Mensch und Mitmensch in Drama Anton Čechovs: Analyse der Dialogtechnik. Göppinger akademische Beiträge, no. 56. Edited by Ulrich Muller, Franz Hundsnurscher and K. Werner Jauss. Goppingen: Alfred Kummerle, 187 pp.

Analyses the dialogue in Chekhov's major plays and argues that his main interest was human conversation itself rather than the convictions of specific characters. His characters are isolated from one another, however, and no real understanding is possible, at least in The Three Sisters and The Cherry Orchard. His mature drama does not allow the audience to identify with his characters but forces them to become active and critical observers.

25 SKAFTYMOV, A.P. Nravstvennye iskaniia russkikh pisatelei. Stat'i i issledovaniia o russkikh pisatelei [The moral quest of Russian writers: articles and studies of Russian writers]. Moscow: Khudozhestvennaia literatura, pp. 339-456.

Includes 1958.20, 1958.21, 1958.22, and 1958.23.

26 STEWART, MAAJA A. "Scepticism and Belief in Chekhov and Anderson." SSF 9:29-40.

Discusses Chekhov's influence on Sherwood Anderson and compares the two writers' approaches to their art. Both deal with cultural failure, both portray characters attempting to "climb out of the void," both "depict the elusive reality of the self."

27 STYAN, J.L. "The Delicate Balance: Audience Ambivalence in the Comedy of Shakespeare and Chekhov." Costerus 2:159-84.

Compares Shakespearean and Chekhovian comedy and argues that both deal with irresolvable paradoxes and "radically opposed literary ideas" which must be kept in careful balance; this balance derives from the sanity and objectivity of each author.

28 WILSON, EDMUND. "Seeing Chekhov Plain." In _A Window on Russia: for the Use of Foreign Readers_. New York: Farrar, Straus & Giroux, pp. 52-68.
Reprinted from 1952.9.

29 ZALYGIN, SERGEI. "My Poet." _SovL_, no. 4, pp. 63-129.
Translation of 1969.25.

1973

1 AVDEEV, Iu.K. "Chekhov. Lika. Levitan i _Chaika_" [Chekhov. Lika. Levitan and _The Seagull_]. In _Chekhovskie chteniia v Ial'te_ [Chekhov papers in Yalta]. Edited by V.I. Kuleshov, A.A. Khrenkova, S.V. Zhitomirskaia, E.M. Sakharova, and N.F. Shevtsov. Moscow: Kniga, pp. 72-77.
Attempts to clarify the relationship between Chekhov's romance with Lika Mizinova and _The Seagull_ by arguing that the play originated during Chekhov's and Levitan's hunting trip of 1895 and by casting doubt on Mizinova's influence.

2 BELKIN, A.A. "Chudesnyi zontik: ob iskusstve khudozhestvennoi detali u Chekhova" [The marvellous umbrella: on Chekhov's art of the detail]. In _Chitaia Dostoevskogo i Chekhova: stat'i i razbory_ [Reading Dostoevskii and Chekhov: articles and analyses]. Moscow: Khudozhestvennaia literatura, pp. 221-29.
Argues that the detail has much more importance in Chekhov's work than in the poetics of other writers. Even such an ordinary object such as an umbrella, frequently encountered in his writings, gives not only a sense of one individual thing but takes on a larger, symbolic function, expressing, perhaps, the evolution of a character's feelings. Often a detail seems utterly inappropriate to the meaning it expresses; thus an umbrella in "Three Years" conveys the theme of happiness.

3 -----. "'Dom s mezoninom'" ["The Artist's Story"]. In _Chitaia Dostoevskogo i Chekhova: stat'i i razbory_ [Reading Dostoevsky and Chekhov: articles

and analyses]. Moscow: Khudozhestvennaia literatura, pp. 230-64.

Makes a close reading of the story, focusing on Chekhov's technique and style and on the story's ideas. "The Artist's Story" illustrates Chekhov's belief that truth is the liberation from illusions.

4 -----. "Khudozhestvennoe masterstvo Chekhova-novellista" [Chekhov's artistic craftsmanship as a short story writer]. In Chitaia Dostoevskogo i Chekhova: stat'i i razbory [Reading Dostoevsky and Chekhov: articles and analyses]. Moscow: Khudozhestvennaia literatura, pp. 173-220.

Argues that the new form of Chekhov's short stories corresponded to the new historical reality in which he produced them. One of his brief stories contains enough material for a novel and can, within its few pages, even show the lengthy process of evolution of a character. His art can reveal the banality that hides behind an attractive facade; it can also reveal the real beauty that lies behind an unexceptional exterior. The descriptions of nature in his works often contain profound philosophical ideas. His most basic qualities as a writer are restraint and subtlety.

5 -----. "'Shchast'e'" ["Happiness"]. In Chitaia Dostoevskogo i Chekhova: stat'i i razbory [Reading Dostoevsky and Chekhov: articles and analyses]. Moscow: Khudozhestvennaia literatura, pp. 265-84.

Makes a close reading of the story, concentrating on Chekhov's use of detail. The integration of all elements in the story shows Chekhov's typically "novellistic" manner and his mastery of the technique of creating a work of universal significance out of the bare facts of ordinary life.

6 -----. "'Student. ["The Student"]. In Chitaia Dostoevskogo i Chekhova: stat'i i razbory [Reading Dostoevsky and Chekhov: articles and analyses]. Moscow: Khudozhestvennaia literatura, pp. 285-99.

A close reading of the story, comparing the final version to earlier drafts and setting it in historical context. "The Student" deals with values such as compassion that survive, transmitted by art, through eternity. Yet the optimistic view of the triumph of goodness is clearly the student's and not necessarily Chekhov's.

7 BIALYI, G.A. "Zametki o khudozhestvennoi manere A.P. Chekhova" [Remarks on Chekhov's artistic manner]. In Russkii realism kontsa XIX v. [Russian

realism of the end of the 19th century]. Leningrad: LGU, pp. 149-68.

Reprinted from 1968.3

8 CHEKHOV, ANTON. Letters of Anton Chekhov. Edited by Avrahm Yarmolinsky. Translated by Bernard Gilbert Guerney, Lynn Solotaroff, and Avrahm Yarmolinsky. New York: Viking, 490 pp.

Contains over 400 letters translated in full or in part and arranged chronologically from 1879 to 1904. Annotated, illustrated, indexed.

9 CHEKHOV, ANTON. Letters of Anton Chekhov. Edited and translated by Henry Michael Heim in collaboration with Simon Karlinsky. Introduction by Simon Karlinsky. New York: Harper & Row, 494 pp.

Contains the complete texts of 185 letters selected "to give a comprehensive picture of his literary, social and scientific interests and views." The letters are arranged in sections, each devoted to one period of his life; each section is preceded by an introduction. Annotated, with bibliography and index.

10 DE MAEGD-SOËP, C. "Romanticheskie elementy v tvorchestve Chekhova" [Romantic elements in Chekhov's work]. In Communications présentées par les slavisants de Belgique au VIIe Congrès International de Slavistique Varsovie--Août 1973. Brussels: Centre Belge d'Etudes Slaves, pp. 5-18.

Argues that even though Chekhov is a realist his works contain many romantic elements. These are parodied in his early writings, but in his later works we find romantic heroines and heroes. The romantic elements in his works suggest the possibility of more humane relationships between people and of another, more humane reality.

11 DROUILLY, JEAN. "Čexov et le sentiment de l'absurde." In Canadian Contributions to the Seventh International Congress of Slavists, Warsaw, August 21-27, 1973. Slavistic Printings and Reprintings, no. 285. Edited by Zbigniew Folejewski, Edmund Heier, David Huntley, George Luckyj, and Gunter Schaarschmidt. The Hague-Paris: Mouton, pp. 139-62.

Argues that the sense of the absurd in Chekhov's work is largely unconscious and arises from his overall approach to life; explores various manifestations of the absurd from his earliest to his last writings. His sense of the absurd is first felt in his portrayal of the banality of everyday life and evolves toward a notion of the fundamental incomprehensibility and absurdity of the universe.

12 DÜWEL, WOLF. "Zum Problem von Inhalt und Form in Čechovs Erzahlungen." ZS 18:357-69.

Argues that there are two basic interpretations of Chekhov--as a realist and as a modernist--and examines both. Duwel takes issue with Gabriele Selge's (1970.21) conception of Chekhov as a key figure in European modernism, arguing that "The Lady With the Little Dog" is a typical example of his realist, humanist art.

13 GEIDEKO, V.A. "Magiia kratkosti i prostoty: zametki o masterstve Chekhova-rasskazchika" [The magic of brevity and simplicity: observations on Chekhov's craftsmanship as a narrator]. VLit, no. 7, pp. 168-83.

Examines Chekhov's innovations in the short story form. His openings are extremely laconic and stress the commonness and everyday nature of character and situation. His endings sometimes resolve the plot, but often do not; his characters are complex and multifaceted.

14 HAHN, BEVERLY. "Chekhov's The Cherry Orchard." CR 16:56-72.

Discusses the play as a comedy, arguing that although the characters are often comic their world is extremely serious. The Cherry Orchard is seen as a modern adaptation of pastoral: in the course of the play Chekhov gradually reveals his ironic view of the end of idyllic country life.

15 KULESHOV, V.I.; KHRENKOVA, A.A.; ZHITOMIRSKAIA, S.V.; SAKHAROVA, E.M.; and SHEVTSOV, N.F., eds. Chekhovskie chteniia v Ial'te [Chekhov papers in Yalta]. Moscow: Kniga, 181 pp.

Contains fifteen articles, six of which concern Chekhov's life in Yalta. Literary studies include 1973.1, 1973.16, and 1973.22; other articles deal with realism, naturalism, and symbolism in his work; with Uncle Vanya; "An Anonymous Story;" Chekhov's journalism; and with his influence on Soviet prose.

16 LAKSHIN, V.Ia. "K tvorcheskoi istorii Vishnevogo sada" [On the creation of The Cherry Orchard]. In Chekhovskie chteniia v Ial'te [Chekhov papers in Yalta]. Edited by V.I. Kuleshov, A.A. Khrenkova, S.V. Zhitomirskaia, E.M. Sakharova, and N.F. Shevtsov. Moscow: Kniga, pp. 78-97.

Discusses the origin and the evolution of the plot and characters of the play. By comparing the differences between the director's and prompter's copies of the play used in rehersal in 1904 with Chekhov's own fair copy Lakshin is able to establish some of Chekhov's final revisions.

17 LLEWELLYN SMITH, VIRGINIA. Anton Chekhov and the Lady with the Dog. Foreword by Ronald Hingley. London: Oxford University Press, 249 pp.

A critico-biographical study that examines Chekhov's relationships with women and the treatment of love in his writings. Chekhov's personality contained two antithetical qualities: a coldness and apparent indifference together with a capacity for passionate feeling. Misogyny is a common theme in his life and in his writings, and his view of heterosexual relationships was uniformly gloomy. His romantic heroine Anna, in "The Lady With the Little Dog," symbolizes the ideal love which Chekhov could envisage but never achieve himself.

18 MAXWELL, DAVID. "A System of Symbolic Gesture in Čexov's 'Step''." SEEJ 17:146-54.

Argues that the structural categories of setting, characters, and plot of "The Steppe" are linked by a pattern of symbolic gesture involving verbal forms based on the root makh- (waving, gesticulating). The frequent occurrence of such forms signals the presence of dominant themes--solitude, aimlessness, despair, and uncertainty--and thus gives the work cohesiveness. Several of his other stories of the 1880s use a similar, if less developed, technique.

19 PAPERNYI, Z.S. "Chekhov i romantizm" [Chekhov and romanticism]. In K istorii russkogo romantizma [On the history of Russian Romanticism]. Edited by Iu.V. Mann, I.G. Neupokoeva, and U.R. Fokht. Moscow: Nauka, pp. 473-504.

Examines Chekhov's attitudes to literature as expressed in his notebooks and letters, arguing that his works present both the sense of the oppressiveness of daily life and the joy of living. The contrast between these two strains runs through many of his works and can be clearly seen in "The Student," with its grim picture humanity as well as its deep faith in human potential. Although Chekhov's poetics seem to be at the opposite pole to those of romanticism, his faith inhumanity and his desire to see people better than they are are romantic traits.

20 PIFER, ELLEN. "Čexov's Psychological Landscape." SEEJ 17:273-78.

Argues that after 1886 Chekhov began using a

technique of "psychological landscape" in which the external setting illuminates the inner worlds of his characters.

21 PITCHER, HARVEY. The Chekhov Play: A New Interpretation. New York: Barnes & Noble, 224 pp.

Argues that Chekhov's plays involve us with the emotional side of their characters; we respond to what they feel about themselves, others, and life in general. Each of the major plays is written according to a similar structural formula and its characters converse in similar fashion. The four major plays are analyzed in detail to demonstrate these principles and characteristics at work.

22 PUSTOVOIT, P.G. "'Turgenevskoe nachalo' v dramaturgii Chekhova" [The "Turgenev principle" in Chekhov's drama] In Chekhovskie chteniia v Ial'te. [Chekhov papers in Yalta]. Edited by V.I. Kuleshov, A.A. Khrenkova, S.V. Zhitomirskaia, E.M. Sakharova, and N.F. Shevtsov. Moscow: Kniga, pp. 113-23.

Compares Chekhov's and Turgenev's dramatic technique generally and argues that both writers rely heavily on pauses and authors' remarks to help reveal character; both create dialogue with a subtext.

23 ROSSBACHER, PETER. "Die thematische Bedeutung vier stilistischer Kunstgriffe Čechovs." WSl 18:296-307.

Examines four of Chekhov's stylistic peculiarities or devices: the use of the words "peace" or "quiet" (tishina, tikhii, pokoi); the image of the setting sun; the "tripling of an adjective, predicate, or adverb;" the common motif of a character pondering the meaning of his existence. Argues that these are related to the major theme of hopelessness, often expressed through the vie manquée of a character.

24 SAGAR, KEITH. "Chehov's Magic Lake: A Reading of The Seagull." MD 15:441-47.

Takes issue with Dorothy Seyler (1965.13), arguing that Chekhov's symbolism is not contrived; like Ibsen he uses symbolism to break through naturalistic conventions. The lake and the seagull function as a pair of symbols: the lake is a kind of prison for the characters who live on its shore; Nina, however, spreads her wings to escape to the rougher waters of the open sea.

25 SCHMID, HERTA. Strukturalistische Dramentheorie: Semantische Analyse von Čechows "Ivanov" und "Der Kirschgarten". Skripten Literaturwissenschaft, no. 3. Kronberg: Scriptor, 519 pp.

A study using the approach of the Prague Linguistic Circle that elaborates a theory for the structural study of drama and applies it to Ivanov and The Cherry Orchard. Schmid argues that plays can be divided into dramas of character, of situation, and of dialogue. Chekhov's are extreme variants of the drama of situation.

26 SHOTTON, M.H. "Chekhov." In Nineteenth-Century Russian Literature: Studies of Ten Russian Writers. Edited by John Fennell. London: Faber & Faber, pp. 293-346.

Surveys Chekhov's career generally and discusses some of his major themes and techniques. His central theme is the study of the state of man's consciousness: he examines specific "cases" that imprison the consciousness and restrict the spirit. Such "cases" can be religion, materialism, indifference, or pessimism, and they appear in both prose and drama.

27 TURBIN, V.N. "K fenomenologii literaturnykh i ritoricheskikh zhanrov v tvorchestve Chekhova" [On the phenomenology of literary and rhetorical genres in Chekhov's work]. In Problemy poetiki i istorii literatury: sbornik statei [Problems of the poetics and history of literature: an anthology]. Edited by M.P. Alekseev, V. M. Zabavina, A.M. Kunakov, and S.S. Konkin. Saransk: Mordovskii gos. universitet im. N.P. Ogareva, pp. 204-16.

Argues that Chekhov is the most difficult to study of all the nineteenth-century Russian writers and that it is necessary to elaborate a basic methodology for the study of his work. The key problem in his work is the notion of the conception and mutations of his genres. Chekhov's mistrust of ready-made systems generally is related to his rejection of the ready-made systems implicit in established literary genres. "One can boldly assert that a dialogue between the living, generically unformulated, and atypical on the one hand and the established, settled, and completed on the other is the basic principle of development in Chekhov's work as a short-story writer."

1974

1 AN SSSR. INSTITUT MIROVOI LITERATURY IM. A.M. GOR'KOGO. V tvorcheskoi laboratorii Chekhova [In Chekhov's creative laboratory]. Moscow: Nauka, 362 pp.

Twenty-three essays by leading Soviet Chekhov

scholars based on new research done in preparation for the 1974 Complete Collected Works and Letters. The essays focus on Chekhov's creative process, his methods of reflecting reality in his art, and his poetics generally. Includes 1974.5, 1974.8, 1974.19, 1974.24, 1974.26, 1974.31, 1974.37, 1974.38, 1974.39, 1974.40, 1974.42, and 1974.43. Besides these are studies of "Peasants," Tatyana Repina, The Island of Sakhalin, "An Anonymous Story," "A Woman's Kingdom," The Shooting Party, "The Artist's Story," and "In the Ravine." Articles on Chekhov's art of letter writing, on his life in Melikhovo as reflected in his writings, and on his influence on contemporary Russian litrary style are also included.

2 BERDNIKOV, G.P. Chekhov. Zhizn' zamechatel'nykh liudei, no. 19 (549) [Chekhov. The lives of remarkable people]. Moscow: Molodaia gvardiia, 512 pp.

A full-length biography that devotes considerable attention to discussing Chekhov's personality and ideas and to his relations with contemporaries. Contains a chronology and a bibliography. Illustrated.

3 BILL, VALENTINE. "Nature in Chekhov's Fiction." RusR 33:153-66.

Argues that Chekhov's works show the unity of all living things but that they suggest this unity in a very non-traditional manner. Tolstoy writes of civilized man's alienation from nature, Turgenev shows modern man's alienation from nature, but Chekhov's works show a harmony between nature and man that derives from the human spirit.

4 BORDINAT, PHILIP. "Chekhov's Two Great American Directors." Midwest Quarterly 16:70-84.

Discusses the work of "the two most successful [American] directors of Chekhov," Eva Le Gallienne and David Ross. The work of the former was strongly influenced by the MAT; the latter, however, broke sharply with traditional interpretations.

5 CHUDAKOV, A.P. "Poetika i prototipy" [Poetics and prototypes]. In V tvorcheskoi laboratorii Chekhova [In Chekhov's creative laboratory]. By AN SSSR. Institut mirovoi literatury im. A.M. Gor'kogo. Moscow: Nauka, pp. 182-93.

Examines the prototypes of the characters in "The Grasshopper" and argues that in determining how Chekhov modified real life material one can see his artistic vision at work.

6 CLYMAN, TOBY W. "Čexov's Victimized Women." RLJ

100:26-31.

Examines Chekhov's portrayal of sympathetic but victimized women. Few opportunities are open to women in his stories; those who engage in philanthropy or concern themselves with purely domestic matters are generally portrayed as insensitive or limited. Those who strive for realization outside home and family generally have his sympathy.

7 DLUGOSCH, INGRID. "Die Personen Anton P. Čechovs: Versuch einer Kategorisierung." WSl 19-20:164-98.

Discusses Chekhov's characters generally and groups them, on ethical criteria such as inner freedom and spiritual independence, into seven loose categories: positive characters, portrayed without irony; positive, passive characters treated with some irony; "absurd" characters; inflexible or dogmatic characters; normal, active characters; slaves of authority; the "men in cases." These types anticipate figures in modern, absurdist theater.

8 DOLOTOVA, L.M. "Motiv i prozvedenie: 'Rasskaz starshego sadovnika,' 'Ubiistvo'" [Motif and story: "The Senior Gardener's Story," "A Murder"]. In V tvorcheskoi laboratorii Chekhova. In [Chekhov's creative laboratory]. By AN SSSR. Institut mirovoi literatury im. A.M. Gor'kogo. Moscow: Nauka, pp. 35-53.

Discusses the genesis of the two stories and shows how they developed from entries in Chekhov's notebooks. The notebook entries establish some links between Chekhov's Sakhalin trip and "A Murder."

9 FEJÉR, Á. "'Dom s mezoninom' A.P. Chekhova." [Chekhov's "The Artist's Story"]. SSASH 20:107-14.

Surveys existing criticism of the story and examines its links with Turgenev's works.

10 -----. "Gospodstvo poshlosti i 'gospodstvuiushchaia ideiia': analiz rasskaza A.P.Chekhova 'Skuchnaia istoriia'" [The triumph of vulgarity and the "prevailing idea:" an analysis of Chekhov's "A Dreary Story"]. In SSASH 20:259-69.

Examines the dilemma of the story's hero, arguing that he is trapped within a vicious circle created by the banality of the life around him. He is neither unfeeling nor insensitive but is simply overwhelmed by life's vulgarity.

11 FORTUNATOV, N.M. "Dvizhenie idei v novelle" [The movement of an idea in the short story]. In Puti

iskanii: o masterstve pisatelia [Ways of striving: on the writer's craft]. Moscow: Sovetskii pisatel', pp. 134-78.

Argues that the theme of a work of art should be understood as a dynamic, temporal phenomenon since it develops in time as the work is read. Thus the form of the work unfolds before the reader and should be regarded as a dynamic process and not in spatial terms. Chekhov's "A Fit of Nerves" and "Ward Six" are examined to illustrate this approach and to show how the stories convey their ideas to the reader.

12 -----. "Muzykal'nost' chekhovskoi prozy" [The musicality of Chekhov's prose]. In Puti iskanii: o masterstve pisatelia [Ways of striving: on the writer's craft]. Moscow: Sovetskii pisatel', pp. 105-34.

Discusses the concept of musicality in prose and takes Chekhov's "The Black Monk" as a case study. The story is written in sonata form: it has a tripartite structure and involves two contrasting themes. This shows that aesthetic principles in any genuine work of art, whatever its medium, remain constant.

13 GERHARDIE, WILLIAM A. Anton Chekhov: A Critical Study. Preface by Michael Holroyd. Epilogue and "Literary Credo" by the author. London: Macdonald, 172 pp.

Reprinted from 1923.6.

14 GILMAN, RICHARD. "Chekhov." In The Making of Modern Drama. New York: Farrar, Straus & Giroux, pp. 116-56.

Examines and attempts to clarify two different readings of Chekhov's plays--as undramatic and subtle compositions in a minor key, and as dramas of social process--and argues that these two views complement each other. Beginning with The Seagull Chekhov presented his notion that life's most crucial moments--the subject of drama--can be its least dramatic ones.

15 GITOVICH, N.I. "O sud'be epistoliarnogo naslediia Chekhova" [On the fate of Chekhov's epistolary legacy]. In PSSP. Pis'ma [Letters]. Vol. 1. Moscow: Nauka, pp. 295-318.

Discusses the collection and publication of Chekhov's letters during his lifetime and subsequently. Describes the main portions of his correspondence which have not survived.

16 GLAD, JOHN. "Chekhov Adapted." CSP 16:99-103.

Argues that the story "Poka ne prishel parakhod" [Until the ship arrives] by the Soviet writer Valentin Tublin is an adaptation of Chekhov's "The Student." Both stories are impressionistic and formally identical although "poles apart" ideologically. The conservatism of Soviet literature encourages young writers to look to the past for models.

17 GROMOV, L.P. "Primechaniia" [Notes]. In PSSP. Sochineniia [Works]. Vol. 1. Moscow: Nauka, pp. 547-603.

Discusses Chekhov's literary work from 1880 to 1882, summarizes critical reaction to it, and lists early works that have not survived. The history of publication and explanatory notes for the sixty-three works of the period are also included.

18 GROMOV, L.P.; SEDEGOV, V.D.; and BARLAS, L.G., eds. Tvorchestvo A.P. Chekhova: sbornik statei [Chekhov's work: a collection of articles]. Rostov-on-the-Don: Rostovskii-na-Donu gos. pedagogicheskii institut, 148 pp.

Contains eleven articles on various aspects of Chekhov's writings, including his relations with Tolstoy, his outlook in the 1880s, the tragic sense in his stories, and on various stylistic matters.

19 GROMOV, M.P. "Portet, obraz, tip" [Portrait, image, type]. In V tvorcheskoi laboratorii Chekhova [In Chekhov's creative laboratory]. By AN SSSR. Institut mirovoi literatury im. A.M. Gor'kogo. Moscow: Nauka, pp. 142-61.

Examines the new techniques Chekhov developed for portraying character. He does not provide detailed descriptions that enable readers to visualize the character; rather he focuses on a few sharp, fleeting details and impressions that reveal the character's inner life. Real life prototypes thus bear little resemblance to their literary counterparts.

20 -----. "Povestvovanie Chekhova kak khudozhestvennaia sistema" [Chekhov's narrative as an artistic system]. In Sovremennye problemy literaturovedeniia i iazykoznaniia: k 70-letiiu so dnia rozhdeniia akademika Mikhaila Borisovicha Khrapchenko [Contemporary problems of literary studies and linguistics: for the seventieth birthday of Academician M.B. Khrapchenko]. Edited by N.F. Bel'chikov. Moscow: Nauka, pp. 307-15.

Examines the inner unity of Chekhov's stories, arguing that they should be studied synthetically rather than analytically since the sum of their parts is something greater than the whole. The image of the city, for example, runs through all of his writings; it evolves, so that the image of the city in any one story can only be appreciated when seen in relation to similar images in other works. The same is true of other elements in Chekhov's work; thus his entire cast of characters should be studied. One must examine the system that operates throughout his work.

21 HINGLEY, RONALD. "Chekhov and the Short Story." In Chekhov: Seven Stories. Translated with introduction by Ronald Hingley. London: Oxford University Press, pp. xi-xxii.

Discusses "The Butterfly," "Ward Six," "Ariadne," "A Dreary Story," "Neighbours," "An Anonymous Story," and "Ionych" against their social background and in the context of nineteenth-century literature. Chekhov is elusive and seldom didactic, but "Ionych" comes closest to conveying his outlook on life.

22 KARLINSKY, SIMON. "Frustrated Artists and Devouring Mothers in Čechov and Annenskij." In Mnemozina: Studia litteraria russica in honorem Vsevolod Setchkarev. Edited by Joachim T. Baer and Norman W. Ingham. Centrifuga: Russian Reprinting and Printings, no. 15. Munich: Wilhelm Fink, pp. 229-31.

Compares the figure of the domineering mother in The Seagull and in Annensky's play Thamyras the Cythara Player. In each a mother neglects her artist-son and manipulates a younger woman who gave him love and support. Both plays deal with the prince an artist pays for failure in art and with the jealousy a talented son can arouse.

23 KASZURKEWICZ, TAMARA. "Strukturnye osobennosti rasskaza Chekhova 'Strakh'" [Structural peculiarities of Chekhov's story "Terror"]. RLJ 100:18-25.

Examines some of the story's apparently "unnecessary" elements or details--secondary characters, nature descriptions, imagery--and argues that here, as in many other of his stories, they serve to broaden and deepen the work's meaning. Chekhov's method works toward a maximum impact on the reader. His technique owes something to both Symbolism and Impressionism.

24 KATAEV, V.B. "Avtor v 'Ostrove Sakhaline' i v rasskaze 'Gusev'" [The author in The Island of Sakhalin and in "Gusev"]. In V tvorcheskoi laboratorii Chekhova [In Chekhov's creative

laboratory]. By AN SSSR. Institut mirovoi literatury im. A.M. Gor'kogo. Moscow: Nauka, pp. 232-52.

Argues that in these two works Chekhov first used a new technique typical of the last phase of his work. In The Island of Sakhalin he attempted to protest by letting the facts speak for themselves and shunned any tendency to a self-righteous expose of evil. In "Gusev" Chekhov also deals with protest; his protestor, Pavel Ivanych, is depicted as scornful of the humanity he ostensibly defends and his relationship with Gusev shows how ineffectual his protest is.

25 KATSELL, JEROME H. "Character Change in Čexov's Short Stories." SEEJ 18:377-83.

Discusses the means whereby Chekhov is able to depict character change within the narrow confines of a short story, taking "On Official Duty" as a case study. The use of significant detail allows complex, lengthy processes of development to be highly compressed.

26 KUZICHEVA, A.P. "'Udivitel'naia povest':' 'Moia zhizn''" ["A remarkable story:" "My Life"]. In V tvorcheskoi laboratorii Chekhova [In Chekhov's creative laboratory]. By AN SSSR. Institut mirovoi literatury im. A.M. Gor'kogo. Moscow: Nauka, pp. 270-78.

Examines the moral judgements made on the main characters of the story and the artistic means Chekhov uses to make them. He depicts vulgarity and how it affects those who rebel against the norms of life.

27 LAFFITTE, SOPHIE. Chekhov: 1860-1904. Translated by Moura Budberg and Gordon Latta. London: Angus & Robertson, 246 pp.

Translation of 1971.14.

28 LEONG, ALBERT. "Literary Unity in Chekhov's 'Strakh'." JRS, no. 27, pp. 15-20.

Makes a close analysis of "Terror," arguing that it provides an excellent example of Chekhov's method of uniting psychological, philosophical, and sociological reality. Terror is a fact on all three levels.

29 MacAULAY, JAMES. "Translation, Style and the Relevance of Information Science." In Chekhov: The Gull. Translated by Bernard W. Sznycer. London: Poets' and Painters' Press, pp. 107-22.

Discusses Sznycer's method of translation used in his version of The Seagull (see 1974.41) which is based on modern communication theory and psycholinguistics. The method involves calculating a "consistency ratio" for each speaker, derived from the average number of syllables per word uttered, and ensuring the ratio is the same in English and in Russian.

30 MAXWELL, DAVID. "Čexov's 'Nevesta:' A Structural Approach to the Role of Setting." RusL, no. 6, pp. 91-100.

Reviews existing interpretations of the story and argues that the ending is optimistic insofar as the heroine does manage to escape from her constrictive environment. Time is an important element in the story: the characters must either move forward with it or surrender to emotional and intellectual stagnation. The story's setting remains static, thus providing a background against which Nadia's progress can be measured.

31 MELKOVA, A.S. "Tvorcheskaia sud'ba rasskaza 'Dushechka'" [The creative history of "The Darling"]. In V tvorcheskoi laboratorii Chekhova [In Chekhov's creative laboratory]. By AN SSSR. Institut mirovoi literatury im. A.M. Gor'kogo. Moscow: Nauka, pp. 78-96.

Examines the evolution of Chekhov's attitude to his heroine, Olga, in the context of contemporary reactions to the story; outlines the genesis of the story and its links with Chekhov's biography. Melkova argues that Chekhov's original concept of her as a wholly ridiculous character changed as he gave her more endearing qualities.

32 MUDRICK, MARVIN. "Boyish Charmer and Last Mad Genius." HudR 27:33-54.

Comments on Chekhov's personality and views as revealed in his letters and discusses briefly some of his most important works. Expanded in 1977.37.

33 MUR'IANOV, M.F. "O simvolike chekhovskoi Chaiki." [On the symbolism of Chekhov's Seagull]. WSl 19-20:105-23.

Examines the meaning of the seagull as a symbol, surveying existing interpretations and opinions and tracing its links to such diverse sources as a poem by the minor poet Vladimir Shuf (1865-1913) and the writings of Solov'ev and Nietzsche.

34 NEWCOMBE, JOSEPHINE M. "Was Čexov a Tolstoyan?" SEEJ 18:143-52.

Argues that Tolstoy's influence was not confined to a short period and that Chekhov's attitude to Tolstoy remained fairly consistent over many years. Even such supposedly "anti-Tolstoyan" stories as "My Life" and "Ward Six" provide no evidence that he tried to break free of Tolstoyism; nor is there evidence, however, that he made serious attempts to disseminate Tolstoy's ideas.

35 PLETNEV, R.V. "Ob odnom rasskaze A.P. Chekhova" [On one story by Chekhov]. <u>NovŽ</u> 115:74-82.

Examines "A Fit of Nerves" within the context of Chekhov's own creative personality and the ideological and aesthetic influences of his predecessores. The Russian literary tradition generally and Garshin's writings about prostitutes specifically helped Chekhov create his hero.

36 POLOTSKAIA, E.A. "Primechaniia" [Notes]. In <u>PSSP. Pis'ma</u> [Letters]. Vol. 1. Moscow: Nauka, pp. 319-526.

Provides explanatory notes for Chekhov's letters written between 1875 and 1886.

37 -----. "'Tri goda': ot romana k povesti" ["Three Years:" from novel to tale]. In <u>V tvorcheskoi laboratorii Chekhova</u> [In Chekhov's creative laboratory]. By AN SSSR. Institut mirovoi literatury im. A.M. Gor'kogo. Moscow: Nauka, pp. 13-34.

Examines the genesis of the tale and argues that at one point in its writing Chekhov considered it a novel. Polotskaia also discusses the question of Chekhov and the novel generally.

38 SHAKH-AZIZOVA, T.K. "Sovremennoe prochtenie chekhovskikh p'es: 60-e--70-e gody" [The contemporary reading of Chekhov's plays: the 1960s and 70s]. In <u>V tvorcheskoi laboratorii Chekhova</u> [In Chekhov's creative workshop]. By AN SSSR. Institut mirovoi literatury im. A.M. Gor'kogo. Moscow: Moscow: Nauka, pp. 336-53.

Examines the "canonical" interpretation of Chekhov's plays that emerged from the post-war MAT productions and surveys the main themes in recent Soviet criticism and stage productions.

39 SHATALOV, S.E. "Cherty poetiki: Chekhov i Turgenev" [Features of poetics: Chekhov and Turgenev]. In <u>V tvorcheskoi laboratorii Chekhova</u> [In Chekhov's creative laboratory]. By AN SSSR. Institut mirovoi literatury im. A.M. Gor'kogo. Moscow: Nauka, pp. 296-309.

Examines Turgenev's influence on Chekhov and argues that it appears not only in isolated areas of similarity but in his poetics generally. "Ariadne" is the story most in the Turgenev manner.

40 SMIRNOV, M.M. "Geroi i avtor v 'Skuchnoi istorii'" [Character and author in "A Dreary Story"]. In V tvorcheskoi laboratorii Chekhova [In Chekhov's creative workshop]. By AN SSSR. Institut mirovoi literatury im. A.M. Gor'kogo. Moscow: Nauka, pp. 218-31.

Examines the relationship between author and narrator in the story, arguing that the author reveals the bankruptcy of the hero-narrator's views by showing why he believes the things he does and by pointing out the discrepancy between his image of reality and reality itself.

41 SZNYCER, BERNARD W. "General Notes." In Chekhov: The Gull. Translated by Bernard W. Sznycer. London: Poets' and Painters' Press, pp. 123-36.

A selection of the translator's notes from his version of the play. Included are observations on the style of characters' speech, characterization, and the theory of translation generally.

42 TVERDOKHLEBOV, I.Iu. "K tvorcheskoi istorii p'esy Ivanov" [On the creative history of Ivanov]. In V tvorcheskoi laboratorii Chekhova [In Chekhov's creative workshop]. By AN SSSR. Institut mirovoi literatury im. A.M. Gor'kogo. Moscow: Nauka, pp. 97-107.

Compares the initial comedic version of Ivanov (1887) with its later (1889) dramatic version using a newly-discovered copy of the play containing corrections Chekhov made after its initial failure.

43 VIDUETSKAIA, I.P. "Sposoby sozdaniia illiuzii real'nosti v proze zrelogo Chekhova" [Methods of creating the illusion of reality in the prose of the mature Chekhov]. In V tvorcheskoi laboratorii Chekhova [In Chekhov's creative workshop]. By AN SSSR. Institut mirovoi literatury im. A.M. Gor'kogo. Moscow: Nauka, pp. 279-95.

In his early work Chekhov relied on traditional means to create the illusion of reality. In his later work he attempted to exclude anything that left the impression of artificiality or contrivance and to make his form "invisible." His methods show up clearly when his work is contrasted with that of a very different type of writer such as Leskov or Tolstoy.

44 VUKULOV, L.I. "Chekhov i gazetnyi roman: Drama na okhote" [Chekhov and the newspaper novel: The

Shooting Party]. In V tvorcheskoi laboratorii Chekhova [In Chekhov's creative workshop]. By AN SSSR. Institut mirovoi literatury im. A.M. Gor'kogo. Moscow: Nauka, pp. 208-17.

Examines Chekhov's novel within the tradition of the serialized "newspaper novel" of the 1870s and 80s, arguing that it was not a parody of such works but a serious attempt to test his capacity to write a novel.

1975

1 ANDREEV, G. "Zagadka Chekhova" [The riddle of Chekhov]. NovŽ 118:57-71.

Discusses Shestov's (1905.9), Kurdiumov's (1934.3), Bunin's (1955.2), and other emigré critics' opinions on Chekhov, arguing that he had a deeply tragic view of humanity. His art has its roots in religion. He was part of the tradition of Christian humanism, "a great writer of Christian culture."

2 BABULA, WILLIAM. "Three Sisters, Time, and the Audience." MD 18:365-69.

Argues that the theme of time is central to The Three Sisters. The play contains many verbal allusions to time and change; the profound changes that occur between the acts also convey the effect of the rapid passage of time; clocks and watches also play important roles. Chekhov creates a vivid sense in his audience of time slipping by.

3 CHUDAKOV, A.P.; DOLOTOVA, L.M.; MELKOVA, A.S.; and OPUL'SKAIA, L.D. "Primechaniia" [Notes]. In PSSP. Sochineniia [Works]. Vol. 2. Moscow: Nauka, pp. 467-559.

Discusses Chekhov's literary career during 1883 and the beginning of 1884; summarizes critical reaction to his work of that period; describes works no longer extant. Individual explanatory notes for the 131 works of the period are also included.

4 DOBIN, E. "Detal' u Chekhova kak sterzhen' kompositsii" [Chekhov's details as the pivot of his composition]. VLit, no. 8, pp. 125-44.

Examines Chekhov's use of details and their links with plot, arguing that this was one of his great innovations in prose. A seemingly trivial detail is repeated and its meaning expanded so that it carries much of the action of the story, allowing him to broaden the significance of the work.

5 DOLOTOVA, L.M.; GROMOV, M.P.; MELKOVA, A.S.; and SOKOLOVA, M.A. "Primechaniia" [Notes]. In PSSP. Sochineniia [Works]. Vol. 3. Moscow: Nauka, pp. 525-605.

Discusses Chekhov's literary career from May 1884 to May 1885 and summarizes critical response to his work of that period. Explanatory notes for the 102 items are also included.

6 EEKMAN, THOMAS. "The Narrator and the Hero in Chekhov's Prose." CSS 8:93-129.

Examines the point of view and its evolution in Chekhov's stories. Takes issue with Chudakov's division of point of view in Chekhov's work into three periods (see 1971.6), arguing that Chekhov uses a much more varied approach. The choice of point of view was largely determined for him by the technical requirements of the type of story he was writing. Contrary to Chudakov's assertions, several of Chekhov's stories of his last years do have a hero's point of view. An appendix categorizes Chekhov's stories from 1886 to 1903 according to point of view.

7 GOR'KOVSKII GOS. UNIVERSITET IM. N.I. LOBACHEVSKOGO. Russkaia literatura XIX v.: voprosy siuzheta i kompozitsii. II mezhvuzovskii sbornik [Russian literature of the nineteenth century: questions of plot and composition. The second inter-university anthology]. Gorky: Gor'kovskii gos. universitet im. N.I. Lobachevskogo.

Contains three articles on Chekhov: one deals with the structural unity of his short stories and examines how repeated details of the setting help create a sub-text; a second discusses the history of Uncle Vanya; and a third examines Chekhov's use of landscape in "Lights," "Enemies," "Champagne," and "On Holy Night."

8 HINGLEY, RONALD. Preface, Introduction, Appendices and Notes to The Oxford Chekhov. Vol. 9. Edited and translated by Ronald Hingley. London: Oxford University Press, pp. ix-xvii, 1-12, and 265-323.

Discusses problems of translating the stories of 1898 to 1904 and on translating Chekhov generally; argues that the translator's intent is "to give Chekhov the kind of language which he himself might have used, had he chanced to be writing in English." The stories of Chekhov's last seven years are placed in biographical and social context. Comments on the composition, texts, and variants of "The Man in the Case," "Gooseberries," "About Love," "Ionych," "A Case History," "The Darling," "The New

Dacha," "On Official Duty," "The Lady With the Little Dog," "At Christmas," "In the Ravine," "The Bishop," and "Betrothed." Explanatory notes to the stories are also provided.

9 JONES, W. GARETH. "The Seagull's Second Symbolist Play-Within-the-Play." SEER 53:17-26.

Argues that the fourth act of The Seagull contains a second play-within-a-play in the game of lotto; this balances Konstantin's play in Act One. There are many parallels between the two plays, although they are well concealed. But the second play demonstrates that the new forms of the symbolist theater could succeed if handled with real skill.

10 LAKSHIN, V.Ia. Tolstoi i Chekhov [Tolstoy and Chekhov]. 2d ed., revised. Moscow: Sovetskii pisatel', 456 pp.

Revised version of 1963.10, it devotes somewhat more attention to biographical factors influencing the work of both writers and to elaborating the values implicit in the writings of each.

11 LANTZ, K.A. "Čexov and the Scenka, 1880-1887." SEEJ 19:377-87.

Discusses the nature of the stsenka genre and examines its place in Chekhov's early work. Chekhov developed this common humor-magazine genre by gradually shifting its action from the external to the internal, changing a traditionally comic and frivolous form into a vehicle for serious art.

12 MALAKHOVA, A.M.; ROSKINA, N.A.; and GITOVICH, N.I. "Primechaniia" [Notes]. In PSSP. Pis'ma [Letters]. Vol. 2. Moscow: Nauka, pp. 337-530.

Provides explanatory notes for Chekhov's letters written from 1887 to the end of September 1888.

13 RAYFIELD, DONALD. Chekhov: The Evolution of His Art. New York: Barnes & Noble, 266 pp.

Aims to give a complete view of Chekhov's work by surveying his literary career chronologically and showing the links between the events of his biography and his writings. Considerable attention is paid to the relationship between the plays and the stories and to demonstrating how the two illuminate one another. Key stories in his development are analyzed as are his major plays. Reprinted in part in 1979.14.

14 STOWELL, H. PETER. "Chekhov's Prose Fuge: 'Sleepy'." RLT 11:435-42.

Argues that the story, with its juxtaposition of contrapuntal levels and its overlapping fragments of its heroine's perceptions, is a "prose fugue." It moves through four levels toward the crescendo of its inexorable conclusion.

15 -----. "Chekhov's 'The Bishop:' The Annihilation of Faith and Identity Through Time." SSF 12:117-26.

Argues that the modernism of Chekhov's plays is also a feature of his stories. His impressionistic technique is demonstrated in "The Bishop;" here the title figure attempts to find an identity for his own existence, but his identity, as well as his mother's, is in question. His very existence may have been a dream of his mother.

16 VOROVSKII, V.V. Estetika. Literatura. Iskusstvo [Aesthetics, literature, art]. Introduction by I.S. Chernoutsan. Moscow: Iskusstvo, 544 pp.

Contains 1905.11 and 1910.10.

1976

1 BERDNIKOV, G.P. "Dama s sobachkoi" A.P. Chekhova: k voprosu o traditsii i novatorstve v proze Chekhova [Chekhov's "Lady With the Little Dog:" on the question of tradition and innovation in Chekhov's prose]. Massovaia istoriko-literaturnaia biblioteka [The popular library of history and literature]. Leningrad: Khudozhestvennaia litertura, 96 pp.

Makes a close analysis of the story, pointing out its typically Chekhovian style and structure and viewing it in the context of his other writings. The characters he creates are at once typical and atypical, representative of many, yet clearly individual.

2 -----. "Zametki o poetike prozy Chekhova i ego khudozhestvennom metode" [Remarks on the poetics of Chekhov's prose and on his artistic method]. Zvezda, no. 7, pp. 185-207.

Examines Chekhov's economical, compact style and agrees with Derman(1959.4) that many of his stories fit the formal criteria for a novel in all but their length. The overall simplicity of his manner arises from his simple plots and his highly economical means of exposition. He transferred his center of interest from the external event to the inner world of his characters.

3 BRAHMS, CARYL. Reflections in a Lake: A Study of Chekhov's Four Greatest Plays. London: Weidenfeld

& Nicolson, 154 pp.

Includes individual studies of the last four plays, commenting on their genesis, their major themes, and on various British and European productions. "[Chekhov's] plays come second only to those of Shakespeare in understanding the human heart, and second to none in forgiveness of its weaknesses."

4 BRIUSOV, VALERII. "Vishnevyi sad Chekhova." In Literaturnoe nasledstvo [Literary legacy] Vol. 85, Valerii Briusov. Edited by A.N. Dubovikov and N.A. Trifonov. Moscow: Nauka, pp. 195-99.

A previously unpublished and unfinished article from 1904 in which Briusov dismisses Chekhov's plays as mere reproductions of reality lacking any profound ideas. Similarly the MAT's approach to drama, attempting an exact reproduction of reality, is a blind alley for Russian art. An introductory article (pp. 190-94) and notes are provided by E.A. Polotskaia.

5 CALDER, ANGUS. "Literature and Morality: Leskov, Chekhov, late Tolstoy." In Russia Discovered: Nineteenth-century Fiction from Pushkin to Chekhov. New York: Barnes & Noble, pp. 238-63.

Surveys Chekhov's writings within the context of the history of his own age and the Russian literary tradition. He was a "reverent agnostic" whose morality was not tied to Christianity. His "Ward Six" subtly takes issue with Tolstoyan ethics.

6 CHERVINSKENE, ELENA. Edinstvo khudozhestvennogo mira: A.P. Chekhov [The monolithic nature of the artistic world: Chekhov]. Literatura, no. 18. Vilnius: Mokslas, 183 pp.

Argues that the work of any original writer is monolithic by nature and that the author's personality is the "dominant" in the system that operates within the monolith. The author's criteria in portraying reality can be determined by certain significant features that repeat themselves in his writings. The main criterion in Chekhov's portrayal of reality is the basic humanity of his characters. His universal standard for this humanity is a civilized, humane, and enlightened attitude (kul'turnost'), which reveals itself in respect for others, sensitivity, intelligence, talent, a capacity for work, and a love of beauty. A detailed analysis of "Ward Six" provides a case study that shows the operation of the principles of this artistic world.

7 GEIDEKO, VALERII. A. Chekhov i Iv. Bunin [Chekhov and Bunin]. Moscow: Sovetskii pisatel', 374 pp.

Attempts to define the essential qualities of each writer by examining the main intellectual currents of ther era and showing how the two writers responded to contemporary issues. Similarities and differences in their styles, handling of plot and composition, use of details, and prose innovations are discussed.

8 GERIGK, HORST-JÜRGEN. "Tennessee Williams und Anton Čechov." ZSP 39:157-65.

Examines the influence of Chekhov on Tennessee Williams generally as well as his specific role in Williams' one-act play The Lady of Larkspur Lotion. The two writers' outlooks have some common features, notably their sense of human isolation and mutual incomprehension.

9 GITOVICH, I.E.; KONSHINA, E.N.; NECHAEV, V.P.; OPUL'SKAIA, L.D.; and ROSKINA, N.A. "Primechaniia" [Notes]. In PSSP. Pis'ma [Letters]. Vol. 4. Moscow: Nauka, pp. 369-557.

Provides explanatory notes for Chekhov's letters written from January 1890 to the end of February 1892.

10 GITOVICH, I.E.; GITOVICH, N.I.; GRIEL'SKAIA, M.P.; KHANILO, A.V.; and NECHAEV, V.P. "Primechaniia" [Notes]. In PSSP. Pis'ma [Letters]. Vol. 3. Moscow: Nauka, pp. 311-486.

Provides explanatory notes for Chekhov's letters written from October 1888 to December 1889.

11 GRISHUNIN, A.L.; MELKOVA, A.S.; POLOTSKAIA, E.A.; RODIONOVA, V.M.; and TVERDOKHLEBOV, I.Iu. "Primechaniia" [Notes]. In PSSP. Sochineniia [Works]. Vol. 5. Moscow: Nauka, pp. 597-677.

Discusses Chekhov's literary work and summarizes critical response to it for the period from March to December 1886. Explanatory notes and the history of publication of the eighty-four stories of the period are included.

12 GROMOV, M.P. "Primechaniia" [Notes]. In PSSP. Sochineniia [Works]. Vol. 4. Moscow: Nauka, pp. 453-522.

Discusses Chekhov's literary career and summarizes the reactions of critics and colleagues to his work for the period June 1885 to February 1886. Explanatory notes for the ninety-eight stories of the period are included.

13 HAMBURGER, H. "The Function of the Time Component in Čexov's 'Na podvode'." In Dutch Contributions to the Seventh International Congress of Slavists:

Warsaw, August 21-27, 1973. Edited by André van Holk. Slavistic Printings and Reprintings, no. 293. The Hague and Paris: Mouton, pp. 237-70.

Includes a theoretical discussion of the time component in the sentence and in the larger text; applies this to "In the Cart."

14 HINGLEY, RONALD. A New Life of Anton Chekhov. New York: Alfred A. Knopf, 352 pp.

A complete biography that aims to give a more intimate picture of Chekhov by taking into account new material--notably letters to Chekhov from several close women friends--as well as the author's experience in translating Chekhov. Succinct discussions of Chekhov's writings and their role in his evolution are included. Considerable attention is devoted to his relationships with and attitudes toward women. An Appendix gives a general description of Chekhov's work, dividing it into two periods (pre- and post-1888), each period having four phases. A bibliography lists Chekhov's works in English as well as English-language critical and biographical studies.

15 HULANICKI, LEO and SAVIGNAC, DAVID, eds. and translators. Anton Čexov as a Master of Story-Writing. Introduction by Leo Hulanicki. The Hague and Paris: Mouton, 204 pp.

Contains translated articles or excerpts from larger works by contemporary Soviet scholars. A variety of critical approaches and topics are represented. Includes portions of 1958.9, 1959.4, 1961.14, 1962.5, 1963.10, 1963.18, 1966.18, 1968.5, and 1970.17.

16 KASZKUREWICZ, TAMARA. "Postroenie psikhologicheskoi temy v rasskaze A.P. Chekhova 'Volodia bol'shoi i Volodia malen'kii'" [The development of the psychologcal theme in Chekhov's "The Two Volodias]. RLJ 105:47-59.

Argues that the basic concern of Chekhov's mature work is the inner world of human beings; discusses how this psychological focus is created in "The Two Volodias." This is done indirectly and impressionistically through careful selection of details in characterization, in dialogue, and in description. His technique is thus objective in that he relies on known externals (as well as on the creative efforts of the reader) to suggest unknown internals.

17 KATAEV, V.B. "O literaturnykh predshestvennikakh Vishnevogo sada" [On the literary predecessors of The Cherry Orchard]. In Chekhovskie chteniia v

Ial'te: Chekhov i teatr [Chekhov papers in Yalta: Chekhov and the theater]. Edited by V.I. Kuleshov, N.N. Solov'eva, E.M. Sakharova, M.N. Stroeva, Z.S. Papernyi, and T.K. Shakh-Azizova. Moscow: Kniga, pp. 131-50.

Surveys existing literature on the subject and argues that Ostrovsky's plays contain many situations and characters similar to those of The Cherry Orchard. Saltykov-Shchedrin also dealt with the decline of the landowning gentry, as did N.I. Solov'ev in his play Liquidation [Likvidatsiia]. But there is no single, dominant source: Chekhov assembled impressions from Russian literature generally, from his own works, and from his own experience. This can be seen when studying the character of Lopakhin in the light of his literary and real-life counterparts.

18 -----. "Chekhov i mifologiia novogo vremeni" [Chekhov and modern mythology]. FN 5:71-77.

Takes issue with critics who see Chekhov as a "non-literary" writer, arguing that he relied heavily on literary traditions. His use of modern "myths" also reveals his literariness: in "The Bishop" he uses the myth of Christ's death and resurrection; in The Seagull, the myth of Hamlet; and in "The Black Monk" the myth of Faust. The reverse process can be seen in MacDonald Harris's novel Treplev, whose hero tries to recreate his life in terms of The Seagull.

19 KULESHOV, V.I.; SOLOV'EVA, N.N.; SAKHAROVA, E.M.; STROEVA, M.N.; PAPERNYI, Z.S.; and SHAKH-AZIZOVA, T.K., eds. Chekhovskie chteniia v Ial'te: Chekhov i teatr [Chekhov papers in Yalta: Chekhov and the theater]. Moscow: Kniga, 216 pp.

Contains twelve articles on Chekhov's plays, their stage performance, film adaptations, and their place in world theater; and eight articles on Chekhov's biography, his critical reception, and assessments of his drama generally. Besides 1976.17, 1976.19, and 1976.27-28 are studies of the MAT's presentations of his plays, reactions of his contemporaries to his plays, the structure of his plays, the premieres and later productions of The Seagull and The Three Sisters, and of a filmed version of The Seagull.

20 KUZICHEVA, A.P. "'Zerkalo' chekhovskoi p'esy: o Chaike" [The "mirror" of a Chekhov play: on The Seagull]. In Chekhovskie chteniia v Ial'te: Chekhov i teatr [Chekhov papers in Yalta: Chekhov and the theater]. Edited by V.I. Kuleshov, N.N. Solov'eva, E.M. Sakharova, M.N. Stroeva, Z.S.

Papernyi, and T.K. Shakh-Azizova. Moscow: Kniga, pp. 96-101.

Examines the role of the play-within-the-play, the literary allusions, and the references to art generally, arguing that these help involve the spectator by holding up a mirror that reflects their lives.

21 MARTIN, DAVID W. "Historical References in Chekhov's Later Stories." MLR 71:595-606.

Argues that the many historical references in Chekhov's fiction represent an important stylistic device. Historical references voiced by characters are more often linked with unpleasant than pleasant feelings; they are, however, very clearly the attribute of the character himself and not necessarily of Chekhov. Thus historical references reveal something of the character's inner life.

22 MELKOVA, A.S.; RODIONOVA, V.M.; SAKHAROVA, E.M.; and SOKOLOVA, M.A. "Primechaniia" [Notes]. In PSSP. Sochineniia [Works]. Vol. 6. Moscow: Nauka, pp. 611-706.

Discusses Chekhov's writings and his relationship to the literary world in 1887. Individual explanatory notes for each of the sixty-five stories of that year and a summary of critical responses to them are also included.

23 PAPERNYI, Z.S. "Siuzhet dolzhen byt' nov..." [The plot should be fresh...]. VLit no. 5, pp. 169-89.

Critically examines some truisms about Chekhov's use of plot, modifies some of these, and argues that most have validity. His plots are internalized, but rather than showing his characters in action they show them in inaction. Unlike Pushkin's "syncretically" complete plots, Chekhov's simple plots, seemingly devoid of incident, develop through a complex system of subtle imagery that reflects the inner states of his characters. The imagery, contained in his details, thus becomes a most important element in the work.

24 -----. Zapisnye knizhki Chekhova [Chekhov's notebooks]. Moscow: Sovetskii pisatel', 392 pp.

Examines the notebooks and argues that not only do they contain the germ of many subsequent works but they also reveal the very essence of Chekhov. Papernyi attempts to explain many cryptic references in the notebooks and to show the importance of remarks Chekhov recorded only for his own benefit. Considerable attention is devoted to entries for "The Lady With the Little Dog", "Ionych," The Seagull, and The Cherry Orchard.

25 POMORSKA, KRYSTYNA. "On the Structure of Modern Prose: Čexov and Solženicyn." PTL: A Journal for Descriptive Poetics and Theory of Literature 1:459-65.

Argues that Solzhenitsyn's prose is innovative and fits into the Chekhov tradition. Chekhov's pronouncements about literature--specifically that it need not be "eventful"--are followed in the main by Solzhenitsyn who, like Chekhov, conveys the effect of "a continuous stream of life" in his writings, especially in One Day in the Life of Ivan Denisovich.

26 ROWE, ELEANOR. "Hamlet in the Age of Chekhov and Blok." In Hamlet: A Window on Russia. New York University Studies in Comparative Literature, no. 7. New York: New York University Press, pp. 107-25.

Discusses Chekhov's interest in Hamlet; surveys Hamletian motifs in his works.

27 RUDNITSKII, K.L. "Chaika: 1898" [The Seagull: 1898]. In Chekhovskie chteniia v Ial'te: Chekhov i teatr. Edited by V.I. Kuleshov, E.M. Sakharova, Z.S. Papernyi, and T.K. Shakh-Azizova. Moscow: Kniga, pp. 61-84.

Describes the MAT's first staging of The Seagull as outlined in Stanislavsky's notes and director's plan.

28 SEMANOVA, M.L. Chekhov-khudozhnik [Chekhov the artist]. Moscow: Prosveshchenie, 224 pp.

Examines a number of Chekhov's works of different periods and of different genres with the aim of elaborating his individuality as an artist. Included are studies of his narrative technique, the titles of his works, his use of factual material, specifically the influence of his Sakhalin journey on his fiction. Chekhov uses static and dynamic details to suggest inner changes in his characters; in his trilogy the multiple points of view correct and amplify one another. Comedy in The Cherry Orchard and Chekhov's use of time are also investigated.

29 SHAKH-AZIZOVA, T.K. "Dolgaia zhizn' traditsii" [The long life of traditions]. In Chekhovskie chteniia v Ial'te: Chekhov i teatr [Chekhov papers in Yalta: Chekhov and the theater]. Edited by V.I. Kuleshov, N.N. Solov'eva, E.M. Sakharova, M.N. Stroeva, Z.S. Papernyi, and T.K. Shakh-Azizova. Moscow: Kniga, pp. 22-35.

Discusses the maintenance and renewal of the "Chekhov tradition" in the Soviet theater, describing new productions of his plays in the 1960s and 70s.

30 TSILEVICH, L.M. Siuzhet Chekhovskogo rasskaza [The plot of the Chekhov story]. Riga: Zvaigzne, 238 pp.

Argues that one of Chekhov's major innovations was in plot and that this transformed the short story genre; investigates his technique of plot construction. The reader's perception of plot is the interaction of the characters in time and space, and these elements are also examined. The interrelationship of plot and genre is also examined.

1977

1 AKADEMIIA NAUK SSSR. Institut mirovoi literatury im. A.M. Gor'kogo. "A.P. Chekhov." In Literaturnoe nasledstvo [Literary legacy] Vol. 87, Iz istorii russkoi literatury i obshchestvennoi mysli 1860-1890-kh godov [From the history of Russian literature and social thought of the 1860s to 1890s]. Moscow: Nauka, pp. 258-356.

Contains six newly-found telegrams of Chekhov to A.S. Suvorin; a collection of photographs taken for inclusion in The Island of Sakhalin; new material on his return journey from Sakhalin; and three reminiscences of him.

2 BIALYI, G.A. "Sovremenniki" [Contemporaries]. In Chekhov i ego vremia [Chekhov and his time]. Edited by L.D. Opul'skaia, Z.S. Papernyi, and S.E. Shatalov. Moscow: Nauka, pp. 5-19.

Examines a number of themes common to the works of Chekhov and other writers of his age such as Tolstoy, Dostoevsky, Garshin, Gleb Uspensky, and others. The notion of rebirth and renewal was common in the literature of this period; literary characters often are led to see the world in radically new terms. The themes of repentance and flight from a world become unbearable are also shared by Chekhov and his contemporaries.

3 BRISTOW, EUGENE K., trans. and ed. Anton Chekhov's Plays: The Sea Gull, Uncle Vanya, The Three Sisters, The Cherry Orchard. Backgrounds. Criticism. New York: W.W. Norton. 412 pp.

Contains the four major plays, two short plays, and fourteen essays on Chekhov, his Russia, and his drama. An editor's introduction discusses problems of translation. Includes, entire or in part, 1908.5, 1949.1, 1949.2, 1952.5, 1956.8, 1960.70, 1964.3, 1967.3, 1968.28, and 1970.14.

4 CHANCES, ELLEN. "Chekhov's Seagull: Ethereal Creature or Stuffed Bird?" In Chekhov's Art of Writing: A Collection of Critical Essays. Edited by Paul Debreczeny and Thomas Eekman. Columbus, Ohio: Slavia, pp. 27-34.

Argues that the play is in fact a comedy whose major theme is the stripping away of artificiality. In keeping with this Chekhov deliberately deflates the romantic image of the seagull. The reference to Maupassant's Sur l'eau strengthens the theme of role-playing and the falsity of the characters' lives.

5 CHUDAKOV, A.P.; DOLOTOVA, L.M.; GROMOV, M.P.; KATAEV, V.B.; MELKOVA, A.S.; OPUL'SKAIA, L.D.; OSHAROVA, T.V.; and POLOTSKAIA, E.A. "Primechaniia" [Notes]. In PSSP. Sochineniia [Works]. Vol. 10. Moscow: Nauka, pp. 331-488.

Discusses the work of the last period of Chekhov's life, 1898 to 1903; describes the publication of his writings, including the A.F. Marks edition of his Collected Works; comments on planned but unrealized literary projects. A summary of critical reaction to his work of the period and explanatory notes for seventeen stories are included.

6 CHUDAKOV, A.P.; DOLOTOVA, E.M.; and SAKHAROVA, E.M. "Primechaniia" [Notes]. In PSSP. Sochineniia [Works]. Vol. 8. Moscow: Nauka, pp. 413-518.

Discusses Chekhov's short stories for the period 1892 to 1894 and sets them in the context of his literary career. Critical reaction to his work of the period is summarized; explanatory notes are provided for each of the nineteen stories.

7 CHUDAKOV, A.P.; GRISHUNIN, A.L.; GROMOV, M.P.; KATAEV, V.B.; KRASNOSHCHEKOVA, E.A.; LAZERSON, B.I.; MEDRISH, D.N.; and SOKOLOVA, M.A. "Primechaniia" [Notes]. In PSSP. Sochineniia [Works]. Vol. 7. Moscow: Nauka, pp. 611-724.

Discusses Chekhov's literary career from 1888 to 1891; comments on critical reaction to his work of the period. Explanatory notes for each of the twenty-one stories are included.

8 CLARKE, CHARANNE CARROLL. "Aspects of Impressionism in Chekhov's Prose." In Chekhov's Art of Writing: A Collection of Critical Essays. Edited by Paul Debreczeny and Thomas Eekman. Columbus, Ohio: Slavica, pp. 123-33.

Discusses the concept of literary impressionism and argues that Chekhov's work shares many of its characteristics. "Sleepy," "The Name-Day Party," and "The Bishop," with their stress on the protagonists' perceptions, provide good illustrations of his impressionism at work.

9 CONRAD, JOSEPH L. "Anton Chekhov's Literary Landscapes." In Chekhov's Art of Writing: A Collection of Critical Essays. Edited by Paul Debreczeny and Thomas Eekman. Columbus, Ohio: Slavica, pp. 82-99.

Examines the evolution of Chekhov's descriptions of nature and their contribution to the "mood" of his stories. His early landscapes were composed according to the principles of selectivity of detail and personification of nature; beginning with "Enemies" his technique began moving away from Turgenev's principles toward his own unique style. The landscape is no longer simply a background but is tightly linked to the psychology of the protagonist.

10 DEBRECZENY, PAUL, and EEKMAN, THOMAS, eds. Chekhov's Art of Writing: A Collection of Critical Essays. Columbus, Ohio: Slavica, 199 pp.

Contains thirteen essays on various aspects of Chekhov's prose and drama with an emphasis on formal studies. Includes 1977.4, 1977.8, 1977.9, 1977.15, 1977.25, 1977.26, 1977.33, 1977.35, 1977.47, 1977.48, 1977.52, 1977.53, and 1977.57. A foreword by Ronald Hingley surveys the themes of death and love in Chekhov's work and argues that, unlike his predecessors, Chekhov deliberately deflated these profound topics.

11 DLUGOSCH, INGRID. Anton Pavlovič Čechov und das Theater des Absurden. Forum Slavicum, edited by Dmitrij Tschižewskij, vol. 42. Munich: Wilhelm Fink Verlag, 314 pp.

Sees Chekhov as a pioneer of the modern whose plays, through their artistic methods and new view of the individual in society, anticipate the theater of the absurd. The MAT's interpretations obscured those very elements that make Chekhov a modern dramatist. The structure of Chekhov's plays generally, and of The Three Sisters specifically, display many absurdist features.

12 DOLOTOVA, L.M.; DUNAEVA, E.N.; GAVRILENKO, L.K.; GITOVICH, N.I.; GRIEL'SKAIA, M.P.; KATAEV, V.B.; and VINOGRADOVA, K.M. "Primechaniia" [Note]. In PSSP. Pis'ma [Letters]. Vol. 7. Moscow: Nauka, pp. 385-702.

Provides explanatory notes for Chekhov's letters

written between June 1897 and December 1898.

13 DOLOTOVA, L.M.; MALAKHOVA, A.M.; and ROSKINA, N.A. "Primechaniia" [Notes]. In PSSP. Pis'ma [Letters]. Vol. 5. Moscow: Nauka, pp. 353-593.

Provides explanatory notes for Chekhov's letters written from March 1892 to the end of December 1894.

14 DRAGOMIRETSKAIA, N.V. "Ob"ektivizatsiia slova geroia" [Objectivization of a character's speech]. In Tipologiia stilevogo razvitiia XIX veka [The typology of stylistic development in the 19th century]. Edited by N.K. Gei. Moscow: Nauka, pp. 383-420.

Examines some of Chekhov's stylistic innovations, arguing that these depart sharply from the existing tradition as exemplified by Tolstoy, Gogol, and others. Evaluations and judgements no longer come from the author but from a character; their validity can be determined within the context in which they were uttered. The boundary between the style of the author's language and that of the character is blurred. The sense of time, likewise, is conveyed through a character rather than by the author. This stylistic system is non-hierarchical and centrifugal, allowing the ordinary and average to become the center of attention.

15 DUNCAN, PHILLIP A. "Chekhov's 'An Attack of Nerves' as 'Experimental' Narrative." In Chekhov's Art of Writing: A Collection of Critical Essays. Edited by Paul Debreczeny and Thomas Eekman. Columbus, Ohio: Slavica, pp. 112-22.

Argues that many of Chekhov's stories of the late 1880s were influenced by Zola's "experimental novel," and that "A Fit of Nerves" serves as a good example of this influence at work. Here the effect of the environment coupled with Vasilev's predisposition to nervous tension determines the progress of the story.

16 ESIN, B.I. Chekhov-zhurnalist [Chekhov the journalist]. Moscow: MGU, 104 pp.

An expanded version of 1960.20, it examines Chekhov's journalism of the 1880s and 90s, including his work in the humor magazines, his later articles in Novoe vremia, and his writings on Siberia and Sakhalin. The phenomenon of the "newspaper story" is discussed, and Chekhov's contributions to it are summarized.

17 FROST, EDGAR L. "The Search for Eternity in Čexov's Fiction: The Flight from Time as a Source of Tension." RLJ 108:111-20.

Examines the conflict between the limitations of time and the limitlessness of eternity within many of Chekhov's characters. This conflict causes tension because few characters have a faith in eternity to counteract the pressures caused by temporality. Time is very much in the minds of his characters, and in order to protract it they do essentially nothing. When an event does occur it comes as a sudden disruption of a surface which appears placid but which in fact is full of tension.

18 GIRSHMAN, M.M. "Garmoniia i disgarmoniia v povestvovanii i stile" [Harmony and disharmony in narrative and style]. In Tipologiia stilevogo razvitiia XIX veka [The typology of stylistic development in the 19th century]. Edited by N.K. Gei. Moscow: Nauka, pp. 362-82.

Argues, on evidence from "The Student," "The Man in a Case," and "The Black Monk," that beneath the apparent smoothness and harmony of Chekhov's style are complex, disharmonious elements.

19 GRISHUNIN, A.L. and POLOTSKAIA, E.A.. "Primechaniia" [Notes]. In PSSP. Sochineniia [Works]. Vol. 9. Moscow: Nauka, pp. 435-537.

Discusses Chekhov's literary career from 1894 to 1897 and summarizes critical reaction to his work of that period. Explanatory notes for each of fourteen stories are included.

20 GROMOV, M.P. "Skrytye tsitaty: Chekhov i Dostoevskii" [Hidden quotations: Chekhov and Dostoevsky]. In Chekhov i ego vremia [Chekhov and his time]. Edited by L.D. Opul'skaia, Z.S. Papernyi, and S.E. Shatalov. Moscow: Nauka, pp. 39-52.

Although Chekhov knew Dostoevsky well he left few overt references to him; however, Gromov argues, his works have frequent "hidden quotations" from Dostoevsky. These can be found in "Neighbours," "A Boring Story," and "The Black Monk."

21 HAHN, BEVERLY. Chekhov: A Study of the Major Stories and Plays. Major European Authors. Cambridge: Cambridge University Press, 351 pp.

A general survey of that attempts to dispel critical clichés about the negativity, formless, and insipidness of Chekhov's writing. The Cherry Orchard, as his best-know work and, accordingly, the source of many of these misconceptions, is discussed in detail. His short stories are surveyed generally and "Lights," "A Dreary Story," and "The Duel" examined at length to reveal aspects of Chekhov's art. "The Name-Day Party" and "The Lady With the Little Dog" convey his attitudes to women; "A Woman's Kingdom" and The Three Sisters show his increasing interest in class attitudes and conditions. His overall temperament is humanist and his attitudes strikingly modern.

22 IONANNISIAN, D.V. "Ritmiko-intonatsionnyi stroi prozy Chekhova" [The rhythmical and intonational system of Chekhov's prose]. SSl 23:17-28.
Describes theoretical models for studying rhythmic and intonational structures of prose generally and applies them to Chekhov's stories.

23 IVANOV, G.V. "Zametki o Chekhove" [Remarks on Chekhov]. RLit, no. 1, pp. 175-78.
Contains two separate studies: the first comments briefly on Chekhov's attitude to Maupassant and argues that Chekhov's "Terror" takes issue with Maupassant's story of the same name in that it finds horror in the ordinary and everday rather than the supernatural. The second study concerns the real-life prototype of the narrator of "A Dreary Story."

24 KATAEV, V.B. "Final 'Nevesty'" [The ending of "Betrothed"]. In Chekhov i ego vremia [Chekhov and his time]. Edited by L.D. Opul'skaia, Z.S. Papernyi, and S.E. Shatalov. Moscow: Nauka, pp.158-75.
Examines variants of the story and notes that in successive versions Chekhov made the ending less specific and precise, thus making the "new life" for which his heroine departs a much vaguer notion. This gives her a broader symbolic significance and underlines the story's general meaning of youth breaking away from tradition.

25 KATSELL, JEROME H. "Mortality: Theme and Structure in Chekhov's Later Prose." In Chekhov's Art of Writing: A Collection of Critical Essays. Edited by Paul Debreczeny and Thomas Eekman. Columbus, Ohio: Slavica, pp. 54-67.
Examines "Sleepy," "The Black Monk," and "The Bishop," arguing that these three stories illustrate Chekhov's approach to the theme of mortality in his later prose. In each one death is demystified and mortality accepted; each uses similar imagery and stylistic devices.

26 KRAMER, KARL D. "Chekhov and the Seasons." In Chekhov's Art of Writing: A Collection of Critical Essays. Edited by Paul Debreczeny and Thomas Eekman. Columbus, Ohio: Slavica, pp. 68-81.

Examines the link between the seasonal setting of a story and its overall effect. In his early work the season reinforced the story's atmosphere; in the late 1880s and early 90s seasonal motifs are all but abandoned; in later works, however, the seasons are again used for more complex purposes.

27 KUZ'MUK, V.A. "Vasilii Shukshin i rannii Chekhov: opyt tipologicheskogo analiza" [Vasily Shukshin and the early Chekhov: an essay in typological analysis]. RLit, no. 3, pp. 198-205.

Argues that Chekhov's early story-scenes [stsenki], with their essentially dramatic structure, strongly influenced Shukshin. Both writers are remarkably concise and both rely heavily on *peripeteia*. Translated: 1978.16.

28 LARKIN, MAURICE. *Man and Society in Nineteenth-Century Realism: Determinism and Literature*. Totowa, N.J.: Rowman & Littlefield, pp. 134-38; 148-54; 167-69.

Examines Chekhov's work within the context of a study of English and European realism as a movement that sees humans as products of heredity and environment. Chekhov's characters are generally social types whose behavior is largely determined by economic circumstances. He set great store on science and education as means of influencing environment for the better.

29 LOMUNOV, K.N. "Tolstoy-Chekhov-MKhAT" [Tolstoy-Chekhov-MAT]. In *Chekhov i ego vremia* [Chekhov and his time]. Edited by L.D. Opul'skaia, Z.S. Papernyi, and S.E. Shatalov. Moscow: Nauka, pp. 218-31.

Discusses Tolstoy's evaluation of Chekhov's plays, Tolstoy's own links with the theater of his day, and Tolstoy's and Chekhov's attitudes to the MAT. Lomunov argues that Tolstoy's dramatic achievement helped the MAT to accept and understand Chekhov by avoiding naturalism and impressionism.

30 MANDEL'SHTAM, O.E. ["Chekhov"]. RusL 5:172-73.

A previously unpublished article in which Mandelshtam notes, in regard to *Uncle Vanya*, that Chekhov's characters are simply thrown together: "cohabitation for Chekhov is a deciding principle. His plays have no action; there is only the fact that his characters live near each other and its consequent unpleasantnesses." Notes by Iu. Freidin and Iu. Levin (pp. 171, 174-75) make textological comments and set the article within the context in which it was written.

31 MARSHALL, HERBERT. The Pictorial History of the Russian Theatre. Introduction by Harold Clurman. New York: Crown, pp. 75-85, 162-63, and passim.

Describes the MAT's production of Chekhov's plays; includes many photographs of the actors and stage sets. Some material on later productions is also included.

32 MATHEWSON, RUFUS, W., Jr. "Thoreau and Chekhov: A Note on 'The Steppe'." UlbR, no. 1, pp. 28-40.

Argues that there is a kinship between the two that finds expression in "The Steppe." This work was influenced by Walden in the central role it assigns to perception. "The Steppe" presents experience "poetically" but carefully conceals its artistry.

33 MAXWELL, DAVID E. "The Unity of Chekhov's 'Little Trilogy'." In Chekhov's Art of Writing: A Collection of Critical Essays. Edited by Paul Debreczeny and Thomas Eekman. Columbus, Ohio: Slavica, pp. 35-53.

Argues that, apart from narrators, characters, and themes, the three stories ("The Man in a Case," "Gooseberries," "About Love") share a similar structure. The "functions" (basic syntactical elements of structure) in each story are the same, but the relationship among their component parts differs, giving each story its unique character.

34 MELKOVA, A.S. "Literaturnaia polemika serediny 1880-kh godov i 'tolstovskie' rasskazy Chekhova" [The literary polemics of the mid-1880s and Chekhov's "Tolstoyan" stories]. In Chekhov i ego vremia [Chekhov and his time]. Edited by L.D. Opul'skaia, Z.S. Papernyi, and S.E. Shatalov. Moscow: Nauka, pp. 301-321.

Examines the literary background to and the variants of Chekhov's "Tolstoyan" stories of 1886-87; surveys the 1886 critical debate over Tolstoyism. Chekhov insisted that Tolstoy's ideas should be carefully studied before making pronouncements about them. His stories of the period reflect his carefully considered attitude to Tolstoy's teachings.

35 MORAVČEVICH, NICHOLAS. "Scène-à-faire and the Chekhovian Dramatic Structure." In Chekhov's Art of Writing: A Collection of Critical Essays. Edited by Paul Debreczeny and Thomas Eekman. Columbus, Ohio: Slavica, pp. 100-11.

Examines the concept of the scène-à-faire or

obligatory scene and its application in Chekhovian dramatic techniques. As his drama departed from the traditional direct-action model toward a play centering on the effect of an event or theme on the emotions of his characters, every scene becomes "obligatory."

36 MOSS, HOWARD. "Three Sisters." HudR 30:525-43.
A general study of the play that argues that its action is the inability to act; stasis is made dramatic by an accumulation of small details that gradually leads to insight. The passing of time is an important theme in the play; the characters would like to reverse it to recover the past. The play's ending is enigmatic and leaves many unresolved problems.

37 MUDRICK, MARVIN. "Chekhov." In The Man in the Machine. New York: Horizon Press, pp. 153-77.
An expanded version of 1974.32.

38 OPUL'SKAIA, L.D.; PAPERNYI, Z.S.; and SHATALOV, S.E., eds. Chekhov i ego vremia [Chekhov and his time]. Moscow: Nauka, 359 pp.
A companion volume to 1974.1 and 1980.26, it contains twenty-four essays by Soviet Chekhov scholars using new research done in preparation for the 1974 Complete Collected Works and Letters. The essays concern Chekhov's relations with his writer-contemporaries; the links of his drama with the theater of his day; and his relations with the press and critics of the 1880s and 90s. Includes 1977.2, 1977.20, 1977.24, 1977.29, 1977.34, 1977.39, 1977.46, 1977.50, and 1977.54, as well as studies comparing Chekhov with Bilibin, Saltykov-Shchedrin, Korolenko, Boborykin, Gorky, Teffi, Voloshin, and Rachmaninoff. Chekhov's relations with newspapers and journals of his day (Budil'nik, Russkaia mysl', and Novoe vremia) are also examined. Other articles deal with his contemporary Russian reception, early translations of his works, and biographical matters.

39 POLOTSKAIA, E.A. "Posle Sakhalina" [After Sakhalin]. In Chekhov i ego vremia [Chekhov and his time]. Edited by L.D. Opul'skaia, Z.S. Papernyi, and S.E. Shatalov. Moscow: Nauka, pp. 117-37.
Examines the story "Murder" in the context of Chekhov's Sakhalin experience and his religious upbringing. Notes that Chekhov found some prototypes for the characters and some material on the psychology of murder on Sakhalin; his religious background helped him create the atmosphere of the story. His artistic use of material from real life differed from his "documentary" use of the same material in The Island of Sakhalin.

40 REED, WALTER. "The Cherry Orchard and Hedda Gabbler." In Homer to Brecht: The European Epic and Dramatic Traditions. Edited by Michael Seidel and Edward Mendelson. New Haven and London: Yale University Press, pp. 317-35.

Argues that The Cherry Orchard fits the traditional pattern of neither comedy nor tragedy. Chekhov's concept of character suggests a greater, human content behind the artificial surface, just as the play as a whole suggests a larger reality beyond itself. Chekhov, like Ibsen, creates a realistic theater in opposition to the theater of symbolism.

41 RÉV, MARIJA. "Čechov et Maupassant: La nouveauté de la vision du monde et de la structure dans la nouvelle russe et française au tournant du siècle." SSASH 23:137-49.

Compares the approaches of the two writers and argues that although their methods are quite different they share a cooly objective attitude to their characters. The subject of love, to which both devote a number of works, provides a case study. Chekhov in fact created a whole new type of short story in which the narrator, who is not identified with the author, assumes central importance. Maupassant generally remained within the confines of Naturalism; Chekhov transcended them.

42 ROMANENKO, VIKTOR. "'Pravda vo vsem i vsegda:' estetika realizma rannego Chekhova" ["The truth in everything and always:" the aesthetics of the realism of the early Chekhov]. In Prizvanie talanta: literaturno-kriticheskie stat'i, ocherki [The vocation of talent: articles and sketches in literary criticism]. Kiev: Radians'kii pis'mennik, pp. 111-215.

Examines Chekhov's literary beginnings and attempts to show how his early works convey his artistic and moral credo. His non-fictional writings clearly express his opinions on a whole range of subjects. The questions of how literature relates to life and of the role of the writer are also raised in many of his stories and letters of the period.

43 ROSTOVSKII-NA-DONU GOS. PEDAGOGICHESKII INSTITUT. Tvorchestvo A.P. Chekhova: sbornik statei, no. 2 [Chekhov's works: a collection of articles]. Rostov-on-the-Don: Rostovskii-na-Donu gos. pedagogicheskii institut, 159 pp.

Consists of nine articles on a variety of aspects of Chekhov's works. Includes 1977.45.

44 SCHOLLE, CHRISTINE. "A.P. Čechov, 'Das Duell'." In Das Duell in der russischen Literatur: Wandlungen und Verfall eines Ritus. Arbeiten und Texte zur Slavistik, no. 14. Edited by Wolfgang Kasack. Munich: Otto Sagner, pp. 151-64.

Examines the story within the context of a general study of duels in Russian literature. "Das ganze, Literatur gewordene Emblem kann in der Diskussion um das Recht des Stärkeren als ein Aufruf Čechovs zur Demut gesehen werden."

45 SEDEGOV, V.D. "Povest' A.P. Chekhova 'Step''" [Chekhov's tale "The Steppe"]. In Tvorchestvo A.P. Chekhova: sbornik statei, no. 2 [Chekhov's works: a collection of articles]. By Rostovskii-na-Donu gos. pedagogicheskii institut. Rostov-on-the-Don: Rostovskii-na-Donu gos. pedagogicheskii institut, pp. 45-68.

Argues that understanding "The Steppe" is crucial to comprehending Chekhov's outlook in the 1880s and to understanding his poetics generally. Sedegov examines the imagery of the work, through which much of Chekhov's outlook is expressed, and discusses the themes of country, loneliness, and happiness.

46 SEMANOVA, M.L. "Rasskaz o 'cheloveke garshinskoi zakvaski'" [A story about "a man of the Garshin temperament"]. In Chekhov i ego vremia [Chekhov and his time]. Edited by L.D. Opul'skaia, Z.S. Papernyi, and S.E. Shatalov. Moscow: Nauka, pp. 62-84.

Examines the portrait of the "Garshin type" in "An Attack of Nerves" and analyzes the story generally. Chekhov depicts the encounter of a sensitive man with harsh reality, a common subject of his works. This encounter awakens Vasilev's sense of himself.

47 SENDEROVICH, MARENA. "The Symbolic Structure of Chekhov's Story 'An Attack of Nerves'." In Chekhov's Art of Writing: A Collection of Critical Essays. Edited by Paul Debreczeny and Thomas Eekman. Columbus, Ohio: Slavica, pp. 11-26.

Argues that the story has a symbolic meaning that derives from the color perceptions, specifically black and white, of its protagonist.

48 SENDEROVICH, SAVELY. "Chekhov and Impressionism: An Attempt at a Systematic Approach to the Problem." Translated by Roger B. Mathison and Thomas Eekman. In Chekhov's Art of Writing: A Collection of

Critical Essays. Edited by Paul Debreczeny and Thomas Eekman. Columbus, Ohio: Slavica, pp. 134-52.

Surveys the history of the concept of Impressionism in painting and argues that analogues of its features can be transferred to literature and to Chekhov's work specifically. Momentary impressions predominate in the psychology of Chekhov's characters; objects are captured at one unique moment; words are used in seemingly haphazard fashion; and space has a spiritual rather than geometrical value.

49 SENELICK, LAURENCE. "The Lake-Shore of Bohemia: The Seagull's Theatrical Context." Educational Theatre Journal 29:199-213.

Examines the theatrical background from which Chekhov drew much of the material of the play, discussing his youthful experiences with the theater in Taganrog, the theaters of Lentovsky and Korsh, Chekhov's friends from the theatrical world, the influence of Suvorin's Tatyana Repina on the play, and other literary sources. The Seagull thus presents many diverse approaches to the theater; Chekhov does not take sides, but uses this material to dramatize the theme of the artist's quest.

50 SHAKH-AZIZOVA, T.K. "Russkii Gamlet: Ivanov i ego vremia" [A Russian Hamlet: Ivanov and its time]. In Chekhov i ego vremia [Chekhov and his time]. Edited by L.D. Opul'skaia, Z.S. Papernyi, and S.E. Shatalov. Moscow: Nauka, pp. 232-46.

Examines Ivanov in the context of "Russian Hamletism" and argues that although Chekhov provided no explanation of the phenomenon he continued to search for its causes in the objective conditions of life.

51 SHUBIN, B.M. Doktor A.P. Chekhov [Doctor A.P. Chekhov]. Moscow: Znanie, 128 pp.

Examines Chekhov's career as a doctor, including his medical training, his early practice, and his attitudes to science in general; comments on doctors and medicine as portrayed in his writings. A chronology of his medical career and a bibliography are included. Illustrated.

52 SMERNOFF, SUSAN S. "The Irony of the Doctor as Patient in Chekhov's 'Ward No. 6' and in Solzhenitsyn's Cancer Ward." In Chekhov's Art of Writing: A Collection of Critical Essays. Edited by Paul Debreczeny and Thomas Eekman. Columbus, Ohio: Slavica, pp. 167-79.

Compares the situation of Chekhov's Dr. Ragin

with Solzhenitsyn's Dr. Dontsova and argues that despite their many differences the two characters and the two works share common features. Both show the influence of Tolstoy; both take the hospital as a microcosm of society; and both take an insider's view of the problems they deal with.

53 STOWELL, H. PETER. "Chekhov and the Nouveau roman: Subjective Objectivism." In Chekhov's Art of Writing: A Collection of Critical Essays. Edited by Paul Debreczeny and Thomas Eekman. Columbus, Ohio: Slavica, pp. 180-91.

Traces some links between Chekhov, the impressionists, and the nouveau roman, arguing that Chekhov's best impressionistic stories have a "detached air of scrupulous observation" that produces "phenomeno-logical objectivity." His prose is dominated by the sense of the enduring present and endlessly recurring cycles.

54 VIDUETSKAIA, I.P. "Chekhov i Leskov" [Chekhov and Leskov]. In Chekhov i ego vremia [Chekhov and his time]. Edited by L.D.Opul'skaia, Z.S. Papernyi, and S.E. Shatalov. Moscow: Nauka, pp. 101-16.

Examines Leskov's evaluation of Chekhov and argues that the two writers, for all the obvious differences in their manner, share a common ironic, skeptical tone. Both were masters of the small form in an age without novels and both writers' works embrace a very broad cross-section of Russian life. Neither placed any great store in Populism.

55 WEAR, RICHARD. "Chekhov's Trilogy: Another Look at Ivan Ivanych." RBPH 55:897-906.

Analyzes a number of details in "The Man in a Case," "Gooseberries," and "About Love," arguing that these three show that Ivan Ivanych is not Chekhov's spokesman; rather, he is pretentious, hypocritical, and overly moralistic. He illustrates the common theme of the trilogy: the "possession" of men by some idea or emotion that prevents them from understanding their fellows.

56 WHITAKER, THOMAS R. "Dreaming the Music." In Fields of Play in Modern Drama. Princeton, N.J.: Princeton University Press, pp. 79-101.

Argues that The Three Sisters, with its counterpoint of oblique responses, conveys "the full music of existence."

57 WINNER, THOMAS G. "Syncretism in Chekhov's Art: A

Study of Polystructured Texts." In Chekhov's Art of Writing: A Collection of Critical Essays. Edited by Paul Debreczeny and Thomas Eekman. Columbus, Ohio: Slavica, pp. 153-66.

Argues that Chekhov's art is highly syncretic in nature, containing elements of music and the visual arts, combinations of diverse verbal genres, as well as myth and folk art. The composition of his works is akin to music. These features link his writings both with primitive art and with the avant garde of the twentieth century.

1978

1 BECKERMAN, BERNARD. "The Artifice of 'Reality' in Chekhov and Pinter." MD 21:153-61.

Discusses the nature of theatrical reality and argues that both Chekhov and Pinter create "reality" through a figure-ground symbiosis.

2 CLYMAN, TOBY. "Chekhov's 'Visiting Friends:' A Satiric Parody." MelbSS, no. 13, pp. 63-70.

Argues that "A Visit to Friends" is based on a reworking of Pushkin's Eugene Onegin. Chekhov's story contains scenes, situations, characters, and elements of plot that parody Pushkin's novel.

3 DEBRECZENY, PAUL. "The Device of Conspicuous Silence in Tolstoj, Čexov and Faulkner." American Contributions to the VIIIth International Congress of Slavists, Zagreb and Ljubljana, September 3-9, 1978. Vol. 2, Literature, edited by Victor Terras. Columbus, Ohio: Slavica, pp. 125-45.

Examines the system of elaborate parallels and contrasts in "In the Ravine;" argues that Lipa is not the positive heroine of the story but that she, or the principles she represents, is the target of Chekhov's satire. In attacking Tolstoyan non-resistance Chekhov uses a Tolstoyan method of "conspicuous silence:" his narrator draws our attention away from the murder of Lips's baby to achieve his ironic purpose. Chekhov's plays likewise frequently employ the device of eloquent silence.

4 EGRI, PÉTER. "The Short Story in the Drama: Chekhov and O'Neill." ALitASH 20:3-28.

Discusses the genre of the short story, its relationship to the drama, and how this relationship is embodied in the plays of Chekhov and O'Neill. In Platonov Chekhov linked several short stories to form a drama; he does this in a more balanced fashion in Ivanov, which is later reworked as "The Duel." O'Neill also uses a Chekhovian manner of composition.

5 EROFEEV, V.V. "Stilevoe vyrazhenie eticheskoi positsii: stili Chekhova i Mopassana" [The stylistic expression of an ethical position: the styles of Chekhov and Maupassant]. In Tipologiia stilevogo razvitiia XIX veka [The typology of stylistic development of the 19th century]. Edited by N.K. Gei. Moscow: Nauka, pp. 421-35.

Argues that in spite of their other differences Chekhov's and Maupassant's works use similar techniques for expressing ethical values. Chekhov's stories do make evaluations of their characters, in spite of their apparently strict objectivity. Maupassant, similarly, provides enough information about his characters to allow the reader to make valid ethical judgements.

6 GITOVICH, N.I. "Primechaniia" [Notes]. In PSSP. Pis'ma [Letters]. Vol. 6. Moscow: Nauka, pp. 369-662.

Provides explanatory notes for Chekhov's letters written from January 1895 to May 1897.

7 GROMOV, M.P., and TVERDOKHLEBOV, I.Iu. "Primechaniia" [Notes]. In PSSP. Sochineniia [Works]. Vol. 11. Moscow: Nauka, pp. 377-440.

Describes Chekhov's career as a dramatist from 1879 to 1888 and discusses the writing of and critical reaction to six plays of the period. Explanatory notes for the plays are also included.

8 HAUBRICH, MICHAEL. Typisierung und Charakterisierung in der Literatur. Dargestellt am Beispiel der Kurzegeschichten A.P. Čechovs. Mainz: Liber, 252 pp.

Discusses the notions of "typical" and "characteristic" and examines their functioning within the system of poetics specific to the short story. The use of the typical and the characteristic in conveying character, time, and space as well as in the language of Chekhov's early short stories is investigated.

9 HERBST, U. "Zum Problem der 'Unbestimmtheiten' in spaten Erzählungen Čechovs unter dem Aspekt einer literaturwissenschaftlichen Stilistik." ZS 23:570-79.

Investigates Chekhov's use of indefinite expressions ("for some reason," "somewhere," "something," etc.) and argues that these not only aid in characterization and help establish a mood but also suggest the existence of a deeper reality beneath the surface of that depicted.

10 HINGLEY, RONALD. Preface, Introduction, Appendices and Notes to The Oxford Chekhov. Vol. 7. Edited and translated by Ronald Hingley. Oxford: Oxford University Press, pp. ix-xi, 1-11, and 225-68.

Discusses problems of translating Chekhov's stories of the period 1893 to 1895; surveys Chekhov's literary work of this period and provides social and cultural background to "The Two Volodyas," "The Black Monk," "A Woman's Kingdom," "Rothschild's Fiddle," "The Student," "The Russian Master," "At a Country House," "The Head Gardener's Story," and "Three Years." The composition, texts, and variants of the stories are discussed and explanatory notes are provided.

11 HYMAN, STANLEY EDGAR. "Counting the Cats." In The Critic's Credentials: Essays and reviews. Edited by Phoebe Pettingell. New York: Atheneum, pp. 235-50.

Discusses The Island of Sakhalin, arguing that the book is "repetitious, too long, and full of pointless statistics." Apart from that, however, it contains many "compelling images" of human resilience and courage.

12 JACKSON, ROBERT LOUIS. "'If I Forget Thee, O Jerusalem:' an Essay on Chekhov's 'Rothschild's Fiddle'." Slavica Hierosolymitana 3:55-67.

Examines Chekhov's portrayal of the Russian Jew in "Rothschild's Fiddle." Here Chekhov links the tragic history of the Jews and the Russians by identifying the suffering of both peoples. References to music and to Psalm 137 help make the story's theme a universal one and create a "poetry of suffering."

13 -----. "Chekhov's Garden of Eden, or, The Fall of the Russian Adam and Eve: 'Because of Little Apples'." Slavica Hierosolymitana 4:70-78.

Examines Chekhov's use of the Biblical story of the Fall in his first published story. He parodies the account in Genesis; still his story is written in a tragic mood. The motifs of humiliation and sadism link the story with Dostoevsky's writings; Chekhov's Trifon Semenovich is identified with Fyodor Karamazov.

14 KATSELL, JEROME H. "Čexov's 'The Steppe' Revisited." SEEJ 22:313-23.

Examines the narrative technique of the work, arguing that its unity lies in its focus on the development of its central character's personality. Chekhov uses a double narrative point of view, supplementing Egorushka's perceptions by those of an adult narrator-observer.

15 KULESHOV, V.I.; PAPERNYI, Z.S.; SAKHAROVA, E.M.; SOLOV'EVA, N.N.; STROEVA, M.N.; and SHAKH-AZIZOVA, T.K., eds. Chekhovskie chteniia v Ial'te. Chekhov i russkaia literatura: sbornik nauchnykh trudov [Chekhov papers in Yalta. Chekhov and Russian literature: a collection of scholarly essays]. Moscow: Biblioteka im. Lenina, 167 pp.

Contains twenty-one articles that include studies of the influence of other Russian writers (Pushkin, Gogol, Dostoevsky, Tolstoy, Garshin, Potapenko) on Chekhov's work; his reception among contemporary critics, his relations with the Russian theater, literary allusions in his writings, and other topics.

16 KUZ'MUK, V.A. "Vasilii Shukshin and the Early Chekhov: An Essay in Typological Analysis." SSLit, no. 3, pp. 61-78.

Translation of 1977.27.

17 KUZNETSOVA, M.V. Tvorcheskaia evoliutsiia A.P. Chekhova [Chekhov's creative evolution]. Tomsk: Izdatel'stvo Tomskogo universiteta, 262 pp.

Examines the evolution of Chekhov's prose. Until the mid-eighties his works were permeated with humor and satire; after 1885 his work changes gradually as he himself seeks out new experiences and creates characters who long for a bright future.

18 LANTZ, K.A. "Chekhov's 'Gusev:' A Study." SSF 15:55-61.

Examines a series of polarities in the story and argues that although they are not resolved in the ending their perfect balance nonetheless creates a catharsis.

19 MARTIN, DAVID. "Philosophy in Čechov's Major Plays." WSl 23:122-39.

Distinguishes between "idle philosophizing" and philosophical statements stemming from "an integration of mind, heart and personal experience." No character can be taken as representative of Chekhov's views, even though some express views similar to his own; the chief importance of the philosophical passages is in characterization. Chekhov's distrust of intellectualism and his stress on the cathartic effect of suffering place him in the Russian tradition of Tolstoy and Dostoevsky rather than in the Western tradition.

20 -----. "Realia and Chekhov's 'The Student'." CASS 12:266-73.

Argues that Chekhov, usually scrupulously accurate when using factual information in his stories, has his student retell the story of Peter's denial of Christ as recorded in the Gospel of St. Luke; in fact the Gospels read at the Good Friday service would have been those of St. John and St. Matthew. Chekhov evidently found St.Luke's version more appropriate to the story's emotional atmosphere.

21 MATUAL, DAVID. "Chekhov's 'Black Monk' and Byron's 'Black Friar'." IFR 5:46-51.

Discusses the sources of Chekhov's story and argues that Byron's Gothic tale inserted into Don Juan should be considered as one of them. There are many similarities of detail in the description and actions of the two monks; the role of music in both stories is also similar.

22 MEIJER, JAN M. "Čechov's Word." In On the Theory of Descriptive Poetics: Anton P. Chekhov as Story-Teller and Playwright. Dutch Studies in Russian Literature, no. 4. Edited by Jan van der Eng, Jan M. Meijer, and Herta Schmid. Lisse, The Netherlands: Peter de Ridder, pp. 99-143.

Attempts to characterize Chekhov as a stylist by examining the way the word functions in his text. He began his literary career at a time when the literary medium was losing its autonomy; his writings "set the word free" and made possible the transition from Realism to Symbolism.

23 PAILER, W. Die frühen Dramen M. Gor'kijs in ihrem Verhältnis zum dramatischen Schaffen A.P. Čechovs. Slavistische Beiträge, no. 122. Munich: Otto Sagner, 210 pp.

Examines Chekhov's influence on Gorky's early plays. Comparisons are made and influences found in dialogue, composition, genre, and general technique. Gorky is seen as continuing the Chekhov tradition in drama.

24 RESSEL, GERHARD. "Redetechnik und Erzählstruktur in A.P. Čechovs Višnevyj sad." WSl 22:350-69.

Makes a linguistic analysis of Chekhov's art of dialogue and outlines the role dialogue plays in the overall structure of The Cherry Orchard.

25 RÉV, MARIJA. "Novizna russkogo rasskaza na rubezhe

XIX-XX vv. i ego vozdeistvie na razvitie slavianskoi i evropeiskoi novellistiki" [Innovations in the Russian short story at the end of the 19th century and their effect on the developement of the Slavic and European short story]. In Hungaro-Slavica 1978: VIII. Internationaler Kongress der Slawisten, Zagreb, 3.-9. September 1978. Edited by L. Hadrovics and A. Hollós. Budapest: Akadémiai Kiadó, pp. 265-72.

Argues that Chekhov influenced the development of the modern short story by making it a more adequate vehicle for reflecting the complexity and contradictions of modern life. He creates harmonious art from the disharmonies of life.

26 SCHAUMANN, G. "Čechov und die Sowjetliteratur der Gegenwart." ZSl 23:84-92.

Discusses the comments of a number of contemporary Soviet writers about Chekhov and argues that his works have provided an example both to prose writers (Granin, Shukshin, Nagibin, Trifonov, and Zalygin) and dramatists (Rozov and Vampilov).

27 SCHMID, HERTA. "Die Bedeutung des dramatischen Raums in A.P. Čechovs Vishnevyj sad (Der Kirschgarten) und A. Strindbergs Gespenstersonate." In Referate und Beiträge zum VIII Internationalen Slavistenkongress, Zagreb 1978. Edited by P. Rehder. Slavistische Beiträge, vol. 119. Munich: Otto Sagner, pp. 149-98.

Argues that both Chekhov and Strindberg were innovators: Chekhov in the lyrical "theater of mood", Strindberg in the "epic theater." The link between these two approaches is found in the conception of space in the works of each dramatist. The emphasis in this new drama has been shifted from the characters to the space in which they live; we see their incapacity to develop that space to its full potential.

28 -----. "Ein Beitrag zur deskriptiven dramatischen Poetik." In On the Theory of Descriptive Poetics: Anton P. Chekhov as Story-teller and Playwright. Dutch Studies in Russian Literature, no. 4. Edited by Jan van der Eng, Jan M. Meijer, and Herta Schmid. Lisse, The Netherlands: Peter de Ridder, pp. 147-209.

Attempts to develop a vocabulary for the structural study of dramatic texts and applies it to The Three Sisters.

29 SCHULTZE, BRIGITTE. "A.P. Čechovs Monolog 'O vrede

tabaka.' Vom Drama des 19. zum Drama des 20. Jahrhunderts." In Slavistische Studien zum VIII. Internationalen Slavistenkongress in Zagreb, 1978. Edited by Johannes Holthusen, Wolfgang Kasack and Reinhold Olesch. Slavistische Forschungen, no. 22. Edited by Reinhold Olesch. Cologne and Vienna: Böhlau, pp. 495-507.

Compares three variants of "Smoking is Bad for You," arguing that the final one (1902) is a "tragic farce" and so represents the first work in the theater of the absurd.

30 SCOTT, VIRGINIA. "Life in Art: A Reading of The Seagull." Educational Theater Journal 30:357-67.

Examines a structural pattern in the play in which the question of identity is linked with the treatment of time. The younger characters are seeking an identity, a problem which the older characters have grappled with in the past. "The children" represent the probable pasts of the adults, and the adults represent the probable futures of the "children." The seagull itself is a rich image, conveying soaring creativity and freedom, Treplyov's desire to murder his faithless Nina, and the younger generation's scavenging on the leavings of the older.

31 SEMANOVA, M.L. "Primechaniia" [Notes]. In PSSP. Sochineniia [Works]. Vol. 14-15. Moscow: Nauka, pp. 739-886.

Discusses the circumstances surrounding Chekhov's journey to Sakhalin, his planning of the trip, his actual itinerary, and his survey of the island's population which led to his The Island of Sakhalin. Explanatory notes for that work, as well as for his "From Siberia," are included, along with an account of the writing of both works and a summary of critical reaction to them.

32 TERRY, GARTH M. East European Languages and Literatures: A Subject and Name Index to Articles in English-Language Journals, 1900-1977. Oxford and Santa Barbara, Calif.: Clio Press, pp. 22-26.

Lists 208 critical articles in English, six collections of letters, and twenty-nine English translations of Chekhov's works appearing in journals of the period.

33 TVERDOKHLEBOV, I.Iu. "Primechaniia" [Notes]. In PSSP. Sochineniia [Works]. Vol. 12. Moscow: Nauka, pp. 309-400.

Discusses Chekhov's dramatic works of 1889 to

1891, including his revised version of Ivanov, The Wood Demon, and five short plays. Explanatory notes for the plays are also included.

34 VAN DER ENG, JAN. "On Descriptive Narrative Poetics." In On the Theory of Descriptive Poetics: Anton P. Chekhov as Story-teller and Playwright. Dutch Studies in Russian Literature, no. 4. Edited by Jan van der Eng, Jan M. Meijer, and Herta Schmid. Lisse, The Netherlands: Peter de Ridder, pp. 9-94.

Points out some inadequacies in existing models of narrative and attempts to establish a descriptive method that takes account of the dynamics of the text. The method is applied to "The Lady With the Little Dog," focusing upon the patterns of semantic organization on different thematic levels. The main thematic issue of the story is Gurov's growing self-knowledge.

35 VITINS, IEVA. "Uncle Vanja's Predicament." SEEJ 22:454-63.

Argues that the emotional ties that bind Vanya to the women in his life render him ineffectual and incapable of leading an independent life. Reprinted: 1981.1.

36 WELTY, EUDORA. "Reality in Chekhov's Stories." In The Eye of the Story: Selected Essays and Reviews. New York: Random House, pp. 61-81.

"Chekhov's perception of our differing views of reality, with its capacity to understand them all, may have done more than anything else to bring about his revolutionizing of the short story." He removed the plot and gave the story a new kind of structure that takes form from within. His own vision of reality is comic, the only frame generous enough to encompass all that he saw.

37 WINSLOW, JOAN D. "Language as Theme in Chekhov's 'Misery'." ReAL, no. 2, pp. 1-7.

Examines "Heartache" as a study in human communication, arguing that each of Iona's encounters develops his ability to communicate and thus helps ease his grief in spite of the lack of response from his audience.

38 YURIEFF, ZOYA. "Prishedshy: A. Bely and A.Chekhov." In Andrey Bely: A Critical Review. Edited by Gerald Janecek. Lexington, Ky.: University Press of Kentucky, pp. 44-55.

Discusses Bely's relationship to Chekhov as expressed in his critical articles and in the fragment of his unfinished mystery play, "He Who Has Come." The latter is linked to Treplyov's play in The Seagull and reflects Treplyov's concern for new forms in the drama. Bely's articles on Chekhov also urge the Symbolists to learn from Chekhov.

1979

1 BAEHR, STEPHEN L. "Who is Firs? The Literary History of a Name." UlbR 2, no. 1:14-23.

Surveys the history of the name "Firs" in Russian literature, arguing that Chekhov probably chose it for its pastoral connotations (via the shepherd Thyrsis).

2 BARRICELLI, J.P. "Counterpoint of the Snapping String: Chekhov's The Cherry Orchard." CalSS 10:121-36. Edited by Nicholas V. Riasanovsky, Gleb Struve, and Thomas Eekman.

Argues that the sounds of the snapping string are central to the play's meaning. The play is a "drama of death" and the string evokes a mood of regret for the passing of time. The play's network of contrapuntal images culminates in the final sounds of the snapping string and the ax against the cherry trees. Reprinted: 1981.1.

3 BOYER, ROBERT D. "Anton Pavlovich Chekhov." In Realism in European Theatre and Drama, 1870-1920: A Bibliography. Westport, Conn. and London: Greenwood Press, pp. 188-94.

Lists 100 books, articles, and dissertations, mainly in English, dealing with Chekhov's drama. Unannotated.

4 BRAUN, EDWARD. The Theatre of Meyerhold: Revolution on the Modern Stage. New York: Drama Book Specialists, pp. 23-30, 32-36, 259-61, and passim.

Describes Meyerhold's roles in Chekhov's plays and comments on his relations with Chekhov. Meyerhold's productions of Chekhov's one-act farces are also described.

5 CHUDAKOV, A.P.; GRODSKAIA, E.A.; PAPERNYI, Z.S.; POLOTSKAIA, E.A.; and TVERDOKHLEBOV, I.Iu. "Primechaniia" [Notes]. In PSSP. Sochineniia [Works]. Vol. 13. Moscow: Nauka, pp. 335-518.

Discusses Chekhov's career as a dramatist from 1895 to 1904; comments on the staging of his plays during that period; summarizes critical and public reaction to his drama. Notes on four major and one short play are also included.

6 DOLOTOVA, L.M.; KATAEV, V.B.; MELKOVA, A.S.; PAPERNYI, Z.S.; POLOTSKAIA, E.A.; ROSKINA, N.A.; and SOKOLOVA, M.A. "Primechaniia" [Notes]. In PSSP. Sochineniia [Works]. Vol. 16. Moscow: Nauka, pp. 383-568.

Discusses Chekhov's non-fictional writing, including theatrical reviews, journalism, obituaries, and scientific works. Explanatory notes for the forty-four items are provided.

7 EHRE, MILTON. "The Symbolic Structure of Chekhov's 'Gusev'." UlbR 2, no. 1:76-85.

Argues that the story presents a symbolic, three-level representation of the universe, with man placed between a lower realm of chaos and an upper realm of "unspeakable magnificence." Unlike the Symbolists, Chekhov believed that the higher realm is immanent in nature.

8 FRELING, ROGER. "A New View of Dr. Dymov in Chekhov's 'The Grasshopper.'" SSF 16:183-87.

Argues that Dr. Dymov is not the "great man" commonly seen by critics but a "somewhat lustreless mediocrity among many flashy artistic mediocrities." There is no sound evidence to suggest his professionial greatness, and as a person he is meek and subservient.

9 FRYDMAN, ANN. "'Enemies': An Experimental Story." UlbR 2, no.1:103-19.

Makes a close reading of the story, arguing that it represents both a culmination of his previous work and a new departure in his prose. The conflict in the story is man-made; the unhappiness of each character does not unite them but only drives them further apart.

10 HUBBS, CLAYTON A. "The Function of Repetition in the Plays of Chekhov." MD 22:115-24.

Argues that repetition is a major thematic and structural element in Chekhov's plays and examines "repeated nonaction" in Uncle Vanya.

11 KATAEV, V.B. Proza Chekhova: Problemy interpretatsii [Chekhov's prose: problems of interpretation]. Moscow: Izdatel'stvo Moskovskogo universiteta, 327 pp.

Criticizes some existing approaches to Chekhov's prose; outlines some new principles of interpretation and applies them to a selection of stories, arguing that they represent a new way of seeing the world. Chekhov created the "story of discovery," which centers on a sharp shift in a character's consciousness. His technique is to individualize each instance by showing the specific factors that gave rise to it. Thus his emphasis is on how his characters have come to have the ideas they have rather than on the ideas themselves. He shows his characters in a quest for truth, a process of trying to understand life and find their way in it.

12 LINKOV, V.Ia. "O nekotorykh osobennostiakh realizma A.P. Chekhova" [On certain features of Chekhov's realism]. In Russkaia zhurnalistika i literatura XIX veka [Russian journalism and literature of the nineteenth century]. Edited by E.G. Babaev and B.I. Esin. Moscow: Izdatel'stvo Moskovskogo universiteta, pp. 119-45.

Argues that Chekhov's originality is due to his approach to art. He focuses not on character as such but on the feelings and moods of a character. Similarly, there is little emphasis on plot because his works most often deal with characters who are isolated from one another and do not interact; thus they cannot provide much basis for a plot. The development in his stories is primarily within the mind of a character. The way his characters perceive life is a major determinant of Chekhov's style.

13 McCONKEY, JAMES. "Two Anonymous Writers: E.M. Forster and Anton Chekhov." In E.M. Forster: A Human Exploration. Centenary Essays. The Gotham Library. Edited by G.K. Das and John Beer. New York: New York University Press, pp. 321-44.

Notes that both Chekhov and Forster minimize the importance of their personalities in their writings so that they become all but anonymous. The "attraction of what lies beyond self" gives them both their elusiveness.

14 MATLAW, RALPH E., ed. Anton Chekhov's Short Stories: Texts of the Stories, Backgrounds, Criticism. A Norton Critical Edition. New York: W.W. Norton, 369 pp.

Contains translations of thirty-four short stories from 1884 to 1902, selections from Chekhov's letters on the short story, an excerpt from Gorky's reminiscences, and eight critical essays. Includes 1957.10, 1961.16, and portions of 1949.6, 1959.5, 1968.21, 1970.11, 1973.17, and 1975.13.

15 MUDFORD, PETER. "Anton Chekhov." In The Art of Celebration. London & Boston: Faber & Faber, pp.

110-22.

Discusses Chekhov's work generally, focusing on his treatment of tragedy in the life of the individual. Time and circumstance work against his characters, yet his works celebrate the goodness of human intentions and hopes.

16 OBER, WILLIAM B. "Chekhov Among the Doctors: The Doctor's Dilemma." In Boswell's Clap and Other Essays: Medical Analyses of Literary Men's Afflictions. Carbondale: Southern Illinois University Press, pp. 193-205.

Surveys Chekhov's career as a doctor and discusses the impact of medicine on his work. His clinical detachment from his characters and his knowledge of psychology owe much to his medical training. The doctors in his works are impotent or imcomplete men who cannot cope with their problems.

17 OGNEV, A.V. "O chekhovskoi stilevoi tendentsii v sovremennom russkom rasskaze" [On the Chekhovian stylistic tendency in the contemporary Russian story]. In Zhanrovo-stilevye problemy v sovetskoi literature [Genero-stylistic problems in Soviet literature]. Edited by A.V. Ognev. Kalinin: Kalininskii gos. universitet, pp. 129-56.

Examines Chekhov's influence on a whole range of Soviet short-story writers and finds it expressed in their economy of means, their "psychologizing" of a story's descriptive passages, and their use of expressive detail.

18 OSHAROVA, T.V. Bibliografiia literatury o A.P. Chekhove [Bibliography of literature on Chekhov]. No. 1, 1960 iubileinyi god [The jubilee year of 1960]. Saratov: Izdatel'stvo Saratovskogo universiteta, 261 pp.

Lists over 2000 items on Chekhov's life, his works, and ceremonies marking his jubilee published in the USSR in 1960. Annotated.

19 PITCHER, HARVEY. Chekhov's Leading Lady: A Portrait of the Actress Olga Knipper. London: John Murray, 288 pp. Reprint. New York: Franklin Watts, 1980.

A biography that focuses on Olga Knipper's years with Chekhov and her work in the MAT. Argues that Chekhov had a romantic image of her as a talented actess and leading lady but never allowed her to cross the barriers he set up around himself. Her roles in Chekhov's plays are also discussed.

20 POLAKIEWICZ, LEONARD. "Čexov's 'Tif':" An Analysis." RLJ 116:96-111.

Examines Chekhov's artistic treatment of illness in "Typhus" and argues that it is not merely a "clinical study" but a complex artistic treatment of universal significance. Chekhov exploits the full sound potential of words to convey the sense of disorientation in his character's mind.

21 POLOTSKAIA, E.A. A.P. Chekhov: dvizhenie khudozhestvennoi mysli [Chekhov: the movement of his artistic thought]. Moscow: Sovetskii pisatel', 340 pp.

Investigates Chekhov's creative process, including the genesis of a number of works and his overall psychology of creation. Polotskaia examines the real-life origin of a number of plots, images, and situations in order to show how these are creatively altered in Chekhov's writings. Then she examines how this material is organized within the individual works by pointing out basic compositional principles; images and motifs that recur from his earliest to his last writings are also surveyed.

22 -----. "Vishnevyi sad: zhizn' vo vremeni" [The Cherry Orchard: life in time]. In Literaturnye prozvedeniia v dvizhenii epokh [Literary works seen against the movement of epochs]. Edited by N.V. Os'makov, U.A. Gural'nik, K.N. Lomunov, U.R. Fokht, and I.E. Usok. Moscow: Nauka, pp. 229-87.

Examines the reception of the play among spectators, readers, producers, and critics from 1903 to the present. The focus is on the variety of perceptions of the play held by different critical schools and different audiences. Most attention is devoted to the play's initial reception in 1904.

23 PRITCHETT, V.S. "Anton Chekhov: a Doctor." In The Myth Makers: Essays on European, Russian and South American Novelists. London: Chatto & Windus, pp. 37-49.

Discusses Chekhov's letters, as translated by Heim and Karlinsky (1973.9) and Yarmolinsky (1973.8). The letters give a vivid picture of Chekhov's attractive personality and reveal that he attained the artistic freedom that was his goal. His plays catch people in thier solitude as they are acting out their inner life.

24 RÉV, MARIJA. "Spetsifika filosofskogo rasskaza A.P. Chekhova: 'Palata No. 6'" [The specific nature of Chekhov's philosophical story: "Ward Six"]. SSASH

25:327-36.
Examines "Ward Six" as a philosophical story and argues that it belongs, in part at least, to the tradition of the Voltairean conte philosophique.

25 ROSEN, NATHAN. "The Life Force in Chekhov's 'The Kiss'." UlbR 2, no. 1:175-85.
Argues that Ryabovich's repressed life force is liberated when he is kissed. His newly-released imagination leads him to identify his "new life" with the von Rabbecks. His dream is shattered when the von Rabbecks do not invite him for another visit, and he is "destroyed" thereafter.

1980

1 AVDEEV, Iu.K., and ROSKINA, N.A. "Primechaniia" [Notes]. In PSSP. Pis'ma [Letters]. Vol. 8. Moscow: Nauka, pp. 343-612.
Provides explanatory notes for Chekhov's letters written in 1899.

2 BIALYI, G.A. "'V ovrage' i Vlast' t'my" ["In the Ravine" and The Power of Darkness]. In Chekhov i Lev Tolstoi [Chekhov and Leo Tolstoy]. Edited by L.D. Opul'skaia, Z.S. Papernyi, and S.E. Shatalov. Moscow: Nauka, pp. 199-214.
Compares Tolstoy's play and Chekhov's story, arguing that both deal with the same "power of darkness"--greed, ignorance, and squalor. Custom has replaced morality in both works. But in spite of the gloomy atmosphere, goodness prevails in both.

3 BROIDE, EDGARD. Chekhov: myslitel'; khudozhnik. 100-letie tvorcheskogo puti [Chekhov, thinker and artist: the one-hundreth anniversary of the beginning of his career]. Frankfurt: Polyglott-Druck, 208 pp.
Examines a series of Chekhov's works (Ivanov, "An Anonymous Story," The Cherry Orchard, "Rothschild's Fiddle," "Ward Six," "The Black Monk," "The Bishop," "The Lady With the Little Dog," "The New Dacha"), arguing that his approach to literature is fundamentally hostile to ideologies of all sorts and is free of preconceptions and prejudices. His manner is humorous, ironic, and skeptical; his works reveal the true complexity of life and show the dangers of trying to fit experience within any ideological framework.

4 CADOT, MICHEL. "Tchékhov et le naturalisme." Silex, no. 16, pp. 116-23.

Argues that Chekhov did not content himself with merely reproducing real life but revealed a sense of life; thus it would be better to call him a "supernaturalist."

5 CHUDAKOV, A.P. "'Tolstovskii epizod' v poetike Chekhova" [The "Tolstoyan episode" in Chekhov's poetics]. In Chekhov i Lev Tolstoi [Chekhov and Leo Tolstoy]. Edited by L.D. Opul'skaia, Z.S. Papernyi, and S.E. Shatalov. Moscow: Nauka, pp. 167-98.

Argues that Tolstoy's influence on Chekhov in 1886 and 1887 was in the realm of ideas; his influence on Chekhov's poetics, particularly on psychological analysis, was much more profound, as critics contemporary to Chekhov realized. 1888 and 1889, crisis years for Chekhov, were also the years of his greatest interest in Tolstoy the artist.

6 CONRAD, J.L. "Sensuality in Čexov's Prose." SEEJ 24:103-17.

Examines Chekhov's naturalistic treatment of sexual passion in six stories of the late 1880s and early 1890s. His later treatment of sexuality is much less graphic, probably because he realized that his talent lay in the subtle depiction of emotion.

7 De PROYART, JACQUELINE. "Aux sources du lyrism Čechovien: pseudo-romantisme, anti-romantisme et romantisme dans le traitement de la nature (1880-83)." CASS 14:149-96.

Examines a selection of Chekhov's earliest stories and their links with romanticism. Although his parodies demonstrate his awareness of outworn romantic devices, his descriptions of nature owe much to the romantic tradition and helped him develop his own lyrical style, independent of all "isms."

8 -----. "Tchékhov et Darwin: limites et portée d'une influence." Silex, no. 16, pp. 101-5.

Discusses Darwin's reception in Russia and outlines Chekhov's acquaintance with his work; argues that Darwin influenced Chekhov's views of nature.

9 DOLOTOVA, L.M.; MELKOVA, A.S.; OPUL'SKAIA, L.D.; PAPERNYI, Z.S.; POLOTSKAIA, E.A.; and SAKHAROVA, E.M. "Primechaniia" [Notes]. In PSSP. Sochineniia [Works]. Vol. 17. Moscow: Nauka, pp. 233-465.

Discusses Chekhov's notebooks and diaries, describing their history and function and commenting on their importance for understanding his work and his personality. Detailed explanatory notes for individual questions are provided.

10 EGRI, PÉTER. "The Reinterpretation of the Chekhovian Mosaic Design in O'Neill's *Long Day's Journey into Night*."

Argues that O'Neill's play follows the Chekhovian model in the way it integrates elements of the short story into the drama.

11 ESIN, A.B. "O dvukh tipakh psikhologizma" [On two types of psychologism]. In *Chekhov i Lev Tolstoi* [Chekhov and Leo Tolstoy]. Edited by L.D. Opul'skaia, Z.S. Papernyi, and S.E. Shatalov. Moscow: Nauka, pp. 69-82.

Compares Tolstoy's and Chekhov's methods of psychological analysis, arguing that Chekhov discovered a new method of depicting the inner world of human beings. Chekhov reveals a character's psychological processes gradually, through seemingly unconnected and random details scattered through the text of the work. His method is synthetic rather than analytic.

12 GANZ, ARTHUR. "Anton Chekhov. Arrivals and Departures." In *Realms of the Self: Variations on a Theme in Modern Drama*. New York and London: New York University Press, pp. 37-56.

Reprinted from 1966.4.

13 GIRSHMAN, M.M. "Povestvovatel' i geroi" [Narrator and character]. In *Chekhov i Lev Tolstoi* [Chekhov and Leo Tolstoy]. Edited by L.D. Opul'skaia, Z.S. Papernyi, and S.E. Shatalov. Moscow: Nauka, pp. 126-39.

Compares the narrator-character relationship in Chekhov and Tolstoy. Chekhov's narrator is on the same level as his characters; he does not judge them, but gives an understanding, sympathetic account of their actions. Unlike Tolstoy's narrator, he exists in the same world as the characters.

14 GITOVICH, I.E.; MALAKHOVA, A.M.; and SOKOLOVA, M.A. "Primechaniia" [Notes]. In *PSSP*. *Pis'ma* [Letters]. Vol. 9. Moscow: Nauka, pp. 239-543.

Provides explanatory notes for Chekhov's letters written from January 1900 to the end of March 1901.

15 GOLOVACHEVA, A.G. "Turgenevskie motivy v *Chaike* Chekhova" [Turgenevian motifs in Chekhov's *The Seagull*]. *FN* 3:8-13.

Argues that Turgenev's *A Month in the Country*

was not his only work to influence Chekhov's play; the question of the role and function of the artist owes a good deal to Rudin.

16 GRECCO, STEPHEN. "A Physician Healing Himself: Chekhov's Treatment of Doctors in the Major Plays." In Medicine and Literature. Edited by Enid Rhodes Peschel. Introduction by Edmund D. Pellegrino. New York: Neale Watson Academic Publications, pp. 3-10.

Examines Doctors Dorn, Astrov, and Chebutykin; notes that they are all cynical, loveless, enigmatic, and find medicine unsatisfying. These unflattering portraits probably represent his attempts to exorcise the impersonally rational, "medical" aspects of his psyche that he felt inhibited the functioning of the instinctive, artistic aspect.

17 HINGLEY, RONALD. Introduction to Anton Chekhov: Five Plays. The World's Classics. New York: Oxford University Press, pp. vii-xxxi.

Surveys Chekhov's dramatic works, their writing and their initial performances. Attempting to explain the nature of Chekhov's drama leads one into negative statements: "it is easier to say what the plays are not than what they are." But they appeal to modern man by their very absence of drama or grandiosity; modern man finds that they provide a catharsis for the tedium of life.

18 -----. Preface, Introduction, Appendices, Notes, and Bibliography to The Oxford Chekhov. Vol. 4. Translated and edited by Ronald Hingley. Oxford: Oxford University Press, pp. 235-87.

Examines Chekhov's literary career during 1888 and 1889, including the writing and publication of "The Steppe" and seven other stories. "The Steppe" begins Chekhov's mature period; several other stories of these years show Tolstoy's influence, although Chekhov was never a committed Tolstoyan. Discusses individually the writing, publication, texts, and variants of eight stories published in 1888 and 1889. Explanatory notes for the stories and a bibliography of English-language translations and critical works are included.

19 HUNTER, JEFFERSON. "Three Versions of Peter's Denial." HudR 33:39-57.

Discusses the use of the Gospel account of Peter's denial of Christ in Rembrandt's painting of the scene, in Bach's St. John Passion, and in Chekhov's "The Student." Unlike the two earlier artists Chekhov sees the story as showing the possiblity of self-knowledge and the ability to be moved.

20 KATAEV, V.B. "'V ssylke:' spor o schast'e i asketizme" ["In Exile:" the debate on happiness and asceticism]. In Chekhov i Lev Tolstoi [Chekhov and Leo Tolstoy]. Edited by L.D. Opul'skaia, Z.S. Papernyi, and S.E. Shatalov. Moscow: Nauka, pp. 215-24.

Examines the opposing points of view of Tolkovy and the Tatar, arguing that in spite of their differences they both have an irrational faith in happiness. Chekhov sides with neither character, but finds some truth in both their positions. The story takes issue with Tolstoyan asceticism, showing that the quest for happiness is a fundamental fact of human life.

21 KUZICHEVA, A.P. "O filosofii zhizni i smerti" [On the philosophy of life and death]. In Chekhov i Lev Tolstoi [Chekhov and Leo Tolstoy]. Edited by L.D. Opul'skaia, Z.S. Papernyi, and S.E. Shatalov. Moscow: Nauka, pp. 254-63.

Discusses Chekhov's portrayal of birth and death, arguing that this provides him a means of making statements about life and death generally. Unlike Tolstoy's works, where the approach of death transforms a characters, Chekhov's works portray death simply as an end. Chekhov makes these eternal themes concrete.

22 LORD, ROBERT. Russian Literature: An Introduction. London: Kahn & Averill, pp. 133-40 and 192-95.

Argues that Chekhov's dominant concern is the "increase of entropy" in human affairs; this is expressed in the common motifs of love and indifference in his stories. He is the creator of the modern short story. His plays are comedies in the classical sense and are on a level with Shakespeare and Molière. Their comic effect comes from the constant shifting of focus "from farce to the deepest tragedy."

23 McDONALD, JAN. "Production of Chekhov's Plays in Britain Before 1914." TN, no. 1, pp. 25-36.

Discusses the critical reception of the five British productions of Chekhov before World War I. The outlook of British audiences at that time was not receptive to Chekhov's art, although critical response was often favorable. George Calderon's writings and productions came closest to understanding the nature of Chekhov's drama.

24 MARTIN, DAVID. "Figurative Language and Concretism in Čechov's Short Stories." RusL 8-2:125:49.

Discusses Chekhov's use of abstract-to-concrete similies whereby he introduces elements of the physical world into his treatment of abstract ideas or emotions. Such figurative language not only helps convey abstractions but adds color and energy to his prose.

25 NIVAT, GEORGES. "La peau de chagrin tchékhovienne." Silex, no. 16, pp. 142-48.

Argues that Chekhov's outlook was thoroughly pessimistic; his writings changed the course of Russian thought by destroying the myth of Russian cultural harmony between the peasantry and the intelligentsia.

26 OPUL'SKAIA, L.D.; PAPERNYI, Z.S.; and SHATALOV, S.E., eds. Chekhov i Lev Tolstoi [Chekhov and Leo Tolstoy]. Moscow: Nauka, 327 pp.

The third in a series of collections using newly-discovered materials (see 1974.1 and 1977.38), it contains nineteen articles and a survey of Soviet writers' opinions on the Tolstoy-Chekhov relationship. Includes 1980.2, 1980.5, 1980.11, 1980.13, 1980.20, 1980.21, 1980.28, 1980.32, 1980.33, and 1980.42. Other articles examine the subject of Chekhov and Tolstoy generally, compare specific aspects of their poetics, compare themes and characters, and comment on the two writers' impact on English and American literature.

27 PAPERNYI, Z.S. "Chaika" A.P. Chekhova. Massovaia istoriko-literaturnaia biblioteka [Chekhov's Seagull. Popular library of history and literature]. Moscow: Khudozhestvennaia literatura, 160 pp.

Examines the genesis of the play, its characters, symbolism, and innovative features. The reasons for the play's failure at its first production are discussed, along with the reasons for its success when staged by the MAT.

28 -----. "Detal' i obraz" [Detail and image]. In Chekhov i Lev Tolstoi [Chekhov and Leo Tolstoy]. Edited by L.D. Opul'skaia, Z.S. Papernyi, and S.E. Shatalov. Moscow: Nauka, pp. 150-66.

Compares Chekhov's and Tolstoy's descriptions of characters and argues that Tolstoy applies here the "principle of apparent profuseness;" Chekhov uses the "principle of imperceptible incompleteness." Yet he learned much from Tolstoy's use of detail, particularly from Anna Karenina. Chekhov's details are never haphazard or superfluous. Because he does not provide a complete character description, his details take on great significance.

29 RUSSKAIA RECH', no. 1, pp. 16-52.
Special issue on Chekhov. Contains three articles dealing generally with Chekhov's style and an interview with the actor O.V. Basilashvili on his role as Andrey in The Three Sisters.

30 SAKHAROV, VSEVOLOD. "Vysota vzgliada" [An elevated view]. Okt, no. 8, pp. 208-14.
Discusses Chekhov's inheritance from Turgenev, noting that he reworked many of Turgenev's themes but always in his own, original manner. His works have fewer tragic notes than do Turgenev's.

31 SENDEROVICH, SAVELY. "The Poetic Structure of Čexov's Short Story 'On the Road'." In The Structural Analysis of Narrative Texts: Conference Papers. Edited by Andrej Kodjak, Michael J. Connolly and Krystyna Pomorska. New York University Slavic Papers, vol. 2. Edited by Andrej Kodjak. Columbus, Ohio: Slavica, pp. 44-81.
Notes the misunderstanding of the story by Chekhov's contemporaries and makes a close analysis to determine its point. It is not about love, as commonly supposed, but about the Russian capacity for faith and the meaning of faith in Russian life. The story has a special poetic composition which, when taken into account, reveals its true meaning.

32 SEMANOVA, M.L. "'Kreitserova sonata' L.N. Tolstogo i 'Ariadna' A.P. Chekhova" [Tolstoy's "Kreutzer Sonata" and Chekhov's "Ariadne"]. In Chekhov i Lev Tolstoi [Chekhov and Leo Tolstoy]. Edited by L.D. Opul'skaia, Z.S. Papernyi, and S.E. Shatalov. Moscow: Nauka, pp. 225-53.
Argues that Chekhov's story was composed with Tolstoy's "Kreutzer Sonata" in mind and was influenced by it both positively and negatively. The two works share a structure similar in many respects, but the views of Chekhov's narrator are distinguished from those of the author.

33 SHATALOV, S.E. "Prozrenie kak sredstvo psikhologicheskogo analiza." [Moral enlightenment as a means of psychological analysis]. In Chekhov i Lev Tolstoi [Chekhov and Leo Tolstoy]. Edited by L.D. Opul'skaia, Z.S. Papernyi, and S.E. Shatalov. Moscow: Nauka, pp. 56-68.
Examines Chekhov's technique of psychological analysis, focusing on his portrayal of a crisis in which a character begins to see the world in a new light.

Chekhov's new conception of personality held that a character's striving for moral perfection could survive even within a hostile environment. Such moments of sudden enlightenment are not unlike those in Tolstoy's works.

34 SILEX (Grenoble), no. 16, pp. 1-195.
Special issue on Chekhov. Contains fifteen articles on Chekhov and the drama and eighteen on his works and biography. Includes translations of 1904.5, portions of 1957.2, 1957.7, 1971.6, as well as 1980.4, 1980.8, and 1980.25.

35 SOVIET LITERATURE, no. 1, 208 pp.
Special issue on Chekhov. Contains material which has appeared previously elsewhere, including two Chekhov stories, reminiscences, tributes by sixteen world writers, biographical and critical essays. An introduction by G. Berdnikov stresses Chekhov's optimism and the social content of his writing.

36 STELTNER, ULRICH. "Zur Evolution des russischen Dramas: Ostrovskij und Čechov." WSl 25:1-21.
Examines Chekhov's plays within the general evolution of Russian drama and in comparison with Ostrovsky's plays, dealing specifically with dialogue and plot.

37 STOWELL, H. PETER. Literary Impressionism: James and Chekhov. Athens, Georgia: University of Georgia Press, 277 pp.
Attempts to define impressionism as a literary category and makes a comparative analysis of selected works of each writer to illustrate its main features. Stowell surveys the development of impressionism in Chekhov's work and examines three stories in detail: "The Lady With the Little Dog," "The Bishop," and "Betrothed." Literary impressionism expresses a new vision of a new world, a world of ambiguity and relativity; Chekhov and James are the first representatives of literary impressionism, and the literary impressionists "discovered modernism."

38 TIME, G.A. "A.P. Chekhov i komicheskii 'malyi zhanr' v dramaturgii 1880-kh--nachala 1890-kh godov" [Chekhov and the comic "small genre" in the drama of the 1880s and the beginning of the 1890s]. RLit, no. 1, pp. 150-59.
Examines the early plays in the context of contemporary vaudeville, arguing that they transcend similar works by other writers. His early plays treat most of the themes of his later drama; they reveal much

about his concept of the comic.

39 TULLOCH, JOHN. Chekhov: A Structuralist Study. London: Macmillan, 225 pp.

Attempts to place Chekhov in a social context, arguing that he had the world view and values of a professional doctor of his time, combining optimism over man's evolutionary progress with apprehension over the repressive forces marshalled against that progress. In "The Duel" Chekhov rejects the "inauthentic" scientist von Koren. The Three Sisters, set in a "degraded world," still reveals his faith in the potential for growth in even the harshest milieu. The Cherry Orchard, also set in a passive world, conveys Chekhov's epic vision through the debates of Lopakhin and Trofimov.

40 TURBIN, V.N. "Vody glubokie: iz zametok o zhizni, tvorchestve i poetike Chekhova" [Deep waters: some remarks about Chekhov's life, works, and poetics]. NovM, no. 1, pp. 216-27.

An essay on Chekhov's personal characteristics, themes, poetics, and influence on contemporary writers.

41 TURKOV, A.M. A.P. Chekhov i ego vremia [Chekhov and his time]. Moscow: Khudozhestvennaia literatura, 408 pp.

A critico-biographical study which links Chekhov's characters with the specifics of the times in which they were created. Considerable attention is paid to the influence of Tolstoy and other Russian and European writers on Chekhov's works and to the reactions of contemporary critics to them. Illustrated.

42 -----. "Raznoglasiia po 'zhenskomu voprosu'" [Disagreements on "the woman question"]. In Chekhov i Lev Tolstoi [Chekhov and Leo Tolstoy]. Edited by L.D. Opul'skaia, Z.S. Papernyi, and S.E. Shatalov. Moscow: Nauka, pp. 264-69.

Discusses Tolstoy's and Chekhov's different views on love and on women as expressed in their remarks on "The Darling" and "The Lady With the Little Dog."

43 VOPROSY LITERATURY, no. 1, pp. 65-155.

Special issue marking the 120th anniversary of Chekhov's birth. Contains four articles: one, by G. Berdnikov, surveys Chekhov's reception abroad; a second discusses Chekhov's relations with Balmont and publishes a number of the latter's letters to Chekhov; others deal with reminiscences of Chekhov's contemporaries and other biographical matters.

44 WRIGHT, A. COLIN. "Translating Chekhov for Performance." CRCL 7:174-82.

Argues that translating a play for performance is quite different from translating for reading since the director needs an extremely precise rendition in order to capture the subtleties inherent in the original. Such a translation of The Seagull, specifically intended for directors and made with performance in mind, has been made by the author and Brenda Anderson and is described. This rendering is exact, has detailed footnotes to aid the director, and is intended only as the basis for a director's work, not as a finished product.

1981

1 BARRICELLI, JEAN-PIERRE, ed. Chekhov's Great Plays: A Critical Anthology. Introduction by Jean-Pierre Barricelli. New York and London: New York University Press, 268 pp.

Contains seventeen articles, both originals and reprints: two on each of Chekhov's last four plays and nine on various aspects of his drama. Includes a slightly revised version of 1949.2 and 1958.2, 1967.10, 1978.36, 1979.2, 1981.10, 1981.17, 1981.20, 1981.21, 1981.23, 1981.24, 1981.26, 1981.28, 1981.32, 1981.35, 1981.38, and 1981.46. Barricelli's introduction discusses Chekhov's "poetic naturalism."

2 BERDNIKOV, G.P. Chekhov-dramaturg: traditsii i novatorstvo v dramaturgii A.P. Chekhova [Chekhov the dramatist: traditions and innovations in Chekhov's drama]. 3d ed., rev. and expanded. Moscow: Iskusstvo, 356 pp.

Considerably expanded from 1972.1, this edition adds several new chapters and substantially revises some of the former ones. The role of The Wood Demon in the development of Chekhov's drama is emphasized and more material is included on his youthful dramatic efforts.

3 -----. "Gogol' i Chekhov: k voprosu ob istoricheskikh sud'bakh tvorcheskogo naslediia N.V. Gogolia" [Gogol and Chekhov: on the question of the historical fate of Gogol's creative legacy]. VLit, no. 8, pp. 124-62.

Discusses Gogol's influence on Chekhov, noting the frequency of Gogolian references in his letters and works. The slaves and tyrants depicted in Chekhov's early works are clearly inspired by Gogol. "The Steppe" also shows the influence of Dead Souls, both in its general conception and in its narrative technique. Even the characters of The Cherry Orchard are portrayed with Gogolian touches.

4 -----. "Tvorcheskoe nasledie A.P. Chekhova i sovremennyi mir" [Chekhov's creative legacy and the contemporary world]. In Klassicheskoe nasledie i sovremennost' [The classical legacy and contemporary life]. Edited by D.S. Likhachev, M.B. Khrapchenko, A.N. Iezuitov, and F.Ia. Priima. Leningrad: Nauka, pp. 204-13.

Discusses Chekhov's literary approach generally; argues that his most original contribution was the portrayal of the awakening of a character's self-awareness and the beginnings of his critical attitude to his surroundings.

5 BERLIN, NORMAND. The Secret Cause: A Discussion of Tragedy. Amherst: University of Massachusetts Press, pp. 109-18 and passim.

Compares The Three Sisters and Waiting for Godot, arguing that the play's movement results in a stalemate which is tragic. The play is pervaded by death and dying, and his characters, like most tragic characters, live lives of doubt and uncertainty.

6 BERTHOFF, ANN E. "Marvell's Stars, Schubert's Suns, Chekhov's Pipe: Recognizing and Interpreting Metaphor." SR 89:75-82.

Within a general discussion of the nature and interpretation of metaphor comments on the ending of "Gooseberries" and the possible metaphorical significance of Ivan's pipe. The pipe is not a metaphor but a means of identifying Ivan: it suggests that he has the leisure to think about human misery. He is troubled by the fact that he has such leisure and thus attacks the notion of human happiness.

7 BIALYI, G.A. Chekhov i russkii realizm: ocherki [Chekhov and Russian realism: sketches]. Leningrad: Sovetskii pisatel', pp. 6-254.

Contains 1981.8, 1981.9, and a third article dealing with Mikhailovsky's views on Chekhov.

8 -----. "Poeziia chekhovskoi pory" [The poetry of Chekhov's time]. In Chekhov i russkii realizm: ocherki [Chekhov and Russian realizm: sketches]. By G.A. Bialyi. Leningrad: Sovetskii pisatel', pp. 174-254.

Surveys the work of the poets of Chekhov's time--Nadson, Sluchevskii, Solov'ev, Fofanov and others--and argues that Chekhov's writings were perceived by his contemporaries against the background of such poetry. Nadson, with his passive and hesitant characters, was a notable element in the background to Chekhov's work.

9 -----. "'Puti mnoiu prolozhennye': A.P. Chekhov" ["The trails broken by me...": A.P. Chekhov]. In Chekhov i russkii realizm: ocherki [Chekhov and Russian realism: sketches]. By G. A. Bialyi. Leningrad: Sovetskii pisatel', pp. 6-101.

Surveys the development of Chekhov's art and outlines its main features. One principle of his writings is "the unreality of real life:" he engages in social criticism by reversing our usual conceptions of what is normal and what is abnormal. His drama follows similar line of development to his prose.

10 BRISTOW, EUGENE K. "Circles, Triads, and Parity in The Three Sisters." In Chekhov's Great Plays: A Critical Anthology. Edited by Jean-Pierre Barricelli. New York and London: New York University Press, pp. 76-95.

Examines the extensive role of the number three in the play's structure its language, and in various of its details as well as the play's recurring circular imagery. The images and ideas are consistently and carefully balanced, particularly in the final scene.

11 DURKIN, ANDREW. "Chekhov's Response to Dostoevskii: The Case of 'Ward Six'." SlavR 40:49-59.

Argues that the story has many allusions to Dostoevsky deeply embedded in its text. Apart from the overall Dostoevskian atmosphere, the characters' speech, their actions, and even the narrative sometimes recall Dostoevsky's works and, specifically, Ivan Karamazov. The characters themselves are in the grip of Dostoevskian illusions which Chekhov forces them to abandon and to confront real life.

12 EMELJANOW, VICTOR, ed. Chekhov: The Critical Heritage. The Critical Heritage Series, edited by B.C. Southam. London: Boston & Henley, Routledge & Kegan Paul, 471 pp.

Outlines Chekhov's reception, with emphasis on his drama, in the English-speaking world through excerpts of critical writing and theatrical reviews from 1891 to 1945. In his introduction the editor argues that Chekhov's reception moved through three stages: 1889 to 1919, when his admirers were chiefly critics who "appreciated his short stories but misunderstood his plays;" 1920 to 1929, when enthusiasm for his work grew among the intelligentsia; and 1930 to 1945, when his plays gained wide popular appeal. An appendix gives major productions of Chekhov's plays in New York and London to 1945, including cast lists. A bibliography of works in English on Chekhov's English and American reception is also provided.

13 GILES, STEVE. The Problem of Action in Modern European Drama. Stuttgarter Arbeiten zur Germanistik, no. 85. Edited by Ulrich Müller, Franz Hundsnurcher, and Cornelius Sommer. Stuttgart: Hans-Dieter Heinz, pp. 211-59.

Examines The Seagull, The Three Sisters, and The Cherry Orchard within the context of a general study of the crisis of modern drama. Chekhov's plays push drama to its limits. The actions of individuals no longer generate the movement forward in time that was traditional in the drama.

14 GOLOVACHEVA, A.G. "Monolog o 'mirovoi dushe': Chaika v tvorchestve Chekhova 1890-kh gg." [The monologue on the "world soul": The Seagull in Chekhov's work in the 1890s]. VLU, no. 2, pp. 51-55.

Examines some of the links between the monologue in Treplyov's play and Chekhov's other writings of the 1890s.

15 GRACHEVA, I.V. "A.P. Chekhov i russkoe iskusstvo kontsa XIX veka" [Chekhov and Russian art of the end of the nineteenth century]. VRL, no. 2(38), pp. 66-72.

Characterizes generally Russian painting at the end of the century and argues that it has a number of parallels with Chekhov's work.

16 GROMOV, M.P. "Talant i metod" [Talent and method]. VMU, no. 1, pp. 32-38.

Notes that medicine and the scientific method generally played an enormous role in Chekhov's work. Repeated experience with individual "cases" allows the doctor--and the writer--to make meaningful generalizations. Chekhov saw no division between art and science.

17 HEIM, MICHAEL. "Chekhov and the Moscow Art Theater." In Chekhov's Great Plays: A Critical Anthology. Edited by Jean-Pierre Barricelli. New York and London: New York University Press, pp. 133-43.

Examines Chekhov's relationship with the MAT.

The Seagull anticipates the MAT's abolition of the star system, but their production of it gave rise to differences with Chekhov that increased with their handling of his later plays. Chekhov's dramatic art was far ahead of the theater of the day, even as an advanced a theater as the MAT.

18 HUBBS, CLAYTON A. "Chekhov and the Contemporary Theatre." MD 24:357-66.
Applies the methods of Beckerman (1978.1) to The Three Sisters and suggests a new reading of the play in the context of the work of some contemporary dramatists. Argues that "the major tension of the play...is between profane ritual and lost myth." His plays elicit a deep response from contemporary audiences accustomed to the literature of existential despair and the theater of the absurd.

19 JACKSON, ROBERT LOUIS. "The Garden of Eden in Dostoevsky's 'A Christmas Party and a Wedding' and Chekhov's 'Because of Little Apples'." RLC 45:331-41.
Argues that Chekhov's first published story was influenced by Dostoevsky's "A Christmas Party and a Wedding." Both involve a loss of innocence and a symbolic expulsion from the Garden of Eden; they have other motifs in common and share certain narrative techniques.

20 KARLINSKY, SIMON. "Huntsmen, Birds, Forests, and Three Sisters." In Chekhov's Great Plays: A Critical Anthology. Edited by Jean-Pierre Barricelli. New York and London: New York University Press, pp. 144-60.
Examines Chekhov's stories about hunting and his treatment of the interaction of man and nature generally. His attitudes depart sharply from the Russian tradition and anticipate many contemporary ecological concerns. Karlinsky discusses a number of scientists and writers who influenced Chekhov's conservationist ideas; these ideas are expressed most notably in The Three Sisters.

21 KATSELL, JEROME K. "Chekhov's The Seagull and Maupassant's Sur l'eau." In Chekhov's Great Plays: A Critical Anthology. Edited by Jean-Pierre Barricelli. New York and London: New York University Press, pp. 18-34.
Argues that Sur l'eau not only comments on the Trigorin-Arkadina relationship but also on the nature of art, the nature of the artistic personality, and the nature of freedom.

22 KIRK, IRINA. Anton Chekhov. Twayne's World Authors Series, no. 568. Russia. Edited by Charles Moser. Boston: Twayne, 165 pp.

Includes a brief biographical sketch and analyses of a selection of stories that illustrate various aspects of Chekhov's method and outlook. The five major plays are discussed briefly. The overall view is of a Chekhov who was neither an optimist nor a pessimist but "a mystery."

23 KOVITZ, SONIA. "A Fine Day to Hang Oneself: On Chekhov's Plays." In Chekhov's Great Plays: A Critical Anthology. Edited by Jean-Pierre Barricelli. New York and London: New York University Press, pp. 189-200.

Examines the failure of the characters in Chekhov's plays to realize their goal of happiness. The frustration of their desires forces them to confront their own identities.

24 KRAMER, KARL D. "Three Sisters, or Taking a Chance on Love." In Chekhov's Great Plays: A Critical Anthology. Edited by Jean-Pierre Barricelli. New York and London: New York University Press, pp. 61-75.

Argues that the principal action of the play revolves around love and analyzes the love relationships of the major characters. Although the sisters' experiences with love are deeply unhappy, they find a strength to endure in their love for one another.

25 MALAKHOVA, A.M.; MELKOVA, A.S.; NECHAEV, V.P.; SOKOLOVA, M.A.; and VIDUETSKAIA, I.P. "Primechaniia" [Notes]. In PSSP. Pis'ma [Letters]. Vol. 10. Moscow: Nauka, pp. 257-531.

Provides explanatory notes for Chekhov's letters written from April 1901 to the end of June 1902.

26 MORAVČEVICH, NICHOLAS. "Women in Chekhov's Plays." In Chekhov's Great Plays: A Critical Anthology. Edited by Jean-Pierre Barricelli. New York and London: New York University Press, pp. 201-217.

Argues that Chekhov's female characters are delicately and perceptively drawn; they play central roles in his dramas. Aside from minor characters there are three feminine types: the jeune fille, an intelligent, poetic creature who is at odds with her prosaic surroundings; the assertive, dominant and usualy older woman; and the humble toiler whose stoic efforts hold families together.

27 NABOKOV, VLADIMIR. "Anton Chekhov." In Lectures on Russian Literature. Edited and with introduction by Fredson Bowers. New York: Harcourt, Brace, Jovanovich, pp. 245-95.

Contains a sketch of Chekhov as a man and as an artist which notes the non-didactic nature of his art. His talent was not for the sustained novel, and his typical character is the Russian intellectual. Three works are discussed: "The Lady With the Little Dog," "one of the greatest stories ever written," shows the typical features of his manner; "In the Ravine" is built on a series of deceptions; The Seagull has a "magnificent" ending.

28 NILSSON, NILS ÅKE. "Two Chekhovs: Mayakovskiy on Chekhov's 'Futurism'." In Chekhov's Great Plays: A Critical Anthology. Edited by Jean-Pierre Barricelli. New York and London: New York University Press, pp. 251-61.

Discusses Mayakovsky's article on Chekhov (see 1914.6) and argues that Chekhov's desire to "liberate the word" was the basis of his appeal to Mayakovsky. Chekhov's attitude to language and his dramatic syntax show that he was in some ways a precursor of the futurists and a pioneer of modern literature.

29 O'BELL, LESLIE. "Čexov's Skazka: The Intellectual's Fairy Tale." SEEJ, vol. 25, no. 4, pp. 33-46.

Discusses the nature of the "tale" (skazka) as practised in the late nineteenth century and specifically Chekhov's "Tale" (later retitled "The Bet"); argues that the work is not narrowly anti-Tolstoyan, as is usually supposed, but is deeply ideological, an "educated man's fairy tale."

30 ORR, JOHN. "The Everyday and Transient in Chekhov's Tragedy." In Tragic Drama and Modern Society: Studies in the Social and Literary Theory of Drama from 1870 to the Present. London: Macmillan, pp. 57-83.

Discusses Chekhov's place in Russian drama and Russian literature generally; argues that his plays present "a new theatricality of everyday life." The Seagull and The Cherry Orchard are tragedies, although they break sharply with previous tragic forms.

31 O'TOOLE, L.M. "Chekhov's 'The Black Monk:' Semiotic Dimensions of Character, Social Role and Narrative Function." Essays in Poetics no. 1, pp. 39-66.

Makes a semiotic study of the story, arguing that it contains a geometric pattern that provides a clue to an analysis of its characters. This pattern is a series of concentric circles centering on the estate that forms the principal setting. Changes in characters' behavior as they move between these spheres helps define them. Reprinted: 1982.25.

32 PEDROTTI, LOUIS. "Chekhov's Major Plays: A Doctor in the House." In Chekhov's Great Plays: A Critical Anthology. Edited by Jean-Pierre Barricelli. New York and London: New York University Press, pp. 233-50.

Examines the impact of medicine on Chekhov's work and argues that in his last four plays his characters are cast as patients; the audience is given their symptoms and has the opportunity to diagnose their maladies. Chief among the maladies is vulgarity.

33 POLOTSKAIA, E.A. "Chekhov: lichnost' i tvorchestvo" [Chekhov: his personality and his work]. In Vremia i sud'by russkikh pisatelei [Time and the fates of Russian writers]. Edited by N.V. Os'makov, U.A. Gural'nik, K.N. Lomunov, and I.E. Usok. Moscow: Nauka, pp. 282-343.

Discusses Chekhov's reception by his contemporary critics and fellow writers; surveys memoir and biographical literature that treats the relationship between his personality and his work. His personality as a writer is such that the reader approaches him as an equal and a friend. Part 2 of the article surveys Chekhov's changing reception among Russian and, to a lesser extent, western critics and public from his death to the present.

34 QUINTUS, JOHN ALLEN. "Loss of Dear Things: Chekhov and Williams in Perspective." ELN 18:210-6.

Discusses Chekhov's influence on the work of Tennessee Williams, specifically pointing out parallels between The Cherry Orchard and A Streetcar Named Desire. The principal theme in both is one of loss. Both plays rely on music for some of their effect; there are similarities between some of their characters as well.

35 RISSO, RICHARD D. "Chekhov: A View of the Basic Ironic Structures." In Chekhov's Great Plays: A Critical Anthology. Edited by Jean-Pierre Barricelli. New York and London: New York University Press, pp. 181-88.

Examines Chekhov's use of ironic discrepancy in his four last plays and argues that the ironies of The

Cherry Orchard are finer and different from those of his earlier works.

36 RUDNITSKII, K.O. "Krasota v p'esakh Chekhova" [Beauty in Chekhov's plays]. Teatr, no. 6, pp. 72-80.

Discusses the role of beauty in the plays generally. "The actual poles between which the space [of Chekhov's plays] exists are not defined so much by the concepts of Good and Evil, Truth and Falsehood, Altruism and Egocentricity, as they are by the concepts of Beauty and Vulgarity."

37 -----. Meyerhold the Director. Translated by George Petrov. Edited by Sydney Schultze. Introduction by Ellendea Proffer. Ann Arbor, Mich.: Ardis, pp. 5-24, 21-35, 43-45, 524-28, and passim.

Translation of 1969.22. Illustrated.

38 SENELICK, LAURENCE. "Chekhov's Drama, Maeterlinck, and the Russian Symbolists." In Chekhov's Great Plays: A Critical Anthology. Edited by Jean-Pierre Barricelli. New York and London: New York University Press, pp. 161-80

Examines some of the traits that Chekhov's plays share with Maeterlinck's and surveys the reactions of Russian symbolists to Chekhov's drama. The plays can be seen as "fragments of Chekhov's life-giving imagination" rather than reproductions of external reality.

39 -----, ed. and transl. Russian Dramatic Theory from Pushkin to the Symbolists: An Anthology. The University of Texas Press Slavic Series, no. 5. Austin, Tex.: University of Texas Press, 336 pp.

Contains 1904.5, 1907.1, and 1914.1. The editor's introduction discusses briefly Chekhov's criticisms of the contemporary theater and comments on some critical interpretations of his plays, notably by symbolist critics.

40 SHKLOVSKII, VIKTOR. "Bronza iskusstva" [The bronze of art]. In Energiia zabliuzhdeniia: kniga o siuzhete [The energy of delusion: a book about plot]. Moscow: Sovetskii pisatel', pp. 286-309.

Discusses a number of aspects of Chekhov's art within a general treatment of his attempts to create a new kind of plot in his stories. Chekhov's plots reflect his quest for truth: he refuses to shape his material to create the traditional dénouement. One of his major themes is ecology: he portrays man within a world which he is destroying.

41 -----. "Gamlet i Chaika" [Hamlet and The Seagull]. VLit, no. 1, pp. 213-18.

Discusss some Hamletian motifs in the play and characterizes Chekhov's art generally. Like Shakespeare he could write simply about life's complexities.

42 SILANT'EVA, V.I. "Povest' A.P. Chekhova 'Step': zhanrovo-kompozitsionnye osobennosti" [Chekhov's tale "The Steppe:" peculiarities of genre and structure]. VRL, no. 2(38), pp. 77-85.

Argues that "The Steppe" is like a series of five story-sketches linked by a common idea: "to show the degree of social and moral malaise in all levels of Russian society."

43 STEFFENSEN, EGIL. "Tema ukhoda v proze Chekhova" [The theme of departure in Chekhov's prose]. SSl 27:121-40.

Argues that the motif of departure is repeated in Chekhov's prose, whether an actual departure of characters from their home or normal environment or a symbolic departure in which the character withdraws into himself (futliarnost') or otherwise abandons participation in life. A series of short stories written between 1886 and 1903 in which this motif figures prominently are examined.

44 STRONGIN, CAROL. "Irony and Theatricality in Chekhov's The Sea Gull." CompD 15:366-80.

Argues that Constantine Treplyov may not, in fact, have actually killed himself at the end of the play. All the characters have acted theatrically throughout the play; Treplyov's gesture should also be seen in this context. The fact that his shot may have missed simply underscores his failure.

45 TRAUTMANN, JOANNE. "Doctor Chekhov's Prison." In Healing Arts in Dialogue: Medicine and Literature. Edited by Joanne Trautmann. Foreword by Edmund D. Pellegrino. Carbondale: Southern Illinois University Press, pp. 125-37.

Discusses The Island of Sakhalin, arguing that Chekhov undertook the journey "to face in reality the most profound metaphor of his life, the prison, and to enact, if possible, the sort of release that neither his writing nor his medicine could give him." His writings are filled with motifs of confinement of various sorts and with the quest for freedom.

46 VALENCY, MAURICE. "Vershinin." In Chekhov's Great

Plays: A Critical Anthology. Edited by Jean-Pierre Barricelli. New York and London: New York University Press, pp. 218-32.

Argues that the complexity and ambiguity of Vershinin is a reflection of Chekhov's own nature. "He [Vershinin] speaks more cogently to the feeling than to the understanding."

47 WINNER, ANTHONY. "Chekhov's Characters: True Tears, Real Tears." In Characters in the Twilight: Hardy, Zola, and Chekhov. Charlottesville: University of Virginia Press, pp. 140-94.

Examines Chekhov's characters within the context of "twilight fiction," i.e., literature produced in an era when the outlines of traditions and assumptions had grown dim or uncertain. Chekhov's characters live in a world without conviction and cannot bridge the gap between their private selves and public realities. "Ward Six" is discussed in detail as an example of Chekhov's art.

1982

1 ANDREW, JOE. "Anton Chekhov." In Russian Writers and Society. London: Macmillan, pp. 152-94.

Surveys Chekhov's literary career within the Russian tradition of social involvement and civic criticism through literature. Chekhov's work, together with Dostoevsky's, puts an end to "landowners' literature." As a self-made man he regarded writing very differently than his predecessors did. Although not a utilitarian, Chekhov was deeply concerned about the present and future good of humanity and tried actively to promote it thorugh his writings and philanthropic activity.

2 BERDNIKOV, G.P. "Sotsial'noe i obshchechelovecheskoe v tvorchestve Chekhove" [The social and the universal in Chekhov's work]. VLit, no. 1, pp. 124-51.

Discusses Chekhov's relevance to contemporary life and surveys some critical approaches to his work. Argues that the specifically social and the universally human exist in a "dialectical unity" in Chekhov's work; one cannot ignore its social content without distorting its meaning.

3 CENTRE NATIONAL DE LA RECHERCHE SCIENTIFIQUE. Les voies de la création théâtrale. No. 10, O. Krejča--P. Brook. Edited by Denis Bablet. Paris:

CNRS, pp. 15-186.

Contains various materials dealing with Otamar Krejča's 1980 and 1981 productions of The Seagull and The Three Sisters. Included are act-by-act descriptions of the production, detailed analyses of specific scenes, an interview with Krejča, an audience survey, and a summary of critical responses.

4 CHANCES, ELLEN. "Čexov and Xarms: Story/Anti-story." RLJ 123-24:181-92.

Explores parallels between Chekhov's early work and the stories of Daniel Kharms; suggests that the latter takes Chekhovian techniques to an extreme which lead to a dead end.

5 CHICHERIN, A.V. "Leksicheskaia osnova chekhovskogo stilia" [The lexical basis of Chekhov's style]. RLit, no. 3, pp. 112-18.

Notes that Chekhov's world consists of a "gloomy" element and a "bright" element and discusses some distinctive features of his style.

6 CHUDAKOV, A.P.; DOLOTOVA, L.M.; GITOVICH, N.I.; GROMOV, M.P.; MELKOVA, A.S.; OPUL'SKAIA, L.D.; PAPERNYI, Z.S.; PODOROL'SKII, N.A.; POLOTSKAIA, E.A.; ROSKINA, N.A.; SOKOLOVA, M.A. and TOLSTIAKOV, A.P., eds. "Primechaniia" [Notes]. In PSSP. Sochineniia [Works]. Vol. 18. Moscow: Nauka, pp. 195-316.

Discusses miscellaneous writings of Chekhov, including juvenilia, humorous album inscriptions, verse, drawings, works of which he was a co-author, and dubia. The place of these items in his literary career is discussed and explanatory notes are provided for each.

7 De PROYART, JACQUELINE. "Anton Čexov et Herbert Spencer: premières investigations." Revue des Études Slaves 44, nos. 1-2:177-93.

Comments on Spencer's reception in Russia generally and focuses on the role he played in Chekhov's works of 1883 when Chekhov first read him Spencer's ideas encouraged Chekhov to be a good doctor and to see the links between science and art. His views on education and its role in human development were also influenced by Spencer.

8 DMITRIEV, Iu.A; FEL'DMAN, O.M.; KHOLODOV, E.G.; RODINA, T.M.; and SHAKH-AZIZOVA, T.K., eds. Istoriia russkogo dramaticheskogo teatra [A history of the Russian dramatic theater] Vol. 6, 1882-1897. Moscow: Iskusstvo, pp. 16-19,39-44, 122-29, and

246-48.

Discusses the role played by Chekhov's drama in the history of the Russian theater; comments on the staging of his plays to 1897.

9 EREVANSKII GOS. UNIVERSITET. Institut mirovoi literatury im. A.M. Gor'kogo, Akademiia nauk SSSR. Chekhov i literatura narodov Sovetskogo Soiuza [Chekhov and the literature of the peoples of the Soviet Union]. Erevan: Izdatel'stvo Erevanskogo universiteta, 479 pp.

Contains thirty-one articles: nine deal with Chekhov and other Russian writers (Leskov, Pisemsky, Gogol, Turgenev, Saltykov-Shchedrin, Blok, Gorky), with Chekhov's poetics and his relationship to romanticism; the remainder deal with his influence on the literatures of the non-Russian Soviet peoples. The introduction, by G.P. Berdnikov, is a slightly revised version of 1982.4. Includes 1982.13, 1982.30, 1982.32, 1982.33, and 1982.37.

10 GOR'KII, MAKSIM. "About Chekhov's New Story 'In the Gully'." Translated by Olga Shartse. In Collected Works, by Maxim Gorky. Vol. 10, On Literature. Moscow: Progress, pp. 83-89.

Translation of 1900.2.

11 GOTTLIEB, VERA. Chekhov and the Vaudeville: A Study of Chekhov's One-Act Plays. Cambridge: Cambridge University Press, 224 pp.

Argues that Chekhov's one-act plays reveal his indebtedness to the Russian popular theater and also reveal much about his theatrical thechnique and his overall view of life. These works use a number of the techniques of his longer plays, specifically techniques of distancing. The development of the farce-vaudeville and Russian comedy generally is discussed; individual studies of his five farce-vaudevilles, his three dramatic studies, his one-act play The Wedding, and his one-act monologue, Smoking is Bad For You, are also included.

12 FONIAKOVA, N.N.; GRUDNINA, I.E.; KHOLINA, A.P., and KURILENKO, R.G., compilers. A.P. Chekhov: materialy literaturnogo muzeia Pushkinskogo doma [Chekhov: materials of the literary museum of Pushkin House]. Leningrad: Nauka, 163 pp.

Lists 1037 portraits, drawings, and photographs of Chekhov, his haunts, and his friends held by the literary museum of Pushkin House, some of which are reproduced. A number of illustrations of his works and photographs of actors in his plays are also included. Annotated. Indexed.

13 GROMOV, M.P. "O Gogolevskoi traditsii u Chekhova" [On the Gogolian tradition in Chekhov]. In Chekhov i literatura narodov Sovetskogo Soiuza [Chekhov and the literature of the peoples of the Soviet Union]. By Erevanskii gos. universitet. Institut mirovoi literatury im. A.M. Gor'kogo, Akademiia nauk SSSR. Erevan: Izdatel'stvo Erevanskogo universiteta, pp. 55-76.

Examines Gogolian traits in Chekhov's early works, noting that they contain frequent paraphrases of Gogol. Many elements of plot and style are also similar. "The Steppe" has much in common with Dead Souls. Above all Chekhov used Gogol's technique of "embodying in an image the conflict between the form of life and its human essence."

14 HARUSSI, YAEL. "Realism in Drama: Turgenev, Chekhov, Gorky and Their Summer Folk." UlbR 2, no. 2:131-48.

Examines The Seagull in the tradition of Russian realistic drama, noting how Chekhov, as well as Turgenev and Gorky, adapted elements usually belonging to prose fiction for their plays. Chekhov "brought his drama as close to life as art allowed."

15 HELDT, BARBARA. "Chekhov (and Flaubert) on Female Devotion." UlbR 2, no. 2, pp. 166-74.

Compares "The Darling" to Flaubert's "Un coeur simple," arguing that Chekhov makes us question our initial favorable reaction to his heroine just as Flaubert makes us doubt the value of the devotion of his heroine.

16 HIELSCHER, KARLA. "Zum Verhältnis der Poetik Gor'kijs und Čechovs." WSlA 9:151-63.

Argues that Chekhov's and Gorky's literary systems are essentially different and that many elements of Gorky's poetics developed in opposition to Chekhov's. These differences can be seen when one examines their evaluations of each other's writings. The views Gorky expressed in his 1898 story "Chitatel'" [The Reader] should be interpreted as his reaction to Chekhov's poetics.

17 HOLLAND, PETER. "Chekhov and the Resistant Symbol." In Themes in Drama. No. 4, Drama and Symbolism. Edited by James Redmond. Cambridge: Cambridge University Press, pp. 227-42.

Discusses symbolism in Chekhov's plays, arguing that he intended "symbols" such as the seagull and the cherry orchard to be accepted as real bird and real orchard. Individual characters in the plays may make symbols of them, but the things themselves resist symbolic status. These views are disputed in 1982.34 and further discussed in 1982.39.

18 HRISTIĆ, JOVAN. Le Théâtre de Tchékhov. Translated from the Serbo-Croatian by Harita and Francis Wybrands. Lausanne: l'Age d'Homme, 191 pp.

Explores the world of Chekhov's drama, arguing that his full-length plays present a coherent vision of human life and the forces that move it. Thus the plays are not examined separately or chronologically but as a totality. His plays are not "actionless:" Chekhov simply presents the action in terms of everyday life and refuses to dramatize it. Chekhov also transported "novelistic time" into the drama; his temporal perspective allows him scope for irony. His plays make brilliant use of space, both of the cramped and confining interiors and, by suggestion, of the vast geographical distances outside. Comments are also made on his characters, dialogue, use of symbols, and other aspects of dramatic form as well as on his links with Russian drama.

19 KAMIANOV, V. "Shchet vremeni: v khudozhestvennom mire Chekhova" [The accounting of time: in Chekhov's artistic world]. Okt, no. 12, pp. 188-94.

Discusses the critical approach to the works of Chekhov as a distinct system or artistic world. Chekhov's world is not easy to penetrate. His main dramatic conflict is between the human and the routine; the real humanity of his characters occasionally and surprisingly is made visible. The behavior of his characters can be seen as an oscillation between their human and their "routine" selves.

20 KATAEV, V.B., ed. Sputniki Chekhova [Chekhov's companions]. Moscow: Izdatel'stvo Moskovskogo universiteta, 479 pp.

Contains stories by nine of Chekhov's contemporaries who published in the humor magazines (N.A. Leikin, V.V. Bilibin, Alexander Chekhov, I.L. Leont'ev, I.I. Iasinskii, K.S. Barantsevich, E.M. Shavrova, V.A. Tikhonov, and I. P. Potapenko). The editor's introduction discusses the work of each of these writers and its relationship to Chekhov's work.

21 KULESHOV, V.I. "Realizm A.P. Chekhova i naturalizm i simvolizm v russkoi literature ego vremeni" [Chekhov's realism and Naturalism and Symbolism in Russian literature of his time]. In Etiudy o russkikh pisateliakh: issledovaniia

kharakteristiki [Studies of Russian writers: investigations and characteristics]. Moscow: Izdatel'stvo Moskovskogo universiteta, pp. 245-61.

Examines Chekhov's relationship with various Russian naturalist and symbolist writers; surveys Soviet studies of the same topic. Some features of naturalism are found in The Island of Sakhalin, and some of symbolism in "The Black Monk."

22 LIEBER, L. "Otsenochnyi 'prostranstvennyi iazyk' v trilogii Chekhova" [Evaluative "spatial language" in Chekhov's trilogy]. SSASH 28:199-312.

Argues that Chekhov, like Gogol, "humanized" geographical space in his works; analyzes the use of space and movement in "The Man in a Case," "Gooseberries," and "About Love." The characters of the three stories exist within a narrowly-circumscribed and oppressive space.

23 LINKOV, V.Ia. Khudozhestvennyi mir prozy Chekhova [The artistic world of Chekhov's prose]. Moscow: Izdatel'stvo Moskovskogo universiteta, 127 pp.

Considers Chekhov's works as making up a system or "world;" examines stories ("Lights," "The Duel") which mark stages in the development of this world. Problems of human relations and alienation are treated in "A Dreary Story." "The Student," "Terror," and others are also discussed, as are Chekhov's technique of portraying character and his plot construction.

24 MALAKHOVA, A.M.; MELKOVA, A.S.; SOKOLOVA, M.A.; TVERDOKHLEBOVA, I.Iu., and VIDUETSKAIA, I.P., eds. "Primechaniia" [Notes]. In PSSP. Pis'ma [Letters]. Vol. 11. Moscow: Nauka, pp. 329-652.

Provides explanatory notes for Chekhov's letters written from July 1902 to the end of December 1903.

25 MANHEIM, MICHAEL. "Dialogue Between Son and Mother in Chekhov's The Sea Gull and O'Neill's Long Day's Journey into Night." Eugene O'Neill Newsletter, vol. 6, no. 1, pp. 24-29.

Argues that the two playwrights saw life in similar terms and dramatized emotional relationships in similar ways. Both are able to find hope even while acknowledging the worst about human beings. The violent mixture of emotions in both playwrights' depiction of mother-son confrontations illustrates this emergence of hope from despair.

26 MELLER, PETER ULF. "A.P. Chekhov i polemika po povodu 'Kreitserovoi sonaty' L.N. Tolstogo" [Chekhov and the polemics over Tolstoy's "Kreutzer Sonata"].

SSl 28:125-52.

Surveys the treatment of the Tolstoy-Chekhov relationship by literary critics; discusses Chekhov's reaction to "The Kreutzer Sonata." A series of his post-Sakhalin stories such as "The Duel," Neighbours," "Ariadne," and "My Wife" can be better understood when seen in the context of the debate over Tolstoy's ideas on marriage.

27 MILES, PATRICK and PITCHER, HARVEY. Introduction to Chekhov, The Early Stories: 1883-88. Translated by Patrick Miles and Harvey Pitcher. London: John Murray, pp. 1-8.

Discusses Chekhov's early stories generally and argues that they are both valuable in themselves and important as a means of understanding Chekhov's development.

28 NILSSON, NILS ÅKE. "Tolstoj--Čechov--Babel': 'Shortness' and 'Syntax' in the Russian Short Story." SSl 28:91-108.

Examines certain "syntactic strategies" in Tolstoy's "Master and Man," Chekhov's "Betrothed," and "The Lady With the Little Dog," and Babel's "Guy de Maupassant." Chekhov's sentence structure is typically paratactic. "A concept such as 'shortness' (szhatost') . . . must . . . be studied not in general terms but first of all on the syntagmatic level (the syntax of the individual sentence and the syntax of the paragraph)."

29 O'TOOLE, L. MICHAEL. Comments on "The Black Monk" and "Peasants." In Structure, Style and Interpretation in the Russian Short Story. New Haven and London: Yale University Press, pp. 161-79 and 203-20.

Analyzes six levels of structure (narrative structure, plot, setting, point of view, fable, character) in twelve Russian short stories. Comments on "The Black Monk" are reprinted from 1981.31. The setting of "Peasants" serves as "a moral touchstone by which to evaluate human actions and a tenuous bridge from an unbearable reality to a potential better life."

30 PAPERNYI, Z.S. "'Pravda bezuslovnaia i chestnaia'" ["The truth, absolute and frank"]. In Chekhov i literatura narodov Sovetskogo Soiuza [Chekhov and the literature of the peoples of the Soviet Union]. By Erevanskii gos. universitet. Institut mirovoi literatury im. A.M. Gor'kogo, Akademiia nauk SSSR. Erevan: Izdatel'stvo Erevanskogo universiteta, pp. 143-64.

Examines the issue of Chekhov and romanticism, arguing that his works look at life directly and puncture romantic illusions about it. In revising "Horse Thieves" for publication in his Collected Works he systematically removed "romantic" descriptive passages. The Three Sisters is a good example of Chekhov's belief that people must be told the bitter truth about life before they can hope to improve themselves. This does not mean that he was a thorough pessimist; he had a firm belief in happiness in the future, but felt that this would only come as a product of a sober, realistic, unromantic appraisal of the present.

31 -----. Vopreki vsem pravilam: p'esy i vodevili Chekhova [Contrary to all the rules: Chekhov's vaudevilles and plays]. Moscow: Iskusstvo, 285 pp.

Examines each of Chekhov's plays, noting their relationship to his stories. Argues that Chekhov scorned the rules of traditional drama by abandoning the central hero, by blending comedy and tragedy to create a new genre, and by omitting the climax in developing his plays. This absence of an event expected to occur is a basic trait of Chekhov's mature stories as well as of his plays. Each play also contains a number of "microplots" which help unify the play by their relationship to the main action.

32 POLOTSKAIA, E.A. "Poetika Chekhova: problemy izucheniia" [Chekhov's poetics: problems of their study]. In Chekhov i literatura narodov Sovetskogo Soiuza [Chekhov and the literature of the peoples of the Soviet Union]. By Erevanskii gos. universitet. Institut mirovoi literatury im. A.M. Gor'kogo, Akademiia nauk SSSR. Erevan: Izdatel'stvo Erevanskogo universiteta, pp. 165-82.

Surveys Soviet studies of Chekhov's poetics and attempts to clarify terminology; finds two major trends in these studies. One trend is the detailed textual study, another looks at the overall structure of his works.

33 SAKHAROVA, E.M. "Chekhov i Blok" [Chekhov and Blok]. In Chekhov i literatura narodov Sovetskogo Soiuza [Chekhov and the literature of the peoples of the Soviet Union]. By Erevanskii gos. universitet. Institut mirovoi literatury im. A.M. Gor'kogo, Akademiia nauk SSSR. Erevan: Izdatel'stvo Erevanskogo universiteta, pp. 107-20.

Examines Blok's remarks on Chekhov, arguing that he had considerable influence on Blok's early dramatic work. Blok's "The Song of Fate" in particular continues the themes of The Cherry Orchard. Blok's essay

"Bezvremen'e" conveys the same sense of Russian life as does Chekhov's "A Woman's Kingdom."

34 SENELICK, LAURENCE. "Chekhov and the irresistible symbol: a response to Peter Holland." In Themes in Drama No. 4, Drama and Symbolism. Edited by James Redmond. Cambridge: Cambridge University Press, pp. 243-51.

Takes issue with Holland (1982.17), arguing that Chekhov's plays are symbolic and, sometimes, Symbolic. Chekhov both interprets reality as reality and also suggests something more profound behind it. These views are discussed in 1982.39.

35 SMELKOVA, Z.S. "Ot nabliudenii nad slovom--k analizu: rabota nad rasskazom A.P. Chekhova 'Krizhnovnik'" [From observation of the word to analysis: work on Chekhov's story "Gooseberries"]. Russkii iazyk v natsional'noi shkole, no. 1, pp. 37-42.

Discusses the notion of a "dominant word" [slovo-dominant] and applies it to "Gooseberries;" argues that a close examination of Chekhov's use of the word "gooseberries" uncovers new areas of meaning in the story.

36 STROEVA, M.N. "Voennaia muzyka" [Martial music]. Teatr, no. 10, pp. 118-25.

Discusses a new production of The Three Sisters by Yury Liubimov and the Taganka Theater in Moscow. This production departs sharply from the MAT tradition; it is deliberately contemporary, abandons much of Chekhov's lyricism, and stresses the threat of war which the characters face.

37 VIDUETSKAIA, I.P. "Ob istokakh rannei prosy Chekhova: Leskov i Pisemskii" [On the sources of Chekhov's early prose: Leskov and Pisemsky]. In Chekhov i literatura narodov Sovetskogo Soiuza [Chekhov and the literature of the peoples of the Soviet Union]. By Erevanskii gos. universitet. Institut mirovoi literatury im. A.M. Gor'kogo, Akademiia nauk SSSR. Erevan: Izdatel'stvo Erevanskogo universiteta, pp. 23-41.

Examines some themes found both in Leskov and in Chekhov's early works, arguing that both writers depict the "disorder" of Russian life. Both writers' works show a similar love of humanity, and both admire talent. Like Leskov and Pisemsky, Chekhov had a breadth of knowledge of Russian provincial life. Like Pisemsky, Chekhov "depoeticizes" reality. Chekhov's early work thus develops the themes of his two predecessors.

38 WILKS, RONALD. Introduction to The Kiss and Other Stories. A Penguin Classic. By Anton Chekhov. Translated by Ronald Wilks. Harmondsworth: Penguin Books, pp. 9-30.

Discusses ten stories written between 1887 and 1902 ("The Kiss," "Peasants," "The Bishop," "The Russian Master," "The Man in a Case," "Gooseberries," "About Love," "A Case History," "In the Ravine," and "Anna Round the Neck"); notes that the most distinctive trait of Chekhov's work is "the evocation of mood and atmosphere, the portrayal of elusive states of mind, fleeting sensations." For all his gloom, however, he was basically an optimist.

39 WOODS, LEIGH. "Chekhov and the Evolving Symbol: Cues and Cautions for the Plays in Performance." In Themes in Drama No. 4, Drama and Symbolism. Edited by James Redmond. Cambridge: Cambridge University Press, pp. 253-58.

Reviews the symbols in Chekhov's plays and comments on Holland's (1982.17) and Senelick's (1982.34) discussion, arguing that the disagreement over the meaning of his "open-ended" symbols shows that they do succeed. His earliest attempts at symbolism were less refined than his later ones, which approach conventional "Symbolism."

40 ZINGERMAN, B. "Prostranstvo v p'esakh Chekhova" [Space in Chekhov's plays]. In Vzaimosviaz' iskusstv v khudozhestvennom razvitii Rossii vtoroi poloviny XIX veka: ideinye printsipy, strukturnye osobennosti [The interrelationship of the arts in Russian artistic development of the second half of the nineteenth century: ideological principles, structural features]. Edited by G.Iu. Sternin. Moscow: Nauka, pp. 298-351.

Examines the settings of Chekhov's major plays, arguing that he uses them to convey his theme of beauty. The landscapes of his plays are similar to Russian painting of the era in their impressionism and overall lyrical mood. The landscape represents a norm of beauty, and his characters are partly defined by their relation to it. The plays also suggest a sense of space in their references to a wider world beyond the narrow confines of their immediate settings.

1983

1 BEN'IASH, R. "Neiavnaia novizna" [Unapparent

innovation]. Teatr, no. 5, pp. 58-62.

Reviews G. Tovstonogov's 1982 production in Leningrad of Uncle Vanya. This production has little lyricism; it stresses the cheerless fate of the characters and the courage Vanya needs in order to carry on his life.

2 BIALYI, G.A. "Anton Chekhov." In Istoriia russkoi literatury [The history of Russian literature] Vol. 4, Literatura kontsa XIX--nachala XX veka (1881-1917) [Literature of the end of the nineteenth and the beginning of the twentieth centuries (1881-1917)]. Edited by K.D. Muratova. Leningrad: Nauka, pp. 177-230.

Surveys Chekhov's entire career, discussing briefly key works in its development and focusing on his innovations in prose and drama and on his analysis of Russian society of his day.

3 BITSILLI, PETER M. Chekhov's Art: A Stylistic Analysis. Translated by Toby W. Clyman and Edwina Jannie Cruise. Ann Arbor, Mich.: Ardis, 194 pp.

Translation of 1942.1. Includes a translators' preface and an index of works and personal names.

4 CHERNIKOV, I.N. "A. Belyi o teatre A.P. Chekhova" [Bely on Chekhov's theater]. VRL, no. 1(41), pp. 86-92.

Surveys Bely's writings on Chekhov's drama (1904.3, 1904.4, 1904.5, 1907.2); argues that Chekhov's drama had a positive influence on Russian Symbolism and on Bely in particular. Bely's remarks on Chekhov's drama are profound and perceptive.

5 CHUDAKOV, A.P. Chekhov's Poetics. Translated by Edwina Jannie Cruise and Donald Dragt. Ann Arbor, Mich.: Ardis, 228 pp.

Translation of 1971.6. A translators' foreword discusses Chudakov's methods and findings.

6 -----. "Istoki chekhovskogo siuzhetnogo novatorstva" [The sources of Chekhov's innovations in plot]. RLit, no. 3, pp. 97-111.

Argues that Chekhov's innovations in plot construction were partly derived from his predecessors in Russian literature. The plotless "scene" [stsenka] was a not uncommon genre in the 1860s and 1870s: V.A. Sleptsov, I.F. Gorbunov, and N.V. Uspenskii produced a number of them. These helped Chekhov create a new kind of literature.

7 DMITREVSKAIA, M. "'Aktery, prav'te remeslo...'"

["Actors, set right your craft..."]. Teatr, no. 12, pp. 37-43.

Reviews a 1982 Leningrad production of The Seagull by G. Oporkov. This production stresses the play's theme of art and the pain that total dedication to it can bring.

8 EMELJANOW, VICTOR. "Komisarjevsky Directs Chekhov in London." TN 37:66-77.

Describes Komisarjevsky's 1926 London productions: his Uncle Vanya minimized the serious elements of the play and stressed its lighter aspects; The Three Sisters attempted to show Chekhov's universality. The Cherry Orchard, although less well received, also helped popularize Chekhov on the English stage.

9 HOLLOSI, CLARA. "Chekhov's Reactions to Two Interpretations of Nina." Theatre Survey 34:117-26.

Compares the interpretations of Nina in The Seagull's 1896 premiere with that of the MAT's 1898 version. In the first, Nina was played as a suffering, struggling, but talented actress and a woman of strength. The second interpretation stressed the tragic element and saw Nina as a woman broken by life.

10 MAJDALANY, MARINA. "Natasha Ivanovna, the Lonely Bourgeoise." MD 26:305-9.

Argues that Natasha in The Three Sisters should be regarded with some sympathy and understanding: she is of the petite bourgeoisie, displaced from her class, despised by her sisters-in-law, and married to an unresponsive and self-absorbed man. Many of her actions should be seen as attempts to ovecome her social and cultural inferiority.

11 MALAKHOVA, A.M.; MELKOVA, A.S.; NECHAEV, V.P.; POLOTSKAIA, E.A.; SOKOLOVA, M.A.; TVERDOKHLEBOV, I.Iu., and VIDUETSKAIA, I.P., eds. "Primechaniia" [Notes]. In PSSP. Pis'ma [Letters]. Vol. 12. Moscow: Nauka, pp. 219-385.

Provides explanatory notes for Chekhov's letters of 1904.

12 NAZIROV, R.G. "Chekhov i Giugo: polemicheskoe prodolzhenie" [Chekhov and Hugo: a polemical sequel]. FN, no. 6, pp. 21-25.

Examines Chekhov's early parody of Victor Hugo, "A Thousand and One Passions, or A Terrible Night: A Novel in One Part With Epilogue;" argues that his "At Sea" was also written originally as a parody of Hugo.

13 NIKEPELOVA, N.A. "Chekhov i Turgenev: osobennosti rasskaza-vospominaniia" [Chekhov and Turgenev: features of the memoir-story]. VRL, no. 1(41), pp. 100-7.

Notes that Chekhov used the "memoir-story" as a means of portraying real life as seen by a specific individual. Turgenev also has many such stories; Chekhov learned from his example, but developed in his own way.

14 OPUL'SKAIA, L.D., ed. Pis'ma [Letters], vols. 1-12. Ukazateli k tomam 1-12 [Indices to vols. 1-12]. In PSSP. Moscow: Nauka, 368 pp.

Contains indices to Chekhov's letters published in Letters (PSSP). Included are indices of his works and of Chekhov's pseudonyms mentioned in his letters, an index of names mentioned, and an index of addressees of letters.

15 PEACE, RICHARD. Chekhov: A Study of the Four Major Plays. New Haven, Conn.: Yale University Press, 192 pp.

Examines the plays in the context of the Russian drama and the social and political issues of their day. Discusses the major characters and argues that the minor characters also have great importance in creating mood and conveying theme. Considerable attention is paid to the literary allusions and to Chekhov's use of sounds and symbols. The Cherry Orchard is seen as a comedy, and Chekhov's notion of comedy is discussed in some detail.

16 POLAKIEWICZ, LEONARD A. "Crime and Punishment in Čexov." In Studies in Honor of Xenia Gąsiorowska. Edited by Lauren G. Leighton. Columbus, Ohio: Slavica, pp. 55-67.

Discusses Chekhov's portrayal of crime and comments on the views on imprisonment and capital punishment expressed in his work. Examines these themes in "The Bet" and "The Head Gardener's Story," arguing that they express Chekhov's deep humanitarian concerns.

17 REKHO, KIM. "Nash sovremennik Chekhov" [Our contemporary Chekhov]. LO, no. 10, pp. 20-28.

Surveys Chekhov's reception in Japan and discusses the views of a number of Japanese writers and scholars as set forth in recent scholarship.

18 RYBAKOVA, M.V. "A.P. Chekhov i redaktor Zhurnala dlia vsekh V.S. Miroliubov" [Chekhov and the editor of the Journal for Everybody, V.S. Miroliubov]. Vestnik Moskovskogo universiteta. Seriia 10. Zhurnalistika, no. 4, pp. 77-79.

Discusses Chekhov's association with Miroliubov

and his journal, noting that "The Bishop" and "Betrothed" were written especially for it; argues that the journal's orientation toward a broader reading public was the basis of Chekhov's attraction to it.

19 SILANT'EVA, V.I. "Konflikt v povesti A.P. Chekhova 'Step'' i narodnicheskoi proze vtoroi poloviny 80-kh godov XIX veka" [Conflict in Chekhov's tale "The Steppe" and in populist prose of the second half of the 1880s]. VRL, no. 1(41), pp. 66-71.

Argues that "The Steppe" is not about the fate of its hero, Egorushka, but is an allegorical work on the fate of Russia and its people. In his analysis of Russian society Chekhov followed many of the traditions of populist prose.

20 SUKHIKH, I. "Zagadochnyi 'Chernyi monakh'" [The puzzling "Black Monk"]. VLit, no. 6, pp. 109-25.

Surveys existing Russian interpretations of the story and makes a detailed analysis of it within the context of Chekhov's other writings. In spite of its apparent differences from his other works it illustrates one of his most fundamental ideas: the moral equality of human beings.

21 "Tovstonogov repetiruet" [Tovstonogov rehearses]. Teatr, no. 5, pp. 45-57.

Contains a transcript of portions of the director G. Tovstonogov's comments during rehearsals of his 1982 production of Uncle Vanya. He comments on Acts One and Three of the play and stresses the complexity of Vanya's character.

22 VALENCY, MAURICE. The Breaking String: The Plays of Anton Chekhov. The Making of Modern Drama Series. New York: Shocken Books, 324 pp.

Reprinted from 1966.22. A new preface by the author comments on the frequent misunderstanding of Chekhov's work and points out his debt to Maeterlinck.

Index